Paul Be

GW01418861

THE

LAND OF THE MIDNIGHT SUN

SUMMER AND WINTER JOURNEYS

THROUGH

SWEDEN, NORWAY, LAPLAND, AND
NORTHERN FINLAND

WITH DESCRIPTIONS OF THE INNER LIFE OF THE PEOPLE, THEIR
MANNERS AND CUSTOMS, THE PRIMITIVE
ANTIQUITIES, ETC.

Volume II

Elibron Classics
www.elibron.com

REINDEER.

THE

LAND OF THE MIDNIGHT SUN:

SUMMER AND WINTER JOURNEYS

THROUGH

SWEDEN, NORWAY, LAPLAND, AND NORTHERN FINLAND.

WITH DESCRIPTIONS OF THE INNER LIFE OF THE PEOPLE, THEIR
MANNERS AND CUSTOMS, THE PRIMITIVE
ANTIQUITIES, ETC.

By PAUL B. DU CHAILLU,

AUTHOR OF

"EXPLORATIONS IN EQUATORIAL AFRICA," "A JOURNEY TO ASHANGO LAND," ETC.

IN TWO VOLUMES.—VOL. II.

WITH MAP AND 235 ILLUSTRATIONS.

THIRD EDITION.

LONDON:

JOHN MURRAY, ALBEMARLE STREET

1882.

LONDON:
PRINTED BY WILLIAM CLOWES AND SONS, Limited,
STAMFORD STREET AND CHARING CROSS.

CONTENTS OF VOL. II.

CHAPTER XIII.

CHAPTER XIV.

CHAPTER XV.

CHAPTER XVI.

CHAPTER XVII.

CHAPTER XXVIII.

CHAPTER XXIX.

CHAPTER XXX.

CHAPTER XXXI.

CHAPTER XXXII.

CHAPTER XXXIII.

CHAPTER XXXIV.

CHAPTER XXXV.

CHAPTER XXXVI.

CHAPTER XXXVII.

LIST OF ILLUSTRATIONS IN VOL. II.

THE LAND OF THE MIDNIGHT SUN.

CHAPTER I.

Winter. — In the North a Sunless Sky. — Short Days in the South. — Beautiful
Nights.—A Snow-storm on the Norwegian Coast.—Making the Land.—Chris-
tiansand.—Ferder Light-house.—Christiania Fjord.—Fog.—Slow Travelling.—
Ice in the Fjord.—Christiania in Winter.

How great the contrast between summer and winter in
the beautiful peninsula of Scandinavia — "the Land of the
Midnight Sun!" In December, in the far North, a sunless
sky hangs over the country; for the days of continuous sunshine in summer there are as many without the sun appearing above the horizon in winter. During that time, even at
the end of December, which is the darkest period, when the
weather is clear one can read from eleven A.M. to one P.M.
without artificial light; but if it is cloudy, or snow is falling,
lamps must be used. The moon takes the place of the sun,
the stars shine brightly, the atmosphere is pure and clear, and
the sky very blue. The aurora borealis sends its flashes and
streamers of light high up towards the zenith; and there are
days when the electric storm culminates in a corona of gorgeous color, presenting a spectacle never to be forgotten.
I have travelled in many lands, and within the tropics, but
I have never seen such glorious nights as those of winter in
"the Land of the Midnight Sun." The long twilights which,
farther south, make the evening and morning blend into one,
are here succeeded by long dark nights and short days.

All nature seems to be in deep repose; the gurgling brook
is silent; the turbulent streams are frozen; the waves of the
lakes, upon which the rays of the summer sun played, strike

no more on the pebbled shores; long crystal icicles hang from
the mountain-sides and ravines; the rocks upon which the
water dripped in summer appear like sheets of glass. The
land is clad in a mantle of snow, and the pines are the winter jewels of the landscape. Day after day the atmosphere is
so still that not a breath of wind seems to pass over the hills;
but suddenly these periods of repose are succeeded by dark
and threatening skies, and violent tempests. On the Norwegian coast fearful and terrific storms lash the sea with fury,
breaking the waves into a thousand fragments on the ragged
and rocky shores. Under the fierce winds the pines bend
their heads, and the mountain snow is swept away and to immense heights, hiding everything from sight.

We will wander together, kind reader, all over the land—
over snow-clad mountains, hills, and valleys, over frozen lakes
and rivers—at times drawn by those "swift carriers of the
North, the reindeer;" we will skirt the frozen Baltic, and go as
far as the grand old cliff of Northern Europe, the North Cape.

On a dreary December day I was near the Norwegian coast,
bound for Christiania. The weather was very stormy, the
wind blowing a gale from the south-east; snow, hail, and sleet
fell alternately. We were nearing the desolate coast, to be
wrecked on which was sure destruction. We steamed slowly;
the anxious and watchful eyes of the captain and of the pilot
were turned in the direction of the land, and we all listened
for the sound of the roaring breakers. We had on board, as
passengers, a dozen sturdy Norwegian captains, who were going home to spend their Christmas: these men knew every
inch of the barren shore. We supposed ourselves but a few
miles from the city of Christiansand, our first stopping-place,
and every time there was a lull in the storm all eyes were
strained to get the first glimpse of the land. Just at noon
the sky cleared, and the snow-clad mountains came into full
view. The engines were stopped, to give the pilot time to
reconnoitre. It was very difficult at first to make out the
land, on account of the snow, but after a little while we found
that we were abreast of the city. The captain could not
have been more correct in his calculations; and we finally

anchored before the town, completely sheltered from the outside sea and the gale.

After a short stay we left for Christiania. A marked change had taken place in the weather, which had become much milder; the wind had ceased, and it was getting foggy, so that the voyage became tedious. Fogs are prevalent on the fjords in winter and early spring. and days are sometimes required for a passage which in clear weather consumes only a few hours.

We lay at the entrance of the Christiania fjord until we saw the light-house of Ferder, and then slowly continued our way, stopping, slackening, or increasing the speed of the steamer as circumstances would permit. The end of the fjord was frozen for a few miles, the ice being nearly two feet thick; but a passage for the steamers had been kept open by means of steam ice-boats, which are kept constantly running. The water of Christiania fjord, on account of its position at the end of the Skager Rack, is colder in winter than that of the other fjords of Norway, the influence of the Gulf-stream being less felt. Navigation is generally closed at Christiania until March, though in very mild winters it sometimes begins later and ends sooner, and *vice versa.* The vessels were dismantled and imprisoned in the ice; people were walking to and fro on the frozen surface, some making their way on skates, others were moving on *kelke* (a little hand-sleigh), the occupant of which pushes himself along with two sticks, shod with pointed iron. At times several were racing with each other, or with the skaters, who were also going home. The men were busy cutting ice, a great deal of which is exported.

The city in winter has a quiet appearance, even when the Storthing is in session and the court is present. The quays are silent, and the numerous coasting steamers, with the loads of passengers, are missing, the travelling season being over. The hotels are deserted, and the amusements are few; now and then a concert takes place, or a theatrical company makes its appearance, and then the theatre is crowded every night. The skating places in fair weather are filled with young people, while children amuse themselves, as in America, by coasting down the hills.

CHAPTER II.

Christmas.—Festive Preparations before the Holidays.—Christmas-eve.—Feeding
the Birds.—Even Animals are more Bountifully Fed.—Early Christmas Morning.—Some strange Old Customs.—The Festival in Christiania.—Dancing Round
the Christmas-tree.—Distribution of Presents—The Author is not Forgotten.—
The End of the First Day.

CHRISTMAS is the greatest festival of Scandinavia. There are
no holidays to which both young and old look forward with
so much pleasure as to the days of yule—days which, in olden
times, were also celebrated by the followers of Thor and Odin.

In the cities Christmas and the following days are legal holidays; but it is in the country that one should witness the re-
joicings. In many districts of Sweden and Norway, among
the peasants and farmers, these continue for thirteen days, and
are called the "Tretten jule dage" (thirteen days of yule).
Then, after a week's interval, come—

> " Tyvende dag Knut
> Danser julen ud."

> (" The twentieth day Canute
> Dances yule out.")

This is the best time of the year for holidays—the season
in which the farmers have very little to do, and the monot-
ony of the long winter needs to be broken. The grain has
been threshed, and the products of the dairy sold. The labor
to be done is that of laying in supplies of wood and hay, the
carpenter and blacksmith work, mending the carts, and repairing harness and ploughs. The dairy-work is lighter than
in the summer, for the cows give but little milk, and the
amount of butter is not more than enough for the use of the
household; the women are busy in the daily routine of weaving, spinning, carding, and knitting.

A CHRISTMAS SCENE.

During these days visits are interchanged, and at almost
every farm a feast or a dance is given, to which the neighbors
are invited; frolics are devised by the young, and the time is
considered auspicious for betrothal.   The more primitive the
district the greater the festivities.   Wherever I wandered, after
the first week in December, I could see nothing but bustle and
preparation for the holidays.

At this season every household vessel of ancient times is
brought out, together with strange old pottery, silver, and odd-
shaped wooden vessels and spoons—heirlooms of the family.
The stranger might well fancy, as he stands in a dimly lighted old log-house in a remote mountain region of Norway, and
drinks *skål* (a health) from an ancient tankard, that he is
among the Norsemen and Vikings of old: for many a chieftain, bold warrior, or hunter has drunk from the same cup;
many a revel has taken place within the old walls; many a
silver goblet has clinked against another while men who were
the terror of many lands swore eternal friendship over their
potations.   The same cup had also been used at many a
marriage-feast, a christening, or a burial.   Some of them are
mounted with brass, others with silver or gold, and others,
again, are gilded; some have Runic inscriptions, others have
none; and some are so old that their history cannot be traced,
having probably been brought by the invading hordes from
Asia.   A few of these cups have been found in the mounds,
and others dug out of the earth.

Each hamlet and farm is busy for two or three weeks at
preparations for the day.   Special care is taken in the brewing of *jule öl* (Christmas ale), which is stronger than that
used at other times.   A great part of the hops that have grown
on the little patch by the house has been reserved specially
for this occasion; or they have been bought long before, and
carefully kept by the wife.   Such a quantity is brewed that
there is no fear that it will give out before the festivities are
over—for every friend and visitor must partake of it, when
offered in a large tankard or wooden cup holding a gallon or
more.   The men go to the mills for more flour, and for several days mothers and daughters are busy baking, and girls who

have the reputation of being good bakers are in great demand. Home-made currant-wine—if the berries grow in the district —has been kept for the occasion. On the highways numerous carts are seen carrying little kegs of bränvin (spirituous liquor) homeward from the heads of fjords, or towns where it can be procured, a man having been specially sent to bring this with other luxuries. The larder is well stocked; fish, birds, and venison are kept in reserve; the best *spige kjöd* (dry mutton, or either beef or mutton sausage) is now brought forward; a calf or a sheep is slaughtered, and, as the day draws near, wafers and cakes are made. The humblest household will live well at Christmas.

In many districts of Sweden the pastor receives the remainder of his tithes in the shape of flour, etc. A few years back one could see on Dopparedagen—two days before Christmas —the assistant pastor, the klockare (organist), and the kyrkvaktare (sexton) going round with large boxes, baskets, or bags, in which to put the tithes; but this custom now prevails only in remote districts, the system of tithes having been generally abolished. The little country stores carry on a thriving trade in coffee, sugar, prunes, raisins, and rice, for puddings; the girls buy trinkets and handkerchiefs for their heads, and the young men get a new hat or a scarf. At that time the servant men and girls of the farmers get the new clothes and shoes that are due them, and all wear their best on the holiday. The Christmas feeding of the birds is prevalent in many of the provinces of Norway and Sweden : bunches of oats are placed on the roofs of houses, on trees and fences, for them to feed upon. Two or three days before cart-loads of sheaves are brought into the towns for this purpose, and both rich and poor buy, and place them everywhere. Large quantities of oats, in bundles, were on sale in Christiania, and everybody bought bunches of them. In many of the districts the farmers' wives and children were busy at that season preparing the oats for Christmas-eve. Every poor man, and every head of a family had saved a penny or two, or even one farthing, to buy a bunch of oats for the birds to have their Christmas feast. I remember well the words of a friend of mine, as we were driving through the streets of Christiania; he said, with deep feeling, "A man must be very poor indeed if he cannot spare a farthing to feed the little birds on Christmas-day!" What a pleasing picture it is to see the little creatures flying round, or perched on the thickest part of the straw and picking out the grain! It is a beautiful custom, and speaks well for the natural goodness of heart of the Scandinavian.

On this day, on many a farm, the dear old horse, the young colt, the cattle, the sheep, the goats, and even the pig, get double the usual amount of food given them, and have so much that often they cannot eat it all.

The day before Christmas, in the afternoon, everything is ready—the house has been thoroughly cleaned, and leaves of juniper or fir are strewn on the floor. When the work is done the whole family generally go into the bakehouse, which has been made warm, and each member takes a thorough wash from head to foot, or a bath in a large tub—the only one many take during the year; then they put on clean linen, and are dressed. In the evening they gather round the table, the father reads from the Liturgy, and oftener a chapter of the Bible, and then a hearty meal is taken. In many of the valleys and mountain-dales watch is kept during the whole of the night, and all are merry; candles are kept burning at the windows, and, as in Dalecarlia, the people flock to church, each carrying a torch. In some districts, immediately after service, the people hurry from church either on foot or in sleighs, for there is an old saying that he who gets home first will have his crop first harvested. Early on Christmas morning the family is awakened by the shrill voice of the mother or sisters singing—

> A child is born in Bethlehem, Bethlehem,
> That is the joy of Jerusalem,
> Halle! Hallelujah!

The second morning afterward the young people strive to finish their work first, whether in the barn or the house. There is a great deal of fun and mischief: doors and windows are nailed during the night by the boys, to give trouble to the girls in getting down; or their shoes are hidden; and the girls play all kinds of tricks on the boys. In the country Christmas is observed more as a religious day.

In some places old-fashioned ways are still kept. On the twentieth day young men often paint or blacken their faces, put queer crowns on their heads or hats, wear large stars on their breasts, and carry long wooden swords. One is furnished with a pouch, and they visit each farm and solicit contributions for a frolic. Now and then they indulge in a great deal of mischief; and if they suspect some young fellow to love a girl, they sing to her the old Herodes song:

> Just as the three kings
>   In yon time had sung to Maria,
> So do we boys sing
>   Now for thee, beloved Karen.*
> It will now no longer do
>   That thou shalt go so lonely;
> One of us as husband take, do;
>   Then thou hast everything lovely.

> "Here nothing will help but decision—
>   With shining swords we are popping—
> Give on twentieth day answer to our mission,
>   Which two of us you are dropping.

They then clash with their wooden swords, and rush out.

On Christmas evening I found myself once more at the pleasant home of my friend Consul H——. The children were delighted to see me, and bright-eyed little Kristine and her young brother beamed with delight when I told her how astonished I had been while in New York to receive a large letter from her. I told her that at first I thought the letter was not intended for me; but there was no mistake, it was directed to Paul B. Du Chaillu, and it had the Christiania postmark. I opened the envelope and found a pair of slippers, which fitted me perfectly. "It is a gift from Kristine!" cried the boys, who did not give me time to finish my sen-

---

* Or any other name for the girl.

tence; "she embroidered them herself." "But how did she discover the size of my foot?" Before the answer came dinner was announced, and I was the only stranger in that large family circle, where young and old were seated together round the table. After dinner the excitement became great among the young folks, for the door of the large drawing-room had been strictly closed against all. Suddenly there was a rush, the door was opened, and a shout of wonder and delight rang among the children. In the centre of the great room a large Christmas-tree was blazing with the light of scores of little wax-candles of bright colors; the branches were laden with gifts. We formed a ring round the tree, holding each other's hands, alternately advancing and retiring while we sung. After the dance and the song we seated ourselves. The faces of the children were beaming with happiness, and they waited to see what Santa Claus had brought them. Their eager eyes watched the tree, and, as each parcel was taken off, there was a dead silence before the name was read, and then a rush to see, and exclamations of joy and wonder, which made those who had as yet received no gift the more impatient and anxious. Indeed, one must have been heavily laden with care and sorrow who could not be happy at the sight of those bright and joyous faces on that festival-night. It made the old young again, and for awhile, at least, drove trouble away. A large parcel was taken from one of the branches of the tree, and everybody was curious to know for whom it was intended, for it was the largest of all. It was for me! I opened the package, all crowding round, and found a beautiful muff, made of the skin of a fox, with the head splendidly prepared, looking as if the animal were alive. It was a thoughtful remembrance from my kind friend and his wife. "It will be very useful to you this winter, when you are travelling in the far North," said the hostess. Very useful it was, indeed; besides, it became an object of great curiosity to the primitive inhabitants of the interior. The fox's head was so life-like that it invariably set the dogs barking at it.

The remainder of the evening passed off quietly, and by ten o'clock all had retired or gone home.

CHAPTER III.

My object in coming to Christiania was to spend the Christmas festivities among the farmers of Gudbrandsdalen. On
the morning of the 26th of December I took the railway for
Lake Mjösen. Norwegian railway travelling is very slow.
We were three hours making forty-two miles. A thick fog
prevented the steamer from starting at the time appointed ;
but when it cleared we raised anchor, and in a few hours arrived at Gjövick, about half-way, further navigation being
stopped by the ice. A drive of several hours brought me to
the head of the Mjösen lake, about 110 miles from Christiania.
It was very dark, and I did not dare to cross the river Logen
on the ice with my sleigh, as I could not see the way, and my
driver did not know the dangerous places. I knocked at the
door of a small house and asked the owner to cross over with
me ; I excused myself for awaking him, by telling him that I
was very much in a hurry.

After three or four hours' sleep I was on my way northward
towards the Dovre fjelds, travelling over a magnificent road.
The sleighs used at the stations in Norway are peculiar, and I
may say very uncomfortable. They can seat only one person,
and the seat resembles much that of a cariole, except that it is
placed upon runners. There is no place for the luggage, so

that, even with a small valise, the traveller's legs must extend beyond the edge, and generally nearly touch the runners. These sleighs, however, are easily managed in the mountains and narrow roads, and very seldom upset. The post-boy or driver stands behind, with his feet on the runners. One must wear heavy top-boots lined with fur, and two pairs of knitted stockings, to prevent his feet from being frozen in cold weather.

STARTING ON A JOURNEY.

The stranger travelling in Scandinavia in winter, especially an American, who thinks nothing of a journey of a thousand miles, is surprised at the great preparations made when a worthy paterfamilias gets ready to start on a journey of a few hours. He cannot help noticing the anxiety of the wife for her husband, and the respect and love of the children amidst the great commotion. Papa must not be hungry, so the box or basket containing the luncheon is carefully prepared, a little flask of spirits or wine being added to warm him on the road, and a bountiful meal is spread before his departure. Above all, he must be carefully guarded against getting cold: the thickest woollen stockings and mittens are selected and warmed; the long coat, lined with wolf or sheep skin, with collar rising above the head and almost covering the face, is brushed; the high loose top-boots, lined with thick fur, are cleaned; the warmest woollen scarf, probably the Christmas-gift of some of the children, is taken from the drawer.

After the meal the toilet begins. Mother and children assist in dressing him; he takes it easy, with a look of satisfaction that he is the lord of such a household, and is happy to receive so much solicitous attention. The woollen sash is passed twice around his waist, his neck is carefully protected, his fur cap put on his head, and his collar raised so that his face is hardly seen. The servant-maid tries to help also, and thinks she has her share in making her master comfortable for the journey. In the mean time the son has harnessed the horse, and after a pleasant good-bye the head of the household departs, thinking how delightful it is to be the father of a large family.

A DROLL SCENE.

The second day of my trip the sky was so blue, and so charged with aqueous vapor, that I was not without misgivings. I was not mistaken—that fine sky was deceitful; in the afternoon, the weather growing milder and milder, the clouds gathered, and before night the rain poured down. I was astonished at such mild weather in the middle of winter—between 61° and 62° latitude—in a valley several hundred feet above the sea. As the evening advanced the rain-storm increased in violence, and the night became so dark that I could not see my way, so I left all to my horse. The poor animal—a post-horse—had travelled many times over the same route, and knew it perfectly, and by himself that night entered the yard at the station of Skæggestad.

Wherever I was known I was heartily welcomed with a *Glædelig Jul og godt Nytaar* (Merry Christmas and Happy New-year). There had been very little snow, and the rain had so washed the road that driving was equally bad with a cariole or sleigh, until the valley reached a higher level, as I travelled farther north. At this time of the year, in Southern Norway, the days are very short; it is not daylight before 8.30 or 9 A.M., and at 3.30 P.M. it is dark. The sun could not be seen on account of the height of the mountains flanking the valley. At two o'clock the red and yellow sky over our heads told that sunset was near. The bright orange clouds, dyed by the rays of the sun, as they floated across the valley and over the snow-clad summits of Kuven, 4746, and of Jetta, 5278 feet above the sea, presented a beautiful spectacle.

After travelling three days the church of Dovre appeared in the distance, and the road had attained a height of 1500 feet. I was nearing the end of my journey. At some miles to the right of the highway, at the base of the mountains, is a ridge of hills, upon which several farms, some of the oldest in the Gudbrandsdal, are situated; among them were Björn, Hofde, Bergseng, Lindsöy, Budsjord, Höye, Buste, and some others; I also recognized Tofte, my place of destination. I alighted at the historic post-station of Toftemoen, to shake hands with my old friend Ivor before going to see his brother Thord. He was not at home; but his house-keeper, who had entire charge of the farm, said that Ivor did not like Toftemoen any more; that he was more fond of Hedalen, and of his big farm of Bjölstad, and that he spent most of his time there. "But," she added, "you must remain overnight with us, and see our neighbors, and to-morrow will be time enough for you to go to Thord. Ivor would be sorry if he heard you did not tarry a day here. We will take good care of you;

you must spend one of the thirteen days of yule with us."
As the table was being set, she remarked, "At Christmas we
always use a table-cloth." After the meal the farm-hands
gathered about the fireplace to chat, and all were served with
a glass of wine. The talk ran upon Christmas festivities, the
parties that were to be given, and what fun was in prospect.
Then we heard the names of the persons who had become engaged, and who were to be married in the spring, and the
usual comments were uttered—such as, "Who would have
thought it!" "How sly they have been about it!"

It was late when we retired. An immense bedroom, gaudi-
ly painted, adorned with ancient furniture, and very comfortable, was allotted to me.

New-year's day—kept in the country as a religious day—
dawned with a heavy fall of snow. A sleigh was made ready
to take me to church; one of the dairy-maids managed to find
room with me by sitting in my lap; while one of the farm-
hands, with a flaming red cap, stood behind and drove. On
account of the stormy weather the congregation was small.
After church I drove to Tofte, and was received by Thord in
the warm but undemonstrative way characteristic of the Norwegian bonde.

Soon after my arrival a bountiful meal was prepared, for
this is invariably a part of the hospitality offered to a stranger.
The table was covered with a snowy cloth, and I was to eat
alone, for such was the etiquette, to show that the meal had
been prepared for the guest. My host remained to see that
the beautiful fair-haired maids waited properly upon me, for
he was a widower. Thord Paulsen (the son of Paul) was one
of three brothers, belonging to one of the very oldest families
of Norway, tracing his pedigree to King Harald Haarfager,
so called on account of his fine fair hair. He swore that he
would never cut it till he had conquered all the provinces of
Norway, and united them into one kingdom. He ruled over
Norway more than a thousand years ago. Ganger Rolf, an
ancestor of William the Conqueror, who in spite of the orders
of Harald Haarfager had committed depredations on the coast
of the kingdom, was banished, and sailed with his fleet and

warriors southward, to France, where he founded a kingdom, afterwards called Normandy.

The farms belonging to the Toftes had been in the possession of the family from long before the Norman conquest of England, and from the earliest time of the settlement of the valley of Gudbrandsdal by the Northmen; and, in order to keep the property intact, marriages among cousins have been continually taking place. In the Tofte family the name of Paul, Thord, and Ivor are always found.

OLD MOUNTAIN STATION OF HJERKIN.

The farm here has also its stories of love and romance. King Harald, about the year 860, was on a journey when he stopped at the farm of Tofte to spend Christmas. On Christmas-eve, Swase, a Laplander, also arrived at the farm just as his majesty was seating himself at table, and invited the king to go with him to his own house, where a Christmas feast had been prepared. The monarch angrily refused. Swase, not daunted, sent back word that Harald had promised to visit his hut. The king yielded; and on entering the hut he met Snefrid (Snow-peace), the beautiful daughter of Swase

who filled a cup of mead for him.   He had already fallen desperately in love with her on account of her great beauty.   She
had a child, whose descendants afterwards became a great family in the northern part of Norway.

Toftemoen, the farm of Thord's brother Ivor, is one of the
oldest post-stations in the country.   The saga runs to the effect that about the year 1100 King Eysten and King Sigurd
met here on their journeys, and quarrelled, each claiming to
have done greater deeds than the other.   They were brothers.
Sigurd was the younger, and on his return from Palestine gave
great riches to Eysten.   Sigurd talked of his battles, his con-
quests, and his wanderings in far lands ; while Eysten boasted
of the many things he had done for Norway—of the road he
was making from Trondhjem over the Dovre fjeld, and of the
inns he had built and supported for the use of travellers.   In
old times farm-stations were scarce in many parts of the country, and when people travelled they had to sleep out-of-doors
or take refuge in the little shelter-houses called *bæstestue*, some
of which still exist in the far North in uninhabited districts.

Thord was fifty years of age, of medium height, with hair
tinged with gray, and a benign countenance without much expression.   There was not the slightest degree of pretension in
his conversation or his manner.   He was very pious, a stanch
supporter of the Church, and very conservative.   His every-
day dress was a black frock-coat, pantaloons, and waistcoat,
made of fine homespun cloth, and he wore a long red woollen
cap, which seemed to be the fashionable head-covering in this
part of the country; his clothes had been made by the tailor
of Dovre, and his boots on his farm, from his own leather.
My host lived in a patriarchal way, like all the bönder of
Norway; and no one seeing him, with his simple manners,
would have suspected he was of so ancient lineage.   Seven
maids and five men-servants (*drenge*) lived with him, but
during the summer months and in harvest-time a great
number of extra laborers were employed.   These maids had
an independent air, for the fact that they worked for their
living did not in the least affect their social position; they
were Northmen's daughters; and it was the custom for every

bonde's wife, daughters, and sons to waive distinction of caste at social gatherings. The fathers of these girls were bönder, the equals of Tofte, and their farms had descended to them from ancient times. One or two were the children of husmænd; but no stranger could distinguish them from the others, and they were treated with as much consideration. They had all accepted situations, either because the farms owned by their parents were too small, or they wished to make money for themselves.

All were fresh-looking, healthy, and strong. Coarse fare, early rising, and plenty of work in the open air seemed to agree with them. Three were really beautiful: all had light-blue eyes and fair hair. Four out of the seven were named Ragnild—a very common name in this part of Gudbrandsdal, and likely to continue; for a child must always be named after some member of the family: the daughters after their grand-mothers, mothers, or aunts, and the boys after grandfathers, fathers, or uncles. In order to distinguish them from each other, the name of the farm from which each had come was added. Thus, Ragnild Mösjordet was Peder's *datter* (daugh-ter), Ragnild Nyhaugen was Ols's datter, Ragnild Angaard was Martin's datter, and Ragnild Ulen was Torstin's datter. Two others were called Marit, a name also quite common; and one was Kari, the diminutive of Catherine. The five farm-hands were strong healthy fellows, whose names were Anders, Ole, John, Lars, and Hans. The ridge upon which the farm is built slopes gently towards the valley, and is situated about one mile from the main-road, near a torrent. The ground is 1910 feet above the sea, and 400 feet above the valley; at the back of it are dark mountains, from which issued several streams. On the estate were two dwelling-houses—that in which Thord lived dating from the year 1783, and the other from 1651. In the older building dwelt Tofte's sister, with her son Paul, a lad sixteen years of age; Thord inherited the farm, but had to make an allowance to her from its produce, which enabled her to live very comfortably. Thord lived in the more modern house, a large and comfortable building. On the first floor was the kitchen, with fireplace, a large table,

wooden benches, and a few wooden chairs. This was the
every-day room, in which the meals were cooked and served,
and the household fabrics spun or woven. Two rooms
communicated with the kitchen, one of these being Tofte's
bedroom, the other used as a dairy in the winter. In the
centre of the house, back of the entrance-hall, was a room
for the male farm-hands, where were beds consisting of loose
straw covered with sheepskins. The guest-room had a low
ceiling and a painted floor, but was a model of cleanliness;
it was only used when particular honor was to be paid to a
stranger, or on gala occasions; a thick round post in the centre supported the ceiling, and on one of the cross-beams were
cut in the wood the figures 1783, the date of the completion
of the house. A large table, a queer-looking old sideboard,
a few chairs, and a stove constituted the furniture. ·This fashion of inscribing the date seemed to have come in vogue only
since about the year 1600. Yet this building appeared quite
new in comparison with some of those by which we were surrounded.

At this very farm, and not at Toftemoen, as strangers suppose, King Oscar, father of the present sovereign, was entertained by Thord's father while on his way from Christiania to
Trondhjem, where he was to be crowned king of Norway. The
old farmer sent word to the king to bring nothing with him,
not even silver, for he had enough for his whole court. The
king and Tofte had a table to themselves, while the suite of his
majesty ate at another table—even the minister of state included. " This table," said the descendant of the Haarfager,
" is only for those of royal blood." Though this story is a
pleasant one to relate and to read, I doubt it. The host probably desired simply to pay special honor to his sovereign—a
custom usual with strangers. Every day he ate with the servants of his household, and could not consistently refuse to
eat with the dignitaries of state of his own country, although
thinking them far below himself.

One house, as was too often the case, remained unfinished;
on the roof of another was the Christmas sheaf of oats for the
use of the birds. These buildings formed a sort of enclosure,

in the centre of which was a large rounded slab upon which salt was placed for the cattle, which in fair weather were sometimes allowed to come out for a little while. The horse-dung was carefully saved, dried, and then put in the yard in little heaps, and I was surprised to see how fond the cattle were of it.

Other houses contained the family stores, such as salted meat, butter, etc., for winter use; and a third apartment was filled with the wool that had been sheared. On the same side of the yard was a high house, with a belfry and a clock. This building was used in summer by the day-laborers, who often numbered thirty or forty, and it was several hundred years old. There was also a large building, resting on thick stone walls, containing sixty cows, and at a short distance was another building for other cows. The stable contained twenty horses, some of them quite handsome. No one can judge of the Norwegian ponies by those seen or used at the post-stations.

The industrious habits of the farmers in this part of Norway were very striking. Everything was done with the precision of clock-work. On many of the farms a bell, placed on one of the buildings, called the hands to or from work. They rose at four o'clock in the morning, winter and summer; at six o'clock the cows had been milked and the horses attended to, and the laborers sat down to breakfast, Tofte presiding, for the farmers and their wives always set the example of thrift and industry. After breakfast the orders were given for the day, and everything was done accordingly—the equality of social customs giving no one the privilege to neglect a duty. Dinner was served at eleven o'clock—the farmer carving, and the wife, or the house-keeper, placing before each person a piece of flat bread and a portion of butter. Potatoes were always served at dinner. At five o'clock a third meal was provided; and the fourth, and last, invariably consisting of *gröt* (a thick mush), was ready between seven and eight o'clock in the evening. After five o'clock, or even earlier, the girls made their toilets, took their places in the kitchen, and engaged in weaving, spinning, knitting, or needle-work. By eight o'clock, or, at the latest, nine o'clock, everybody was in bed. Above the parlor was a large bedroom, which was a pattern of cleanliness, containing a bed shaped like a bunk. In one corner of this room I saw the old silver crown which had been put upon the heads of many brides of the Tofte family. The bedroom was used only by guests, and it was assigned to me. In the upper hall robes and fur clothing hung upon the walls.

The view from the windows was peculiar, the farms and their buildings forming each a cluster which appeared darker by contrast with the snow; and on the mountains, on the other side of the valley, the sæters appeared like black spots, resembling huge boulders. When I retired for the night, Thord, generally accompanied by two of the maids, would escort me to my room, to see if it was warm and comfortable. My host's first inquiry in the morning was if I had found my bonde bed comfortable, and if I had rested well. I ate breakfast alone, for Thord took his at six o'clock with the farm-hands. I was served with fried bacon, mutton, potatoes, butter, cheese, plenty of milk, and excellent coffee; and a pleasant girl waited upon me.

It was charming, when evening came, to be seated with the whole household in the kitchen round a huge wood-fire the flames of which lighted the entire room. The hard work was then finished, and, as it was Christmas-time, the people of the farm were dressed in their best. The floor of the kitchen had been scrubbed, and everything made tidy; a heap of firewood lay in a corner, and we were to have a dance. Supper was had earlier than usual; afterwards a few neighbors came in. With some difficulty I persuaded the girls to sing. Among their songs were these:

PER AND LISA.

And Lisa she was stiff, and said to Per this way:
"It is no use that thou courtest me,
Because if anybody courts I will not listen to it—
No, never, here in the times of this world!"
        "Oh, by the cross, is that so?
        Ha! ha! ha! ha!
        That was a funny little song."

And Per he sniffed, and said to Lisa this way:
"It is no use that thou go here and puff;
I never think of making myself trouble
For thee or for other girls."
      " Oh, by the cross, is that so?
      Ha! ha! ha! ha!
      That was a funny little song."

And Per and Lisa sullenly separated in a hurry,
And I don't know where they wandered;
But, however, I know that before the year was out
So married they each other.
      " Oh, by the cross, is that so?
      Ha! ha! ha! ha!
      That was a funny little song."

MY LITTLE NOOK AMONG THE MOUNTAINS.

I know a little nook among the mountains,
A little nook that is my own;
Where no vanity has taken root,
No innocence changed its color.
Wherever fate may me throw,
I long back again to my nook,
My little nook among the mountains.

There have I got a captive shut in,
Who must make itself content
Within the little narrow space,
For I have dazzled mind and senses.
Wherever fate may me drive,
I long back again to my nook,
My little nook among the mountains.

My little Hildur is the captive,
And Love with flowery bands
Has tied her, heart and foot and hand,
To the hut and the singer and the song.
Wherever fate may me drive,
I long back again to my nook,
My little nook among the mountains.

THE BOY AND THE GIRL.

THE BOY.

When a girl gets to be fifteen years
She has whims;

But when she gets twenty, and gets a beau,
She makes herself particular;
But if she goes single, in ten years more,
So, you may trust me, you will see
She will consent.

THE GIRL.

So high the bachelor of twenty
He puts his nose;
The best girl of the village
He must surely have;
But when ten times he has got "No!"
So, you may trust me, he is in no hurry
To try the fun.

THE BOY.

There is 'bout women so many a saying
To the worst;
But every bachelor marries well
As soon as he can.
If his woman then is a little mad and angry,
Her words do not go into bone and marrow,
That I have found.

THE GIRL.

Of men one can't always speak
The very best;
But every girl, of course, a man
Wants by her to fasten.
If he is a little angry once in awhile,
Yet the girl thinks he is good
'Most all the time.

THE BOY.

I should like to marry now:
Will you have me?
Don't be afraid—I will never beat you,
Or tease you.
Sometimes I may make wry faces,
But all my time I surely will
Love you.

THE GIRL.

Oh yes! I guess I shall have a man
As well as others;
When such a suitor offers he is
Not shown away.

Little quarrels there may be,
But thine forever I shall be:
Here is my hand.

After the singing the chairs were put aside, and the good Thord, in order to put life into the party, started a dance with one of his maids; but he made only two or three turns, for he was a sufferer from asthma. His son and nephew then danced with each girl of the household. Then we played blind-man's-buff, and many of the maidens had to redeem their forfeits by kissing me. Some of them were bashful, and objected at first; but they had to do it, amidst the merriment of all the company, who seemed to enjoy this part of the fun amazingly.

A strong feeling of conservatism, of holding fast to old customs—a hatred of any appearance of pride—are characteristics of the bönder; these are more apparent in some districts than in others. Often when Thord dined with me he was not hungry. "Why do you not take your meals with me?" I asked; "you certainly cannot eat two dinners within half an hour of each other."

"Oh," said he, "if I did so, I am afraid the servants of the house and neighbors would call me proud; they would say that I am ashamed of them before strangers; they would think that I slighted them."

To Thord, and many other farmers, I have often said, "Why do you not paint your dwellings white? they would look so much prettier, and more picturesque." The answer was, "We would like to do so, but what would the people say? They would think that we wanted to appear better than they are, and were ashamed to be bönder, or that we tried to imitate the city people." This intense conservatism is often a drawback to improvement, for those who would like to make changes dare not begin; hence the social forms of a more primitive state of society, which have been lost in other countries, still prevail here.

From one farm to another I went, here in the mountains, there in the valley, remaining a few hours in one house, overnight in another, welcomed everywhere; drinking the home-made jule öl (ale) from horns so old that the worshippers of

Thor and Odin had used them for toasts on their return from successful raids, and on the occasion of a marriage, or a burial, when they sung the songs celebrating the virtues of the braves who had died on the battle-field to enter full-armed into the happy halls of the Valhalla.

The ancient drinking-horns, now so rare, were from the ure-ox, now extinct. The engraving represents one in my posses-

OLD DRINKING-HORN. THIRTEEN INCHES HIGH.

sion, given to me by the museum of the city of Bergen, and comes, without doubt, from the heathen times. Drinking from one of these requires a peculiar knack, otherwise the contents are sure to fall on you. There was great merriment when, for the first time, I drank from one of them and the contents fell upon the bosom of my shirt.

Next to the drinking-horns are the wooden tankards; they are hooped like small kegs; many of them are beautifully carved, and some are four or five hundred years old. There is another form of hooped wooden vessels which is extremely rare. I saw only two of them, both made in the shape of coffee-pots, and one lined with silver hoops. These two drinking-vessels are the most curious specimens I have obtained. One of them is in the collection of Mr. Joseph W. Harper, one of my publishers, as a token of remembrance of many years of friendship.

On several farms ale was offered to me in old solid silver tankards, which held nearly half a gallon; but these vessels, which have replaced the older ones, date from later periods, very few of them being older than the sixteenth or seventeenth centuries. These tankards are often exceedingly heavy, some of them weighing several pounds.

WOODEN TANKARD.

As the thirteen days of yule drew to a close, I found myself at a farm-house in one of those small transverse valleys which fall into the Gudbrandsdal. It was late, and we were seated near a bright fire. Now and then a large wooden cup, filled with strong yule ale, was passed round. We suddenly heard the sound of music far away, but as we listened it came nearer and grew more distinct. Without warning the door opened, and a crowd of maskers filled the room. It was a surprise-party. Every one was dressed in female costume. The fiddlers and accordeon players

SILVER-MOUNTED PITCHER.

struck up the national mountain tunes, the maskers began to
talk to us in feigned voices, and all fell to dancing.   Many of
the company knew me by sight; one of the girls seized my
hand, and, although I was no dancer, I had to join the frolic.
When the dance was over the girls began to make love to us.
I was made a target for several of them.   "Oh, Paul, what
are you doing here this winter? It is nice of you to come and
spend Christmas among us."   "Paul, I love you!"   "Paul,
come to see us."   "Paul, is it true that you have been to
America since we saw you, hardly two months ago? can it
be, America is so far away?   Take me to America with you
when you go back."   "Paul, do you think I am an old woman
or a young one? do you think I am pretty or ugly?"   "Paul,
I want to marry you; say yes or no without seeing my face."
"Paul, I am sure you will make a good bonde."   "Who are
you?" I asked; but the girls, afraid of being found out, fled
to mingle with the crowd.   The host opened a trap-door in
the middle of the floor leading to the cellar, warning the people to be careful not to fall in, and several large wooden bowls
filled with ale were brought up; after these had been passed
round there was more dancing; and, when the maskers were
ready to depart, a woman took my arm, and I went with her
like a lamb, for I wanted to enjoy the fun.   From farm to
farm the masked party went, singing and dancing, until all
were tired.   Two girls and their brother, who had just arrived,
unmasked themselves and said, "Paul, come to our farm to
sleep."   I accepted the invitation, and was warmly welcomed.
We were all weary, and a crowd slept in the same room the
best way we could, in the old-fashioned style still practised in
Wales, and among the Dutch of Long Island and New Jersey
some thirty years ago, or in Pennsylvania and at Cape Cod,
and in many primitive parts of Europe to this day.

The 6th of January, the last of the thirteen days of yule,
found me at the farm of Hans Bredevangen, a warm-hearted
young fellow, who, besides his farm, had a country store, and
kept the relay-station.   He would have been a good match for
some fair damsel, but no one had captivated him.   On the
other side of the Logen River, a little higher up the valley, at

the base of the Svart (black) Mountain, rising 4389 feet above the sea, and about 3500 feet above the valley, was the farm of Selsjord, belonging to Hans's brother-in-law, Jakob, where we were going to spend the thirteenth day of yule. The weather could not have been finer; the air was crisp; the days were already sensibly longer, and on many of the farms the people had been watching the sun on the mountain-tops day after day—the children noticing with delight its daily descent lower and lower towards the valley, and counting the days when sunshine should reach the farm-house and the fields: the farmers were looking forward to the coming spring; the women were thinking of the sæters.

It is an error to suppose that among the bönder there is no ceremony or etiquette. On the contrary, we were invited by Hans's sister and brother-in-law at once up-stairs to the guests' room. I was startled by meeting there a bevy of young and beautiful girls. This was a young girls' party, and all were daughters of bönder — pictures of health, strong, with rosy complexions, light-haired, and very good-looking. Some of them were quite handsome. I suspected that this party was given as a trap for Hans; his sister evidently wanted to see him married. This I thought a dangerous place for Hans, or for a bachelor like myself. I was not sure if I also was not to fall a victim to the wiles of these fair damsels of Gudbrandsdal. They were dressed in their best—as they always are when they go visiting—with high-necked dresses of homespun material, and round their throats nice little white collars fastened by small gold or silver brooches; they wore their newest shoes, and their brightest colored or striped stockings; their hair was partly hidden under pretty calico handkerchiefs, clean and nicely ironed, and tied in a graceful knot under the chin.

Among the beauties were Karoline, Rönnog, Marit, Mari, Pernille, Fredrika, two Annes, and others. Some were the daughters of well-to-do farmers; more the children of poor parents; two were engaged as maids on the farms, for it is no disgrace to try to gain an honest livelihood, and wealth had nothing to do with friendship. They all knew Hans, who persuaded them that I was one of the best fellows in the world. One or two I had met before—were old acquaintances—but many of the party were strangers to me; nevertheless, we soon became sociable. We have remained good friends—some of them to this day—and sometimes we write to each other.

As we were chatting the good wife came to set the table, which she covered with a white cloth used for grand gala occasions. Dinner was then served, and, as was often the case, neither the host nor hostess took their repast with us—they wanted to show special honor. A high pile of flat bread was placed in the centre, by the side of which were a plate of fresh, soft, home-made brown bread, a large cheese, and an immense cake of butter, weighing at least thirty or forty pounds, so that the guests could help themselves as they pleased. When there is a little feast, butter is one of the luxuries. We clasped our hands, and then bowed our heads, asking a silent blessing before we drew up to the table. Hans and I sat together. Jakob and his wife remained standing, for etiquette required them to wait upon their guests, and to urge them to eat. If one wants to make a farmer in Scandinavia happy, he must eat the most he can.

We had soup, salted fish, roast mutton, sausages, and an immense plate of boiled potatoes. Now and then a large wooden bowl, filled with ale, as a loving-cup, was passed round. The dessert consisted of two huge bowls of rice, boiled with a large quantity of milk, sweetened, and mingled with raisins, forming a sort of very thick soup. These dishes were put in such places that those near them helped themselves. We all had silver spoons, instead of the wooden ones which are used on ordinary occasions. As the dinner proceeded our hearts warmed, and we became more and more talkative; and long before the meal was over all were as friendly with me as if they had known me for a long time. While eating I perceived that one of the girls was intensely in love with Hans, and I could see by the sly glances which the maidens now and then gave to each other that they enjoyed the fun: it was well known that she was desperately in love with my friend, who had seated himself away from her, and paid to every other one as much attention as he could, but none to her. She became so jealous that she could not even eat, and two or three times tears filled her eyes. Hans did not care to marry. Four years have passed away since our dinner, and I hear that the girl and Hans are still single.

After dinner we thanked the host and hostess, shaking hands with them, and then with each other; and after coffee had been served a little dance was started, and as there were no musicians, the dancing took place with singing accompaniment. Afterwards rings and blind-man's-buff and other games were played. In the evening three men who had been celebrating the day by too much drinking, and had heard of this quiet party, came to enjoy the fun; but they were not allowed to enter. Finally sleighs came, and the party broke up. "Paul," they all said, "do not go to Christiania yet; stay with us plain bönder folks a little longer; spend the twentieth day of yule here. You have plenty of time yet to go to Lapland, and see the Laplanders; it is too dark there now:" and we bade each other good-night. As Rönnog and Marit, who were sisters, got into their sleigh, they said to me, "Come to Skjena; father and mother will welcome you: we have folks in America. Come to-morrow."

Hans, on the following morning, invited all the guests who had been at Selsjord and the neighbors to come to his house in the afternoon, to take coffee and participate in a sort of kettledrum. I observed Fredrika, Hans's servant-maid, who was strongly built and powerful, but with soft and gentle manners. She was doing the honors of the house as if she had been the hostess. Hans having no wife, it was her duty to attend to the guests. A stranger would have taken her for the mistress of the house. The coffee-pot was constantly replenished from a large kettle kept over a slow fire. I had hardly drunk one cup of coffee when Fredrika filled it again: her eyes seemed to be everywhere. The time passed rapidly, and it was dark before we were aware of it. Soon a sleigh was at the door, and Anders (Andrew) Pedersen (the son of Peter), Fredrika's brother, was to drive Rönnog, Marit, and myself to Skjena, the home of the girls. The evening was fine,

the stars shone brightly, and the mountains looked majestic
in the stillness of the night. As we passed the farms we saw
the dim light of a lamp through the small panes of the windows, and now and then a farmer reading his newspaper, or
the big Bible was on the table, and the father was reading it
to the family.

Skjena is a very old farm, and I was welcomed by Engebret,
the father, and Marit, the mother, and the rest of the family.
The greeting was so warm that I could not help feeling at
home. At once there was a great stir; keys were in the
hands of two or three of the daughters, who went one way or
another; a large pile of flat bread was brought out, potatoes
were cooked, slices of bacon were fried; and a large bowl of
home-brewed ale and a pitcher of milk were produced. One
is not supposed to know that these preparations are going on
for him. Soon Anders and myself were invited to enter a
little room next to the kitchen, where a fire had been lighted
in the old stove, and a table nicely spread. There was a bed
in the corner. This was a sort of reception-room, and a number of photographic portraits of the family and their friends
hung upon the walls. I asked Rönnog if she would give me
her picture, as she was the only sister who had one to spare.
She answered she was willing if I would give her one of mine.
We were left to take care of ourselves, but members of the
family once or twice came back to urge us to eat and drink
more, and we finished with a cup of coffee. Retiring to the
kitchen, we saw a pretty picture of the home-life of the
bönder. Four daughters were busily knitting stockings,
the mother was spinning, the father reading the Bible, and
Fredrik was seated by the fire. In one corner was the bed of
the old couple, and I noticed the whiteness of the sheets. A
smile from all welcomed us when we entered the room, and
as usual we shook hands with the father and mother and all
the family, and thanked them for our entertainment.

Anders then made preparations to return home. He could
not be induced to remain till the next morning. I said
to him, "Are you going to leave me here alone?" "Yes,"
he replied, "I must go to work early to-morrow morning.

Christmas is over now. I have plenty to do." As he was getting into his sleigh I quietly put into his hand a little money, which I thought would be somewhat more than an equivalent for the drive; but, though a poor man, he returned it. "No, indeed," said he, as if I had wounded his pride— "No, indeed, Paul—we are friends." I could not induce him to take it. One must know the bönder of Norway as I do to appreciate the manliness of their character. Under their apparently rough exterior beat as noble hearts as ever lived.

As he bade me good-bye, he pressed my hand with such a powerful grasp that I was on the point of uttering a scream of pain. On my return to the kitchen the girls lighted a lantern and disappeared, and a short time afterwards returned; they had gone to prepare a room in the next house, to which I was conducted by Rönnog and Marit. My small bedroom, looking out on the main road, was warm and comfortable, and I was left alone in the old log-house, where generations of the Skjena family had lived and died, and I fell asleep on a luxurious feather-bed furnished with snowy sheets.

Early the next morning Rönnog brought me a cup of coffee with cake, lighted a fire in the stove, and said, "I hope, Paul, you have slept well. You know this is a plain bonde bed. While you are dressing we will have breakfast ready for you. Come to the next house:" and with these words she disappeared. I was sorry when I had to leave these good people. To this day we are great friends, and the last letters I received from Gudbrandsdal are from Hans and Rönnog, and I give their exact translation, so that you may know the style of a bonde's daughter, and that of an honest straightforward tiller of the soil. The handwriting of both is excellent.

LETTER FROM RÖNNOG.

Dear Paul,—Eight days ago I received a letter from thee, which made me very happy to read through, and see that thou art well and hearty, which we hardly had expected now, when it is so long since we heard anything from thee. And the same good news I can give thee—we are well, both young and old, and that is certainly the best thing one has in this world. I and Fredrik have recently been to the burial of Thron Loftsgaard, and it was a very nice affair, and I was there three days; and this man died very suddenly; he took sick one day and died the next. I will tell thee that last summer I was sæter girl, and there I had it pleasant; but, then, one day the *grayleg* (wolf) came sneaking forward, and then thou mayst believe I got afraid that he should kill my creatures. He killed five sheep in this place, but none of mine. If thou hadst come to the sæter thou shouldst have got much cream and thick milk; then I hope thou wilt come here next summer, and thou shalt be welcome at Skjena again. This winter it has been very cold, so that it has not been such severe cold in nineteen years; but now it is good winter weather. I can greet thee from my brother Ole. We have recently had a letter from him, and he was well. Hans Bredevangen and M—— go the same now as when thou wert here; they are still unmarried. Fredrika Bredevangen is now under good way to be married to Amun Selsjord. The mother of Fredrika has long been in bed, and she is yet there. Fredrik shot two reindeer last summer—one was a cow and the other a calf: many deer were shot here last season. I must not forget to send thee my hearty thanks for the remembrance thou sent me; it was very unexpected for me to get a present from thee. Now I have got nothing more to write which can interest thee, therefore come to an end with these simple and hurriedly written lines, with the wish that they may find thee well and contented: with a friendly greeting to thee from us all of the house, but first and last thou art greeted from me.   Live well.   RÖNNOG E. SKJENA.

LETTER FROM HANS.

MY DEAR NEVER-TO-BE-FORGOTTEN FRIEND, PAUL DU CHAILLU,—Your welcome letter of November I have received with gladness, for which I thank you. It was received New-year's Day with the enclosed presents to my sister Marit, and to my pige* Marit. They ask me to thank you many times. They think it was very interesting to receive a present from that so much spoken of and berömte (praised) land, America, and so much the more when the present is from you. The newspaper you sent, *Harper's Weekly*, has also been received. I see in it an engraving representing you driving with a reindeer in Lapland, which must have been very pleasant to do. Here in old Norway there is not much to tell one about. We have now finished Christmas, which, as you know, lasts very long here, as you must remember from the fun we had at Selsjord the thirteenth day of yule. At Christmastime I drank to the health of my good friend Chaillu with my *venner*† *og veninder* (Norske pigerne), Norwegian girls, who send their hearty greetings. I see that next summer you will come to Norway again, and also to Gudbrandsdalen, when it shall be very pleasant to meet again, especially now when we can talk and understand each other better. We shall make a few trips to the sæters. I learn by your letter that you will soon publish a book on your travels in Scandinavia, which I hope will be as interesting and entertaining as the publication of your travels in Africa, which book I have read.

Herewith is enclosed a pair of mittens which my pige Marit sends you as a present, *som de faar slide med hilsen* (which you may wear with health). I must finally wish you a good and happy New-year.

You are in the most friendly manner greeted by your friend,

HANS BREDEVANGEN.

---

* Pige, girl; pigerne, girls.   † Venner, male friends; veninder, female friends.

CHAPTER IV.

THE winter was an exceptionally mild and pleasant one, with great variations of temperature. On my way to Stockholm I had for *compagnons de voyage* in the railway carriage an old gentleman, his wife, and three daughters. The gentleman wore a long loose coat lined with wolf-skin—the warmest after that of the reindeer—reaching to the ankles, with a collar which, when raised, completely enveloped the head. He also wore a thick fur cap, and heavy loose boots with fur inside. The ladies were literally packed in furs, and wore exceedingly thick soft knit veils, which completely hid their faces, besides heavy cloaks, closely drawn. The fan-lights over the doors of the car were shut, and the father constantly inquired of his wife and daughters if they were warm and comfortable, although it was thawing weather, and the thermometer stood several degrees above freezing-point. Not a breath of air entered that compartment, which was filled with six persons, all wrapped in furs. As the old gentleman was in constant fear that his family would catch cold, I could not ask to have the windows partly opened; and if I had opened one of them without asking permission, objections would have been raised at once. All of them seemed to regard me with perfect amazement, for I wore only my winter overcoat, with no fur boots, and felt uncomfortably warm. After a short

OSCAR II.

time I began to suffocate, and my temples to throb for want of fresh air. I wondered how people could bear such a close atmosphere; but, happily, at one of the stations the whole party left the train, whereupon I let down one of the windows and breathed freely.

On my way across the peninsula from Christiania to Stockholm by rail, on the 10th of January, the country was bare of snow. At Stockholm, Lake Mälar was not frozen, and the port was free of ice. The people everywhere longed for snow, for the transportation of iron ores or the hauling of timber was at a stand-still; land traffic was delayed; game, which is sent in enormous quantities to the city from distant forests, was scarce, and fuel in the inland towns had become dearer.

Carl XV. was now dead, and Oscar II. was king.

Stockholm had not the cheerful aspect it presents in summer; its gardens and parks were deserted, the delightful strains of music which caught the ear being heard only in the cafés; the merry sound of sleigh-bells and the gay crowd of skaters on the Mälar were yet to come. Sleighing lasts more or less for three or four months in cold winters. The theatrical season had come, and in the evenings the cafés were filled with people. The city nevertheless looked wintry.

All the houses now had double windows (a rare occurrence in Christiania), at the base of which, between the two, a layer of cotton was spread to absorb moisture. French instead of sliding windows are used in Norway and Sweden. One of the panes of each is free, and opens for ventilation. The rooms are uncarpeted, just as in summer. The modes of heating in Norway and Sweden are different in the cities; in the former iron stoves are used — in Sweden the rooms are warmed by long white porcelain stoves, which reach almost to the ceilings. Some are round and others square; the door is of copper, which is kept bright and shining. The amount of wood required during the day is very small; kindling three fires a day is sufficient in very cold weather. When the wood is burned to charcoal, and the disagreeable gases gone, the sliding valve is closed, to retain the heat of the brick and porcelain walls. I am surprised that these stoves have not come in vogue in America.

Porcelain stoves are built in the manner shown on page 36: a is a damper, moved in and out by the cord c; b is the fireplace, where the wood-fire is built; d is a flue, carrying the smoke into the chimney *e*. The inside of the stove, containing the flue, is built of brick, and only the outside covering is porcelain. When a wood-fire is built in the fireplace the hot smoke is carried through the flue, thereby heating the stove through. When the wood is consumed the damper is shut, entirely preventing the heat from escaping into the chimney. The stove, therefore, retains its heat for many hours, even in the coldest weather.

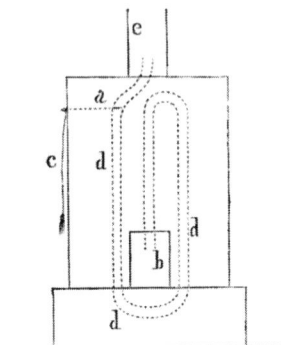

PORCELAIN STOVE.

From Stockholm the highway to the far North skirts the shores of the Baltic, and of the Gulf of Bothnia as far as Haparanda—and still continues north, as we have seen in summer, up to Pajala—the distance being over 128 Swedish miles. The main road passes over many fjords, across hills and valleys, through large forests of pine and fir, affording in summer charming landscapes, which are succeeded by dreary districts of swamp and morasses—then winding its way by wild and lonely lakes, past tracts of cultivated land and sylvan scenery, and through clean and pleasant towns, villages, and hamlets nestled near inlets of the sea, or picturesquely situated by the river-side, full of life in summer but quiet in the winter.

With a moderate amount of snow, when the sleighing is good, the journey can be made in a fortnight without any hardship. Many of the post-stations are very comfortable, and several towns are met on the way. But I intended to roam through the vast region extending from the Baltic to the North Cape; to cross, in the depth of winter, in the latitude of about 69°, the range of mountains to the coast of Norway, hoping to encounter storms which would give me an idea of the fury of the winter winds that sweep the altitudes within the arctic circle; then visit the islands of Lofoden, to see the great cod-fisheries of Norway; and afterwards to make a tour by sea to the other side of the North Cape as far as the Varenger fjord; then, with reindeer, to return to Haparanda in time to see the sudden transformation of winter into spring. This trip was not a small undertaking, for it was to involve more than three thousand miles of sleighing, several hundred miles of sea travel, and about five months of time. Such a journey to many would be long and tedious at such a time; but to me it was full of novelty and instruction, and I look back upon it as among the most enjoyable months of my travels.

From Upsala to Haparanda there are seventy-one post-stations, many of them very comfortable, with tidy rooms and clean beds, and tolerably good food. In winter the bedrooms are always kept warm at night by means of porcelain stoves. How welcome is the sight of the station when hungry, or after a hard day's travel! How cheerful is the blazing fire in the stuga, and how comfortable and warm the feather-bed!

For one wishing to travel fast and cheaply the mail-coach is the best conveyance. There are no stoppages, night or day; horses are always ready at the station at the time the mail is due, and they are among the best; but seats must be secured days beforehand.

On a dark evening towards the middle of January I left the old University town in company with a friend, a delightful companion, Herr A——, a doctor of philosophy, who was on his way to the city of Sundsvall, where he resided. We left in a comfortable coach drawn by two horses. Shortly after our departure a few flakes of snow fell, the forerunner of one of the grandest and most continuous snow-storms that had fallen in Sweden for a hundred years. Faster and faster they came down; the snow increased rapidly as we advanced northward, making slow progress; but by travelling the whole night we reached Yfre, the third post-station from Upsala, at five o'clock A.M. After three hours' sleep, and a good breakfast, we started again refreshed. The Swedish sleighs procured at the stations are very comfortable, and quite an improvement on those of Norway. They seat two persons, and are very much like the sleighs commonly used in America. After leaving Yfre we entered large forests of pine and fir.

From the city of Gefle the snow became deeper and deeper, and the horses floundered through it at every step. The storm had been remarkable for its stillness, and the forests of pine had become exceedingly beautiful. The mercury being hardly below freezing, the flakes were large and damp, and as they fell remained on top of each other, and clung on the branches of the pines; and I often drove through a mass of white pyramids during the night.

The aurora borealis was sending streams of light upward, with waves swaying to and fro over us, and everything was very distinctly seen. The lofty trees and all the shrubs were covered with a white mantle, the branches bending under the weight. The pines of Scandinavia have a pyramidal shape. Not a particle of green could be seen, and each tree was topped with a sharp-pointed pinnacle of snow several feet high. The spectacle was superb, and thousands upon thousands of these lined each side of the road as far as the eye could reach. I thought I was travelling in fairy-land, in the stillness and marvellous beauty of that winter night. At times I fancied I could see minute sparkles of light coming from the snow, and became so excited by the scene that I told my companion that if I had come all the way from America to see such a sight, and nothing more, I should have been perfectly satisfied. He caught my enthusiasm, and said that such forest scenery was not often seen in Sweden. Here in the South the storm had stopped for awhile, though we heard by telegraph that it was still raging fiercely farther north.

Numerous crate-like sleighs, packed with game, were on their way to Stockholm from Jemtland and the forests of Norrland. We were all travelling in the same narrow track, and each vehicle turning to the right, the horses sinking down almost to their necks, and often having to make great efforts to extricate themselves from the snow, jerking the sleigh, and sometimes upsetting it and throwing us out. Only those who were absolutely forced were travelling at this time. The drivers had dogs which warned the people of their approach.

The meeting of the mail-coach was a cause of excitement. On this road they carry two passengers inside and one outside;

the postman carries a big sabre, and sometimes an old army pistol: as for many years no highway robbery of the mail has occurred, these precautions seem needless, though in old times the mail-coaches were attacked when it was known that they carried large amounts of specie. Any one who tries to pick a quarrel, or to stop the mails in a drunken frolic or otherwise, is severely punished. In a short time we got acquainted with the mail passengers while exchanging civilities in the shape of cigars: my friend returning the compliment by passing round his flask, one of the Swedes remarked that in the cold climate of Scandinavia something stronger than water was necessary. "Oh," said another, "have you ever heard of any great man, either as a master intellect, a great writer, or a great soldier, who has drank only water all his life?" "I never have seen a whole-souled, generous, unselfish man yet that did not take a glass of wine," said the third companion. As it was too cold to discuss the subject on the high-road— and I must own that I was trying in vain to remember one— I laughed, and said I did not recollect if there were any great men who had drank only water. I concluded it was better not to discuss the subject.

How strange are these little Swedish towns in the depth of winter! At Hudiksvall we found the streets blocked up with snow, and lighted by the old-fashioned square oil lamps, suspended by cords. There I witnessed another illustration of the honesty of the people. When I reached the station of Gnarp, I found that the driver of the other sleigh had forgotten to transfer my satchel, containing all the money I had provided for the journey. There was a large amount of silver coin for small change, and any one could tell the contents by the weight, and I had not a copper with me. My companion seemed to take for granted that everything was all right, and that it would only occasion a loss of time. A man was sent back to recover the missing bag, and he returned at four o'clock in the morning with the satchel and its contents.

The weather became colder, the mercury marking 17° below zero during the night. The forest now presented a new appearance as we approached Sundsvall; there was not a particle of snow on the pine and fir trees, and the dark-green of their branches contrasted beautifully with the white mantle which covered the earth. The horses and dogs of the northern countries like the snow; now and then the horses take a bite of it, and the dogs, when thirsty, also eat it, and both roll themselves in it: they seem to enjoy the dry cold atmosphere of winter. The magpies would often follow us.

On the fourth day we reached Sundsvall. My thoughtful companion had telegraphed from Hudiksvall, and soon after our arrival we were seated at the Stadhuset before a good dinner which he had ordered; and over a glass of good old wine we recounted the adventures of our journey to the friends who had come to welcome him back. The snow was every day getting deeper. The distance between Sundsvall and Hernösand is about thirty-five miles, and it took me three days to accomplish this short journey. A few miles north of that town is Åland, a hamlet composed of several farms. The landscape was bleak, and the fjord was frozen; but in summer the groves of birch, the green meadows, and the waters of the sea present a charming picture. The traveller, as he drives along, will see a white-painted house at a short distance from the relay-station, between the highway and the rocky shores of the Baltic. This was the pleasant home of a jägmästare—superintendent of the forest of a district—a mighty Nimrod—a gentleman to whom I had letters of introduction. From the station I wended my way slowly through the deep snow towards that house with my letters.

As I entered the gate I saw a maiden of about eighteen years, a true child of the North, with fair hair, soft blue eyes, and rosy cheeks, who was playing with the snow, and with a little shovel was sending it in all directions. She was making a pathway, and seemed to enjoy the fun. The gentleness and grace in all her motions, and delicacy of her features and skin, at once showed that she was a young lady of refinement, while the *naïveté* of her manners indicated that she had been brought up in the country. As I approached she stopped and looked at me, as if to say, "What do you want, sir?" Bowing to her, I inquired if the jägmästare was at home. "Yes," was the answer, and with great composure she begged me to follow her to the house, and leaving me in the parlor she disappeared. Soon afterwards the jägmästare came and read my two letters of introduction—one a general letter from the Director-general in Stockholm to all the jägmästares, and the other from a colleague of his.

"Welcome here!" said he, with great warmth, extending his hand, "*very* welcome." He was over middle age, with a pleasant countenance but determined features, and genial in manner. He had read accounts of my travels and gorilla hunting, and received me at once as a brother sportsman. The young lady whom I had met soon came back with refreshments. I was asked if I could travel on snow-shoes, and was told that I must learn to walk on them, and also to drive reindeer. "My daughter can go on snow-shoes," said the father with a sort of pride, "quite as well as a Laplander." "Yes indeed," she said, "I love to go on them, it is such fun! I love winter." "Will you teach me to go on snow-shoes?" "Yes, certainly, with great pleasure. I am sure you will learn quickly." "It is necessary," said the father, "that you should learn to walk on them in order to go bear-hunting, for the snow is very deep in the forest." "I can scull also," said the daughter with a sort of girlish pride, "and in summer I like to row on the fjord, and ramble into the woods in search of wild-flowers." Looking at her, I thought the girl a flower herself—a picture of health, and as fresh as the budding of spring. The dress she wore had been woven and made by herself; the pattern was very pretty, and the material handsome. Brought up at home, she had learned to be industrious, and enjoy the more her hours or days of freedom.

"If you return early perhaps we shall be able to go after a bear; one is ringed about thirty miles from here; but if you are late he may either be shot or have left his winter place," said the jägmästare, a great part of whose conversation ran on bear-hunting, and how they are ringed. The bears in Scandinavia sleep all winter; but in the autumn, before the snow comes, they look out for places where they want to hibernate, and are then exceedingly shy, often spending several days going round and round their chosen place. In the far North they remain as much as five or six months hidden and without food.

Before I left, the good jägmästare exacted a promise that I should come again on my return from the North, and go to his sæter; then he added, "At all events, come back before I am too old to go with you." Since that time I have been twice to Åland, and each time warmly received; but I have not yet succeeded in going to the sæter or in hunting bears with him, for in both cases the season was over. I shall always remember Åland and the white house of the jägmästare, and hope that at a not far distant day we may meet again and go bear-hunting.

The large snow-ploughs which one sees in summer lying by the way-side were now dragged over the road by four, five, or six horses, driven by two or three farmers, to level the track. The laws in regard to the highways are very strict, and after a snow-storm the farmers have to furnish horses, and break and flatten the road for a certain distance. These ploughs are a triangular frame of heavy timber, eight or ten feet wide and about fifteen feet long; the work of the men and horses is very hard, the men having to walk. Often during the night when it was mild and foggy, or it had snowed, or the wind had blown snow over the road and obliterated the traces of preceding sleighs, we had to drive very cautiously; for when a mistake occurred, and we lost the ploughed track, we went deep into the snow. In that case the intelligent horse was left to himself, and knew what to do; most carefully he moved, and when he sunk in going to the right he immediately made the next step to the left, and *vice versa.* His sagacity was so remarkable that it made me forget in part the weariness of the drive. Occasionally we got at quite a distance from the road, the first intimation being the animal sinking up to his neck. After walking in several directions, trying the snow with his feet, and sinking repeatedly, the driver finally found the road by the firm snow. We then wondered how we could have got so far from it.

The snow kept increasing every mile northward. We tum-

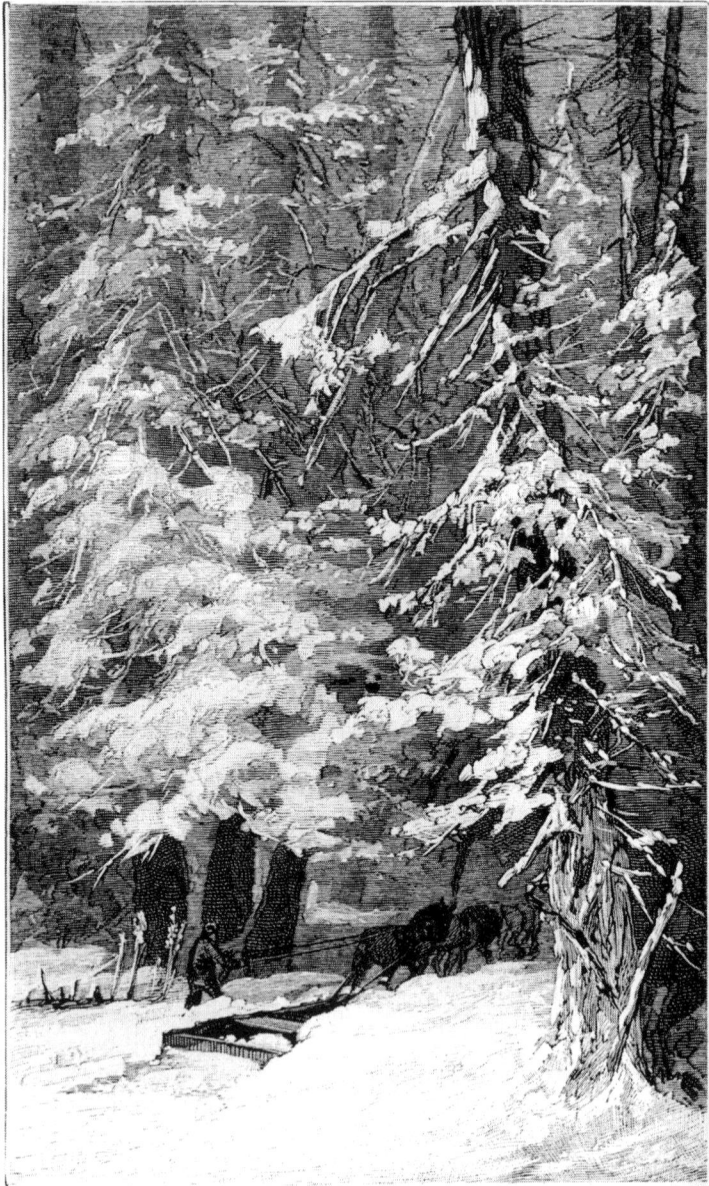

THE SNOW-PLOUGH.

bled on one side or another, upsetting before we were aware
of it. At each effort our animals made to extricate themselves we were almost thrown out of the sleigh. The poor
brutes would sink to their necks, and sometimes almost to
their heads. Each horse stepped in the track of the one that
preceded, so that, if the plough had not passed over, the tracks
would have been perfectly honey-combed: the holes were
often more than fifteen inches deep. At the end of the day's
travel, which averaged about eighteen hours, I felt so sore
and tired that I was glad to rest. The snow was so heavy
inland that some of the Lapps had to come to the coast with
their reindeer or they would have perished; they had to feed
on the moss hanging from the branches of the pines and firs.
At last the fences, the shrubs, and the huge boulders were
hidden from view; twigs of fir and pine had been planted
to show the way; these, of course, are always put over the
fjords, lakes, and swamps, and many thousands of young
saplings are thus destroyed every year. The telegraph wires
were nearly out of sight. Snow-ploughs were levelling the
road everywhere; farther south they were drawn by three
horses, but here the number had increased to six, and three
or four men had charge of each plough. These were followed
by wooden rollers, which packed the snow more closely. The
struggles of the horses became so great, in their efforts to extricate themselves, that in some cases blood came from their
nostrils. I myself had to stop. Farther north the ploughs
were laid aside, and the snow was left to settle by its own
weight for a day or two before they would be used again. The
farmers did not understand how I could travel for pleasure
in such weather, and why I wished to go so far away. Few
persons were out-of-doors, but the thick smoke from the chimneys showed that there were cheerful fires, round which the
families were gathered. All the winter outside work was suspended; the hauling of logs in the forest was stopped. The
snow still increased as I advanced towards the north, and there
was more than twelve feet on a level. This is enormous, when
we consider that two feet is about the maximum that falls in
twenty-four hours. Here the strength of the great snow-storm

had lasted a week, from Sunday to Sunday. Some of the houses were covered to their roofs; and galleries were necessary in many places to give light to the windows, with trenches to reach the doors; others were blocked up by drifts against the doors, and exit had to be made by the windows. Here we had reached the maximum of snow, which gradually diminished afterwards; and twenty miles farther we came to the small town of Umeå, which I found obstructed with snow. At the relay-station a card was waiting for me, upon which was written in French the following message from a doctor of philosophy: "If you have time, let me hear of your arrival, for your friend, Director U——, has asked me to do all I could to be agreeable and useful to you." This was another of the many illustrations of the acts of thoughtful politeness of which I had been the recipient from educated Scandinavians.

Though only a year and a half had elapsed since I had seen the little town, time had worked great changes in the place. The former governor of the province was dead, and universally regretted by all who knew him. At the agricultural school of Innertafle my old friend and his wife received me most kindly. "You cannot go farther to-day," said they, at the same time helping me to divest myself of my winter garb; and a short time after their daughter, a sweet little girl, presented me with a little pocket-book, which she had embroidered with pearls especially for me, and which she intended to send to me in America.

Since my departure from Upsala there had been at times great changes in the weather. At Innertafle the temperature had moderated so much that I was afraid it was the precursor of another snow-storm. If more snow were added to the already prodigious quantity which had had no time to pack, I dreaded the prospect. These great snow-storms generally take place when it is not very cold, and when the mercury ranges from 2° to 11° below the freezing point. In February, the coldest month of the year in those regions, such mild weather was unusual. The following morning was gray, and the thermometer marked only 5° below freezing. The atmosphere was foggy, and, as the fog fell on the groves of birches which surrounded the house, it adhered to the branches, which appeared as if they had been covered with a dew which had crystallized upon them, presenting a very beautiful and fairy-like appearance. These birches of Scandinavia are exceedingly beautiful, with their white trunks and branches gracefully bending towards the ground. The following day the mercury ranged from 5° to 7° below freezing, and we were between lat. 63° and 64°.

From Innertafle I travelled all night; and at five A.M., after twenty-two hours of driving, tired and hungry, I came to the station of Innervik. The two previous stations were filled with travellers, and there were no vacant beds. I might have slept on the floor, or on a bench, or on the table, but preferred to go forward. At Innervik I found comfortable quarters, and fell into a dreamy sleep, in which I thought I was bumped about in the sleigh, just as one sometimes feels the motion of a ship a day or two after landing. The hamlet of Innervik takes its name from the bay, and is distant about a Swedish mile from the small town of Skellefteå. From the farm I could see the frozen sea below, looking now like a vast field of snow. The weather had become colder again, the thermometer remaining steady at 20° below freezing, and a piercing wind warned me that another cold wave was coming over the land. The little seaport of Skellefteå has quite a number of streets, and the houses were large and comfortable. I was struck, while walking in the streets, with the number of pretty young ladies with oval faces, rosy cheeks, and light and graceful carriage. They were certainly, I thought, more numerous in proportion to the population than at any place I had visited before.

In the North some small towns have a large building called the stadshuset. It is a hotel, containing a spacious hall for entertainments, and a number of rooms for travellers, with a restaurant and a café, private dining-rooms, and often a billiard-room. The cooking is generally very good and the rooms comfortable, and altogether superior to post-stations on the road.

After leaving Skellefteå the cold spell was of short duration, and when I reached Piteå it had become mild again. We were now out of the great snow belt, which in Sweden is between lat. 61° and 64°. The weather was so mild for February that in the morning it was only 7° below freezing; from hour to hour it became milder, and in the afternoon, when I arrived at Piteå, the thermometer stood at freezing-point, and remained so for a few hours; it rose in the evening to 36°, at 6 o'clock P.M. it was 34°, at 8 P.M. 30°. The air was perfectly still, and not a cloud could be seen, but the horizon was hazy. At about 7.30 I noticed a soft and luminous atmosphere towards the north, the forerunner of the aurora borealis. Soon afterwards a wide arc of haze, full of light, appeared, through which the stars could be seen. The clearness of the sky above and below the arc was remarkable. The highest point of the lower edge seemed to be about 35° above the horizon, and within was Jupiter and other stars shining brightly. The whole body began to show signs of motion; the tremor became more and more perceptible from one end to the other of the bright hazy mass; its motion increased, and it became more luminous, and swayed to and fro in undulating waves. Within half an hour another arc was formed under the first, the centre of the second being 15° or 20° below the other. Through the body of this also stars could be seen, and between the two arcs, and above and below, the sky was clear: the second at first showed hardly any signs of motion, and its brightness was as that of the Milky Way. Sheets of glimmering light streamed from the horizon, disappearing and reappearing. The light became more and more brilliant, quicker and quicker became the motion of the waves; they swayed to and fro from one end of the arc to the other; the discharges of the electric glow became more intense, varying in brightness—the quicker the motion the brighter the light—indicating that a great magnetic storm was raging.

Soon changes in the centre of the luminous body began to be noticeable; the waves as they rolled began to change from white to bluish, from green to violet, and then came almost a blending of all the colors. The lower arc in the mean time had shown signs of motion, and of the electric storm; sheets

of light from the horizon became more vivid as they shot upward—a spectacle of great beauty. The upper part of the
swaying mass was fringed with a magnificent dark-red border,
singularly contrasting with the color of the lower part, till the
whole arc became of a fiery red; then the waves began to
move more slowly, the flashes of light became dimmer, and
the great storm was coming to an end; the red mass was
broken into numerous fragments, which were scattered over
the sky, and finally nothing was left over our heads but the
blue starry heavens of that winter night.

Life in many towns by the sea is one of great dulness; they
seem dead, on account of the stagnation of trade; the farmers
do not come to the villages for news or business; few sleighs
are passing to and fro, but now and then a load of wood comes
in; goods are seldom transported from Stockholm, for it would
be too tedious and expensive, and everybody waits for the
summer season. The only time when there seems more activity is when a fair is to take place in the interior; then the
merchants are sending goods for sale; but this bustle lasts
only a day or two.

The Swedes are passionately fond of cards. In the sitting-
rooms are sometimes scattered a number of little tables where
ladies and gentlemen play together. In the hotels, or at their
own houses, men occasionally pass the whole night in gaming.
It is a custom to play together for a given number of days in
a week, in which there are often heavy stakes, and frequently
a considerable amount of money changes hands; but I was
told that at the end of the season the players generally came
out about even, as the partners are changed.

They also have singing clubs, which meet on Sunday afternoons. While in Piteå I was invited to the home of a
teacher who taught English in one of the schools, and could
speak it well. At his house every Sunday afternoon about
twenty ladies and gentlemen met to practise the singing of
church music, and some exceedingly pretty ballads which are
taught in the schools. Some of the voices were beautiful, and
the performances of this little society would have been creditable to any company of trained artists: two pleasant hours

were spent in this way. The climate of the country seems to benefit the vocal organs, and during the long winter months little musical sociables are constantly taking place. Now and then a ball is given, almost always in the large room of the stadshuset; in such cases tickets are sold, or an admittance fee is charged to defray the expenses. Almost everybody goes—especially the marriageable damsels, with their mammas; all gentlemen are in full dress: there are seats around the ball-room for the ladies. One meets the old and young—for even old married couples like to have a dance, and it is quite common to see a married man or an old gentleman dance with a young girl, or *vice versa*. Waltzes and galops are the favorites. One of the peculiarities which struck me was that, immediately after a dance was over, the gentlemen would quietly return their partners to their mammas or friends, and then disappear in the next room. They smoked, drank, ate, or talked, till they were again called by their engagements for the next dance. Now and then they brought in some refreshment for the ladies. After these intervals they seemed to enjoy the fun with renewed vigor.

From Piteå the snow continued to diminish greatly in depth the farther north I travelled. After Luleå the Finnish was only spoken by the farmers. At these stations no one thought of locking his trunks, as it would not look well. At Jemtön the servant-girl brought me a gold locket which she found on the floor of the kitchen. I had dropped it from my satchel the evening before while showing them the curiosities which it contained. I said, playfully, "Why did you not keep it?" She replied, "How, then, could I ever walk erect and look people in the face?"

I had hardly left this station the next morning when I was startled by a call, and as I looked back I saw a small white-headed urchin, whose cap had just tumbled from his head, running after us as fast as he could; I stopped my horse. He had in his hand a white pocket-handkerchief of mine which I had dropped on the road. It would have been a nice thing for him to keep, but his boyish heart was too honest; he handed it to me breathless, and ran back as quickly as he came; and though I called him, to give him a few öres, the little fellow, who was not afraid to return what did not belong to him, feared to come back to get a bit of money.

At Saiwits the station-master knew Swedish, and his farm being very comfortable, I concluded to remain a couple of days. This man, Kivijärvi, was considered by all a lucky fellow to have secured the heart and hand of Maria Fredrika over all his rivals. He had married a wife who had brought to him her farm; for in Sweden, as well as in Norway, as soon as a woman marries all she has goes to her husband, so that all the girls who have or are to inherit farms have no trouble in getting married. Such will have many admirers, for here, as elsewhere, wealth has its charms. But to a stranger it did not seem to matter much, for the owner of an estate works as hard as any of his hands, and the wife as much as any of her maids. The farm had eighteen cows, quite a number of sheep, and a goodly number of acres of grazing and grain land. There were two dwelling-houses—one for the reception of strangers and friends. I found the people here were very shy.

While here a woman came and asked me if I had met her husband, who had gone to Norway and had remained there: she had heard indirectly from him. During my journey in Scandinavia I found several poor women with their children who had been deserted by their husbands and fathers, who, under the pretext of going to America to see how it looked before bringing their families, never wrote, and were never heard of again.

The weather, which had remained cold for a week, and varied from about 1° to 18° below zero, began to moderate, and then came on the mildest temperature I had met since I left Christiania: the mercury stood at eight o'clock A.M. at 36°, at noon, 45°, and at three P.M. fell back to 38°.

From Saiwits we came to Nikkala, the last station before Haparanda. I was welcomed by the farmer, for he had heard of me, and had wondered if I would stop with him. Fresh logs were thrown into the fire, and the cheerful flames lighted the kitchen, where coffee was made and served in the parlor. I was a guest, and for the first day it would not have done for me to remain all the time in the kitchen.   Flower-pots with carnations, roses, geraniums, etc., were at the windows.   The mother, Matilda Serlota (Charlotte), and the daughter, Maria Matilda, a perfect blonde, and really a good-looking girl, and Abram (Abraham), the son, and Maria Kajsa, the maid of all work, with the husband, composed the family at that time. When I asked the daughter to write her name and those of her people in one of my memorandum-books, used for the purpose of judging of the education of the people, I learned here, as I had farther north, that the young among the farmers wrote badly, sometimes unintelligibly, and many of the old people did not know how to write at all, but old and young knew how to read.

From Nikkala to Haparanda the distance is about six miles.   There was but little snow; it had drifted badly in many places, showing that we were in a windy region; in others the road was bare, and nowhere was the snow two feet deep on the level.   Dreary, indeed, appeared the frozen sea in its white mantle, and the long low granite promontories, clad with fir and darker pines, coming down to the ice-bound shore.   But beautiful was the pale-blue sky in contrast with the white robe which covered the country, and the pale rays of the sun did not seem to give any heat.

Late in the afternoon on the 17th of February, 1873, I came to Haparanda, at the mouth of the Torne River, after a journey of 740 miles from Stockholm over the deepest snow I had ever crossed.   I had been over five weeks on the way, but felt none the worse for the journey.   I had now reached the extreme northern part of the Gulf of Bothnia.   The coast was low, fringed by birches, and the gulf looked like a vast white plain.   The farms were few and far apart, and there was an oppressive dreariness about the whole landscape.

CHAPTER V.

In winter the country between the Gulf of Bothnia and the Arctic Sea is subject to violent winds, which sweep northward over the frozen surface with no obstacle to lessen their fury. We left Haparanda in a storm so severe that our horse could hardly proceed; and, as it increased, our sleigh was often in danger of upsetting. The snow flew in thick cloudy masses to a great height, curling and recurling upon itself in vari- ous fantastic shapes. The wind whistled round us, and it was fortunate that our clothing and everything else was made fast, for one of the large heavy reindeer gloves worn over my thick woollen mittens was blown away as I changed hands to drive, and was so quickly buried in the shifting drift that I could not find it again. My driver at the second station was a stout girl of twenty, strong enough to wrestle any man, but shy, modest, and gentle. I could not tell how she looked, for her face, like mine, was entirely wrapped up. When I entered the post station-house at Korpikylä I was quite dizzy, and for a moment could not walk straight. The gale had now risen to such a height that it was impossible to travel farther that day. During the night it blew with still greater fury, howling so wildly round the house that I could not sleep. Towards morn- ing the storm abated for a few hours, but the wind rose again,

and blew with greater fury than before. Grand, indeed, was
the sight, as I stood on the banks of the Torne River watching
the spectacle. The tempest swept over the land with incredible force; the snow rose in thick clouds, forming deep drifts
and hillocks, which shifted constantly. This great storm, the
grandest of that year in that region, lasted, with the exception
of a few lulls, over three days. During that time the temperature ranged from 7° to 22° below zero.

As soon as the people began to move from farm to farm
the news was spread that the stranger from America had returned, and on Sunday the farmers came pouring in from the
whole neighborhood—even from the other side of the Torne
River. The winter costumes were not so picturesque as in
other places. The men wore long overcoats lined with sheepskin; the women's dresses consisted of a body of black cloth
with a skirt made of thick homespun, a long heavy jacket,
having sheepskin inside, and a warm hood. Many of our
guests remained all day, and nearly all of them invited me to
visit them. They sung for me, but their voices were inferior
to those of the Swedish peasantry. The amazement of these
good people was great when they heard I was going north.
After the storm the thermometer ranged from 22° to 27° below zero morning and evening to 30° at night, and from 13°
to 18° below zero in the afternoon—the atmosphere being
perfectly still. I was no more a stranger with the people, and
had to stop at several farms on the way. They knew the time
I was to pass, and did not wish me to continue my journey
without stopping awhile at their houses. Coffee, bread-and-
butter, cheese, and dried mutton were set before me, and I
was plied with questions as to my purpose in going so far at
this inclement season. "It is no fun to live with the Laplanders—
ers—stay with us this winter, Paul," said they; "we will teach
you how to go on snow-shoes, and we will hunt bears when the
time arrives."

The cheerful open fireplace of the farms of Sweden and
Norway had given place to the clumsy thick stone structure
of the Finns.

One who has never travelled in winter in northern lands

can have no conception of the clearness of the atmosphere when the temperature is from 30° to 40° below zero. Then there is not a breath of wind, generally not a cloud in the sky, the blue of which is very light. The outlines of the distant forest-clad hills are of a peculiar light purplish blue of indescribable softness, and are so sharp and distinct that they are seen from a greater distance than in more southern countries. There are also many different shades of color in the sky—pale blue one day, deeper the next. This dry still cold is so healthy that it never even parches the lips, no matter how long one remains out-of-doors; during the whole of that winter mine were not sore once; it seems to give strength to the lungs and banishes all kinds of throat diseases.

Soon after leaving Korpikylä, coming to a farm along the road I saw a little girl watching for some one. As soon as she saw my sleigh she rushed through the snow towards me, and bade me come in. Her name was Hilda Karolina. Hardly had I entered the large room when she put her arms around my neck, gave me a kiss, and told me that every day she had put on her snow-shoes and run out to look for me. Though we could not talk much to each other we managed to become good friends. She was a true child of the North, with flaxen hair, deep soft blue eyes, reminding one of the sky, very white skin, and rosy cheeks—healthy, strong, and consequently happy—far happier than many children clad in costly garments, and surrounded by so many playthings that they take no pleasure in them.

A little farther on was a humble log-house, where lived Greta Maria, a poor widow, and her four daughters. They were standing on the porch watching for me, for they would not let me pass without inviting me in. I entered the plain, small, but very clean room; and while the mother and daughters were spinning we talked. The old lady wore glasses, and age had made her handsome and dignified. Some of her daughters found employment among the farms, or worked by the day. All the women know how to spin and weave, and work in the fields also. Greta and the daughters then with her supported themselves by weaving for others on their loom at

home, and by buying a little stock of spun cotton thread and
making white or colored handkerchiefs; or at other houses
they made woollen cloth. They got along very well, enjoying good health, though without even a cow; a few goats furnished them most of the milk they wanted, and some sheep
the wool they needed for their garments. They were satisfied
with their common healthy fare, and by economy managed to
have always a little coffee in the house, to offer to a friend
or stranger. They lived on coarse flat bread with sour milk,
cheese, and sometimes butter, hardly ever tasting meat; the
dried flesh of the sheep or goats they killed every year was
kept for festive days, such as Christmas or Sundays, or for the
entertainment of strangers. Now and then they would eat
fish, which they had caught and salted in summer, or game
presented to the mother by some one who was trying to win
the heart of her handsome flaxen-haired daughter Wilhelmina,
who was considered the flower of the family. They asked me
all sorts of questions. They were apparently perfectly contented, and loved their simple home and northern climate;
they did not repine against their lot, for their religious belief
was that whatever God did was the best for them; on the
shelf was a well-worn Bible and other religious books several
generations old. They did not care about the allurements and
wealth of the world. "There is another life," said the old
woman to me; "let us be good, and love God with all our
hearts." When the weather was fine she never missed going
to church, though it was at a considerable distance. I could
not leave without taking a cup of coffee; but it was mixed
with roast barley, for they could not afford to have it pure.
Wilhelmina bit off a piece of rock-candy, which she gave
me, to put in my mouth while drinking the coffee; her rosy
lips and white teeth seemed to me such charming sugar-
crackers that I had no objection to the way the sugar was
broken. While I was taking coffee all kinds of advice was
given me for the journey; for, though it was 35° below zero,
it would be colder still; in order not to freeze my nose and
ears I must rub them with snow now and then, and use my
mask often; I must always hang up my stockings to dry in

the evening, so that they will not be damp in the morning; I must take the grass out of my shoes and dry it well, and not forget to hang up my shoes. The earnestness of their recommendations showed that they came from the heart. Saying good-bye, I put a little money into the hands of the mother. "No," she said. "Yes," I answered, and jumped into the sleigh; the two tucked the robes around me. "Welcome back, Paul!" were the last words I heard, and soon we were out of sight.

As my eyes rested on the dark beautiful distant forest-clad hills, I thought I had never before seen such effects. Now and then we drove on the frozen Torne River, to shorten the way, passing by many little farms and poor cottages. Here a farmer is considered well off if he possesses a farm valued at 1000 to 1500 dollars; the buildings alone in America would cost several thousand dollars. The little station-house of Niemis was almost buried by drifted snow; the well was surrounded by a heavy mass of ice, which kept increasing every day as the drippings of the bucket fell upon it. I entered the dirty room where the family lived. The old man put on his long coat lined with sheepskin, which had seen its best twenty or thirty years ago; he had pride enough to wish to hide his worn and dirty clothes; he then put on his fur cap, and was dressed. His wife put on her old sheepskin jacket, with the hair inside; while Kristina, a daughter of sixteen or seventeen, rushed to the well for a bucket of water to wash her face and hands; she then undid the tresses of her hair, which fell in a thick, wavy, amber-like mass over her shoulders, and combed it in such a hurry that much was torn out; then she tressed it again, and put a clean bodice and skirt over the dirty one, and finished her toilet by putting on her Sunday shoes. The mother, in the mean time, swept the room, and put more wood in the open fireplace. A new-comer made her appearance—a former acquaintance of mine, the mother of the farmer—an old woman of eighty years, yet with hair almost black falling loosely over her shoulders, combed perhaps twice a month; she reminded me of an old gypsy: she squeezed me in her arms to show the depth of her feelings, and how glad she was to see me once more; and I felt that, notwithstanding her age, she was still strong. I could not free myself until she released me, and I shall long remember that tight embrace. Their cow-house was a curiosity; it was a small log-house, almost buried in the snow; four cows were there, and they were so thin that their ribs and bones protruded. The hay crop had been poor. As in all similar houses, a large iron pot was encased in masonry, and used to cook the coarse marsh-grass for the cattle. During the winter months the cows do not go out at all; every aperture is closed against the entrance of cold. I could not leave these good people without partaking of a cup of warm milk, for which they would take no money.

I continued my route with a new horse and sleigh, the snow increasing in depth as I went on. At Ruskola I was received with open arms by my friends Carl John Grape and his wife, who wanted me to tarry, to learn how to go on snow-shoes and to speak the Finnish language. Carl's farm was a very good one. I could not help noticing how industrious the people were; Selma Maria was a model of a farmer's wife, a thorough house-keeper, always busy—cooking, washing, weaving, spinning, baking, sewing, knitting, or making butter from morning till night. The children had to be looked after, and taught to read, that they might learn their catechism. Selma, Såfia (Sophie), Hilda, Emma, Carl, Thilda, Amelia, were the names of these children, and they looked like a flight of stairs, so closely did they follow each other. A maid and two men servants made the remainder of the family, besides two or three other farm-hands paid by the day. A poor girl is often hired to do house-work, or weaving or spinning, for a few days, that her family may be helped a little: in summer Grape would often hire one or two extra, unnecessary hands, simply to help his poor neighbors. Eva Maria, the maid, was quite a belle in the neighborhood; she had rather high cheek-bones, florid complexion, fine teeth, with youth and health, and was the maid of all work, having entire charge of the cow-stable and the milking. The most remarkable thing was that she was rich, possessing 1800 or 2000 kronor (about 500 dollars) in her own right, being an orphan girl. Many were trying to make love to her, and several had proposed marriage, but she laughed at all her suitors, and wanted to be free and independent; not seeing why she should marry to be afterwards poor, since all her little fortune would belong to her husband. "No, indeed," she would say, "I am not going to get married; I prefer to work all day long;" and then merrily sung and laughed. Eva Maria was kind and amiable to every one, even to those who wanted to be lovers, and these were plenty, for she not only had money but was intelligent and industrious—in a word, quite a prize.

While in Ruskola another violent tempest swept over the country, preventing further travel. The frozen Torne seemed to be enveloped in a cloud of white dust, and for twenty-four hours there was no cessation of the blustering wind; at times it snowed very heavily, and the thermometer stood only $7°$ below freezing. After the storm huge drifts of snow made the roads impassable. Grape advised me to wait a few days before continuing my journey; "for," said he, "we do not plough the roads here: let other people travel first, and then the road will be in better condition."

For several weeks I had applied myself with all my might to the study of the Finnish language. Each syllable is very distinct, making it easy to acquire; but a greater number of words are often necessary to express an idea than in English. Two things are essential to a traveller who wishes to see thoroughly these northern countries—he must know how to travel on snow-shoes, and how to drive reindeer. With these two accomplishments he can roam where he likes.

The snow-shoes used in Scandinavia are very unlike those of the Indians of North America, and are far superior for speed and comfort, requiring no spreading of the limbs. At the first glance one may think them clumsy, on account of their great length. Those used in a mountainous or wooded country are the shortest, and generally six or seven feet long; those used by the Finlanders on the banks of the Torne are much longer, averaging some ten or twelve feet. The longest are those of Jemtland, where they sometimes measure fourteen to sixteen feet. They are made of fir wood, about one-third of an inch thick at the centre, which is the thickest part, and four or five inches wide. There is a piece of birch at the centre, and over this is a loop through which the instep of the foot is passed; the part near the foot is convex, so that the weight of the body cannot bend the shoe downward. The under part is very smooth, with a narrow furrow; both ends are pointed.

The boots of the Finlanders are specially adapted to snow-shoes, they being pointed, without heels, and so large that the foot can be surrounded by Lapp grass. With two pairs of home-made woollen stockings one can defy the cold, but the foot must be perfectly free. In travelling, one always carries a good stock of Lapp shoe-grass. Grape gave me a very beautiful pair of snow-shoes (now, with one of my sleighs, in the rooms of the American Geographical Society of New York). They were admired by all who saw them when I travelled north. Ruskola was a very good school in which to take the first lessons, the Torne being frozen and covered with snow, with a surface smooth and easy for a beginner. While there I practised on snow-shoes several hours a day. If a man has to travel in a flat country he must have two staves, at the end of each of which is an iron spike, and a little above this wicker-work, about ten inches in diameter, to prevent the stick from sinking deeper; when the snow is soft, these serve to propel the person forward.

Snow-shoes must not be raised, but slid one after the other, unless when going down a hill; then the feet are kept side by side, if possible. The natives can easily go ten or fifteen miles an hour when the snow is firm and in good condition. For a beginner the great difficulty is to keep the two shoes exactly parallel, and prevent them from becoming entangled with each other. On a level surface the walker cannot hurt himself in falling on the deep snow — a great advantage over skating, for ice, as many know by experience, is not a pleasant bed to fall upon. The first day, after two hours' practice, I could slide on the Torne River a thousand yards without falling. It is very difficult to walk on the crusted

A LAPP GOING DOWN-HILL ON SNOW-SHOES.

snow without a great deal of practice, as the shoes tend to slide too far apart, or the lower or upper ends overlap each other. The ascent of hills is made in zigzag, and is hard work for those not accustomed to it. But the most difficult of all is to descend the steep hills, as the momentum and speed are very great; it is even quite dangerous in mountainous regions, and where boulders are uncovered; it is safe only for those who have practised from childhood, for the speed is as great as in coasting. I have often trembled at seeing Norwegians or

WALKING WITH SNOW-SHOES.

Lapps come down the mountains. In descending, the two shoes must be parallel and close together—a very difficult task, and almost impossible on rough ground. One must have a long stout staff for a rudder and guide, to be used on the right or left, as occasion requires, and the body must be bent forward. I have never been able to descend in this manner. In going down a steep hill he who cannot imitate a Scandinavian or Lapp must ride a staff, resting upon it as heavily as he can, taking care, also, to keep the shoes even. The staff acts as a drag, and prevents him from going too fast. I was

not successful the first time I tried. I had not slid a yard before my shoes left me and went to the bottom of the embank-
ment, and I found myself seated in the snow. I had not bent
my body forward enough for the momentum of speed. I tried
again, but with no better success. I have frequently seen the
children in Norway practice jumping on their snow-shoes.
Sometimes, where one side of the road was higher than the
other, they would leap over to the other side, and land upright, often from a height of seven or eight feet, and even
more, enjoying the excitement amazingly.

On Sunday I went to the old log-church of Matarengi,
built two hundred years ago. The day was so cold that the
clergyman read the service and preached in a heavy fur coat,
and every one in the congregation was dressed in furs.

I left Ruskola with the thermometer standing at 34° below
zero. As the horse stood before the door, with my snow-shoes
tied to the sleigh, Grape called me into the guest-room. He
then opened a bottle of old wine, and he and his wife drank to
my health and the success of my journey. The good fellow
was sorry to see me depart. As I drove along, admiring the
marvellous shades of the distant hills, I saw now and then a
woman getting a bucket of water from an almost frozen well,
or hurrying from the cow-house; or a man was taking a load
of wood from the shed by the farm. I enjoyed those winter
scenes in the highest degree. The dry and bracing atmosphere seemed to give me additional strength. What a glorious contrast was it with that of the miasmatic equatorial Afri-
can jungle, where a white man's life is a continual struggle
against death!

At the end of the day I reached the station of Pirtiniemi,
where in the summer I had crossed on a ferry-boat to the
other side of the lake, to meet the highway. The thermometer stood at 32° below zero, and the night was superb. The
flashes of the aurora borealis darted high into the heavens,
and the stars twinkled brightly through that clear blue sky.
Pirtiniemi was indeed a poor station to spend the night in.
All the family and wayfarers were in the kitchen, which was
far from clean. Some were sitting around the blazing fire,

smoking and chatting; while several others were asleep on
skins on the floor, but the color of the robes on the beds was
very dingy and uninviting. The wife could speak Swedish,
and immediately on my arrival there was a great bustle; coffee and the best supper they could afford were prepared. The
large room for travellers was clean, and a big fire was immediately lighted in the oven-like fireplace; the structure, however, was not in order, and the thick masonry would not get
heated, as there was nothing to prevent most of the heat escaping up the chimney. The bed was brought near the fire, and
when made presented a nice appearance. I was to sleep between two fine soft robes of hareskin, as white as snow, and
other robes of fur were spread over me. In spite of the fire
the mercury stood at 18° in the room during the night. The
farmer excused himself for the poor accommodation he had to
offer me. The house was very old; they were going to build
a better one—indeed, it was already partly built; but "we
must go slowly," said he. "I bought this farm for nine hundred rix-dollars, and I owe six hundred on it; the times have
been hard, and there is the five per cent. interest on those six
hundred rix-dollars to be paid every year."

I slept splendidly, though when I awoke the mercury marked 15° below zero in my room, and 34° outside. The wife had
a sister in America, and that seemed to be a bond of friendship
between us. "Try to see her," she said, "when you go back.
Tell her that we are all well, and that God is kind to us."
The sister lived in Michigan, which State seemed to the wife
about as large as her parish, and fancied that in New York
every one knew her sister. "Don't you remember," said she,
as I was ready to start, "the girl who drove you to the next
station the summer you were here? But now you would hardly recognize her, for she is a big girl. How happy she was
when back again, and showing the little silver piece you had
given her! It was the first one ever owned by her. What
you did on the way was told: how you gave her some biscuit
that had been brought all the way from America, and some
candies. Go and see her, for she often speaks of the stranger
who gave her money, and wonders if he will ever come back;

she has often said that she would like to see him again. How
glad she will be! The boy who will drive you to-day knows
the way to her house, which is on a farm in Korpilombolo,
not far from the church. Good-bye! Welcome back on your
return! Happy journey! Take great care of yourself, for it
will be very cold in the far North, and you will have to sleep
on the snow."

When I stopped at that farm-house in Korpilombolo and
entered the door, a large, bright, beautiful girl met me. Suddenly a smile came over her face, for she recognized me, although I was dressed like a Laplander. She was my dear
little driver of the year before, but she had grown much since
then. Soon after my arrival the house was crowded with the
neighbors. The clergyman, a strong healthy young man, a
native Finn, came also. I found him exceedingly agreeable.
Soon a man was pointed out to me who had returned in the
summer from the United States, where he had remained only
a year, getting so home-sick that he came back to the land of
his ancestors. How strong is the love of home or country in
the hearts of many! No hope of gain could have made that
man stay in a strange land. He loved and dreamed of the
long days in the land of the midnight sun; the long nights
of his northern home; the snow; and the birch, fir, and pine
forests. The farther he was from them the more beautiful
they appeared to his vision, and his friends were much dearer
to him than strangers.

But, when years have elapsed, how disappointed are we on
our return! Father and mother are dead; sister and brother
have left home; old school friends are scattered, or, if still
living, the bloom of boyhood or girlhood has given place to
deep furrows on the face, the buoyant spirit of youth has gone,
the gray hair shows the ravages of time; the laughing girl
with whom we gathered flowers has become a sedate matron;
the fields do not seem so large as they used to; the trees are
not so big, the fences not so high, the rocks less towering; the
barn is much smaller, and the river has dwindled to a brook;
the great school-house has shrunk to a small room. The eyes
of childhood magnify everything. At that time of life the

days, months, and years were much longer, and vacation seemed
as if it would never end. Now time passes away more swiftly.
It was spring yesterday; it is summer to-day; and the winter
will come to-morrow. How much quicker does time fly as we
grow older!

After leaving Korpilombolo we took the winter road, marked
by branches of trees, made a short cut over frozen marshes
and swamps, through forests and fields, and arrived at the post-
station of Otanajärvi. The weather was fine, though cold;
even in the afternoon the mercury remained at 30° below
zero; the snow was gradually increasing in depth, but the
drifts were getting scarcer. At Sattajärvi I found that some
one had preceded me on the way, and that the people had not
forgotten Paulus, but were waiting to welcome him. The
reception-room was soon filled with people. "Here is Paulus
again," said they, as they looked at me with amazement, "all
the way from Stockholm! Did you ever see such a man?
Paulus, where are you going?" "To Norway, to North Cape,
to live with the Laplanders, and to the Norwegian fisheries."
A shout of exclamation arose at these words. "Go and live
with the Laplanders? It is true, we see; we had read this in
the newspapers, but we did not believe it."

"Where is my friend Kristina?" said I. (The reader remem-
bers, perhaps, the girl whom the people wanted me to take to
America on my first visit.) "Why, have you not seen her?
She lives in Pirtiniemi." "No," said I; "it is too bad."

"Paulus, you are not going to-day? Indeed, we shall not let
you go; you must stay some time with us. We hear that you
have been in America since we saw you." "Yes," said I,
"but only for a few days." This speech made them look
with still greater wonder upon me. "What are you going to
do? You will find people talking only Finnish or Lappish,
and you will have a long journey to Norway." "Yes," said
I, "I shall have trouble. It is hard to travel in a country if
one cannot talk with the people." More logs were thrown
into the fireplace, a meal was served, and we continued to talk
to a very late hour.

The following morning a young Finn girl was brought to

me. The people of Sattajärvi had given me a guide in summer,
and they wanted me to have one also in winter. They said,
" Paulus, we bring you a girl to go to Norway with you. She
has been there before, and can talk Norwegian, which you can
understand, so she will be able to interpret for you." They
all seemed happy to have found somebody to help me. It
never occurred to these primitive, kind-hearted people that I
could violate the trust put in me.

Elsa Karolina was a young and pretty girl of seventeen
years. Her mother was dead, and her father lived a few miles
from Sattajärvi, and was very poor. Two of her sisters had
migrated to Norway, where one was married; she had come
from there herself a few months before, over the mountains,
with Lapps, to Pajala, to be confirmed, for here was the church
where she had been baptized, and where she must obtain the
certificate necessary for her in any other district. She seemed
glad at the prospect of going with me, and was even willing to follow me to America. How beautiful is the trust of
that primitive life which, in its simplicity, does not see the
evil, treachery, trickery, and rascality of a higher civilization!
Why should she be afraid? why should the people fear for
her? I promised that, wherever I landed on the coast of Finmarken or Norway, I would make arrangements to let her go
to her sisters. They believed me, and that was enough.

The good people of the little hamlet of Sattajärvi rejoiced
when they heard I would return from the North in the spring;
they said, " You must then stay many days with us, Paulus."
At Pajala a large and comfortable school-house had been built
since I had left; a teacher and his wife lived in the building,
and a fine piano adorned one of the plainly furnished rooms
of the family.

Here we found the snow much deeper than at Haparanda.
There had been several heavy falls, which made it of a depth of
five or six feet in the woods. I could go to Norway over the
frozen Torne, through Jukkasjärvi, and then over the mountains to the Ofoten fjord, situated about lat. 68° 40'. This
route would leave me unacquainted with a large tract of country northward, where the Laplanders were the most numerous

in winter. I concluded to continue my journey by ascending the Muonio River to Lake Kilpisjärvi, of which it is the outlet, and then over the mountains to Lyngen fjord, above lat. 69°, almost opposite the Lofoden Islands, thus seeing the country I had not explored in summer. In winter the distance from Pajala to Muoniovaara is twelve Swedish miles. There are three stations on the way — Kaunisvaara, Killangi, and Parkajoki—the distance between each two being about three miles. The winter road makes a short cut across forests and swamps, and there is no highway. Now and then we met a queer-looking conveyance used to carry hay, a sled very much like a crate, with men dressed in reindeer skins. The horses seemed about as lazy as the men, and went as slowly as they possibly could, using their own intelligence to get over the difficulties of the way. I had to awaken several of these men to make room for me to pass. The weather had now become charming, and the thermometer remained all day at or within a fraction of 13° below freezing.

At Kaunisvaara—which small hamlet is situated about half-way between the Torne and the Muonio—we waited for two hours. All the horses were either in the woods drawing timber, or in the fields taking in loads of hay, which had been stored at a distance. The people were busy hauling it to their farms, for in summer very little transportation takes place. Our route was through a forest of fine fir-trees till we came to Arkavaara, on the banks of the Muonio. The owner of the place and his wife were Swedes. "You had better stay for the night," they said, " and go on to-morrow." The invitation seemed so honest that I accepted it. A substantial dinner, an excellent bed, and a hearty welcome were given to me. On the next day, when I mentioned paying, I was at once stopped, and was told that the invitation to stay was to enjoy the pleasure of my company. Often at these farms are inns, and one never knows exactly what to do; but it is safe to offer payment. The road lay over the frozen Muonio, and, with the exception of myself, the travel was done entirely with reindeer; as there was a great deal of traffic, the track was very good for a horse. The Finns at home were dressed in homespun and woven clothing, and only used the Lapp dress when travelling.

It was late when I reached Muonionalusta, but the lights twinkled through the windows, showing that the people of the hamlet were not asleep. The inmates of one of the houses came out and bade us welcome. There was quite a company of people inside. On our arrival more logs were thrown into the open fireplace, and room was made for us to warm ourselves, for the night was very cold. The men and women were smoking, and having a little chat before going to bed. This farm belonged to Lars Johanson. The people seemed happy when they heard I was to spend the night with them. The two daughters, Lovisa and Sophia, immediately went to work, and, while we were chatting, prepared a meal of reindeer meat for me; coffee was roasted, and the good farmer Abraham brought in another armful of firewood. The people here consume a vast amount of fuel. None of the residents were bashful, and numerous questions were asked of Elsa Karolina concerning me. When bedtime came the neighbors left, and immediately preparations for sleep took place. The sofa-bed was opened, a sliding-drawer was pulled out, the hay was shaken up afresh, and reindeer and sheep skins were put over it for me; other skins were spread on the floor as beds for the family. Then all took off their shoes and stockings, and hung them on a cross-pole, near the ceiling, by the fireplace. Father and son now bade us good-bye, and left. Elsa Karolina and one of the daughters slept together, while the eldest daughter slept near me, bundling with her sweetheart, this being the lovers' day.

I had had only one unpleasant adventure since leaving Stockholm; but one, indeed, since my arrival in Scandinavia. Coming before a fine-looking house, well painted, and thus showing at once that it belonged to a family of more than ordinary refinement, my driver alighted, and said that we must go in, as it was the house of his mother-in-law. I had hardly entered before an old lady made her appearance, and welcomed me in the kindest manner. Then my little girl driver of the summer before came in, and I gave her a gold ring, showing her the silver one she had given me. The good hostess invited me to dinner, and to spend the night. Four sperm candles were lighted; and when I remonstrated against such a waste, she said there could not be too much light to see a man from America. In the mean time my companion had disappeared, and when he came back he was tipsy, to my great annoyance. He gave as an excuse that he had caught cold, and had a great pain in his head. The dinner was served, and I had hardly commenced when the door opened, and the two daughters made their appearance; one gave such a look at my humble luggage in the corner of the room that I saw at once I was not welcome. I said "Good day;" she hardly deigned to answer, and glanced at her brother-in-law in a manner which showed that he was not in her good graces. She unmuffled herself, seeming more and more angry, went into the next room, said a few hasty words there which I could not understand, came back through the room, slamming the door, returned with a pillow, leaving the door wide open, and rushed into the apartment in an angry mood. The fork dropped from my hand as she said "This is not the station-house." "I know it, madam," I replied; "I came here to see a little friend; your brother-in-law brought me here, and your mother invited me to stay." "You can sleep but one night here; there is no room for you." I said nothing, but got up from the table and ordered the horse to be made ready. The mother and other daughter were mute, and seemed afraid. Then she said, "Will you not stay here for the night, and go to-morrow?" "No," said I. I thanked the mother, and gave to the servant a piece of money which was more than I would have paid at a hotel for my dinner: I was glad to go back to my friends. The next day, probably feeling the impropriety of her reception, the daughter came and excused herself, and said she would be glad to see me. Such was the end of that unpleasant adventure, which, no doubt, was occasioned by her dislike for her brother-in-law, and the state of drunkenness in which she saw him: she thought perhaps that I had made him so.

Muoniovaara was only a short distance, and I was received by my old friends, the family of Herr F——, with a hearty welcome. The father had gone to Haparanda, to attend the fair at Torneå, and they seemed quite astonished when they heard I had not met him on the way; but I was well received by his kind-hearted wife, his two amiable daughters, and his two sons, one of whom was now on a visit from Karesuando, where he resided, being the länsman of the district. They said that, though their father was not at home, they would try to make me have a good time. They succeeded splendidly. The last sheep was killed, and I could see by that and sundry other preparations in the kitchen that these hospitable people intended that I should live on the fat of the land.

CHAPTER VI.

MUONIOVAARA now presented a very different aspect from that of summer. The yard was crowded with queer-shaped Lapp sledges, to which were attached magnificent reindeer, and Laplanders, in their quaint winter garments, were talking to each other. How comfortable was their dress: no clothing is warmer than reindeer skin, and it is well adapted to the climate. It is convenient either when the wearers are riding in their sleighs, travelling on snow-shoes, or breasting the violent wind-storms which they encounter in their wanderings. Experience has taught the Lapps that it is very important that nothing they wear should impede the free circulation of the blood, which maintains the animal heat of the body.

WINTER COSTUME.

The winter kapta is made of reindeer skin with the hair attached; it is loose, reaching below the knee, with a narrow aperture for the head to pass through, and fitting so closely around the neck that cold air and snow cannot enter. The sleeves also are loose, but at the wrist the skin is without hair, or furnished with a cloth band. Under the kapta they wear one or two very thick woollen under-garments, and often over

LAPP WINTER COSTUME.

these a vest made of soft reindeer skin. In very cold weather
another warm kapta is worn beneath the outer one, but with
the hair inside. The breeches are made of skin from the legs
of the reindeer, which is considered the warmest part; these
are worn over thick close-fitting woollen drawers, and are fast-

ened around the waist by a string, and, if short, are tied above the knees. Near the ankles the hair is removed, and the leather is made very soft, so that it may go inside the shoe. Nothing can be better adapted to keep the feet warm than the Laplander's shoes, made of skin, soft and pliable, taken from near the hoof. They are sharp-pointed and graceful, and, as they are not made fast, convenient for snow-shoes. Some are lined at the seams with red flannel or cloth; the upper part, which fits above the ankles, is without hair. They are made large enough to allow two pairs of the thickest home-knitted stockings and the Lapp grass to be worn without pinching the feet. Sometimes their socks are made of cows' or goats' hair; these are warmer than those of wool, but are not strong. Great care is taken that neither stockings nor grass are damp. The foot must be completely wrapped with grass to the ankle; the shoe is then put on, the lower part of the legging is put inside, and a long band attached to the shoe is wound round and round, preventing the entrance of either air or snow. These shoes can be used only in cold dry weather. I do not remember a single instance during that winter when I suffered from cold feet, but I always had one of the natives arrange and prepare the shoes, and put them on for me. In the spring, when the snow becomes wet, hairless boots well greased are worn instead, both by Finlanders and Lapps.

The head-dress of the Laplanders varies according to the district: at Muoniovaara it is square at the top; the upper part is either blue or red, and is filled with eider-down, while the thick wide border, often made of otter-skin, can be turned up in frosty weather; the down, which is several inches thick, was too warm for me. A mask of fur is put over the face for protection, but this covering is used only in very windy weather. Their mittens are of the warmest description, made from the skin near the hoof; they are very loose, with room for a thick pair of woollen ones inside; and as they lap over the lower end of the sleeve of the kapta with these, I never suffered from cold hands that winter.

The very appearance of the yard at the farm showed that I was in Lapland. The conveyances are peculiar: the *kerres*—

used either to carry people or merchandise, over which is a
skin fastened with strings—is very much the shape of an
open boat, and is made of narrow fir planks, very strongly
ribbed inside, about seven feet long, two and a half at the
broadest part, varying but little in width. The keel is very
strong, about four inches wide, but varies much in thickness,
as they wear out in time by constant rubbing. The higher
they are the quicker one can travel; as in case snow is well
packed or crusted the sides hardly touch it, and the keel then
acts like a runner under a skate. It was absolutely necessary
that I should learn to drive reindeer, and how to remain in
those little Lapp sledges. *Pulkas* (in Norwegian, *akja*), built
for fast travelling, have keels about two and a half inches
thick. The higher these are the more difficult it is to learn
how to balance one's self, and consequently not to upset.
The pulkas are used also to pack goods. There are regular
posting pulkas, which are more neatly finished, the forward
part being decked for about a third of the length, forming
a sort of box with a trap opening, the top covered with seal-
skin. Their shape is quite graceful, the keel high, and they
are made for rapid locomotion. The back is often cushioned,
and ornamented with copper buttons. All have on the forward part a strong leather ring, to which the trace is fastened.
They are ribbed inside very strongly, and are capable of with-
standing any amount of bumping and knocking. Others, called
låkkek—larger, but of the same form—were covered above
like the deck of a vessel, and answered for trunks; one had
the top covered with seal-skin, and contained the clothing, jewellery, Bible, hymn-books, handkerchiefs, and a great part of
the wearing apparel of the family, or coffee, sugar, flour, and
other provisions which required to be well protected. Each
is drawn by one reindeer, and carries a single person. The
harness is very simple, the common one consisting of a collar
around the neck, at the lower part of which a single strong
twisted or leather trace is fastened, to which the conveyance
is attached. No bit is used, and the rein is made of strong
plaited leather straps, and fastened to the base of the horns.
There are also fancy harnesses, ornamented by bright belts.

The harnessing must always be done with very great care, for the reindeer is easily scared, and often makes sudden springs at slight noises.

The rider seats himself, holding the rein twisted around the right hand. The line must not be held tightly, and the middle part should not quite touch the snow, for it is dangerous should the rein get under the sleigh; in this case the driver's arms may become entangled, and he be dragged some distance before he can loosen the cord around his hands. A novice, therefore, must be constantly on the watch. If you want the reindeer to stop, the rein is thrown to the left; if you wish to go fast, then to the right; as for myself, I have never been able to make a deer go slow—they never walk unless very tired. You must make up your mind to be upset a great many times before you learn to drive reindeer.

The most difficult and dangerous time in driving is when descending steep hills, as the speed of the sleigh is greater than that of the reindeer. The Lapps sit astride with their knees bent, using their feet as rudder and drag. To a novice this practice is very dangerous, and might lead to his breaking his legs. They never would allow me to try to come down in this manner, and even they, with their constant practice, sometimes rupture themselves from this cause. In going down I used a short stick, the point of which I would force into the snow with all my might, this acting as a drag. But sometimes the hills and mountains are too steep even for the Lapps. In that case the reindeer is tied behind the conveyance; they cannot bear to be pulled by the horns, and consequently make strong efforts to free themselves, and in so doing greatly lessen the speed. It is also very difficult to learn how to balance one's self, so as to keep the equilibrium of the pulka and prevent upsetting; the greater the speed the more difficult is the task. For example, when a deer, after swiftly going down a hill, turns suddenly in a sharp curve, the rider must bend to the other side, or he will be overturned. I could not have found a better place than Muoniovaara in which to learn to drive reindeer. These animals are not housed like horses. Those belonging to Herr F—— were in the woods,

and when needed the servants had to go after them; neither
are they fed, for they have to find their own food. In the
early morning, that I might take my first lesson, two men with
lassos started for the forest on snow-shoes after the reindeer;
for those broken to the harness are sent to feed with the rest
of the herd, often remaining days and weeks before they are
again required. The herd had been left at a distance of about
six miles from the farm. The men returned with five superb
strong animals having magnificent horns.

THE FIRST DRIVE.

The harnesses used were fancy ones of brilliant colors. Herr
Gustaf, the son, was to accompany me and be my teacher.
After being seated I was shown how to twist the rein around
my hand and wrist. When I remonstrated, I was told I
must not hold it otherwise, because, if I should upset, the animal could not run away without me: a cheerful prospect, I
thought! Gustaf was to lead; I was to come next, and the
man-servant was to follow to keep watch over me. The reindeer were brought to the side of the dwelling-house, near a
hill that led down to the river. The young ladies did not
join the party, but as we were ready to start I saw them peeping between the curtains; their roguish eyes were full of fun,
for they knew what would happen, and I did not. The signal given, my leader threw himself into his pulka, and off his
reindeer started. Mine followed at the same speedy rate;
my sledge swung to and fro, and I had gone but a few yards
when I was thrown out, and rolled over and over till the
creature stopped. This was the first upsetting but not the
last. When I got up and looked for Gustaf he was far ahead,
but the man behind was at hand to help me. "No one who
had never driven a reindeer could come down that hill at full
speed without upsetting," said he, as he tried to console me
for the mishap. It seemed to me railway speed, though I was
told that my animal was quite a slow one, and one of the
most tractable. We had hardly made another start when I
was out of the sleigh again. At the foot of the hill Gustaf
was waiting, and said it was a splendid place in which to learn

to drive a deer. I did not then see it in that light; but he was right, on the principle that when you go to sea for the first time it is better to encounter a storm at once, and then you will not be sea-sick afterwards. After reaching the river we drove on a level surface, over a well-furrowed track, made by those who had crossed to the other side. The first reindeer went slowly, and I followed in its wake, upsetting only four times in a ten minutes' ride. On our return I was upset a few times more, but was perfectly satisfied with my first lesson in the art of reindeer driving—especially as I had no bones broken. The animals were then taken back to their pasture-grounds.

Next morning a man started after some of the fastest deer owned by my host. After an absence of about four hours he returned with three magnificent ones, with great spread of horns, and faster than the fastest horse. We were going to make a visit to an encampment of Laplanders about twenty-five miles distant. Herr Gustaf wore his finest dress, the robe being almost pure white, and his gloves and shoes were of the same color. When ready to start, the whole family came out to say good-bye, and to see us off. It was just the kind of weather that makes reindeer lively—30° below zero, with not a breath of wind.

While some one held my deer I got into the pulka; the line was handed to me, and I twisted it around my wrist, when immediately, and before Gustaf was ready, his animal started: he had just time to throw himself across his sleigh. This sudden start was the signal for a wild hurried stampede, each reindeer trying to outrun the other. We went at great speed. Gustaf succeeded in stopping his runaway, but not before tumbling over; this barred the way of mine, which made a sharp turn to the right, keeping up his swift gait. I came near a post, and, if my sledge had struck against it, I should have been thrown out, and probably badly hurt. Happily I escaped this danger, but was shot out of my sleigh heels over head, and rolled over and over till the rein slipped off my wrist, and the animal started as if a fire had been lighted at his heels. I got up, rubbed the snow from my face and out of my mouth, and looked for my courser, but he was out of sight, and I saw Gustaf driving as fast as he could after him. Behind was the servant, who also had been upset.

When the deer are fresh from the woods the starting is always the most difficult; when they have not been used for weeks, and when the weather is cold, they are wild and unruly. Gustaf returned with the animal, which he had caught after a mile's chase. I could now understand why the thong must not slip from one's hand. We were all mortified, for we wished to have started in grand style. The next time Gustaf rolled the cord around my wrist himself, for he did not want to run after the reindeer a second time. "Now," said he, "the animal cannot run away without you, and when he sees that you are out he will stop." I found by experience that, being of light weight, I was often rolled over and over for some time before they came to a stop.

The track over which we travelled was furrowed deeply by pulkas, and this helped to steady ours. There had evidently been a great deal of travel over it, and we went at-times at the rate of fifteen miles an hour. Before we came to the declivity of a hill the animals always quickened their paces, and, by the time we came to the descent, the speed was so great that everything passed before my eyes as quickly as if I were going by railway at the rate of twenty or thirty miles an hour, and the reindeer with their trotting pace sent the granulated snow into our faces. While going fast the animal invariably carries the neck forward. I could hear all the time a sound as if two pieces of wood were knocking against each other; this was produced by the feet. Every time the hoof touched the snow it spread open, and as it was raised the two sides were brought together again. Going down hill, the pace was so rapid that the animals' feet seemed hardly to touch the snowy ground; they knew that if they did not go fast enough the pulka would strike against their legs.

At first, every time I reached the base of a hill, or when we had to go round a sharp curve, I was sure to upset; but finally I understood what to do; and when my sleigh was on the point of upsetting I managed to bend my body half out, and thus avoided being thrown. This constant watching made the drive very exciting. We drove over some little lakes, and through forests of fir, pine, and birch; but in these our leader alighted, and led his reindeer, for fear that we should knock against the trees, as I was not an expert.

INTERIOR OF A KATA IN WINTER.

We followed a well-furrowed track, each of us leading our animal; we soon heard the barking of dogs announcing our approach to a Lapp encampment, and found ourselves before a kåta (tent). The people were friends of Herr Gustaf, and we were heartily welcomed. They could talk Lappish, Finnish, Swedish, and Norwegian. Several women were inside the kåta, seated on skins, and all were, as usual, busy. Lapp women are very industrious; upon them devolves the labor of making the clothing for the family. One was weaving bands of bright colors, another was giving the final touches to a garment, while a third finished a pair of shoes: they are very expert, also, in embroidering cloth or leather. The thread they use is made of the sinews of the forelegs of the reindeer.

The reception is always formal. The left side of the tent was given to us as guests, while the family and the dogs were huddled together on skins. After the usual salutation, the Lapps gradually became sociable. A vessel full of snow was put over the fire, and, when it had melted, the water was put into the coffee-pot, then the coffee was ground and boiled, a piece of dry fish-skin being used to clarify it. Silver spoons, of a rounded shape and with twisted handles, were furnished to the guests. After partaking of their kind hospitality we left them, as we intended to stay with another family, great friends of Gustaf, who were in much better circumstances, and whose encampment was only a short distance off. It was now impossible to drive on account of the trees and the deep holes made in the snow by the reindeer, so we walked in front of our animals, now and then having to pull hard to make them follow. We soon discerned through the trees a Lapp kåta, the place where we intended to stay. The father of the family was a well-to-do Laplander, possessing over a thousand reindeer.

The furious barking of half a dozen dogs warned the inmates of the tent of our coming. A short, thick-set, middle-aged, blue-eyed man came out, ordered the dogs to keep quiet, and, recognizing Gustaf, bade us enter. The door leading into the tent was pushed aside, and we found ourselves in the midst of a large family. The left side of the tent was again given to us, nice bear-skins being first laid over twigs of young birch-trees, which were used as mattresses. Several of the family had blue eyes, and the skin of the protected parts of the body was very white; their faces were quite red, owing to exposure to the cold winds and their open-air life, reminding me much of a sailor's complexion. As usual, coffee was at once made. We were hardly seated when a pinch of snuff was offered to us: this is etiquette with them.

The encampment was in a wood, and the tent was made of coarse heavy vadmal, and about twelve feet in diameter at the

A WINTER ENCAMPMENT.

base. There was a blazing fire in the centre, the smoke escaping by an aperture above. Two kettles filled with meat were boiling, for they were preparing the evening meal; and the tent was so crowded that I wondered how we should all be able to sleep comfortably. Numerous pulkas and kerres were scattered around, snow-shoes were either lying on the ground or standing upright against the trees. Harnesses were hanging here and there, and quarters and pieces of frozen reindeer meat were suspended from the branches. A kind of rack had been built about six feet from the ground, where frozen meat was piled. There was also a store of smoked meat and tongues, buckets full of frozen milk—for some of the deer are milked until Christmas, as was stated by the host himself— and bladders of this congealed milk or blood, and reindeer feet. The skins of animals recently killed were drying, stretched on frames so that they could not shrink. Saddles, empty pails, kettles, iron pots, wooden vessels, and garments were scattered about.

THE REPAST.

After the meat was cooked it was put on a wooden platter, and the father, as is the custom, divided it into portions for each member of the family. The fattest parts are considered the best, and I noticed that these were set aside for us. Then we began our meal, using our fingers as forks.

The fire was kept blazing, for it was 40° below zero; and, besides, we wanted the light. While eating, many questions were asked: after our meal both men and women smoked their pipes, and during this time I had to go through a regular catechism of questions on religion, which reminded me of a Sunday-school. They wanted especially to know if I believed in the Trinity. After a long chat, the night being far advanced, the time to sleep had come; then, singing hymns in praise of God, they dressed themselves for the night, putting over their garments a long reindeer gown, extending below the feet—almost a bag. No matter how severe the weather may be, one does not feel cold in such a garb.

Lapps rarely remove their clothing during the winter, and generally only with the change of seasons. When they go to church they often put the new dress over the old one. Of course vermin swarm in these fur costumes; when they become unendurable, the custom is to expose the garments to the air when the temperature is thirty or forty degrees below zero, so that all noxious things are destroyed. In summer this effectual remedy cannot be applied; but the Laplanders who are more cleanly wear woollen under-garments, which they can wash. Bathing is, of course, impracticable in winter, and not extensively practised even in summer.

Several skins were spread as a mattress for us, and others given for coverings. The fire had gone out, and we were in complete darkness; the air was perfectly still, and I could hear from time to time the booming sound of the cracking of the ice on the surrounding streams. A little later I thrust my head now and then over my furs; I could see the blue sky and the bright stars. All was as still as death, for there was not a breath of wind to stir the branches of the surrounding trees, and the reindeer were at a distance. The dogs awoke me several times, for they would try to get under our coverings. As the people were afraid of wolves, some remained with the reindeer the whole of the night. When we awoke my thermometer marked 37° below zero; nevertheless, I had rested very comfortably. Immediately after our awaking one of the servant-girls was set to make bread without yeast, a small loaf, prepared specially in our honor, being baked in charcoal. Inside the tent and all around it on the ground were small boxes, packages, and skins, to prevent the wind from blowing in; young branches of birch-trees were piled up several inches thick, upon which skins were spread, and upon which the family ate and slept.

The people wanted me to see the killing of a reindeer. In the morning a man went into the wood and returned with a deer he had lassoed. The animal, by a twist of the horns, was laid on his back, and remained quiet in that position; then a sharp narrow knife, somewhat of the shape of a stiletto, was thrust deeply between the forelegs till it pierced the heart, and was left there. The poor creature rose, turned round once or twice, then tottered, and fell dead. The blood was removed from the cavity of the chest, where it had accumulated, and put into a bladder, and the intestines were carefully cleaned for food; the animal was skinned, the parts between the eyes, over the forehead, and on the lower legs to the hoof were cut separately—these being, as I have said, considered the best for gloves and shoes; the hide was stretched over a frame to dry.

The Laplanders are very fond of dried powdered blood, which is cooked in a kind of porridge mixed with flour, or diluted with warm water and made into a pancake. The meat is cut in large pieces, and put over a rack to freeze. Bladders are always preserved, as are also the sinews, which are used as thread; the horns and hoofs are kept for sale, to be manufactured into glue.

After the morning meal every man and woman, except the host and hostess, put on their snow-shoes, which I noticed were much shorter than mine. They then started into the forest to look after the reindeer and relieve the night-watch. This family had two servant-maids, who were not paid in cash, but at the rate of three reindeer a year. The average pay of a man-servant in this district is five or six deer.

Each dog followed his master or mistress. These dogs are the useful friends of the Laplanders; in order to keep them hardy, strong, and healthy, they are treated roughly, never overfed, and are not allowed to rest till their owner does; indeed, they often seem to get only the food they can steal. Every man, woman, grown child, and maid-servant has his or her own dogs, which obey and listen only to the voice of their owners. They are exceedingly brave, and not afraid of wolves and bears, which they attack without fear, but with great cunning, taking care not to be bitten by them, and choosing their time and place to bite.

The Lapp dogs somewhat resemble the Pomeranian breed; they are not large, and are covered with long thick hair. Some look very much like small bears, and I have seen a few with the same dark-brown color, and without tails. These are said to belong to a peculiar variety, and to have come from ancestors whose tails at first were always cut off. It is won-

derful to see how these dogs can keep a flock of reindeer together; occasionally, for some unknown reason, a panic seizes
a herd, and it takes all their cunning and a great deal of running to prevent the deer from scattering in all directions.

Our friends were much afraid of the wolves, and were constantly on the watch at night over their deer. In some years
the wild beasts are exceedingly numerous. Reindeer bulls
often defend themselves with success against such enemies;
but when a pack of wolves rushes into the midst of a herd
the latter are scattered in all directions, and then the owners
have to go long distances to bring the herd together again,
often losing great numbers. The wolf and the järf (glutton)
are the greatest enemies of the reindeer, and the Laplanders
have to be constantly on the hunt for these wary foes. When
the snow is on the ground, and especially when soft and newly
fallen, they pursue the wolves on snow-shoes, easily overtake
and spear them, or kill them with clubs; the wolves cannot
escape when the snow is deep.

The life of a Lapp is one of constant vigilance ; young and
old are continually on the lookout, and walk with their dogs
around the herd. If the wolves are not hungry they will not
dare to come near, but if in want of food they will attack a
herd in spite of all precautions. Often the deer detect by
their sense of smell the approach of their enemies ; in that
case the herd moves away. The Laplanders then know what
to expect, and with their dogs pursue the wolves, keeping the
deer together at the same time.

The process of lassoing reindeer is interesting ; sometimes
the lasso is thrown thirty or forty feet, and when the animal
is strong the pursuer is often thrown on the ground ; but as
the animal runs the rope draws tighter and tighter, and the
deer falls as it gets more entangled in the coils.

The snow-shoes of the Laplander of these regions were much
shorter than those of the Finlanders—those for an adult béing
about six feet long ; very long ones would be clumsy in wooded or mountainous districts ; they were usually four or five
inches wide, and about half an inch thick. Deer-skin, or, in
the spring, seal-skin is sometimes used for shoes when the snow

becomes soft; the latter does not stick to the skin. I was told that a Laplander, if the snow is in good condition, can travel one hundred and fifty miles in a day of eighteen hours; if the country is only slightly undulating, they can sometimes go fifteen miles an hour, and even more.

The process of teaching a reindeer to draw a sleigh or carry burdens is tedious and difficult; and, even after being well trained, the wild nature of the timid and restless animal shows itself frequently. The training commences at about the age of three years, and is not completed before the fifth; they are good for work till they are fifteen or sixteen years old. A daily lesson is given to make them know their master, and to accustom them to the lasso, of which they are at first afraid. They are given salt and angelica, and are subjected to no ill treatment when under training. Two men came into camp with a young reindeer, and soon afterwards the work of teaching him to draw a sleigh began. A long very strong leather rein was attached to the base of his horns, and the rest of the harness was carefully attended to; the trace attached to the sleigh was several yards in length, the trainer himself being at quite a distance, thus placing the animal and the sleigh far apart. As soon as the reindeer was urged forward he plunged wildly and kicked, and it required all the strength of the man to hold him. After repeated rests for the animal and driver the lesson was recommenced, and continued till the man was utterly exhausted. To an unpractised eye most reindeer look alike, but the Laplander knows every one of his flock.

It was with sincere regret that I parted from Herr F——'s family, and from Muoniovaara; their many acts of kindness to me, a perfect stranger, will never be forgotten. The young ladies and their two brothers accompanied me for some distance on the river: the former had dressed themselves in the costume of the Laplanders, and drove their pet reindeer. Finally the time for separating came, and beyond the icy river we bade each other good-bye. "Come again, and you will always be welcome. Do not fail," said the länsman, "to come back to Karesuando for Påsk (Easter), for you will see a great number of Laplanders."

CHAPTER VII.

THIS part of the arctic region, especially on the coast, is inhabited by Finlanders, Lapps, and Norwegians; in many districts there is a mixed type, as they have intermarried much.
Russian Lapland is here wedged in between the frontiers of
Norway and Sweden. The best feeling prevails among those
peoples. The Laplanders and Finns are very friendly, the
former often visiting with their families, and staying, both in
health and sickness, at the farms. In return for their kindness
the Lapps will, during the summer months, take the reindeer
of the farmers with their own to the mountains to pasture;
or, while staying with them, will either make their shoes and
gloves, or give them frozen reindeer meat. All Swedish, Norwegian, or Finnish farmers in Lapland must own reindeer, as
they require a certain number for winter use; but these thrive
only when kept under the same conditions as those of the
Lapps—that is, they must have the necessary freedom to roam,
without which they are sure to degenerate, and become useless.
The males are generally used for draught. Along the coast
of Bothnia, north of Luleå, I met some drawing sleighs with
pretty heavy loads; and others, farther north, dragging two or
three trunks of pine or fir trees; I saw several eating bread
and hay, but their principal food must be the lichen. When
I was travelling in summer I noticed that in the Finnish for-

ests there are magnificent lichens; the Swedish and Norwegian Laplanders always try to get their reindeer across to these
in winter, to find good pasture, and the chances are they will
not be detected in those uninhabited districts. The Laplanders who belong to Finland do not complain of them, for they,
in their turn, often smuggle articles to Norway by sea, through
their Swedish or Norwegian friends; but in both cases care
must be taken not to be found out by the authorities. The
punishment is a fine, to be paid in reindeer to the länsman;
for a second offence the fine is greater; but I have never
known of a herd being confiscated, though this could be done
according to the law.

The journey on the Muonio as far as Karesuando presented
nothing striking. At the station of Kälkesuaanto we stopped
for the night; the room for travellers was very small, and
Elsa and the daughter of the house slept on skins on the floor
near my bed. Living at this place, to my surprise, was comparatively dear. About two miles from Kälkesuaanto was a
comfortable farm, belonging to a skogvaktare (keeper of forest) called John Puranen, and a good stopping-place, for the
wife was a Norwegian, and an excellent house-keeper. She
and her husband, a servant-maid, and a man-servant composed
the family; for a wonder, the couple had no children. My object in remaining at the farm was to go among the Lapps
to see a Laplander named Pehr Wassara, who was one of the
richest in herds in Sweden—he owned over 3000 reindeer;
my friends at Muoniovaara had sent me to him, and I was to
inquire where he was. The Finnish länsman, an elderly man,
had just arrived, and stopped here. We were acquainted, for
we had dined together at Muoniovaara. As we were chatting,
while drinking a cup of coffee I said to the wife, "By-the-
way, I want to go and see Pehr Wassara, for I hear he is some-
where in the neighborhood." "Where?" said the old länsman, inquisitively. Without thinking, I answered, "I hear
that he is about a mile and a half from here." I saw at once,
by the sober faces of the family, that I had, unfortunately,
aroused the worthy officer's suspicions. Pehr Wassara was
trespassing on forbidden ground, and he had been caught here

several times before; but to all the länsman's inquiries about
the offender the people gave an evasive answer, that they did
not know exactly—for Pehr was a good friend of the farmer,
and both reaped the advantage.   I saw that I had made a
blunder, and guessed at once that Pehr was probably a smuggler in the forests of Finland.   I had innocently made that
inquiry before an officer who was looking after him or any
other trespasser.

REINDEER DIGGING IN THE SNOW.

Early the following day, with the mercury at 10° below
zero, I was driving with a guide, on my way, as I supposed, to
the encampment of Pehr Wassara, when unexpectedly the länsman joined us.   Entering a forest after a long drive, we found
ourselves suddenly in the midst of a number of holes several
feet deep, dug by reindeer.   The track of the furrows of the
other sleigh was soon lost, and the route became abominable.
Down into the depths we would go—up again—then on one
side, then on the other.   From the top of a mound we were
pitched into a hole, bumping against a tree, the boughs or

branches often striking against our faces; to avoid these we had to keep ourselves flat in the sleighs, in constant danger of being upset. Several thousand reindeer had evidently been here, and we were completely lost in their excavations. Wherever we turned we could not discover either fresh reindeer tracks or furrows of sleighs to lead us to an encampment. I began to suspect that our guide did not want us to see Pehr Wassara or any other smuggler: the old länsman was apparently of the same opinion, for he ordered him to go in a certain direction. We succeeded in getting out of the honeycombed track, and into a clean smooth region. As we entered another wood we came suddenly upon a large herd of reindeer, which apparently had just halted. I could not help seeing, by the look of despair of our guide, that the discovery was not agreeable to him. The länsman had fallen upon trespassers; for when we saw the fresh furrows of sleighs and imprints of snow-shoes we knew we had come among one of Pehr Wassara's herds. The creatures composing it were of all sizes, many having superb horns. Strange, indeed, was the appearance of that dark forest with the multitude of reindeer under the foliage.

The animals had just been left, and I witnessed an interesting sight. The snow in this district was not very deep—not over four feet. Under that thick cover was buried the rich moss of which the reindeer is so fond. All except the younger ones were busy digging, first with one forefoot then with the other; the holes gradually became larger and larger, and the bodies of the animals were more and more hidden; they would not stop till they had reached the moss. Wherever I turned my eyes they were seen doing the same work, for they were evidently hungry. The Lapps have to find places where the snow is not more than four or five feet deep, otherwise the reindeer cannot reach their food. The number seemed countless. We followed the tracks of the snow-shoes, and after awhile found ourselves in the presence of three Lapp women, who had evidently just arrived. The women were quiet and self-possessed; they knew they had been caught on forbidden ground, and that if the länsman

chose he could fine them. My old companion seemed to try
to appear furious, but the women listened to him calmly. I
felt sorry, for there was not the usual welcome, nor the invitation to spend the night or to partake of coffee—nothing but a
cold reception. The men had evidently taken themselves out
of the way of the officer of the law, and left the women to
do the best they could. They said they did not know they
had crossed the frontier, and that it was simply a mistake;
they were ordered to leave the place, and recross the boundary. The länsman told them he was coming again the next
day, and that if they were seen on this side the herd would
be confiscated. Then we left with no kind words, no invitation to come again.

The place of the encampment was well chosen, on a spot
where the wind had almost entirely blown away the snow.
The tent was not yet put up, but a fire was lighted. The
reindeer had just been unharnessed, and numerous kerres,
akja, and låkkek were lying close together, loaded with the
frame of the tent and the woollen canvas, with frozen meat,
cooking utensils, wooden vessels, etc.

On the way back, another strange sight presented itself.
Where had the reindeer gone? None were to be seen. Had
they been taken away? As I approached the herd I discovered that all of them had dug holes so deep that I could see
only their tails, which swayed to and fro. This was certainly
a landscape I had never seen before.

It was wonderful how our guide now knew a good track!
We met no more holes and places where reindeer had been
before; we drove over an entirely new path, our little boat-like
sleighs leaving their furrows behind.

This hard day's work, with the constant jumping, knocking
against trees, and tumbling into the deep holes of the honey-
combed ground, was too much for the länsman; he came back
very tired and quite unwell, and was soon after seized with a
high fever, which continued the whole of the following day.

Farther on I crossed the Palojoki River, where we had been
in summer, and passed several farms and the hamlet of Kuttainen, when the spire of the church of Karesuando, the most

northern one in Sweden, burst upon our sight, while to the north the bluish birch-clad hills added to the quiet beauty of the scenery, and the houses came in view.

I was now 280 miles from Haparanda. Soon afterwards I came to the modest post-station, the humble but best farm of the hamlet. The seven or eight farms which made the place, scattered wide apart, possessed about sixty milch cows (for the pastures here are very good), six horses, sheep enough to supply the inhabitants with wool, and about 240 reindeer. Now and then there was seen a hay-stack resting on an elevated platform, which prevented the snow from covering the bottom of the stack.

The parsonage was at some distance, and easily recognized by its red buildings. Scattered about were queer-shaped solitary houses, belonging to the nomadic or fjeld Laplanders, in which they kept their garments, ornaments, flour, etc. The station was very comfortable, and the location unsurpassed. The dwelling-house was composed of two large rooms—one in which the family resided, and the other the stranger's room. The cow-house was opposite, and built very low, in order to keep it warm; the old-fashioned wooden bucket at the well, with its long pole, was entirely surrounded by a thick mass of ice.

Karesuando is situated in lat. 68° 30′, on the banks of the Muonio River, and 972 feet above the level of the sea; a little farther north is Enontekis, at an altitude of 326 feet more. These hamlets are the coldest places in Sweden where meteorological observations have been taken; the mean temperature throughout the year at Enontekis is about 4° or 5°; at Karesuando, about 6° below freezing-point, the mercury falling sometimes as low as 40° and 45° below zero.

Here, as in some other parts of Sweden and Norway, the cattle are strangely fed. Every farmer keeps as many animals as he can, though the hay crop is often short. The fine hay is kept for the horses, and the coarser grass for the cows; but this marshy grass is so hard to chew that it has to be soaked in boiling water. The reindeer-moss, an excellent fodder, is also used extensively; but it has to be cooked, and is often mixed with the grass, with the addition of sheep or horse dung. The cattle here looked far better than in many of the districts farther south. Occasionally barley ripens, but the crop is so uncertain that the people seldom plant it. Potatoes grow so fast that the tubers are small, all the strength going into the stem.

At the parsonage the pastor and his wife asked me to be their guest; I expressed my thanks, saying that I came to study the people, and wished to be among them, but that I would come often. I was not allowed to leave that day before I took dinner with the pastor. He was a quiet, undemonstrative man, with a benign countenance, and was much respected by the people, among whom he had lived for a number of years.

All over Swedish and Norwegian Lapland churches are scattered, so that the Laplander may easily attend a church, enjoy the privileges of religion, and partake of the Lord's Supper; and, when his days are ended, his body is carried thence to the graveyard. Near the church are schools where the children are taught, and the clergyman imparts the precepts of religion.

Vittangi, Jukkasjärvi, and Karesuando, in Torneå Lappmarken, are the three most northern churches of Sweden, around which is always found a hamlet. There, as in Karesuando, the Lapps have built many small houses, where they store the various articles they do not care to take with them. On Sunday many Lapps attend the church from their different encampments, either on snow-shoes or with reindeer; those who live far away often start the day before—the Finns from distant villages also join the congregation. The Swedish and Norwegian Lapps are all Lutherans. Here, also, the men were seated on one side of the church, and the women on the other. When I returned to the farm the whole congregation followed me.

At that time there were several young persons who had come to pass their religious examination before being confirmed at Easter (which is here one of the great festivals of the Church), and that year it was to take place on the 9th of April.

They were all dressed in their best clothes, the women in a gown of reindeer skin reaching much below the knees, with pantelettes and shoes of the same material. The women wore

SORSELE LAPP GIRLS AND BOY.

queer little bonnets of bright colors, made of pieces of wool and silk; some of the belts around the waist were ornamented with silver: they also wore large glass beads around the neck, and the fingers of many were ornamented with odd-shaped silver rings. Their great pride is to have two, three, or four large bright silk handkerchiefs about the neck, hanging down behind. The more they have, the more fashionable they are considered. The men were dressed very much in the same way, except that they wore square caps and shorter gowns. One of the characteristics of the Laplanders is that they are not bashful, though they are not forward. I never met even a bashful child; so we all soon became good friends. The men and women smoked and snuffed a great deal. The large room was packed with people, and all were animated.

In our farm-house there was a white-headed Lapp, nearly eighty years old, who passed all his time, Sundays as well as week-days, in reading the Bible, especially the Psalms, and the Prayer-book. He had ceased wandering over the mountains, being unable to bear the fatigue. He loved to remain near the church and the surrounding graveyard, where his forefathers had been buried. He was now looking beyond the grave and death, which he knew was near, but which did not frighten him. That cold icy grave of the north, covered with snow a great part of the year, and over which no flower would ever bloom, had no terrors for him. "It is," he said to me, "to be my quiet bed, over which the storms will blow without disturbing me. My spirit will go where God is, and where the Lord Jesus Christ, in whom I trust, doth live."

At the solitary farms and little hamlets of Lapland the sickly are left, and the kind care of the farmers is repaid, as I have said before, by presents from Lapps, and by taking care of their reindeer. In these hamlets, sometimes very far from home, the young people are confirmed, and finish their religious education. In the church they are baptized, and around it they are buried. The church to them is a sacred and beloved spot; they repair to it with joyful hearts, and all those who can, at certain times of the year make it a point to participate in its religious services. The Laplanders always come and partake of the Lord's Supper at *Påsk* (Easter) before they go with their herds into the mountains for the summer, to be absent several months.

At their religious reunions or festivals marriages are often arranged; girls are allowed to marry at the age of sixteen. Matches are often determined by parents beforehand, and the bridegroom must give the father or mother of the bride a certain number of reindeer; but sometimes engagements take place between lovers without the consent of the old folks. If the presents given to the parents and relatives of the bride are thought to be insufficient, I am informed they say so without scruple. At the betrothal feast the engagement ring is presented, and frequently a silver spoon. After the wedding another feast often follows, with the usual excesses of eating and drinking. When a child is born a reindeer is given to it; it is a custom also for the family to give one to the person who soonest observes the first teeth. The offspring of these animals become the child's own, and are not counted when there is a division of the property. The sponsor, too, often gives a reindeer to the child.

Many of the young Lapp girls I have met in my different journeys were fresh and blooming; but I frequently noticed how much older they appeared than they really were, in spite of the good health they all enjoyed, and which insured for them a ripe old age. Girls of fourteen or fifteen years of age appeared sometimes to be eighteen and twenty. This was no doubt due to their laborious and wandering life, and exposure to the dry cold winds; their premature development might also be attributed to their early and hard work. As they grow older they become very ugly and wrinkled. The old women—with their long uncombed hair hanging over their shoulders, their unwashed faces, and the entire absence of any desire to please—are certainly among the most hideous specimens of humanity. Among the younger, I frequently could not, from the face, distinguish a boy from a girl when the head-dresses were off.

At this time of the year I saw so many Laplanders together that I could well observe the characteristic type of their features. With few exceptions they had broad and short faces, with prominent cheeks; the chin was very short; nose usually flat between the eyes, sharp and *retroussé*, as shown

in our engravings from photographs. A number had dark
hair, that of others was blonde; but reddish dark-brown was
common. There were few eyes really blue; most were of a
light green and grayish; some had dark, and two or three had
hazel eyes. Their lips were thin; the skin of their faces was
reddened by the cold winds, but the protected part of the neck
and body was quite white by contrast. The fact is that the
Lapps have a very white skin, and those who have described
them as a dark-skinned people have made a mistake.

ÅSELE LAPP WOMAN—FRONT VIEW.

During my stay we became good friends; I gave them
many silver rings, and all the Lapp girls and boys said they
would never part with them. Like the Finns, they were fond
of large, round, glass beads, which they wore around their
necks. I had several pressing invitations to come and see
them during the summer. At night they slept among their
friends at the different farms, on deer-skins spread on the floor.
    The following measurements will give a fair idea of the
size of the Karesuando Lapps:

ADULT WOMEN.				ADULT MEN.			
5 ft.	½ in.	4 ft.	9¼ in.	5 ft.	0 in.	5 ft.	4½ in.
4 "	11 "	4 "	7 "	5 "	3 "	5 "	1 "
4 "	11¼ "	4 "	5¾ "	4 "	10 "	5 "	3 "
4 "	8¼ "	4 "	8¼ "	5 "	1½ "	5 "	"
4 "	11 "	4 "	10 "	5 "	1 "	5 "	½ "
4 "	6 "	4 "	5¼ "	5 "	4 "	4 "	10½ "
4 "	8¼ "	4 "	7¾ "	4 "	7 "	4 "	10¼ "

Those which have been given in other parts of the narrative, in the first volume, indicate the general size of the Laplanders.

ÅSELE LAPP WOMAN—SIDE VIEW.

In the school, at a farm-house near the parsonage, about seventy girls and boys were seated on the floor—the teacher or catechiser being in the centre of the room, in front of a little table. He called one after another, making a long and searching examination to see if they were strong in the faith, and if they knew their catechism well. The room was crowded with old men and women, who seemed much interested in the questions and answers. The children appeared humble and timid as they stood before their teacher, knowing that every one present was attentive.　The pastor also examined them.　As I listened to the questions my thoughts wandered to other lands with a denser population, blessed with a fertile soil and genial climate, having wealth and great resources, with numerous large towns and thrifty villages ; I thought of the millions in those countries who could not even read, and I could not but compare them with the wandering Lapland-

ARJEPLOUG LAPP (TWENTY-FIVE YEARS OF AGE).

ers, who at least can read, and many of them can write.　Here teachers travel from hamlet to hamlet, as the population is too scattered for a regular school-house.　Honor is due to Sweden and Norway for their long and earnest endeavors to carry education to their remotest and most thinly inhabited regions.

The district of Torneå Lappmark contains about 1200 square miles, and has two *socknar* (parishes) with parsonages.　The church at Karesuando belongs to the parish of Enontekis, which is divided into four *byar* (districts or hamlets): Köngemä or Rorto has 59 families; Lainio-wuoma, 65; Romma-wuoma, 25; Suonta-vaara, 44. Each have tracts of their own on which to pasture their herds, and here the Swedish länsman executes the laws.

JOKKMOKK LAPP (TWENTY-FOUR YEARS OF AGE).

The Lapps leave for Norway after Easter, and return be-tween the end of August and the middle of September, following the track of Kilpisjärvi, and going towards Balsfjord, Tromsö, and Marknäsdalen. They follow another track, and on the Norwegian coast are found at Ankenäs, Bardö, Ibestad, Målselven, and Tranö och Senjen. They return in the autumn, and wander in winter by Lake Torne towards the region of the upper Muonio. The tract of land lying west of Karesuando, and to the most northern part of Sweden, contains the greatest number of Laplanders—about 1100—who possess 80,000 reindeer. There are also 300 farmers, chiefly Finlanders, scattered over the region.

Jukkasjärvi, the parent church of the most northern part of Sweden, was built in 1603, and the parish, by the census of 1870, contained 626 Laplanders. It is divided into four districts or hamlets: Kalas, with 31 families; Rautas, with 20; Saari-vuoma, with 19; Tallma, with 28.

I greatly enjoyed myself here, for the winter is the travelling season, as then the rivers, lakes, and marshes are frozen, and one can roam over the roadless land with rapidity by reindeer, or may go eastward to the White Sea and the land of Samoïdes—to Siberia, if he chooses; westward and northward, over the mountains, to the Norwegian coast. In Sweden and Norway there are post-stations, where reindeer are procured, and *fjeldstue* (houses of refuge), built by the Norwegian and Swedish governments to shelter travellers. Karesuando can be reached with horses, the journey being quite easy as one travels on the river; but to go farther reindeer must be used.

The following are the calculated distances: From Karesuando to Bosekop, on the Alten fjord, 175 miles; from Karesuando to Skibotten, on the Lyngen fjord, 133 miles; from Jukkasjärvi to Skibotten, 210 miles. There are several other winter tracks leading to different parts of the Arctic Sea. From Torneå Lappmark an extensive traffic is carried on with the Norwegian coast, not only by the Laplanders but by Finlanders. The parishes of Karesuando, Kautokeino, Karasjok, and many hamlets on the banks of the Muonio and upper Torne rivers, and the farms scattered over the country, contribute their quota of dairy products. I have no doubt that even in this far North a greater population could be supported; a larger crop of grass could be obtained by improving the drainage; more horses and cattle could be raised, especially as the latter feed so much on the lichens: the production of butter is even now increasing every year.

While in the remote and wild regions of the North, I always made it a point to let some official or well-known person take cognizance of my intended journeys, and trusted to them for guides, as well as to secure the services of the right persons. The people were so kind-hearted that in all cases I found either the governor of the province, the clergyman of the parish, the doctor, judge, jägmästare, länsman, the principal merchant of the place, or the leading farmers ready to help me, and do all they could to further the object I had in view. Without their help I should often have been unable to undertake interesting journeys; their letters of introduction, also, were of great value. I felt, too, that if people knew where I had gone, it would act as a check on the evil-doer, if any one were disposed to act badly, and that my whereabouts would be known in case of any accident or sickness.

I had come to Karesuando at a good time, for the inhabitants were making preparations to cross the mountains to attend a fair at Skibotten, a little hamlet near the head of the Lyngen fjord. There were six stations between the two places. Finlanders and Laplanders were ready for the journey. Butter, frozen reindeer meat and smoked tongues, skins, Lapp shoes and gloves, and frozen ptarmigans were already packed. Fish, coffee, sugar, flour, tobacco, and sundry hardware, provisions, goods, and oil were to be brought back. Many had already gone on with their products; from Karesuando alone more than twenty kerres had left. They could not wait for me, for they had heavy loads, and their animals would go slowly, so I could soon overtake those who had started. The pastor had sent a messenger in search of a Laplander that he recommended. One does not always know where to find these people, and oftentimes, when found, the herd from which the draught deer are to be chosen is at some distance. A strong reindeer can draw from 200 to 400 pounds, according to the country. Every load in Swedish and Norwegian Lapland is drawn in the boat-like sleigh, and by one animal only. Among the Samoïdes several reindeer are harnessed together to a sleigh. If the country is mountainous, a spare reindeer is taken in the descent of very steep hills. My Laplander having arrived, I was ready to leave.

H 2

CHAPTER VIII.

Departure from Karesuando.—The Lapp Pehr.—Vuokainen.—Large Numbers of Travellers.—An Obstinate Reindeer.—A Runaway.—A Lapp Woman comes to my Help.—Lost for awhile.—Arrival at Sikavuopio.—Shelter House of Muk-kavuoma.—A great Storm.—Making Ourselves Comfortable.—Ready to Cross the Mountain Range.—Preparing for the Worst.—A Perfect Hurricane.—Sufferings. —A Mask of Ice.—We come to a Halt.—Continuing the Journey.—Down the Hills.—Great Speed of Reindeer.—Thrown out of the Sleigh.—In a Predicament. —Reindeer on the Ice.—Deep soft Snow.—Reindeer exhausted with Fatigue.— Preparations before going down a Steep Gorge.—Dangerous Descent.—Helligs-koven.—Another great Storm.—Arrival on the Norwegian Coast.—Skibotten.— The Fair.—The Lyngen Fjord.—The Hamlet of Lyngen.—A Parsonage.—District Doctors.—Hard Life of a Doctor.—The City of Tromsö.

Four kerres, with reindeer harnessed and ready to start, stood on the frozen Muonio by the shore near the parsonage. Three of these were for Pehr, Elsa, and myself, and the fourth one contained our luggage, which had been made secure with a skin over it, so that there was no fear of our losing anything in case of upsetting. Elsa had only a sack, in which her whole wardrobe, composed of two home-made dresses, two pairs of woollen stockings, a pair of leather shoes, and two or three fine handkerchiefs, was packed. After dinner the worthy pastor and his wife accompanied us to the sleighs, and gave some advice to my Lapp regarding the journey.

Though our reindeer started with great speed, they soon slowed and became tired; perhaps they had been used recently, and were inferior to those at Muoniovaara. The track was exceedingly good, and our kerres were almost buried in the deep furrows made by preceding ones, for evidently there had been considerable travel. Towards eleven o'clock at night our animals were very weary, and we stopped at a farm called Vuokainen or Vuokaimo, at the head of Lake Kellotijärvi, a broad expanse of the river, which afterwards takes the name of Köngämä. A strange sight met us as we approached the yard—about a hundred loaded kerres were standing in front, and the farm-house was crowded with Finns and Lapps, who were lying close together on the floor, all fast asleep. The fixed odor of the room was very disagreeable. A lamp hung from the centre, and threw a dim light over the packed and snoring crowd. In the next room, on the only bed, was the wife of the farmer, with a babe two or three days old. Even there, on the floor, were people fast asleep. "If my wife could get up," said the husband, "I would give you the bed; but she cannot." To our reindeer we gave some moss, which we bought for a small sum, and started again.

The next stopping-place was at the farm of Sikavuopio, twelve miles farther. At first Pehr was unwilling to start, but I said I would rather have slept on the snow than breathe the air of that crowded room. Our reindeer were obstinate, and twice they turned back in spite of all the skill of Pehr; he had to get out of his kerres and lead his animal for awhile; then we started in the usual wild way. This time I brought up the rear, when my reindeer gave a sharp turn that would have upset me had I lacked experience; then he started at full speed back for Vuokaimo, and soon afterwards I found myself dashing against the numerous sleighs in the yard. A Lapp woman came to my rescue, and led the beast back quite a distance—far enough to be sure that he would not take a fancy to return. I followed in what I supposed to be Pehr's track, but soon found that, in spite of my extra speed, he was not to be seen. I began to feel anxious, being alone, and not knowing where I was going, and without a mouthful of provisions with me. I stopped, and shouted "Pehr!" but no answer came; and then I continued on my way. Soon in the distance I saw, over the snow, something black; I shouted "Pehr! Pehr!" again, and was glad to hear another shout of "Paul! Paul!" It was my leader, who had become anxious at not seeing me, and was coming back with Elsa Karolina. I had gone on the wrong track, as he suspected. The outlines of the hills on our right were almost as distinct as dur-

ing the day, on account of the aurora borealis. It was 26°
below freezing at three o'clock A.M. when I reached the farm-
house of Sikavuopio, where I found the people fast asleep.
The three beds were occupied — the two farm-girls were in
one; the children, huddled together like rabbits, had another;
and the man and his wife were in the third. Though the
room was intensely warm, they were all wrapped in skins.
The strangers' room was occupied by my friend the Finnish
länsman, who insisted on my taking his bed. When I refused,
he offered me half of it, which I also politely declined. The
farmer's wife got up, and spread for me two deer-skins on
the floor, with some sheepskins for blankets; Elsa went to
sleep with the other two girls.

From Sikavuopio the hill-sides were clothed only with
birch-trees. In a couple of hours we came to Vittangi, near
the river, which there forms a lake. The dwelling-house, with
another low building for three cows, constituted the farm; and
the family consisted of a man and his wife and two grown-up
daughters. The farmer himself was going to Skibotten, to sell
butter, shoes, skins, and several hundred ptarmigans, which he
had trapped during the winter. I tarried two hours, not only
to rest the reindeer but to stretch my limbs—for the seated
position required in the Lapp sleighs is very tiresome to one
unaccustomed to it—and I left the farm thankful for the kindness shown us. The landscape became more and more beautiful as we approached the head-waters of the stream, and the
farm and station of Mukkavuoma. Our course was over Lake
Kilpisjärvi, the source of the Muonio. Several feet of snow
covered the ice. We were evidently among the first, for there
were no furrows, or the wind had obliterated them. The sky
began to grow gray, and a storm apparently was coming; the
breeze increased, and flakes of snow began to fall; the squalls
increased in force and frequency. These were the forerunners
of a series of great storms—in fact, the greatest I ever experienced. The dark clouds were flying very fast over our heads,
and the sky became wild and peculiar. I hurried my reindeer
to his utmost speed by striking his flanks, in order to keep
pace with Pehr, who saw what was coming, and wished to

reach the farm of refuge before the storm should burst upon us. It was well that we hurried, for we had hardly reached Mukkavuoma when the wind blew furiously; the snow was driven in thick clouds, the hills were hidden from view, and before us was nothing but a thick misty haze.

Mukkavuoma was composed of two farms, not far from each other, overlooking Lake Kilpisjärvi. The farm-house, like others, consisted of two rooms — one in which the inmates lived, the other, with an open fireplace, for strangers; the latter was given to us. Elsa was quite ill with a burning fever, this constant and hard travelling having been too much for her; the länsman himself was so tired that he could hardly move. How welcome is such a spot to the weary traveller during winter! How quickly he hastens to seek its shelter when he sees a threatening snow-storm ready to overtake him!

One by one some of the Finns we had left behind on the way made their appearance. Long before dark the storm had greatly increased, and the wind blew a gale. We felt how comfortable it was to be under shelter, and how cheerful was our blazing fire, as through our little glass window we watched the storm. The spectacle was so grand that I went out into the yard, for I love to feel a great tempest beating upon my face: there is something exhilarating to me in the strong wind. Our sleighs were now buried in the snow; our reindeer, tied together, were standing perfectly still. The hostess soon came in with four large trout from the Kilpisjärvi, which we roasted for dinner on a bright charcoal fire; besides, we had two ptarmigans, which had been cooked, in the mean time, in the next room. These birds were very abundant, more than two thousand having been trapped by our host during the past winter. The coffee-kettle, black from smut, was brought in, and coffee was served to us in large cups. After dinner another bed was placed in the room for Elsa; the länsman insisted on my taking the other one, but I was determined that he should have it himself, as he was oldest; a reindeer skin on the floor was quite enough for me; I put clean dry stockings on my feet, new grass in my shoes, so that my feet would be warm, and my extra long deer robe over the other; then I lay down and

slept comfortably. Several times during the night I was awakened by the noise of the wind, which howled dismally about
our little house.

Next morning the weather was calm. In the other room I
found Pehr fast asleep, with his dog by his side, and a number
of men on the floor snoring heavily. The farmer's wife was
grinding coffee; the kettle was on the fire, and the dregs of
the day before were boiling in the water. When the people
got up the coffee was served, and those who had a little bränvin mixed some with it, and offered it to those who had none.
Then one by one they made their preparations for departure,
first eating a hearty meal. As the charges were very high to
travellers—even those who slept on the floor having to pay
twelve skillings—every one had brought his own provisions.

The distance from Mukkavuoma to Helligskoven, in Norway, was about thirty miles. The country was mountainous,
and the driving rough. Everybody had left the hospitable
fjeldstue of Mukkavuoma, notwithstanding the threatening appearance of the weather. Pehr was anxious, thinking that we
were going to have another storm, and he well knew with
what force the wind blows on the highest point which we had
to cross; we therefore prepared ourselves for the worst. My
stockings were dry, and my shoes had been carefully and firmly tied around my reindeer pantaloons; the belt at my waist
was well secured, Pehr himself attending to my toilet; I put
on a mask and a heavy hood; my gloves were fastened at
the wrists, and I was ready for bad weather.

We had not left Mukkavuoma two hours, when signs of a
great storm gathered fast around; the wind increased in violence, heavy squalls burst upon us in quick succession, and at
last we found ourselves in the midst of a perfect hurricane,
while the mercury fell to 8° above zero. We were, however,
gradually reaching higher land, and were nearing the summit
of the range, though our reindeer travelled very slowly. No
traces whatever of those who had preceded us could be seen,
and Pehr was guided only by the outlines of the surrounding
hills and mountains, which showed themselves now and then
when the gale moderated or the wind varied in violence. The

TRAVELLING IN LAPLAND.

storm continued to increase, and swept down upon us from
the higher mountains and hill-sides with a force which I had
never witnessed before. The fine snow flew so thickly that
at times the atmosphere became almost dark. I could see neither Pehr, who led, nor Elsa. I could not even see my own
animal, and I let him take his course, knowing that he would
instinctively follow his leader. At last I began to fear that we
might be separated and lost. I had very little food with me,
and only a small supply for the reindeer. Occasionally came
a short lull, and in the intervals the wind would blow with
the greatest fury. The fine snow-dust was getting through
the open spaces of the mask into my eyes. The small particles then adhered to each other, gathering on my mustache,
eyebrows, eyelashes, and hair, and at last formed a mask of ice
which blinded me. Every few minutes I had to break this,
that it should not become so thick that I would be unable to
see. The ice was scarcely removed when it would form again,
causing me great pain whenever I broke it. At last I became
very anxious, for I had not for a long time seen even dimly
any other member of our party. I shouted for Pehr and
Elsa, but my voice was lost in the midst of that furious wind.
I became still more alarmed. To be lost in such a region in
a storm was no pleasant prospect. Suddenly through the
mist I discovered what appeared to be figures of reindeer
and men. They were standing still, afraid to move farther,
and my animal stopped in their midst. They were a large
party of Lapps and Finns, my companions of Karesuando,
Kuttainen, and Mukkavuoma. I was glad to recognize Pehr
and Elsa among them. We could go no farther, for it was
now impossible to see anything ahead, and there was danger
of mistaking the passes which were to lead us to Norway; besides, our reindeer needed rest, and from excessive thirst they
were eating the snow ravenously. I shall never forget how
the storm raged as we lay by a rock with our backs to the
wind. For three hours we remained still, frequently almost
buried, the thermometer being at 15° below zero. The wind
was so terrific at times that hardly a particle of the several
feet of snow that had fallen during the winter months re-

mained on the ground. It flew in dense bodies, carried hither and thither; a hill was no sooner formed than it scattered in thick heavy masses; we were fearful of being buried under one of these hillocks, which were as dangerous as those formed by sand in the desert of Sahara.

The object my companions seemed to have in view was to shelter me as much as they could from the fury of the wind; they would surround me as a protection; one of them especially, Ephraim Person, from Kuttainen, tried to keep a large bear-skin over me; but it was of no avail, the tempest was so powerful. Then, gradually, the wind became less violent, and we continued our journey. As we had to go over many mountain-tops and ravines, one of our party proposed that we should travel close together, for fear of getting separated. I noticed, by the quickening steps of my animal, that we were approaching the slope of a hill. I was not mistaken, and we descended a long steep declivity with fearful speed. Suddenly my reindeer sank above his flank into a bank of unpacked snow, and before he had time to spring out my sleigh dashed rapidly ahead of him, and, suddenly stopping, threw me out; fortunately I leaped in quickly, and the animal again started at what I thought a greater speed than before.

One of the Finlanders just in front of me was less fortunate. His sleigh, moving faster than his deer, struck upon the legs of the animal, and he was thrown out; I saw the danger at a glance, but, being unable to stop, went rushing down in the same track. My sleigh struck his, and by the force of the collision I was pitched head foremost into the snow. To add to the confusion, my animal became mad and charged upon me; but I was soon on my legs and in again, following the Finn, who had started once more, and was going at a rapid rate towards the base of the hill. Then came Elsa's turn to be upset; but soon she recovered her seat, and we reached the bottom without further mishap. The adventure was exciting and glorious. At the foot of the hill the snow covered thinly the frozen stream, and the scene became rather ludicrous. There was not snow enough to prevent the reindeers' hoofs from touching the ice, so it was an impossibility for them to advance a step; the awkward attempts they made were quite amusing. We were compelled to get out of the sleighs and lead the animals, and it was with considerable difficulty and great loss of time that we succeeded in crossing. It is impossible for reindeer to travel over ice.

As we ascended the mountains on the other side the snow became deeper; a part of the way led us through very narrow ravines, in which it was so deep and soft that our boat-like sleighs ploughed heavily through it, sinking sometimes into it above their sides. I could not but admire the adaptation of the reindeer for such travelling; their hoofs, between which grows long hair, spread in the snow as soon as their feet touched it, and although the depth must have been in places eight or ten feet, they seldom sank as deeply into it as their knees. They moved so quickly that there was no time for them to sink deeper. At times, however, when passing through a very soft and heavy snow-drift, they would sink even to their bellies.

Our progress now was exceedingly tedious. In ascending the hills, our reindeer became very tired from their struggles in the snow; they were heated; their mouths would open, and they panted for breath, sometimes even protruding their tongues. They were often so exhausted that they would drop upon the snow and lie on their backs, apparently in great suffering, then breathe very hard, and be so utterly helpless that a stranger would think they were about to die. After resting a few minutes in that position they would regain their breath, rise to their feet, eat snow, and set off again. There were many steep and short hills, up which it was impossible for them to run, and we were often obliged to get out of our sleighs to let them rest.

We came to the worst part of the journey, on the brink of a narrow ravine, and stopped, for the descent was very abrupt, and preparations to insure safety had to be made. I felt rather concerned when I saw the difficulties to be encountered on the route, which was somewhat crooked; in some places the ridge over which we were to drive was quite narrow, the

gneiss rocks were bare, and the track very steep and dangerous. The prospect was not a cheerful one. I had some objection to being pitched into the snow, and no inclination to
be dashed against rocks or boulders at the risk of a broken
head. I remembered, for the first time, the recommendation
of my London bankers, who, as I left London, said, "Travel with
a placard on your back—'To be forwarded to Baring Brothers!'"

Pehr and the other Finns waited for those who were behind. While resting I watched the weary reindeer eating
snow as fast as they could. The way by which we were to
make the descent was entirely new to me. After every one
had arrived the preparations began. Numbers of sleighs were
lashed together by a long and strong leather plaited cord,
which was first secured to the forward part of each; then,
passing along the middle, was made fast; after which it was
attached to the next in the same manner, and so on; four
others were connected with mine. In this way eight or ten are
often fastened together. With the exception of the leader,
each reindeer was secured to the rear of his sleigh by a leather
cord from the base of the horns: almost every sleigh had a
deer behind. Each man remained in his vehicle, the distance
apart being small. Pehr was to take the lead. The spare
reindeer were for the first time harnessed, and the tired ones
put behind. Pehr had to start the whole train, which, when
once put in motion, would go with great velocity; he rode
with his legs outside, turned back somewhat, with his feet
touching the snow. Every man but me seated himself in
the same posture, the feet acting as rudder and drag in the
snow. I was not allowed to ride in that way, for they said my
legs would surely be broken. Ephraim, of Kuttainen, attached
his conveyance behind mine, and also had a reindeer to act as
a drag; in that way he would be able to watch and direct my
movements. When everything was ready Pehr looked back
and gave the signal, and started his reindeer down the hill in
a zigzag course. This required great dexterity, as we flew
over the snow with astonishing speed. At times the sleighs
would swerve on the declivity, but we went so fast that we
were soon out of danger.

GOING DOWN A STEEP DECLINE.

I was anxious in the highest degree. If one of those cords had broken we should have been precipitated far below, or dashed against the rocky sides. I admired the simplicity of the arrangements, which were dictated by the fact that rein-deer cannot bear to be pulled by the head, especially by the horns; each one, therefore, makes an effort to disengage him-self, and by so doing acts as a brake on the ones in front, so that no sleigh is likely to be overturned. But what a speed, with a precipice on our right! In two or three places we went for a short distance over the bare rocks; I was afraid the reindeer would miss their foothold, and was intensely excited, for I might at any moment have been thrown out headlong. Pehr and my other companions were accustomed to this route, and knew what they were about. After reach-ing the bottom of the ravine we allowed the panting animals to rest. We were now on the western shed of the mountains, and had just ended the most thrilling ride I had ever taken.

Though protected from the wind, we could hear it whistling through the branches of the leafless birches, for we had again reached the level of tree vegetation; as we descended, the for-est became thicker and the trees larger. It was dark when we came to the mountain shelter-farm of Helligskoven. How welcome was that house of refuge to us! All of us were stiff from cold and our seated position, and we had also been the whole day without food: it was the hardest day's travelling I had ever experienced. We were so tired that we were not hungry. Pehr produced a bottle of sherry wine, which had been packed in the sleigh surrounded by a thick deer-skin, and the eyes of my friendly and kind-hearted companions brightened as a glass was given to each. I felt at once that it did me good, for our feet had been dangling in the snow a great part of the time without snow-shoes. Our simple fare consisted of coarse, hard, black, flat bread, with butter, cheese, and coffee, though the latter was salted.

A single room offered the only accommodation for the fam-ily and the travellers; there was no open fireplace, but a large stove; poles were fastened under the ceiling, on which to hang our clothes, stockings, and shoes. Coffee was drank, cup after cup, with real enjoyment, and soon all were fast asleep, some on the floor, others on the plain beds, without straw or hay.   The storm, which had somewhat abated on our arrival, increased after midnight, and continued through the next day; but during one of the lulls we started, for we could not wait, as the fair would last only three days, and I did not wish to desert my travelling friends, all of whom had been such good and thoughtful companions.   Our sleighs were lashed together again, and we bade good-bye to Helligskoven, which had been built by the Norwegian Government as a place of refuge.   Not far from the farm two or three short fir-trees raised their heads among the shorter birches.

Soon after our departure the gale intensified, and became almost a repetition of the storm of the day before.   Then it began to snow heavily, and we were obliged to stop, as we could not see our way, and had lost our reckoning: the wind had the effect of making me dizzy.   When the storm ceased the men did not know exactly where we were, and had mistaken some of the outlines of the mountains.   They put on their snow-shoes and went to reconnoitre; they soon came back with the pleasing news that we were only a little out of the way.   The weather cleared suddenly, and became very cold.   Being obliged to take off one of my gloves, my hand instantly became almost like marble, and useless; I rubbed it at once with snow, and quickly replaced it in the mitten. The snow became less deep; and when we came to a small lake, which we tried in vain to cross in order to shorten the distance, we were forced to skirt the shores, as the late storm here had blown the ice bare.

The fir-trees had for some time been about us, and were thicker and thicker as we descended the mountain and reached warmer regions.   It was quite dark when, at 8 P.M., we came to the hamlet of Skibotten, and stopped in front of a large painted house by the fjord.   We had been four days on the way.   Through one of the windows I could see a blazing fire in the kitchen.   I entered, and addressing myself to two young girls, said, "Can you give shelter to a hungry and tired stranger, who has just come from Sweden over the mountains?" "Welcome art thou! Whence comest thou?" "From America." "The more welcome, then, for we have a sister in the State of Minnesota." From the kitchen I was taken into the next room, both the girls helping me to remove my Lapland robes. The owner of the house, their father, came in and greeted me. I was soon enjoying a substantial meal, for I had not eaten for many hours—not since we left Helligskoven. The people looked at me with astonishment, and asked if I did not fear to travel alone in such a wild country. "Are you not afraid you will be robbed or murdered by the mountain Lapps? How would people ever know if you were killed for the sake of your money?" They then told the story of some foreigner who had not been heard from, and who was supposed to have been murdered; his name they could not tell: of course nobody had been killed, but many of the inhabitants on the coast are strongly prejudiced against the mountain Lapps. The conversation ended by their advising me to be careful, and not trust myself among those dreadful Lapps who live in the inaccessible mountains.

The fjord was frozen at its upper extremity, and during the two days I remained here the mercury averaged 22° to 24°.

The hamlet of Skibotten is situated near the head of the fjord. Three fairs take place here every year, that of March being the least important. A few log-houses had been built by the merchants who come only to sell and buy goods, the houses at other times being unoccupied. Laplanders and Finlanders were still arriving; all had experienced great difficulty in crossing over on account of the storm, and we heard that many had returned home, or remained at the mountain farms, frightened by the severe weather. The fair lasted from Saturday until Tuesday, business being suspended on Sunday. Saturday and Monday were the great days, after which all may be said to be ended.

Several houses of farmers and fishermen had been turned into inns, and most of the people were satisfied to find a sleeping-place on the floor. Coffee was made everywhere, a large cup, well salted, costing three cents, and strangers could procure a meal very cheaply. These people work so hard to get money that they do not squander it; many had brought their provisions with them, and paid only for lodgings or coffee. I treated Pehr and my companions to several meals—an attention which very much pleased them.

Scattered at the back of the houses were numerous kerres loaded with frozen meat, ptarmigans (ten thousand of these birds are sent to this part of the coast every winter), butter, skins, shoes, gloves, etc., each owner having his sleighs grouped together. The bargains were made on the spot, and the articles after being sold were stored in the log-houses. When the sellers had received their money, they wandered from store to store to buy what they wanted.

I had now brought Elsa Karolina within a short distance of her home, for one of her sisters lived near. I gave her a few presents, a little money, and a gold ring to remember me by. I have often wondered since what has become of my interpreter and fellow-traveller over the mountains to the Lyngen fjord.

I did not desert my companions of the fjelds; the storm had made us all fast friends; we were a good part of the time together, and I took great interest in their bargains, and was as delighted as they were when I heard they had sold what they had brought at fair prices. I treated them to many cups of coffee, they returning the compliment, and we passed the time in a very agreeable way. Faithful Pehr received more pay than I had agreed to give him, and we parted on good terms, all wishing to their friend Paul a successful journey, and Ephraim making me promise to come to his home, which was but a few miles from Karesuando, on my return.

How austere and impressive was the winter scene at the Lyngen fjord, with its small glaciers and snow! At some distance from Skibotten was the hamlet of Lyngen; the landscape surrounding the place was extremely picturesque, the hills were clad with birch-trees. By the church was the parsonage. How tidy were the rooms! how hospitable were the pastor and his family! In the parlor windows the flower shrubs bent their tops towards the outside light, and seemed to look at the snow.

Not far from the parsonage, high up and overlooking the lovely landscape of the fjord, was the new home of the doctor who had met me at Skibotten, and I had come to make the promised visit. He had been appointed doctor of the district but a short time before, and had just bought the farm. When I arrived he was not at home, but his young and amiable wife received me with great kindness, and bade me await her husband's return; she was expecting him every minute: he had gone to see some patient. While waiting for him, his wife having gone to prepare a meal, I looked around. The house was a picture of neatness; there was evidence of refinement everywhere in this plain unpretending home—books, music, engravings. In a short time the doctor came. He was cold and tired, for the sail had been a long one, as the patient lived far away. The district to which he had been appointed by the Government was a large one.

Throughout Scandinavia there are *distrikts læge* (doctors of a district) who receive yearly a certain amount of remuneration from the State, varying according to places; for the population is so scattered that, were it not so, large tracts of country would be found without medical help, for doctors could not make a living. The fees they receive are regulated by law, according to the distance travelled from their residence. Hard, indeed, is the life of country doctors, especially of those whose districts are on the fjords or by the sea-coast. The only way of locomotion they have is by boat. Often they have to sail or row some twenty or thirty miles, or even more, and encounter all sorts of weather; and great praise is due them for their lives of self-denial. I did not wonder they were so highly esteemed by the people.

From the hamlet of Lyngen, or Lyngseidet, a short valley crosses the peninsula to the Ulfs fjord, over which there is a good driving road. After a sail through a magnificent, ever-changing panorama, on the 25th of March I arrived at Tromsö, one of Norway's charming little towns, with a population of 5000 inhabitants. The houses are painted and cheerful, there are some very pretty villas, and the situation of the place is beautiful; the smiling landscape is quite in contrast with the weird mountains. This is a very thriving seaport, and sends expeditions yearly to Spitzbergen and other places in the far North for seals. There are some wealthy and enterprising merchants, several banks, and fine schools. It is the residence of the Stiftamtmand, and of the bishop of the diocese.

My journey over the mountains beyond the arctic circle, between 69° and 70° lat., was over. I had met many a storm on the Atlantic; the tornado of the equator had often passed over my head or struck the ship which bore me, but of all the wind-storms I ever encountered that of the mountains we had just crossed was the grandest. As I look back to those days I fancy I can hear the shrieks and howling of the wind, and remember how I crouched upon the rocks for safety, while the tempest beat upon me as if the elements had obtained the mastery over the world, and chaos was coming again.

CHAPTER IX.

The Lofoden Islands.—Their Picturesque Appearance.—The Voyage from Tromsö. —A Magnificent Sunset.—The Raftsund.—Svolvær.—Thousands of Fishing-boats. —Migration of Cod.—Henningsvær.—A Great Fishing-place.—A Kind Merchant. —Lofoden Hospitality.—Care of the Norwegian Government over the Fisher-men.—Hospitals.—Fishing Regulations.—Telegraphs.—Comfortable Clothing of Fishermen.—The Finmarken Boats.—The Start.—Return.—Price of Cod.—Cleaning the Cod.—Fishing Lapps.—Going after Cod.—Signal for Departure.—The Fishing-grounds.—Net-fishing.—An Afternoon with the Fishermen.—Line-fishing.—A Kind Woman.—Stamsund.—Manufacture of Cod-liver Oil.—Rev-erence of Fishermen for God.—A Sunday at Church.—A Worthy Pastor.—Love-making on Sunday Afternoon.—Departure from Lofoden.

There is a group of islands not far from the Norwegian coast, beyond the arctic circle, between lat. 67° and 69°, called the Lofoden. They are unsurpassed in their wild beauty; a tem-pestuous sea beats almost all the year against their rocky walls; the warm Gulf-stream laves their shores. As one sails among them their fantastic forms are ever-changing in appearance, some of their peaks appearing like needles against the blue sky. Their outlines stand out clear and sharp, and their pur-ple color grows dimmer and dimmer as they fade away from sight, like a vision of the sea. No wonder that in ancient times the mariner regarded them almost with reverence, and believed that a malström* should guard their approach from the south, so beautiful are they. Looking from them towards the main-land, a hundred peaks can be seen on the mountains clad with snow and glaciers, and from the bare brow of the

---

* In consequence of the great masses of water which the tides force through the narrow sounds between the islands of Lofoden, the current becomes extremely strong, and forms the so-called Malström, which is strongest between Lofoden Cape and Mosken; this, without being of the significance ascribed to it, can in winter, during westerly gales, run in strong whirls, and with a speed of twenty-six miles an hour, according to official statistics.

I 2

coast the Lofoden appear like a gigantic uneven wall rising from the sea.

Nowhere have I seen such beautiful sunsets as in those regions. In the spring the glow is so bright that it seems to typify the fire of youth. In the autumn the sunsets are the finest; but, as if foreshadowing the repose of nature before winter comes, their golden hue is more mellow. In summer the midnight sun shines for awhile over the mountains and the sea that washes their shores. In winter furious snow-storms clothe the lofty hills in white, while the gales dash the waves against the immovable walls; but occasionally there comes a clear bright night when the aurora borealis, in all its varied beauties, crowns the Lofoden with a halo of glory. Some of the islands are quite large, and possess fertile tracts, and their shores here and there are lined with hamlets and farms, protected from the stormy sea. The approach, either from the north or south, is very fine.

From Tromsö the sail southward is at times grand in the extreme: jagged wild mountains, alpine in their appearance, their abrupt sides denuded of snow, with here and there a small glacier, are numerous; the West fjord, formed by the Lofoden group on the west and the main-land on the east side, grows narrower towards the north, and gradually loses itself in a labyrinth of islands and the Ofoten fjord.

On the 31st of March, about seven o'clock P.M., as we came towards Lodingen, situated on the island of Hindö, a scene of indescribable splendor was before us; it was one of the finest sunsets I had ever seen. Towards the east were the towering mountains of the main-land, their hollows appearing like golden valleys surrounded by white snowy peaks, while island after island rose from the sea in the soft light. The sight was so extremely beautiful that I could not restrain my enthusiasm. When night came, the fantastic forms of the mountains appeared still more strange; the stars were reflected in the quiet sea, for there was not a breath of wind; it was a fitting close of the last day of March on this bleak, barren, stormy country of the North.

Among the many beautiful sails is the one on the Raftsund,

FISHING SETTLEMENT ON LOFODEN. From a Photograph.

formed by the islands of East Vaagen and Hindö; there the
scenery is exceedingly beautiful, and the sound gradually nar-
rows until it looks like a river, flanked by towering mountains
rising from the water's edge. The sea is deep, and of a green
color. The landscape grows grander and grander. Everywhere rise fantastic peaks of all imaginable shapes, towering
above the level of the water. Glaciers and patches of snow
cling to the mountain-sides, and beautiful cascades pour down
the dark weather-beaten rocks. The ragged mountains and the
deep fissures increase the wildness of the scene. Moraines are
seen here and there, and boulders seem ready to topple down.
Now and then a little log-hut is passed.

On a clear morning, the first of April, I emerged from
this sound into a lake-like bay studded with islands, and
neared the island of Svolvær, steaming in the midst of hundreds of fishing-boats coming back under sail, and loaded
with codfish newly caught. The Lofoden are famed for their
cod-fisheries, which begin in the latter part of January and
last until the beginning of April. At that time the rocky
and deserted islands become full of life; thousands of fish-
ing-craft come, and hundreds of small vessels are seen nestled
safely among the islands. The codfish, in untold numbers,
make their appearance, whence no one knows, to spawn. They
begin to arrive in January, and leave at the end of March or
at the beginning of April, migrating towards the North Cape
and along the Finmarken coast; they then disappear for the
year.

How wonderful is the migration of fish! Whither do they
go? How well they know the time for returning to deposit
their ova! The codfish are found in large numbers along
the coast; they occur in vast shoals only from the Lofoden
Islands northward along the Finmarken coast. High above
the fishing settlement of Svolvær are twin rocks, looking,
as the people said, as if they were kissing each other; they
incline towards each other somewhat like the arms of an in-
verted V. Fishing establishments are located on small islands lying at the base of the towering consorts, but so over-
shadowed by the high shore that they can only be seen at

a short distance; they are often clustered so closely as to protect each other from the wind, and thus enjoy excellent harbors.

We remained but a short time at Svolvær; and after a
pleasant sail we cast anchor before Henningsvær, my place of
destination.   Several sharp whistles warned the people of our
arrival.   From the deck of the vessel no sign of a habitation
was seen, when suddenly boats emerged from behind the
rocks, and speedily came along-side.   I left the steamer and
soon entered a natural canal formed by two islands, Henningsvær and Hellandsö, where an unexpected sight burst upon us:
a fleet, hitherto unseen, was at anchor, and in large numbers.
Seventy-five sail had come here this year—sloops, schooners,
and cutters—with crews aggregating 328 men.   Most of these
vessels bought their fish directly from the fishermen; several
had stores, and sold sugar, coffee, ship-bread, tobacco, and
many other things.   There were 688 fishing-boats, 351 of
which had come to fish with nets, the remainder with hook
and line; the crews of all numbered 3337 men.   Craft laden
with fish, some almost to the water's edge, were going to and
fro, stopping along-side of a vessel to make a bargain, pulling
their loads on board, or making for the land.   Immense quantities of cod were piled one upon another on the shore, men
were busy opening and cleaning them, and tens of thousands
of the fish were hanging upon poles to dry.   Numerous log-
houses were surrounded by barrels filled with cod livers, and
every rock was covered with heads.   Hundreds of boats lined
the shores, crowding the narrow channel.   Great numbers of
eider-ducks, as tame as those on farms, were swimming to and
fro, seeming to know that no one would harm them.

We pulled along until we came in front of several large
houses, where we landed.   Here was the great establishment of
the place, belonging to a Norwegian, the richest man of Nordland, who was worth 300,000 or 400,000 dollars, at the least.
I had made on board the acquaintance of the clergyman and
länsman, who at this time resided here, and they presented
me to the hostess, who kindly offered me the hospitality of
the house, and said I could stay as long as I wished.   This invitation was the more acceptable, as there was no other place

where I could have found shelter. The goodness of her heart
was marked on her face. Her husband was one of those self-
made men who have acquired a large fortune, and have not
changed their ways since they started in life. He spent the
day in his store, buying and selling fish. He welcomed me,
but did not talk much, his mind seeming intent on his business, for it was just the height of the season, and he was an
extensive exporter of fish. A large room was shown me, and
soon dinner was served. For a wonder, there were no children in the family. A young niece and another lady friend
did the honors, and helped the hostess in her arduous duty of
house-keeping. Several persons were at dinner—mostly captains of the craft engaged in the fishery. The lensmand, the
clergyman, and doctor were guests during the fishing-season,
for only two or three families dwell on the island the year
round. Henningsvær is the largest fishing-station on the Lofoden—there are years when over 800 boats go there to fish.

The warehouse of my host was a sight worth seeing: long
deep rows of freshly-salted codfish, six feet high, were packed
together, to be afterwards laid on the rocks and dried. There
are three different ways of curing the cod. The first, and the
most common, is to cut the fish open, flatten, and salt it, putting it afterwards on the rocks to dry. The second is to open
the fish, tie them two and two, without being salted, and hang
them on frames. The third is to divide each in halves, connected only by the gills; the spine is then taken out, and the
fish hung upon the frames: this method is much the quickest, as the air now operates directly on the exposed flesh of
the fish, soon making it as hard as wood. It takes one to two
months to dry the fish, according to the season.

In sight was the island of East Vaage, with its towering
peak, Vaagökallen, 4000 feet high. At its base were several
islands, among them Henningsvær. The settlement is built
on both sides of the channel formed by two islands. The
houses of the fishermen are of logs, generally with a single
large room, around the walls of which are bunks, as in the
forecastle of a ship. These rooms could hold from twenty to
twenty-five men, two or three sleeping in the same bunk; but,

as there were no women to take care of the premises, the beds were far from being inviting. The houses appeared to be very dirty, and vermin were said to abound. The surroundings were worse; the ground was saturated with blood and offal—fish-heads lay drying on the rocks in every direction; barrels full of rotten livers, salted roes or tongues of cod, and fish hanging out to dry by thousands, combined to make the smell far from agreeable. Each boat pays one hundred and twenty codfish for lodgings during the season, and each house brings four hundred and eighty; all the houses on the island, and the island itself, belonged to my host.

The Norwegian Government exercises a paternal care over the men who form such an important part of its population, and who contribute so much to the wealth and prosperity of the country. If it were not for the fisheries many districts of that rocky coast would be uninhabited. Small hospitals are built on several islands; during the fishing-season doctors sent by the State attend to the sick, giving their advice free; medicines only are paid for, and at a rate that merely covers their cost. A very small duty is paid on the fish sold, and the revenue from this source is applied to defray the expense of medical attendance. There was a project for building a large hospital on Henningsvær.

The sale of spirituous liquors and of intoxicating drinks is, wisely, entirely forbidden; and during my two weeks' stay I saw but a single intoxicated man; he had brought his liquor from some point outside the fishing jurisdiction. This abstention from intoxicating drinks recalls to mind the warning given in the old laws of the Vikings ("Vikingabalk"):

> Wine is Valfader's* drink, and
> An inebriation (rus†) is welcome to thee
> If thou can sensibly bear it.
> The one who is reeling ashore can brace up;
> But to Ran‡ reelest thou here (on the sea).

---

* Valfader, the name given to Odin.   † Rus, intoxication, inebriation, a drunk.

‡ Ran, the fickle daughter of Ægir, the god of the sea, called the enchantress, from her peculiar power of enchanting mariners, drawing them to the bottom, and never letting them return. Hence the dread of the people of going to her, and the admonition against drinking while on the deep.

Formerly no nets or lines were laid, nor any fishing permitted, from Saturday afternoon until Monday morning. But a law has been passed (1869) allowing the fishermen to raise their nets till seven o'clock Sunday morning. The maximum fine for fishing during the prohibited time is one thousand dollars.

A naval officer, called *opsynschef*, has the supreme oversight of everything. Under him are lensmend who enforce the rules regulating the fisheries, and arrest those who violate them. There is a circuit judge, holding court at different points, who decides questions in dispute among the fishermen, and punishes any infraction of the laws. Vessels of the navy cruise as police; telegraphic lines connect the main fishing-stations, and the number of fish caught is known every day, not only here but in every port of Norway. Everything seems provided to enable the State to gather her harvest from the sea.

The fishing season commences at the end of January; from the 24th of January to the 8th of February, the fishermen cannot put out from shore before seven o'clock; afterwards, to a date to be fixed, they cannot go before six o'clock; from the 22d of March to the 14th of April, five o'clock. The cod-fisheries are virtually closed after the 14th of April. The fleet of fishermen is classified in three categories: *Liners*, those who fish with lines and numerous hooks; *Garn*, those who fish with nets; and *Dybsagn*, those who fish with a single hook or line. The fishing-grounds in Lofoden are divided into twenty-one districts; at each of these all the boats have to start together, and all must return the same day, and about the same time, if possible. Every fishing district has its own letter, and each boat has a number; the name of every fisherman being registered, with his place of residence, birth, etc., so that in cases of disaster the crew of any missing craft can be identified. Formerly the men were obliged to remain during the whole season in the fishing district they had chosen; but now they can go from one district to another, though they must report at once before beginning to fish.

I was surprised at the very comfortable clothing of the fishermen; none suffered from cold on account of the thinness of their garments, nor were any ragged; all wore thick stockings, and had water-proof clothing, tarpaulins, and comfortable sea-boots. It spoke well for the humble households of these fishermen, and for the thrift and industry of their families, that almost everything they had was home-made; they all had homes, however humble, either on the fjords by the coast, or on some little island. Every one retired early. The steadiness and good behavior of those hardy sons of the sea I have never seen equalled in any other country. During my sojourn in Henningsvær there was never any fighting or quarrelling, and the lensmand was the only man there to preserve law and order. At all these fishing-stations everything is as safe as on shore; the doors are left open, chests are never locked, and no one would ever think of stealing the fish that were drying.

Two kinds of boats are used; one is open, from thirty to thirty-five feet long, and six to six and one-half feet beam; the Finmarken boats are longer—they have a house on the poop—being from thirty-five to forty feet and more in length, and from seven to seven and one-half feet beam; a pole several feet long is attached to the rudder, and held by the last rower, who steers as well as pulls, thus saving the labor of one man. Their cabins are about eight or nine feet long, affording protection at sea and sleeping accommodations, as the men do not return to land every day. The engraving from one of my photographs (given opposite this page) shows the structure of the boats. There are also little craft used for transporting the fish from the shore to the vessels; these are not more than nine feet long by four feet wide.

The morning after my arrival I was up at four o'clock to witness the start of the fishing fleet. I stood by the flag-staff on the highest point of the island. No one is allowed to leave before the flag is hoisted. The fishermen came one by one, and all were seated in their boats for some time before the signal was given. At five precisely the flag was hauled up by the lensmand, and the air was filled with a heavy booming sound from several thousand oars dipping into the water at the same time, and working with astonishing regularity, which

THE FISHING-STATION OF HENNINGSVÆR.

continued for quite awhile. As they moved away the boats
began to scatter, and by the time they reached the fishing
banks — about seven or eight miles from Henningsvær, and
covered with from sixty to one hundred fathoms of water—
they were widely apart. From the height I could see the
light-house on the island of Hellandsö, which lies opposite, and
forms the canal-like port. Lonely indeed now seemed the low
islands; the landscape, so beautiful when seen from a distance,
was melancholy and dreary when near at hand.

At ten o'clock, one by one, the boats came back, and by
noon the whole fleet was in, with an immense number of
fish. Life had returned to Henningsvær. Boats moved to
and fro, going from vessel to vessel, the fishermen trying to
make the best bargains they could, and everybody was busy.
On the decks were piled the fish just caught; these were cleaned on board, washed, salted, and laid in the hold one on top
of another. These vessels would, after the fishing season, go
home to some solitary farm by the fjord, and their cargo would
be dried on the rocks. The price of the fish varied somewhat
every day, according to the catch; that day it was seven Norwegian dollars* per hundred, without livers, eggs, and heads; it
is sometimes less. Great
numbers of ducks and
gulls were feeding upon
the mass of offal thrown
upon the water. On that
day the catch was said to
have reached nearly three
hundred and fifty thou-
sand codfish; I have been
told that sometimes it
goes as high as half a
million a day. Many
boats landed their loads

EIDER-DUCK.

along the shore, where men were busy preparing the fish.
Those engaged in this work were dressed in large pantaloons,

* The Norwegian dollar is worth $1 12.

aprons, and cuffs of leather. One man cut off the heads; another took out the intestines, and cast them on one side; others put the heads, the livers, and the eggs by themselves; the latter were carefully put in barrels and salted—a barrel containing the ova of 300 fish; these were sold for nine dollars: they are sent to France or Italy, where they are used for catching sardines. The livers were put in barrels by themselves, sold to the merchants, and kept till rotten, when cod-liver oil is made from them. Two barrels of fat livers are said to yield a barrel of brown oil. The tongues were salted, and kept by the fishermen for their own use. The heads were scattered on the rocks to dry, to be used to feed the cattle at home, or to be sold with the bones for fish manure, a manufactory of which is close at hand, on another island.

A few days ago I was roaming over mountains covered with snow, and on frozen lakes and rivers; my coursers were reindeer, and my dress that of a Laplander. Now I was clad like a Norwegian fisherman.

I had deliberately made up my mind from the time I landed in Scandinavia to see everything for myself, and not to trust to hearsay for descriptions, so I concluded to go on fishing excursions. The lensmand kindly chose the craft in which I should go. When I came out a profound silence reigned over the fishermen's houses, and nothing was heard but the shrill cry of the gulls; the boats were by the shore, ready to start. The quietness of the scene soon changed; the men came, and within a short time all was activity. I was fortunate in my arrival here, for it was the first fine weather of the winter. Before this there was a continuous series of gales and snow-storms, and the year had been one of the most tempestuous known for a long time. My boat had upon it the letter H—which signified that it came from Henningsvær—bore the number 87, and was manned by six persons. It belonged to Evert Arntsen Kildal, from Melö, a place on the Nordland coast. He was a leading man in the church, and had the reputation of being a good Christian. The crew was composed of two strong elderly men, two younger, of about twenty, and one boy fourteen years of age, who was serving his apprenticeship. These fisheries of Norway are splendid schools for the making of sailors, and it is no wonder that they are considered among the best by the maritime nations of the world, not only for seamanship but for their honesty, good temper, and respect for discipline. All eyes were watching the flag-staff. Suddenly the flag was hoisted, and thousands of oars struck the water. We pulled to get out of the channel, and, as the wind was favorable, the boats steadily approached their fishing-grounds. The crew were guided entirely by the positions of the surrounding mountains, and with great accuracy came to their lines.

Every fisherman has his distinct buoys, representing the different objects that he may need to recognize. We went to the first one—a pine roller about four feet long—to the centre of which was tied the thick line which held the net. As the line was pulled in, two men stood by, each drawing one side of the net into the boat, which is the hardest work; two others behind placed the nets in good order; near the pullers there was a man who hooked the fish and threw them into the boat. There were some twenty nets tied together in fours, each net twenty fathoms long, and two to three in depth. Eight minutes were passed in raising one set to the surface, and it required fifty minutes to hoist the whole number. The length of time in hauling depends, of course, on the number of fish caught, and on the weather. Though some cod were taken, they were not plentiful, partial migration to some other ground having taken place. We caught only a few more than three hundred, the catch sometimes being more than double this, and heavily loading the boats.

A consultation was now held as to where to cast anew, and seeing others going towards a northern point our crew concluded to go that way also, and leave their nets there for the night. In what direction fish will migrate is only a matter for conjecture, and success during the season depends entirely upon striking the right places. The wind was ahead, and our destination was about ten miles distant; it was a hard pull, consuming five hours in reaching the ground. The boats were evidently too heavy for the crew to row, and they would sometimes take advantage of or beat against the wind. During this time the men inspected their nets, and four, with their drawing-lines, were replaced by new ones that had been brought. Then we began to sound: the first trial showed no bottom at one hundred and twenty fathoms, the length of the sounding-line; the second, a little farther on, gave one hundred fathoms. All along the nets at intervals there were glass balls, about four and a half inches in diameter, each securely enclosed, and attached by a cord about three feet long; these were to keep the nets afloat, while stones at the bottom kept the lower part downward. We finished by casting the first buoy, one man throwing the net while another threw the float from the stern of the boat. When they reached the last of the nets it was let down, with a heavy stone attached, four buoys being arranged on the upper surface, there to remain till the next day. At three o'clock we reached Henningsvær, none of us having touched a mouthful of food since our start. The fortunate ones that day were those who had lines. The average of each of such boats was about three hundred codfish. In the nets two salmon had been caught—a not uncommon circumstance.

I was invited to spend the remainder of the day with my new friends, three other boat's-crews being in the same house. I accepted on the condition that I should partake of their regular fare. The dinner was composed of a sort of porridge or pudding made of ship-bread, liver, and fish. I put on the best face I could, but cannot say I enjoyed the meal.

Wood is very scarce and dear, as it is brought from the other islands or from the main-land; they use as little as possible, and mix pieces of fat with it to promote combustion. Some of the men treated me to a cup of coffee, which I could not refuse. We spoke about the prospect for the fishing season now about to close; they calculated that the fishermen would average sixty or seventy dollars each; in some very fortunate boats the men would make ninety or a hundred dollars. The captain, or one who owns the boat, is entitled to a certain number of fish, and those who own the nets also have a share. We talked over fishing adventures, the terrible storms often encountered, and the narrow escapes they frequently had. Two or three years before one hundred and twenty-three men were drowned in less than an hour. All spoke very kindly of my hostess, and exclaimed "God bless her!" I learned that in one part of her house she had a store-room, and many a poor fellow went in there by the back-door. She kept flour, coffee, sugar, bread, and many other things; and often when the men could not obtain credit from her husband they came to her. She had friends among the fishermen, and knew those who were poor and had large families to support: many had left that house slyly with a parcel of sugar, coffee, or bread, and not unfrequently a little money for the wife. "She does everything so quietly," said they, "that nobody knows anything about it; but when we see some one leave her house by the back-door, we always know that she has been doing some good deed."

One of the beautiful characteristics of the Norwegian fisherman or seaman who has never left his native land is his reverence for God; he is seldom heard to utter an oath. During the years I have been in the country I never heard any one of them swear, no matter how angry he may have been, or how great the provocation. They reprove the offender without cursing him. In this respect they are better than their brethren of Southern Sweden, and more docile withal.

The next day I went hook-fishing, and consequently had to take another kind of boat, and go with another set of men. Each of these craft generally carries twenty-four lines. The captain with whom I went was Hans Mikel Nikolaisen, from Tennevold, in Ebestad, a place not far distant from Tromsö. He was a married man, with three children, and his eyes glowed with happiness when he talked to me of his wife and little ones. His boat was much smaller than the other one, the fishing by hook being much lighter work, and the whole crew consisted of two Sea Laplanders and three strong men. The Lapps were easily recognized by their short reindeer costumes, with hair inside, and Finland boots. The wind was good from the very start, and we rapidly passed the light-house on the island of Hellandsö. About a thousand boats were scattered within a few square miles, near Henningsvær, for there were boats from other stations; after four hours we came to the place where our lines were and lowered the sail. Several buoys were taken into the boat, and then began the hauling of the lines by the help of the little roller along-side. There were four lines attached to one another, each being one hundred fathoms long; the hooks were four to six feet apart, generally one hundred and twenty on each line, and at intervals a buoy was attached to the line to prevent it from getting snarled, and sinking too deeply. The lines of all those who fished by hook contained on an average, per boat, about twenty-four hundred fathoms in all. An immense number of these lines are cast into the sea every day with the nets, occupying the waters for miles. We had not pulled in over two hundred fathoms of our own when we found they had drifted into a net, and that some of our hooks had caught it—an awkward yet common accident—but we were able to free the hooks without much trouble. We continued to haul in the fish, which were very abundant. Once again a part of our line became entangled, this time with three or four belonging to other fishermen, and great care was necessary to separate them. The men know well their own lines, as, for greater certainty, each one is marked from place to place with the letter of the district and the number of the boat. The work was hard and tedious, for the tides and currents had done considerable twisting for several different fishermen. After the lines had been separated they were thrown back into the water with the fish attached to them. The end of our third one came to the surface, and we saw that it had been cut by a knife, and the rest lost with all its fish, probably about seventy-five. Sometimes, when too badly mixed up, lines have to be cut and hauled into the boat; in that case the men bring them ashore, and give the fish found on them to the owner, who is always known by the marks on his tackle. We then went to the other buoys, and hauled in another line, capturing in all three hundred and seventy-three large codfish.

After our fishing was over we went to several of the boats near us, and made inquiries about our lost line. In one or two cases, as we came along-side of the boats, my men looked suspiciously into them. Sometimes, when they find lines entangled in their nets, they draw everything on board, being obliged to do so to separate them, and return the fish. Some of the boats had parts of lines not belonging to them, which they intended to take ashore. When the fish are stolen the tackle is thrown away, but this very seldom happens. Evidently many of the crews mistrusted each other, and I was told that some fishermen would take fish that did not belong to them simply by way of retaliation, thinking that others who had found their lines had done the same. Of course it is very difficult to prove any theft of this kind; but, when caught, the culprits are severely punished by the judges. We cast out again, our hooks being baited with young herrings cut in two. There was a general complaint this year of the scarcity and dearness of the bait. There are men whose only business is to catch bait and sell it to the fishermen; my host had a small steamer employed for this purpose during the fishing-season. When the fishing-ground is near the line fishermen return to the shore and go again, and so also do those with nets.

Another sail, two hours long, from Henningsvær, brought us to Stamsund. The dark rocky hills which tower over the little fishing settlement give it a gloomy appearance, though there are several farms on the island. The harbor is made perfect by many small islands near the shore, among which boats wind their way. Here the fishing-boats were few, for most of the fish on the banks near the islands had migrated, and they seldom return the same season; only a few small vessels were completing their cargoes before leaving. I noted a comfortable house, owned by the leading merchant of the place, used also as an inn. Several buildings were supported partly on piles near the water's edge, and dwellings built of logs were scattered here and there between the rocks at the foot of the hills, and near the boulder masses that have been torn from the side. Vessels and boats were at anchor in the narrow basin, or among the islands, and the place presented a far wilder aspect than Henningsvær. There were birch-trees on the island, and they are said to be common in one of the valleys. Near the settlement by the sea is a low dale with two or three farms.

My object in coming to Stamsund was to visit Herr M——, a celebrated manufacturer of cod-liver oil which enjoys such great and well-deserved reputation in the United States. The room where the oil is made was not very large, but everything was extremely clean. Several men were engaged in separating the good livers from the bad; all were fresh from fish caught that day. The fat and healthy livers were whitish, while the diseased ones were greenish, and the lean ones red. I was surprised to see the number of diseased and lean livers. The season for the best ones would soon be over, and it happens that the cod arrive at Lofoden when their livers are in the finest condition. The men were very particular in selecting the choicest kinds. After they had been assorted they were put into a large tank, washed thoroughly in warm water, and then placed over an open wire net to let the water drip away. I noticed that extreme care was taken in all stages of the preparation of the oil. There were five large, high, rounded kettles or vessels, surrounded by steam at a pressure never exceeding five pounds. By this process the livers boil very slowly for eight hours, after which the oil is filtered twice through cotton, and put in large tin vessels tightly soldered. The product was clear and white, and appeared to me perfectly pure; but the process does not end here. The oil is shipped to Christiania, where it undergoes chemical treatment which frees it from the microscopic globules of blood, and from stearine; it is then filtered through paper, and is ready for the market. Some sort of brown oil is made from most of the residue, and what is left after this is manufactured into a fertilizer, said to be very rich. The process has nothing of the repulsiveness of the method by which brown oil is usually made, namely, by letting the livers rot, skimming the oil, and afterwards boiling it.

I wished very much to visit the most southern of the islands, the inhabitants of which are said to be very primitive; but steamers touch there but two or three times a year, and then only during the fishing-season, so I preferred returning to

Henningsvær; for, though the weather had every appearance of remaining fair, the falling of the barometer indicated that a change was at hand. I busied myself in taking views of the Lofoden, and of the fishing-quarters. One evening I witnessed one of the grandest displays of the aurora borealis that I ever saw in the North; the corona was superb, and its brilliant red crown seemed to hang over these islands.

There is a church at Henningsvær, and, during the short fishing-season, a resident clergyman. On Saturday no nets or lines are put out, the law not allowing sufficient time in which to return to and raise them on Sunday. Buying and selling cease; the captains come ashore; the fishermen shave themselves and put on their best clothes; and all feel that a day of rest has come.

Sunday, April 6th, the last service of the season took place on the island of Henningsvær. The church was crowded with over three thousand fishermen, every one with his Church-service book. None wore amulets or pictures, for they trusted first in God and then in themselves in the hour of danger. The clergyman gave a most impressive sermon. It was to be the last of the season, and the congregation would soon be scattered; and when it returned in another year, he said, some then present might be missing. With tears flowing down his cheeks, showing the depth of his feeling (for he was a thoroughly good man, with no sham about him), he told them that after this life there was another; that soon death might come, and they must think of their souls, putting their trust in the Lord Jesus Christ. He finished with an earnest exhortation to love God, to hate sin, and follow after righteousness: it brought tears to many eyes, and made every one thoughtful as he went away.

It was really beautiful to see so many men, bred among the rocks of the North amidst storms and privations, come to pay homage to the Creator. I doubt very much if such a sight could be seen in any other Christian country. There was not a fisherman on Henningsvær in his cabin on that day, unless detained by sickness. In the afternoon the room of the worthy pastor, who, by-the-way, was a very handsome man, was crowded with fishermen, who came to say good-bye, to thank him for his teachings, or to make some religious inquiries. I also made him a visit, and admired his urbanity to these hardy sons of the sea; he was, indeed, a gentleman. During our conversation he told me that he had sold that season 15 large Bibles, at 4 marks; 15 Testaments, at 20 skillings; and 150 books of Psalms, at 6 skillings.* Sunday was the day on which they generally bought them, and willingly, with their hard earnings. They are too proud to ask for one as a gift, but now and then, in a delicate way, the good clergyman would say to a man with a very large family, or who had had an unsuccessful fishing season, "I want you to give this Bible, Testament, or hymn-book to your wife, as a little remembrance from me."

The afternoon was passed in social enjoyment; neighbors visited each other, and talked of home. The younger folks paid their attentions to the maids of Herr D——, and to two others in the neighboring houses. Women were at a great premium, for these few were all — the fishermen not having brought wives or daughters; so the girls had many admirers on Saturday evening and Sunday afternoon; lads, wherever there was an opportunity, would pass before the houses to catch a glimpse of the fair ones; if so fortunate as to meet one, they would address their compliments to her and try to make love, for which there was little chance, as some person on the watch for a favorable time would be sure to interrupt. Nature, in this respect, is the same all the world over.

The fisherman's life is arduous. At dawn of day he goes out, and, when he has to row against a head-wind, often comes back tired and weary. On their return, after the first meal, all are very busy outside; those who do not clean and prepare the fish cut bait for the lines, replace the lost tackle, and repair the nets.

The barometer was not mistaken, for the threatened storm came on the 8th, with a very high wind, at times almost a hur-

---

* The new coinage at that time was not in use—5 marks, or 120 skillings, made one dollar.

ricane. No boat was allowed to leave. Dark clouds gathered in the north-west, and violent squalls drove them overhead; snow fell heavily, and after awhile the land was covered with a thick white mantle to the sea. I went to the highest point of Henningsvær, where I could see the angry waves, as they struck against the rocky cliffs, breaking in foaming spray along the shore, and then dashing themselves into a thousand atoms, apparently harmless; but every billow that struck against that shore was stronger than the rock, and left its mark behind. On the point of Hellandsö the light-house stood unharmed, for the surf could not reach it; and, when night came, its bright light shone like a star over the horizon. Everything in the port was still; the sea there was smooth; the wind blew over the masts of the vessels, and no one would have dreamed, in looking on that quiet narrow channel between Henningsvær and Hellandsö, that outside a tempest was sweeping over a heaving sea. Part of the channel, however, is not well protected against a south wind. At Easter the gale was still unabated, and on the following Sunday it raged with a fury that made one feel thankful to be on land.

The climate in these islands is subject to great variations; violent storms are succeeded by very fine weather, and still, clear days. The temperature was remarkable for this season of the year, being milder than on the main-land. On the 31st of March the snow at the foot of the hills on the latter extended to the sea, while in the Lofoden it was several hundred feet above. On the 1st of April, on deck, the mercury stood at 52° while we traversed the Raftsund; in 1871, in the same region, at the end of July, the mercury stood at 40°, and 43° at the warmest time of the day, with the wind blowing from the north-east. In some of the sheltered nooks at the base of the mountains at Stamsund, where the stones reflected the heat of the sun's rays, daisies blossomed on the 7th of April; and I was assured that the year previous some were in bloom at the end of February. For the last six days the thermometer ranged in Henningsvær from 42° to 45°, and one day reached 52° in the shade, without any influence whatever from the sun's rays; and on the 7th of April, at Stamsund, the lowest point was from 38° to 40°. This was the finest and warmest weather they had had that year.

The steamer *Nordstjernen* (Star of the North) had arrived in the midst of a very tempestuous time, and lay quietly at anchor outside, protected by the mountains there. The sea was smooth, though the wind swept between the islands with great force; but there was no space for it to rise. For four days no one was allowed to go fishing. The catches even before had been small, and the fishermen who were going north had already left by hundreds, many of them intending to stop for Easter at Tromsö. Hard, indeed, would be their journey in their little open boats—gales and snow-storms, rain and sleet, cold and wet these hardy sons of Norway must encounter; but the sea is their element, and the wind the music they love. They are still the true descendants of the Vikings.

The steamer waited for the storm to moderate; the gale was at its height on Friday and Saturday, 11th and 12th. I left the Lofoden on the 13th of April, bidding farewell to those who had been so good and kind to me. The deck of the vessel was literally packed with fishermen, and their heavy wooden chests were piled everywhere; so also were numerous nets and lines, and cooking utensils. Every one was good-natured—laughing, talking, and looking forward to the Finmarken fisheries. They were going to sleep wherever they could on deck, for hardly any of them had taken second-class tickets; they wanted to save their money, and were satisfied with third-class. In a few days the Lofoden would be entirely deserted —boats and fishermen gone—and on the shores of many an island not one would be left to watch the sea.

CHAPTER X.

Climate of Scandinavia.—The Gulf-stream.—Temperature of the Sea.—Summer Heat.—A Temperate Strip of Land.—Prevalent Winds.—Table Showing the Temperature beyond the Arctic Circle.—Highest Temperature on the Norwegian Coast.—The Coldest and Warmest Months.—Number of Rainy and Snowy Days. —Foggy Days.—Thunder-storms.—Temperature of Northern and Southern Sweden.—Temperature of the Wells.—Fall of Rain in Sweden.—General Remarks on the Temperature between Haparanda, Stockholm, Petersburg, Copenhagen, Christiansund, Yarmouth, and Valentia.

In the first volume we have spoken of the vegetation of Scandinavia. We will now, before proceeding farther, give a general idea of the climate, which is remarkable, especially in the far North, when compared with that of other lands in the same latitude. In countries like Norway and Sweden, which reach from lat. 55° 20′ to North Cape, 71° 10′—an extent as great as that from the most northern part of the State of Maine to Florida—one must, of course, find a great diversity of climate and vegetation. The boundaries include more territory than those of any other country in Europe except Russia, its total area amounting to 294,000 English square miles. An oblique line from Northern Germany through France and Spain would equal the length of the Scandinavian peninsula, but its greatest width is not more than seven hundred miles.

The Gulf-stream sweeps along the Norwegian coast and prevents the formation of ice; only the upper extremity of the fjords are frozen in winter, this being due to the lesser density and greater freshness of the water from incoming streams. On the two following pages are the maps showing the temperature of the sea between Norway, Sweden, Scotland, and Iceland. The sea is warmer than the air from September to May, the reverse being true from June until the

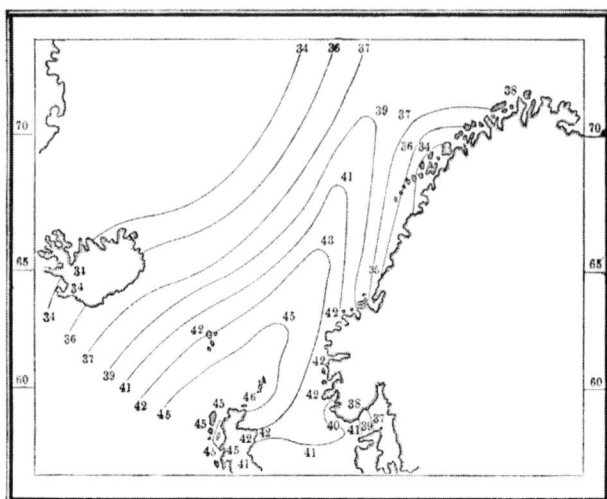

SEA-TEMPERATURE IN DECEMBER, JANUARY, AND FEBRUARY.

end of August. The Gulf-stream is warmest in summer in the south, the mean temperature of the water during the months of June, July, and August averaging, on the Skager Rack, 62°; in some places I have found it 75° near the shore. It flows

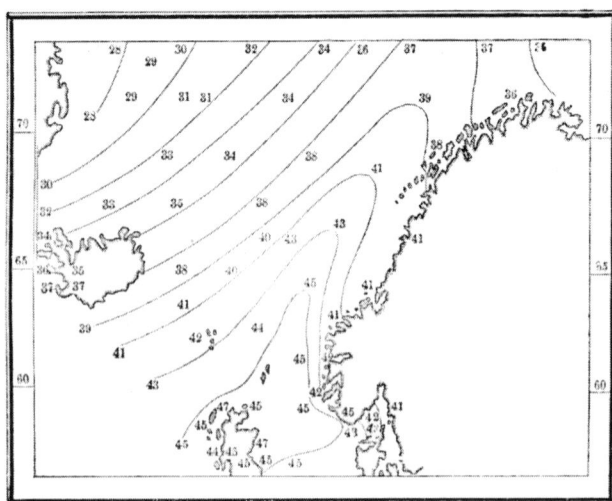

SEA-TEMPERATURE IN MARCH, APRIL, AND MAY.

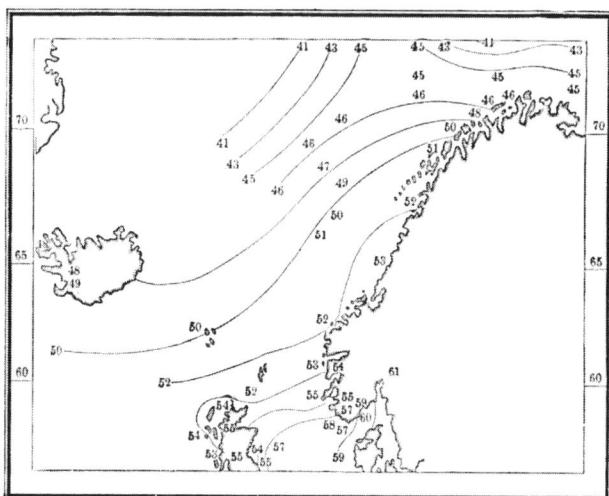

SEA-TEMPERATURE IN JUNE, JULY, AND AUGUST.

more rapidly as it proceeds northward, and is warmest on the
coast of Norway, between Lindesnæs and Lyster, in lat. 57° 59′
and 58° 6′, where the mean temperature is 48° or 49°, falling
gradually to 46° or 45° as it reaches North Cape, and thence

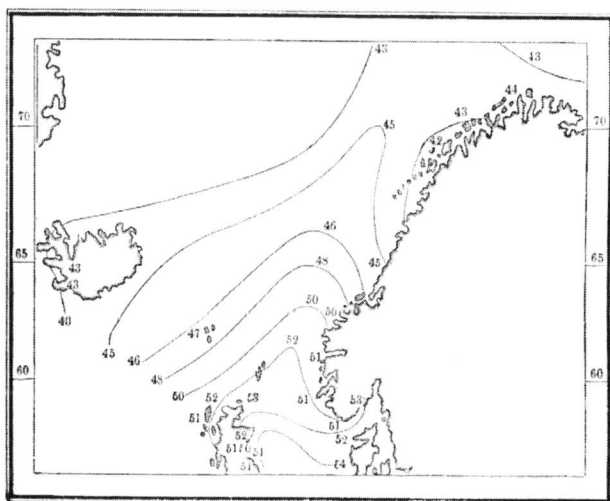

SEA-TEMPERATURE IN SEPTEMBER, OCTOBER, AND NOVEMBER.

losing its heat farther east. The temperature of the sea is at its maximum in August, and minimum in February—both, therefore, coming later than the extremes of the air temperature : the yearly variation in the former is greatest on the southern coast of Norway, and smallest farther out where the sea is deeper. It is especially in winter that the influence of the Gulf-stream is felt. In summer the sun's heat regulates the motions of the atmosphere; the effect of this is greater inland than on the coast, thus causing a variation of pressure and northward air-currents.

During the autumn the warmth of the sea diminishes: at North Cape in September and October, and November being about 43°. Later the reverse is the case; the temperature of the sea on the Skager Rack is about that of the air, 38°; and the Christiania and some other fjords grow gradually warmer as the current flows northward to Hellisö, lat. 60° 45′, attaining there a mean temperature of 42° to 43°. At North Cape the water is the coldest in March and April, its mean temperature being 48°.

The absolute temperature variation of the air in inner Finmarken and South-east Norway is 126°; at Finmarken fjords, on Dovre, and in Christiania, 108°; on the Finmarken coast, Nordland fjords, the north side of Dovre, along the Lange fjelds and mouth of Christiania fjord, 90°; on the coast from Tromsö to Christiansund, and Bergen to Lindesnæs, 40°; on the whole west coast, 54°. The number of days having a daily mean below 32° follow the same course.

On a narrow strip of the coast from Folden fjord to Lindesnæs the mean daily temperature never sinks below the freezing-point. In Central Scandinavia the daily temperature is below zero during more than seven months; thence this number decreases, so that at the Bothnia and on the Finmark coast it is six months; at Vesterålen, along the Nordland coast, Trondhjem, in inner Sogne, at Christiania, and Stockholm, four months; and, finally, at the outer Trondhjem fjord, Romsdal fjord, Sogne, Hardanger, and Arendal, two months. This shows the warming influence of the sea.

On the west coast, in Northern Norway, and at the Christiania fjord, southerly to south-westerly winds are prevalent. In the whole country to the south-west the prevailing breezes are from the south, although easterly winds occasionally occur. The average warmth generally lessens as one gets farther north, but in Norway the heat decreases most towards the east; thus, on the west coast, from Stadt to Lyster, the yearly average is 45°, which in Sweden is found only as far north as Gothenburg and Wexiö.

The contrast between the inland and coast climate is most apparent when observing the yearly variation of temperature in different places. Though the summers in the far North are short, there are days when the heat is greater than that of the country farther to the south.

THE RESULT OF TEN YEARS' OBSERVATIONS OF TEMPERATURE BEYOND
THE ARCTIC CIRCLE.

	Lati- tude.	Jan.	Feb.	Mar.	April.	May.	June.	July.	Aug.	Sept.	Oct.	Nov.	Dec.	Mean of the Year.
	Deg. Min.	Deg.	Deg.	Deg.	Deg.	Deg.	Deg.	Deg.	Deg.	Deg.	Deg.	Deg.	Deg.	Deg.
Vardö.......	70 22	18	20	23	29	35	41	47	48	41	29	26	21	32
Hammerfest..	70 40	23	22	26	30	37	46	53	51	45	36	31	24	36
Kåfjord......	69 57	18	15	20	29	39	48	54	54	45	39	25	22	34
Tromsö......	69 39	22	21	25	31	38	48	49	50	45	37	28	23	35
Bodö	67 17	26	37	29	30	41	50	54	54	49	41	31	28	39

The heat in the sun is far greater in proportion to the shade than in any other country, sometimes being twice as much.

The days of the year when the temperature is the same beyond the arctic circle are about as follows:

Vardö...............................April 27 .... October 27
Hammerfest........................May 5 .... October 15
Kåfjord ....April 25 .... October 12
Tromsö...............................May 2 .... November 1
Bodö.......... ....May 3 .... October 22

The greater heat in summer and the greater cold in winter are both found inland, while the coast has milder winters and cooler summers. The smallest variation on the Scandinavian peninsula, 12°, is observed from Stadt to Hiteren and Lofoden.

On the coast of Norway the highest temperature in the summer may reach 77° to 80°, while a short distance inland it is 82° to 86°; at Christiania, 88°; and even on the top of Dovre,

2098 feet above the sea, 84°. Near the Justedalsbræen, in winter, the climate is pretty mild, in consequence of the large rainfall caused by the glacier, which comes down in the shape of snow. In the far North the cold reaches 40° to 45° below zero, and in Central Sweden sometimes 40°.

The coldest days occur generally between the middle of January and the middle of February, and earlier in the east than the west; the hottest weather is between the middle of July and the middle of August. The part of the country having the greatest rain and snow fall is from Sogne fjord to Stadt, where the yearly fall is 72 inches, while Christiania has only 20 and Dovre about 13 inches. On the coast the greatest fall occurs in autumn—in Christiania, in August. The number of days with rain or snow is in Dovre only 90 ; on the coast of Skager Rack, 100 ; in Bodö, Tromsö, and Vardö, about 120 ; Christiania, Romsdal, and the Helgeland coast, 140 ; Bergen and fjords to the north, and Vesterålen, 160 ; and Lofoden, 180 days in the year : while inland it rains or snows every fourth day, it does so at Lofoden every other day ; in Vardö it rains 54 days, and snows 71 ; in Dovre there are 42 rainy and 48 snowy days ; in Christiania there are twice as many rainy days as those in which snow falls ; in Bergen, five times ; and in Lofoden, one and a half times as many. Finmarken is generally free from snow in summer. Vardö and Bodö in July and August have no falls of snow, but it has been known to fall in July. In Lofoden snow has fallen three or four times in July within ten years. In Dovre and Vardö it falls as frequently in May as in October ; in other places this happens only in April and November ; and on the west coast only in March. The fall of snow varies each year considerably. I have known more to fall in one week in my trip northward than during the rest of the winter, and found much less in the Dovre fjelds in January than in September of the previous year. Measurement of its depth is quite difficult, being greatly affected by the temperature ; for, though much in quantity, it is often light and spongy ; while at other times, though less in bulk, it is dry and compact, and affords excellent sleighing.

The number of foggy days is, at Vardö, 18; Lofoden, 13; Christiansund, 7; Dovre, 10; Ålesund, Skudenæs, Mandal, and Sandösund, 20; Bergen, 40; and Christiania, 62. A marked yearly peculiarity must be noted here. In the east, from Lindesnæs to Christiania, most foggy days occur in winter; on the west coast, on the contrary, almost exclusively in summer; in Bergen they are divided pretty evenly the year round, but occur most often in June.

Thunder-storms are rare, occurring on the west coast only in winter, and after strong westerly winds, generally near the sea; but in South-eastern Norway they take place only in summer, and as often inland as near the coast. Beyond the polar circle they are seldom noted. I learned that snow and hail, which generally accompany the thunder-showers, do very little damage, and that the lightning rarely strikes.

In Sweden the mean temperature for the year in the far North is 34°, while in the South it is from 44° to 46°. At Stockholm it is 41° to 43°. The wells, which give a pretty accurate idea of the earth's temperature, show about the same figures; in Central Sweden they have a yearly average of about 43°; while in the north they are often found covered with ice all summer, and swamps are frozen hard to a depth of five to six feet. Lakes are ice-bound in the south for about 115 days, in the central part 150, and in the north 230. The annual fall of rain is less than in Norway, and is, as a general rule, pretty evenly distributed throughout the country. On the west coast it is about 21 inches; in the interior, in the central part, 16; on the south-east coast 13; and in the north 12. In the southern part of Sweden the winter climate is quite even, and might be compared with that of parts of Western and Northern New York, but in the summer the nights are much cooler than in the United States, and the heat of the sun is not so powerful; consequently Indian-corn does not ripen.

From the meteorological observations noted down in the daily records (1879) — for Haparanda, Stockholm, St. Petersburg, Copenhagen, Christiansund (Norway), Yarmouth, and Valentia (Spain)—I note the following remarkable facts: in June, 1879, the warmest average weather for the month was

experienced in these places in the following order: first at
Stockholm, then Copenhagen, St. Petersburg, Yarmouth, Valentia, Haparanda, and Christiansund. The hottest day, however, was in Haparanda, on the 5th of June, 66°. In July
the latter place had the highest mean temperature of the
month, though I-have only the records from the 1st to the
15th; it had also the highest mean of a day, 68°. In August,
Stockholm, Christiansund, and Copenhagen had the highest
temperature, being 62°—Valentia, St. Petersburg, and Haparanda being the lowest. In September, Copenhagen, Yarmouth, and Valentia were the warmest. For October, 1878,
I have only the data of the last half of the month : Haparanda
was the coldest, then Stockholm; next followed Copenhagen,
then Valentia, Yarmouth coming fifth in the scale. In January of that year St. Petersburg, Haparanda, and Copenhagen
were the coldest; Valentia and Yarmouth the warmest. As
a general rule, Haparanda is the coldest locality during the
winter.

CHAPTER XI.

NORDLAND, TROMSÖ, AND FINMARKEN PROVINCES.

The three Northern Provinces of Norway.—The Wildest Scenery on the Coast.—
Population.—Products of the Soil.—Occupation of the People.—Fishing.—Great
Number of Fishermen.—Homes on the Coast.—Steamers everywhere.—Impor-
tance of the Cod-fisheries.—Number of Cod caught.—The Herring-fisheries.—
Number of Men employed.—Spring Fisheries.—Migration of the Herring.—How
Herring are caught.—Immense Catch of Herring.—Summer Fisheries.—Number
of Herring caught.—The Spitzbergen and Nova Zembla Fisheries.—A Sea-faring
People.—Norwegian and Swedish Mercantile Navy.

NORWEGIAN Nordland includes that part of the country
which extends from about lat. 65° to 70° on the coast, and
comprises the old province known under the name of Haloga-
land, and which is now divided into Nordland and Tromsö
provinces, while Finmarken is farther north. The scenery on
the shores is the wildest on the coast of Norway, and culminates in its savage and weird grandeur between the cities of
Bodö and Tromsö; there the loftiest mountains are found;
the highest being between the Lyngen and Ulfs fjords, with an
altitude of 6500 feet, and present the characteristics of the
Alps. Glaciers and snow-clad peaks are seen from the sea.
The abrupt sides of these elevations often cause landslides and
avalanches of snow. At the bases of these wild, abrupt, and
jagged slopes are sometimes rich wooded land and luxuriant
pastures, with here and there a driving-road, and sometimes
wild bridle-paths, leading from one fjord to another.

Sailing along that apparently forsaken coast, noting the towering dreary mountains in the background, and remembering
how short are the summers and long and stormy the winters,
one can hardly believe that fine agricultural land and extended
forests are to be found there. In Nordland the population
is about 100,000, of whom 7000 are fishermen, and 15,000

farmers.   The number of horses is 7500; of cattle, 55,000; of sheep, 108,000; of goats, 24,000; of swine, 5433.   Nordland produces 350,000 bushels of grain, and 1,100,000 bushels of potatoes.   In the province of Tromsö there are about 53,000 inhabitants, among whom are over 5000 fishermen, and as many farmers.   There are over 26,500 head of cattle, 58,000 sheep, 4500 horses, 1800 pigs, and 10,000 goats.   An average of 120,000 bushels of grain and 400,000 bushels of potatoes are raised yearly.   This part of the country was settled by the Vikings, several of the chiefs being mentioned in the sagas. There are also several old churches of stone, among which are those of Ibestad and Trondenæs.

Contiguous to Tromsö lies Finmarken, the most northern province of Norway.   The Arctic Sea washes its rocky shores on three sides; its territory has an extent of coast, not including the fjords, of about 350 miles, and covers an area of 2600 square miles, or the seventh part of the territory of Norway. Finmarken proper commences at about lat. 70°, at a point between Kvænangen and Alten fjords, and extends along the coast to the Russian boundary by Jakob River.   Its most southern point inland lies near the mountain Beldovado, while the most northerly is North Cape.   A straight line from Beldovado to North Cape measures about 190 miles.   In comparison with the country farther south Finmarken is a low land, as its greatest area lies less than 1000 feet above the sea.

The highest mountains are the Gaiser range, reaching about 3000 feet, but they are entirely without snow in summer.   In the interior of this province bare rocks are not very common, being generally covered by glacial gravel; while in the riverbottoms nearest to the sea fine sand is quite prevalent.   In the Tana, Alten, Laxe, and Eiby rivers gold is found, though not in paying quantities.   Five large fjords wind their way far inland—the Alten, the Porsanger, the Laxe, the Tana, and the Varanger—and between each two lies a huge stretch of rocky land, forming peninsulas, upon which the Laplander and their reindeer roam.   On the Alten and Laxe rivers there are quite considerable deltas, with clay beds rich in phosphoric acid, making them very fertile for the growth of grass.

Islands dot the sea, in many places protecting the coast, which appears from a distance to belong to a land of desolation entirely uninhabited. On the boundary between Tromsö and Finmarken is the Jökel glacier, the only one in Scandinavia which, like those found in Greenland, sheds pieces. The Tana is the largest river, and is navigable by boats as far as Ulvefos, 210 miles from the sea; its longest tributary is the Karasjoki. The Alten and Pasvig rivers are considerable waters, the latter rising in Enare Lake. The lakes north of the Gaiser mountains empty into the Porsanger fjord through the Laxe River.

This bleak province has nearly 24,000 inhabitants, which number includes 6700 fishermen and 2800 farmers. There are over 9000 head of cattle, 20,000 sheep, 2500 goats, and 400 pigs. Not much grain is raised, but over 30,000 bushels of potatoes. In these two most northerly provinces twenty-eight per cent. of the population are pure Lapps and Finns. Of Lapps proper there are in Norway 17,178; of Finlanders, 7637; of Lapp and Finnish half-breeds, 909; mixed Norwegians, Finns, and Lapps, 2961, among whom the Nomads are only 1577; the merchants are almost always Norwegians. The yearly average of marriages according to population was in Finmarken seven and six-tenths for every thousand inhabitants; in Tromsö, six and one-fifth. The people intermarry closely, and the mixed offspring of the three nationalities form an excellent race. The inhabitants of the Lyngen, Alten, and Skjærvö parishes are better educated, and have finer dwellings.

Fishing is the chief occupation of the inhabitants: many of the farms are owned by fishermen. Wherever there is a good harbor one is sure to see some houses, or a fishing-village consisting of several families who have settled together. Each merchant owns several homes for fishermen, resembling those of Lofoden; every man pays one dollar for the season, and when four or five merchants are settled together there is quite a village. Sometimes two or three families dwell in one place all the year round: they have a few cows, goats, or sheep, which feed chiefly on the heads of fish, which are cooked for them.

In other places the settlement consists of a single merchant's family, with his own men and servants; the warehouse stands on piles by the sea, and the effect is that of a little hamlet. The larger steamers stop during the fishing season at many such places, and there are smaller ones of lighter draught which ply among the fjords and land at the various establishments.

The cod-fisheries are of the utmost importance to Norway; the people live, and even get rich, by them. There are three varieties of the common species, namely, the sea cod (*Gadus morrhua*), the fjord cod (*Gadus virens*), and the ling (*Molva vulgaris*), also of the cod family; the last two are often very large, frequently attaining a length of six feet. In Tromsö the number caught averages 5,000,000, and in Finmarken 12,000,000; including the Lofoden fisheries, the catch averages about 38,000,000 or 40,000,000; on the whole Norwegian coast, 50,000,000: these figures are for the season. A great deal of brown cod-liver oil is made.

Next in importance are the herring fisheries. The herring (*Clupea harengus*) is plentiful all along the Norwegian coast, but only on that part lying between Lindesnæs and Lofoden is it the object of any extended fishing. As far back as history goes, or from about the ninth century, these fisheries have been of great value; but they have also been subject to greater variations than the cod-fisheries, and only at a comparatively later period did they yield any proper article of trade. In 1416 a Hollander, Beuckel, devised the art of salting the herring, and, when soon afterwards the knowledge reached Norway, this industry at once attained great prominence. They are divided into two principal classes: the spring or large herring-fisheries, which take place in the beginning of the year, when the herring, in immense shoals, go inshore to shed their roes, and the summer and autumn fisheries, at which time the fish is smaller, when they run in near land to feed on the enormous masses of *Copepoda* (very small crawfish), *Annelida*, and *Mollusca*, which are plentiful at that time of the year on certain parts of the coast.

The spring fisheries extend from latitude 57° 59′ to 60° 25′;

the herring rarely goes east of Lindesnæs, and but seldom north of Stadt. The time and places of their arrival are very irregular, but usually their season is from January till March. At the same time, also, occurs the fishery for large herring, but generally only on the Nordland coast and by Lofoden. The summer herring-fishery is still more uncertain, and occurs at different dates here and there along the coast from Lofoden to the southward ; it very much depends on the whereabouts of the food sought by the fish. In this season the herring has, as said, no roe or milt, but fat, and is therefore called fat herring : it is also smaller than the spring herring.

The different names and sizes of the herring depend, according to Professor G. O. Tars, on their various ages ; the largest, the " storsild," being six years old. The irregularity in the time of the arrival of the herring, and its periodical disappearance from long stretches of the coast, are hardly caused by any decrease in the mass of fish, as the number caught by man is insignificant in comparison with what is eaten by other enemies of the fish. There is very little probability of its having taken to other runs or sought another coast, but it is more likely that in summer it has found its food farther out at sea, and about the shedding period has not had time to get inshore, and therefore has been obliged to shed its roe on the more distant banks (where the fish has been seen lately) when it did not appear on the west coast at the usual time.

The herring is caught with nets, the meshes of which are about an inch in diameter. These nets are 60 to 75 feet long and 12 feet deep, and are kept at a proper depth by stones and floats, generally of cork. These nets are tied together, set at night, and taken up in the morning. A series of three yields ten, twelve, and sometimes as high as twenty barrels of herring, but the average catch is about six barrels. Each boat carries five to eight series, or fifteen to twenty-four nets. The crew consists of four or five men and boys.

Another mode of catching the herring is with a seine about 750 feet in length and from 90 to 120 feet in depth, which is used to enclose the immense shoals. Several small boats and a larger vessel, in which the men lodge—generally twenty-five to thirty — form a seine gang. The foreman having charge of the work, and often owning the whole or part of the equipment, is called the seine boss. The complete fishing outfit costs from 6000 to 8000 kronor. The work is done in the following manner: when the herring comes inshore, in a bay or sound, the seine is drawn around the mass of fish, whereby a so-called herring-lock (*sildelås*) is formed. The approach of the herring is generally indicated by the large fish or birds following the shoals, or in the night by a lead and line, with which a trained fisherman can feel if they have arrived in sufficient numbers. The catch depends, in a great degree, on the skill of the seine boss. When two or more seine gangs have worked at making the lock, the catch belongs to that gang which first gets down its seines. Disputes are settled immediately by the *opsynsmand*. When the herring is locked, the men hurry to empty the enclosure by means of a smaller seine or drag-net, which is drawn towards the shore, where the fish are taken up with hand-nets and emptied into the boats, which, after being filled, are sent out, and the fish sold to owners of trading-vessels. It is by no means rare that several thousand barrels are enclosed within the seines, and it has happened that 20,000 to 30,000 barrels have been taken in a single catch, the value of which is very considerable. Sometimes, however, the seines are torn to pieces when bad weather occurs before they are emptied.

Part of the fisheries have of late been managed by vessels of 40 to 60 tons, each carrying four to five boats'-crews, and accompanying the latter over whatever course the fish may take. The spring fishery is often attended by risks, though perhaps not so much so as that for the cod, and is generally more uncertain than the latter. Many a time the fishermen lay-to and consume their provisions, waiting in vain for the herring, and finally have to go home empty-handed, while at times the fishing is so rich that small fortunes are made. The fish are usually sold immediately to merchants, who, with their vessels, are always lying in wait for the fishermen; and as soon as these little vessels, holding from 400 to 500 barrels, are full, they repair at once to the salting establishments, erected either in the towns or near the best fishing-grounds. Here the fish are gilled, which is done by making a cut with a sharp knife over the throat of the herring, whereupon the windpipe and entrails are drawn out with a quick motion, and a little blood escapes. This process is usually done by women. The fish are then packed between layers of salt, in barrels which hold about 480: for a barrel, one-quarter barrel of salt is used. Two skilled gillers can clean and fill thirty barrels a day. Later, the herrings are sorted and repacked.

The summer fisheries, or those for fat herring, begin shortly after the close of the spring fisheries; but the best herring appear in August and September; the fish are then caught partly by nets and partly with seines. Those taken by the latter are left enclosed a couple of days before being removed, so as to allow them to get rid of their food. As the summer herrings are smaller, the nets and seines have smaller meshes, generally three-quarters of an inch in diameter. The nets are 90 feet long and 24 feet deep, and six nets are tied together. When using the seines, the fishermen have to pay the owners of the adjoining coast a percentage of their catch for the right of drawing to the shore, and also have to indemnify such owners for any damage done to their crops. This percentage in the Bergen provinces is six per cent. of the catch—in all other places three per cent.

The aggregate number of barrels of herring caught annually is 1,312,000—it has reached as high as 1,800,000; of sprats (*Clupea sprattus—brisling*), 342,000; the number of mackerel caught is about 5,000,000. The average value of the catch is: cod, $5,000,000; herring, $3,503,000; other fisheries, $193,000; total, $8,696,000.

To Spitzbergen and Nova Zembla are sent yearly about 30 vessels for seal-fishing, with 268 men, the value of the catch being 44,778 specie dollars; for seal-catching at Jan Mayen Land were sent 15 vessels with 684 men, the value of the catch being 184,000 specie dollars: 1,200,000 lobsters were exported alive to England, and also 140 tons of salmon on ice. The number of seals caught was 63,700; and of whales, 36.

The herring migrates, and is known to have disappeared for years from many districts, but sometimes appears in immense numbers on the west coast of Sweden. The herring fisheries along the east coast are carried on by more than 3000 boats, and in 1873 the catch was about 150,000 barrels. On the island of Gotland 2000 people with 600 boats are engaged in these fisheries. The Baltic herring is a smaller variety of the common kind. On the banks in the Kattegat or the North Sea are employed vessels of 65 to 200 tons burden, with crews of 12 to 14 men. The mackerel-fishery is carried on along the west coast by about 1500 men with nearly 400 boats.

The number of men employed in the fisheries for cod is about 60,000, in the herring-fisheries 50,000, and then come the mackerel-fisheries with 3000, making, with the sailors of the merchant marine, a grand total of nearly eight per cent. of the whole population who live by maritime pursuits.

The Norwegians are pre-eminently a seafaring people, and outrank every other nation in Europe in that respect. England employs a far greater number of seamen in her mercantile navy; but many of the crews of her ships are often chiefly composed of men alien to her soil; besides, many Norsemen are found in foreign bottoms, and vessels on the great American lakes are frequently manned by them. But it is in her fishermen, who are the most hardy of sailors, that Norway outstrips her rival, who is popularly known as the "Mistress of the Seas." Besides the thousands engaged in the large fisheries, there is a numerous home population that almost subsists by fishing.

From the latest statistics (1877) the merchant navy consisted of 8064 vessels, with an aggregate carrying capacity of 1,493,041 tons: 7791 were sailing-vessels, with a tonnage of 1,446,172 tons, and 273 were steamers, of 46,869 tons. In that year of commercial depression the ships earned by foreign freights 98,444,000 kronor, or about 26,600,000 dollars. Of this sum, 21,000,000 kronor represent the freights of the carrying-trade between Norway and foreign countries; between the United States and other countries, 25,000,000 kronor; and last year more than 1000 Norwegian vessels came to the port of New York, at one time more than 250 barks being seen lying along-side the docks.

The foreign trade was carried by

5049 sailing-vessels with a capacity of..............	1,371,300 tons;
95 steamers " "	38,974 "
Only 47 vessels had a tonnage of over..............	1,000 "
" 1 vessel " "	1,500 "
" 2 steamers " "	1,500 "

In domestic traffic were engaged 163 steamers, only two exceeding 500 tons, the greater number carrying between 20 and 100 tons.

Engaged in the whale and seal fishery were

15 steamers with a capacity of.....................	3643 tons;
55 sailing-vessels " "	2200 "

The sailing-vessels were manned by 58,911 men; the steamers by 3229.

The coasting trade is open to vessels of all nationalities, upon the same conditions as of Norway, and people are at liberty to buy their ships anywhere.

The mercantile navy of Sweden is much smaller than that of Norway. At the end of 1873 it consisted of 3900 vessels of 434,310 tons, manned by 24,750 men; of these vessels 565, carrying 51,590 tons, were steamers. This only included vessels of ten tons and over.

CHAPTER XII.

THE trip by steamer from the Lofoden was a continuation
of gales and snow-storms, against which our vessel with difficulty made its way. We had occasionally to cast anchor for
a few hours, both by day and by night, being unable to proceed. This voyage of a day in fair weather often takes a
week in a gale. At Tromsö we had to stop until a snow-
storm abated. There were there several thousand fishermen,
who were waiting for safer wind in order to continue the
journey northward with their boats, or for steamers, either
to go home or to some fishing-place on the coast of Finmarken. Many evidently were making up for the solitary
life they had led, and I thought the sudden increase of population was not very conducive to the good of the place.
The lower part of the town, by the fjord, was entirely in possession of the new-comers, many of whom spent their money
freely, to the joy of the store-keepers and others.

At the important fishing-village of Skjærvö, which possesses
a splendid harbor—the best between Hammerfest and Tromsö
—we were obliged to cast anchor, on account of a violent wind
and snow-storm. Thence we steamed slowly towards the fishing settlement of Loppen, on the island of that name; across
to Hasvik, on the island of Sörö; and then up the long sound
to Hammerfest. The streets of Hammerfest were filled with
snow, and the port with fishing-boats at anchor; these had

come from the south and the Lofoden, and were waiting for the storm to abate so that they might continue their voyage along the coast. The streets were crowded with idle fishermen and Sea Laplanders, in their dresses of reindeer skins. They did not know what to do with themselves while waiting for a change.

The thermometer seldom falls to 20° below zero; even in the depth of winter it stands for consecutive days several degrees above freezing-point. The discharge of a gun on board the steamer at midnight notified our passengers to go on board; the stars were shining; it was the first clear weather for several weeks here, and the tenth day of an almost continuous snow-storm. But the improvement was maintained only a few hours. We also had to wait for a lull in the storm.

The route in winter is through the Magerö Sound, steamers not doubling North Cape. On the little island of Fruholmen, latitude 71° 5′ 45″, is situated the most northerly lighthouse on the globe, guiding the mariner along that desolate and dangerous coast, and warning him of danger. We passed a fine mountain, called Kjerringen (old woman), and Cape Stikkelvaagnæringen, with its sharp pyramidal mountain peaks. An indescribable feeling of utter desolation impressed me as I looked on that bleak land; the steep sides of the mountain seemed striped with black and white, which made the scene appear still wilder. The whole coast, from a distance, seemed to rise vertically. The dark gray sky was in unison with the dreary landscape; the wind was cold and piercing.

But even on that bleak island of Magerö the Norsemen have settlements. Suddenly masts of vessels appeared; fishing-boats were seen at anchor, and houses stood near the shore. It was the fishing-station of Honningsvaag. Kjelvig is the most eastern station on the island; and its church, vessels, and houses soon came in sight. Though the sound was quiet the wind blew a gale on the mountain-tops; there the snow flew in thick clouds, which suddenly came together, whirling, like a water-spout, in a spiral column, which, in turn becoming broken, sent its particles from Magerö far over the sea.

Here are the highest tides on the Scandinavian coast. At

the Kattegat the tides are feeble, but they increase gradually towards the north. At Stavanger they rise three feet; at Trondhjem, eight, and at the North Cape and Vadsö, nine feet.

From Kjelvig we sailed across the Porsanger fjord to Cape Sværholdtklubben. This fjord extends southward as far as 70° latitude, and is the largest within the arctic circle, having a length of about 85 miles; its shores are dreary; here and there one sees a Lapp hut. Farther inland some of the hills are clad with small birches. There are two or three fishing settlements and two churches. Cape Sværholdtklubben forms the extremity of a long peninsula, dividing the Porsanger from the Laxe fjord, averaging a height of about 1000 feet at its eastern extremity. The scenery is wild near the cape; ragged mountains rise like walls near the abrupt shore, torn in many places, and with huge masses of rock piled up at their base. As we rounded the cape an immense number of small gulls, frightened by our steamer, flew wildly above and around us; the air was thick and every crevice in the rocks white with them; I had never before seen such numbers of birds together; there must have been hundreds of thousands, perhaps millions. The fishermen there ask, "Who is the biggest king in the world?" "The king of Sværholdt; because he has the most subjects." This bird, the *Larus tridactylus*, is the smallest species of gull, and the number of eggs they lay in the crevices of the mountains and on the plateaus must be simply innumerable. The captain fired a gun, and the view above our heads became extraordinary, in some places the birds being so numerous as to hide the sky.

Then we came to the little fishing settlement of Sværholdt, which takes its name from the cape, and is protected by it; with north or north-west wind the landing is difficult. A single family dwells here all the year round. The year before, in mid-winter, their house was burned, and one of the children was lost; no trace whatever of him was found; the people to this day do not know whether, in the darkness of the night, he fell into the water or was burned.

On the eastern shore of the Laxe fjord, near its entrance,

and almost opposite Cape Sværholdtklubben, is a narrow bay-like arm of the sea, called the Eids fjord. From the deck of the vessel we could see beyond a narrow low tract of land, the Hops fjord, a small eastern branch of the Tana fjord: the Eids is shallow, while the Hops is deep. The distance between these two being very small, the Storthing has been asked to make an appropriation to cut a canal to connect them ; this would be of great advantage to the fisheries in bad weather. The configuration of the land reminded me forcibly of that of the island of Magerö, and showed that, when the country was still beneath the sea, the Kjorgosj Njarg, the name of the massive rock, which is indented with bays and fjords, was an island.

On the Laxe fjord is the thrifty fishing settlement of Lebesby, with a church. The northern coast of the Kjorgosj Njarg is the wildest in Finmarken, the cliffs being very rugged. The strata of the rocks were seen distinctly ; masses had fallen down near and into the sea in large slabs. One of the great sights is the gammel Finkirken (old Lapp church), situated at the foot of the high hills near the sea. I took this at first for the ruins of an old stone church or monastery, the end walls of which still remained, and I really believed it was an ancient ruin, whose pillars or walls only were standing. The illusion was complete until I came near it ; then I noted quite a distance between the two walls, though the slab structure gave the appearance of masonry : it was simply nature resembling the work of man. Finkirken certainly is one of the greatest curiosities of Northern Europe. At the head of the Kjölle fjord a picturesque wooden church and a few houses formed the settlement. The church is at about lat. 70° 55' ; this, with that of Kjelvig, are the two most northern churches in Europe.

Continuing to skirt the shores, one doubles Nordkyn, lat. 71° 6' 50'', the northern extremity. Kjorgosj Njarg is the most northern point of Europe, and is over 700 feet high. In the distance, westward, is North Cape, appearing like a black mass rising perpendicularly from the sea. From Nordkyn the coast gradually becomes lower, and ice was thick at the head of the fjords. Fishing-stations, where there are a few vessels, continue to be seen, while bright-painted churches testify that the seafaring population has places of worship on that oft-desolate coast. Then one enters the Tana fjord, which pierces through the mass of rocks for a distance of about forty-five miles; its mountains are high, in some places reaching a height of from 2000 to 2300 feet. Here the geological formation is chiefly of sandstone quartz, of white, red, and yellow strata, and is crumbling everywhere. Its upper end is filled with sand-banks formed by the Tana River. This fjord is remarkable for the forest of birches lining its shores to the south; it has several branches.

Crossing the Tana fjord, one sails along the Vargack Njarg, another huge knoll, bounded on the west by the Tana fjord and river, the sea, and the Varanger fjord. From Tana Horn the elevation of the coast continues to decrease, and is not more than three or four hundred feet. Some fishing-stations are passed, and one comes to Vardö, the most important town on the coast of Finmarken. We entered that crowded port in the midst of a violent snow-storm. The place is built chiefly on two bays extending in opposite directions, separated only by a narrow tract of land in the shape of an elongated promontory; an island farther at sea partly protects the shores. The two harbors afford protection, one from the south-eastern, the other from the north-western gales. The port is not good, and it is said to be the most unsheltered town on the whole of that northern coast: to judge by the strong wind blowing through its streets, and the huge snow-drifts, I should say that its reputation is well deserved. It is the coldest place in Finmárken, the mean temperature of the year being only a fraction of a degree above freezing-point; but in cold winters it is exceeded by Kåfjord and Nyborg—the latter situated at the inner end of the Varanger fjord.

There were but few vessels, but hundreds of fishing-boats were stranded on the shores, and a great number were at anchor. The fleet had been unable to get out for more than three weeks on account of storms, and no bait had been caught. The place has a population of about 1200 inhabitants, and during the fishing season it is much larger. It had an unfinished appearance; some of the houses were painted, others not, and, owing to the ground, there was no symmetry in the arrangement of the streets. The city is situated on the island of Vardö, and at the most eastern extremity of the Vargack Njarg. Here are seen three very interesting shore-lines, formed of large pebbles, which have been mentioned in Chapter XVIII. of the first volume.

Those large fishing settlements presented a singular sight. Scattered about were hundreds of poles on which the fish were hung to dry. Near the bay were several manufactories of brown cod-liver oil, and projecting over the water were the wharf-houses of the merchants, partly built on piles.

Vardö is the only fortified place on the northern coast of Norway. On the way to the fort (Vardöhus) the wind was so high that we could hardly stand against it, and the flying snow so blinded us that at times we could not see our way. Over the gate leading in was the date 1737. On one side of the house of the commandant of the fort the snow was piled above the door, and the first-story windows were hidden from view. We had to enter by the kitchen, where we found the official engaged in making a pair of boots for one of his children. He had a large family to support, and strict economy was necessary. He received us kindly, and I admired his manliness, for he was not in the least ashamed that we saw him playing shoemaker.

The fort had twenty old-style cannon in battery, and the garrison was composed of twenty soldiers—seamen, no doubt, for, on account of the small pay, six of the garrison fish for the commandant, three for the lieutenant, and two for the doctor; the fish are divided between the fishermen and the respective officers for whom they are caught. This was primitive enough, and showed plainly that the Norwegians did not wish the expenses of their army to fall heavily upon the people. The barracks reminded me much of those of the Cossacks on the island of Torneå.

From Vardö can be seen, on the other side of the bay which forms the entrance to Varanger fjord, Cape Njemetski, the most northern point of the Gikker Njarg—the last njarg on the coast, unless we except the Kola peninsula (almost an island), and the shores of which form one of the most desolate regions of Russia in Northern Europe.

Continuing to skirt the coast, about seventy miles farther one comes to Vadsö. This last town on the Norwegian shore, with a population of 1800 inhabitants, is divided into the Finn and Norwegian quarters; there are also a few Lapps. It is the seat of a court, and the judge is the chief functionary of the place. Like all fishing-stations, it is filled with framework used to dry the fish. Cod-liver oil, and guano from fish-heads and bones, are manufactured. A small steamer is engaged in the whale fishery in an unusual way. The whales—which are numerous on this part of the coast—are killed by a gun which discharges a peculiar harpoon with an explosive shell. The creatures thus taken are towed into Vadsö. Many have been obtained in this way during the past few years. The large Norwegian coasting steamer goes no farther, but there is generally a small one plying weekly in the fjords. Vadsö is the last telegraphic station. Who would think that even on this lone coast the important news of the world flashes every day over the wires, and is made known to the inhabitants? The postal telegraph has always been used, with but one uniform rate all over the country, and from this northern part of the land a message to the most southern point of Norway costs but one krona. In Sweden it is the same, and, though the distances are so great, the government is no loser; the rates will become still lower as soon as the receipts allow a reduction.

The schools are good; Greek, Latin, Hebrew, French, German, and English are taught. In this district some of the teachers have to know the Norwegian, Finnish, and Lapp languages. In many of the inhabitants' houses pianos, guitars, violins, and concertinas are found. The homes of the merchants are large and exceedingly comfortable, and their hospitality unbounded. I was invited by a fellow-passenger on board the steamer, Herr W——, to stay at his house. Kindness to strangers seems to be the law of the land, and I was introduced everywhere.

During winter the inhabitants, having nothing to occupy their minds, sometimes labor under intense religious excitement. All through the past season there had been among the Finns a time so threatening that, had it not been for fear of the law, it might have ended seriously. The clergyman was not fanatical enough for these people, so they preached in their rooms; force and threats were used against those who did not seem to be strong in the faith; many declared that they had the spirit of the Lord and power of prophecy; others believed that some were possessed of devils; the clergyman was unwilling to go with them, and in their excitement they threatened him. For awhile the Norwegian inhabitants wore sober faces, not knowing how things might terminate, and fearing that perhaps it would end in bloodshed, as it had in Kautokeino some years before, where people were killed by the fanatics, and the soldiers had to be called upon to quell the disturbance and punish the assassins, who thought they were doing God's will by murdering those who did not believe as they did. History repeats itself.

The catching of lodd (*Mallotus arcticus*) at the fishing settlements produces great excitement, and the young people are continually on the watch for these little fish. When the shoals are pursued by cod they take refuge near the shore. While we were in Vadsö an immense number of them were caught, to the great joy of the population; they had been waiting for them in order to commence the fishing-season, which was late that year on account of the very stormy weather that had prevented them from going out, and without lodd they had no bait to fish with.

The emigration from Finland into Norway is increasing, and every year new settlers establish themselves on the coast. A strong tide has begun to set towards the United States, the people coming from Finland in sleighs, and starting for America in the spring. Several hundred had left by the way of Vadsö the year before, the steamers taking them either to Trondhjem, Bergen, or Christiania.

The long days came on with remarkable rapidity: the sun was below the horizon in these regions till the latter part of

January; and now, on the 25th of April, in clear weather, I could read a newspaper by the window at midnight.

I found here the largest specimens of reindeer I had ever seen ; these had come from the country of the Samoïdes, where they are said to be larger than in Norway and Sweden.

The Varanger is the last of Norway's fjords, and the only one on the coast of Finmarken which runs east and west. It lies between 69° 30′ and 69° 50′, and is a most remarkable one. Its northern shore is almost entirely bare of vegetation, and even brush-wood is very scarce; but the southern, known under the name of Sydvaranger (South Varanger), has a remarkable growth, and is called *Rafte siden* (timber side); many of the houses of Vadsö and other places have been built of timber from that forest. Large trees have become scarce near the sea. On Kjö, Bugö, and Neiden fjords, southern branches of the Varanger, birches occur, and heather covers the rocks; the grass is luxuriant; the trees grow larger and larger towards the ends of the fjords, and thriving forests of fir and pine are continuous. Three large rivers, the Jakob, Neiden, and Pasvig, all abounding with salmon, throw themselves into the fjord. As one ascends the latter stream—the largest of the rivers which rise in Lake Enare—the hills are covered to their tops with trees. These forests are said to cover an area of 230 square miles, almost untouched by the axe, except near the water, and many trees are large enough for timber. One wonders at the possibility of the trees attaining dimensions in such a high latitude—69° and 70°—fully comparable with those of more southerly parts of the country. The nearer the sea the less the altitude of the trees, and the better the quality of the wood; the farther north, the poorer the timber becomes. Birch, alder, and asp abound, the latter often attaining three feet in circumference: in many parts fires have made sad havoc among the trees. The shores on the west side of North Cape, though less covered with forests —which doubtless were destroyed in former times—enjoy a much warmer climate than those on the eastern side; for, as has been seen, on Alten fjord, in the same latitude as the Varanger, barley, rye, and fruits grow, while here these are not planted. The water of the sea is gradually getting colder, and the winds from the east are also bleaker. The population has very much increased of late years in this extreme north-eastern part of Norway, in spite of the barren soil, on account of the fisheries and easy communication. Two new parishes have been created in South Varanger. The population, which hardly numbered 100 at one time, has increased, according to the last census (1865), to 1171 individuals, comprising 194 Northmen, 68 Nomad Lapps, 339 Lapp farmers, 539 farmers, mostly Finlanders, and 31 of mixed races. Two churches have been built; a doctor and lensmand have been appointed; schools have been established.

The adjoining coast, known as Russian Lapland, abounds in fish. There are many settlements, employing several thousand boats in the fisheries. A vast number of fish are caught, even by Norwegians; but, as the men are not allowed to land, they often encounter violent storms with great loss of property and life.

Pasvig, the last regular port and fishing-station on the Norwegian coast, takes its name from the Lapp word *basse* (holy): probably the Pasvig Lapps, in former times, had here a place for sacrifices. It has an excellent harbor, nearly circular, surrounded by rocks. The entrance is narrow, but it is said that it can be entered during all winds.

The most eastern part of Norway is bounded by the Pasvig River, which flows into the sea opposite Vadsö, and by the Jakob River. A knowledge of this region now shows that for a certain distance eastward the coast is open all the year round. In regard to the ice-bound coast of Russia, I will simply say, were she so inclined, that country could establish a harbor on her own possessions; that the Kola fjord does not freeze; that the sea remains open, as on the Norwegian coast, for a considerable distance, and forests grow on the banks of its rivers and lakes—facts which show that it is not necessary to conquer the northern part of Norway in order to have an open port all the year round.

From Vadsö to Nyborg—a hamlet made up of a few scattered farms on the brow of a hill, belonging to fishing Lapps, at the inner end of the Varanger fjord—the distance by water is about thirty-five miles. On the shores are seen two or three fishing settlements, a few Lapp gammer, and the church of Næsby. Several boats, each with two women as rowers, came to our steamer, while at times women alone were seen crossing the fjord.

On the 25th of April I found myself at the head of the Varanger fjord; for a distance of about three miles the sea was frozen, and our steamer had to lie along-side the ice. Sleighs were in waiting to take the mails and passengers.

In a pleasant white house, not far from the shore, lived the Norwegian lensmand, Brun, with his charming family, consisting of wife and two grown-up daughters: books and newspapers came by the weekly or semi-monthly mail, and, with a piano, enabled them to pass the time pleasantly in their solitary home, for they had to depend upon themselves for society. It was very late in the season, and the Laplanders and their reindeer had left. "If you had been here only a week before, you would have had no difficulty in going south," said the lensmand. I ought not to have been later than the 1st of April. "You must stay with me for a day or two, and I will see if any Lapps are still in the neighborhood and are willing to take you." How agreeable was the hospitality of that kind-hearted family, how cosy and comfortable was my bedroom, how luxurious was the feather-bed! I appreciated all the more the luxuries of a civilized and genteel life after the roughing of the winter.

Near Nyborg some Sea Lapps' dwellings are seen on the ridge of a hill. We will enter a *gamme*—as the sod-houses of the Lapps are called—belonging to Matis (Mathias) Johnsen Laiti—a long, narrow, low house, built entirely of sod. It was divided into three rooms, the entrance being through a low wooden door into a centre room, in which were winter garments hung on poles, a pile of fire-wood, and a heap of sea-weed. In the room on the left, about twelve feet long and ten wide, the family lived. It was paved with flat slabs; in one corner was a bed made of small branches of birch, kept together by large logs. At the foot of the bed was a

A STONE AND SOD GAMME.

small cow, and in the opposite corner another, each about three feet in height. The wife was seated on the bed, dressed in a coarse kind of woollen chemise with long sleeves, woollen pantaloons, and Lapp shoes, wearing on her head one of the queer cask-like caps before described. Between the cow and the bed was a calf: three sheep and two small children completed the family, the owner being absent. Everything was scrupulously clean, and there was a little gutter to receive the dirt of the cattle. The structure of the house was tent-like; there was a strong frame of poles supporting the turf, from the middle of which, under the opening for the smoke, were four poles to which was attached a huge iron pot full of sea-weed, covered by birch-bark. This sea-weed had been cooked for the cows; I tasted it, and found it was not at all salt. The cattle in this part of the world have learned to eat horse-dung, raw fish, dry fish-heads boiled, sea-weed and grass, and even boiled lichens. The rest of the furniture consisted of a few kettles, a coffee-pot, a lamp, and a few chests. These sod-houses often last ten or twelve years, but require frequent repairs, and new layers of turf.

Not far distant from Matis's gamme was a small farm belonging to Mikel Iversen, a well-to-do person. The building was long and narrow, one part built of logs, the remainder of layers of turf. In the wooden part was the parlor, kitchen, and bedroom all in one; the roof was made of poles covered with birch-bark, over which was placed earth. The cattle here were kept by themselves. Two cows, two little oxen, and eight sheep formed the wealth of the family. The master with the two oxen had gone for sea-weed; but soon after my arrival he made his appearance with a small cart, having two old-fashioned wheels of solid wood, drawn by his two oxen— dwarfish and wretched-looking creatures.

Near by was the farm of Ole Persen Maja. The dwelling-house was built entirely of logs, and reminded me very much of those belonging to poor Scandinavians in other parts of Sweden and Norway; but inside it made some pretension to luxury and comfort. The little room had two wooden beds, a cast-iron stove, a clock, and three chairs; and here, also, as among the humbler dwellings we have just seen, everything was exceedingly clean. The wife wore the usual coarse vadmal gown, but had a close-fitting cap upon her head, and looked wonderfully like a man. Maja was considered very rich by his neighbors; he owned a horse, with a special stable for him, and his four cows and sheep had also a building for themselves.

Being unable to procure any reindeer, the obliging lensmand concluded that he would go with me part of the way, try to see some Lapps, and help me out of my dilemma.

CHAPTER XIII.

Lapland.—Extent of the Country.—Swedish and Norwegian Lapland.—Character
of the Country.—Moss Tracts.—Summer and Winter Wanderings.—The Life of
the Mountain Lapp.—Population of Lapland.—Numbers of Reindeer.—Size of
Herds.—Honesty of the Laplander.—His Severe Training.—Hard Life.—Physical
Structure of the Lapps.—Fine Climate of Lapland.—Diseases of the Country.—
Long Life of some Lapps.—Food.—Contentment of the Lapps.

BEFORE proceeding on our journey southward, we will give
a general outline of the country inhabited by Laplanders, and
known under the name of "The Land of Lapps," which comprises the northern part of Scandinavia; these people are also
found in the north of Finland, and in Russia to the most eastern extremity of the peninsula of Kola, and as far as the White
Sea.

Russian Lapland has an extent of about 13,000 square miles;
Swedish, 10,500; Finnish, 6,000; Norwegian, 3,500: in all,
33,000 square miles. Some parts of Russian Lapland are covered with large forests of coniferous trees; these occupy about
3,000,000 acres, while the hills and valleys towards the north
are chiefly clad with dwarfed birch, but there are also extensive tracts of tundra, or treeless desert.

In Norway and Sweden the Lapps are found as far south
as 62° in the provinces of Herjedalen and Jemtland, and in
Hedemarken and Trondhjem, but very few inhabit these two
large Norwegian provinces. Going northward, their number
increases steadily, and by far the greatest population is found
in Norway in the amts or provinces of Tromsö and Finmarken. The Russian Lapps, according to Friis, are not nomads
in the sense that they roam around with herds of reindeer, for
they own but few of these; still, although they live in houses
of timber or earth, every family changes its dwelling-place
three or four times a year. In the spring they go to their

summer quarters, which are by a lake or the sea; some move again in the middle of summer to other fisheries on rivers or lakes. In August they move to their fall stations, where, besides fishing, they also hunt reindeer, birds, martens, squirrels, otters, and bears. About Christmas they move into their winter homes, which generally are in small hamlets. Their mode of living prevents them from having many reindeer.

These Laplanders call themselves Sabme or Same (plural, Samelats); by the Swedes they are called Lapp (plural, Lappar); by the Norwegians, erroneously, Fin (plural, Finner); and the Finlanders are known by them as Kvæn (plural, Kvæner). The Laplander is unlike the Esquimaux, and I have found that they differ materially from the descriptions I have read of them; though by many regarded as branches of the same Mongolian or Turanian stock, I think, with Retzius, that the Lapps and Esquimaux are of entirely different races—the former being short-headed (*brachycephalic*) and straight-jawed (*orthognathic*), while the Esquimaux are long-headed (*dolichocephalic*) and prominent-jawed (*prognathic*). Finland is called *Suomi*, and the people *Suomalaiset*, by the Finlanders. These two words bear a close resemblance to the Lapp words, and suggest people of the same origin. The two languages are said to have some similarity; but a minor people, for obvious reasons, usually adopt the language of the dominant race. Physically, at this day, they are unlike, the Finlander being far the taller, and in personal appearance more allied to the Scandinavian and Teutonic races, as well as their equal in intelligence. But, whatever may be the different characteristics of all those northern people (which it is not the object of this work to consider), the traveller is now and then surprised at finding, when least expected, some of the same features among the Scandinavians, Germans, Scotch, and other Europeans—namely, high cheek-bones, nose *retroussé*, flat between the eyes, and face short and rounded—which show resemblances to the Mongolian type.

Swedish Lapland is divided into districts, named after the provinces where the Lapps are found. The country is exceedingly well watered, rivers and lakes being found in every direction; swamps abound, and forests cover an area of over twenty million acres. From the eastern mountain range valleys from 150 to 200 miles long descend to the sea; the hills which separate them average from 400 to 600 feet in height, and, with the lower ground, are covered with forests and swamps. Reindeer-moss is plentiful, and there during the winter the Swedish Laplanders retire.

We have seen that in the extensive territory occupied by the Swedish and Norwegian Lapps law and order prevail, as in other parts of the land; lawlessness and brigandage are unknown, the wildest and least inhabited districts being as safe as any other in this most honest land. All the Laplanders belong to certain parishes, where they pay taxes and tithes, their children receive religious instruction, births and deaths are registered, and the number of reindeer they possess is known. The moss-tracts have to be carefully husbanded, not too much time being spent at one spot, while others must be avoided, to allow a crop to mature. I have been told that it takes from seven to ten years for it to grow again, and in some districts even longer than this. The healthy and growing moss has a greenish-white tinge, and is soft and somewhat spongy. When it ceases to develop it becomes dry. The finest I saw was on the Palajoki.

There are many mountain districts in Norway and Sweden, especially in the first country, where great herds of reindeer could be pastured in summer. Year after year will a family roam over the same tract as did their ancestors, here sleeping with the back resting against the same boulder, there under a huge rock pitching the tent, partly protected from the weather.

The Fjeld Lapp's time is engaged in adding to his herd, to which he and his family devote all their energies, for their welfare depends on the growth of the animals. It is difficult to ascertain exactly the increase or decrease of reindeer according to the districts; for the people often change, and there has been of late years in the North a large emigration of Norwegian Lapps to the territory of Sweden, especially to Karesuando; but, taken as a whole, the population and the reindeer are increasing. There is a greater number in Norway than in Sweden, owing to the number of stationary bönder (farmers), and Sea Lapps, which far outnumber the Nomads.

According to the late census, there are

In Sweden (1870).........	6,702	Laplanders, with	220,800	reindeer;
" Norway (1865).........	17,178	"	"	101,768	"
" Finland (1865).........	615	"	"	40,200	"
" Russia (1859).........	2,207	"	"	4,200	"

With those that belong to farmers and others, I think we may safely say that the reindeer number about 400,000. The Samoïdes have the largest and finest breeds, which are not numbered among those of the Lapps. In Kautokeino there are Lapps who own 2000 reindeer; in Sorsele, in Sweden, one is said to own 5000, and others 1000 and 2000. Some of the Forest Lapps have 1000. In Luleå Lappmark there are herds of over 2000; in Finmarken of 5000, and some Lapps have owned as many as 10,000. A herd of 2000 to 2500 is said to give about 200 to 250 calves yearly.

Every owner has his own mark branded on the ears of all his reindeer, and no other person has a right to have the same, as this is the lawful proof of ownership; otherwise, when several herds are mingled in the mountains, the separation would be impossible. According to custom no one can make a new mark, but must buy that of an extinct herd; if these are scarce, the price paid to the families that own them is often high; the name of the purchaser and each mark have to be recorded in court, like those of any other owner and property. The tax paid is according to the pasture-land occupied.

There are sometimes hard feelings between Laplanders and Norwegian settlers in the thrifty inhabited districts of the fjords near the coast, especially in the province of Tromsö, on account of the damage done by the reindeer to the meadows or crops. I was told by some Laplanders that on the Alten fjord the farmers upon whose grounds they have to pass by the fjords, in order to go to pasture, ask an extortionate price for the right of way. I hope the Storthing will see that this abuse is remedied if the complaint be true.

The Laplander is so honest that his kåta is often left with no one to take care of the food, coffee, sugar, garments, silverware, etc., and these are at the mercy of the first thief among them that comes along. But pilfering is very rare, and the tent is almost held sacred. Reindeer thieves are occasionally found, and they have to be guarded against; these are generally the Fisher Lapps, or the bönder who have settled down; it is hard for them to resist the temptation to take from a herd which is left to itself. Once two men were recommended to me as guides by an official; I learned at the same time that although one of them had been in prison for stealing reindeer, I could trust him. I went with him over the inhabited districts with perfect safety. I never have had a disagreement with any one of them in regard to pay or anything else. I have often been amused, on my return to the Norwegian coast, at the people wondering how I dared to go alone into the mountains among the Lapps, and in more than one instance names of persons never heard from were given to me as a warning; but the fears were groundless, as my experience amply proves.

The Laplander, by the severe training he undergoes from childhood, sleeping on the bare ground, or resting against a stone, suffering hunger, and being exposed to great changes in the weather, has very great powers of endurance. In summer he has constantly to follow his herd, which is for the greater part of the day on the march, as they are not then obliged to dig to get to the moss. He is also compelled to go through swamps and bogs, or to cross patches of soft deep snow, to swim or pass rivers swollen by melted snow or the flow from glaciers, as I have frequently done: often hungry, and obliged to milk a reindeer for subsistence, when he comes to the kåta he is generally overcome with fatigue, and, changing his wet clothes, falls into a sleep brought on by sheer exhaustion. Frequently he wanders over a tract of nearly one hundred miles, remaining three or four days in a district, then moving six or seven miles farther. In winter he travels over dreary wastes, during violent storms, suffering from hunger and cold. On the watch, night and day, for bears, wolves,

and gluttons, perhaps he is suddenly awakened, after sleeping an hour, and summoned for the protection of his stock
against enemies which may scatter the herd and reduce him
to poverty.   All this makes the Mountain Laplander one of
the hardiest of men, and his physical structure shows at once
that he is equal to the demands of his life.   He is of short
stature, compactly but slightly built, with strong limbs—his
light weight allowing him to climb, jump, and run quickly.

Consumption, cancer, chills and fever, and affections of the
liver and kidneys, are unknown.   The water is as pure as in
granitic countries, and the drinking of sour milk prevents many
complaints elsewhere common.   But acute diseases are prevalent—often brought on by the perspiration which comes when
ascending steep mountains being suddenly checked by the
piercing winds of the summit.   I am surprised, after having
been subjected to such exposure on the mountains of Scandinavia year after year, that I have yet to know what a rheu-
matic pain is.   I have seen Lapps use the fat coming out of
cheese, which they keep before the fire, to rub on their sore
spots and sprains.   They are subject to measles, and sometimes get small-pox from the sea-shore people.   Hernia is not
unfrequent, owing to their driving with the legs reversed and
acting as a drag on their sleighs.   Ophthalmia is quite prevalent, on account of the cold winds and the glare of the snow;
in the spring great care has to be taken with the eyes, as the
reflection of the sun is very bright in April, May, and the beginning of June; without blue or green goggles one easily
becomes snow-blind.   The men and women are active to a
great age.   Their life in the open air and constant wandering on foot preserves the elasticity of the muscles; their
simple habits, the keen, invigorating, dry air, and the pure
water (which is without lime) all contribute to secure lon-
gevity to those who have been able to pass the severe or-
deal of childhood.   Many attain very great age, some more
than a hundred years.   When I was in their country in
1873 there were Laplanders living who were born in the
years 1773–1775.   Although the Lapps live chiefly on animal
food, barley-flour is almost always found in the kåta, to be

used for mush, unleavened bread, or blood-pudding. They often mix their milk with sorrel-grass (*Rumex*). They are great drinkers of coffee, inveterate smokers and snuff-takers. The vice of drunkenness, once so prevalent, has now almost entirely disappeared at home; but whenever they go to a town, and can procure spirituous liquors, they generally have a frolic for a day or two.

In Norway the first Christian instruction among the Laplanders began about 1640; in Sweden in 1606; even in faraway South Varanger a school-master named Isaac Olsen, as early as 1703, and under great difficulties, converted the Laplanders of that district. Happy, and contented with his lot in the world, endowed with a religious nature, which a barren and lonely land contributes to intensify, the Lapp believes in God, in his Bible, in the Lord Jesus Christ as the Son of God, and in a future life. From those dreary wastes his songs of praise and prayers are uttered with a faith which ceases only with his breath, and he departs rejoicing that he is going to the "better land."

THE PASVIG. THE MOST NORTHERN RIVER IN EUROPE.

CHAPTER XIV.

THE Laplanders may be divided into the following classes,
according to their habitat and manner of life: 1. The Mountain or Nomad Lapps, who live upon the increase of their herds,
and wander with them all the year round from pasture to pasture, living in tents—these possess by far the largest number of
reindeer; 2. The Sea Lapps; 3. The Forest Lapps; 4. The
River Lapps; 5. The Fisher Lapps. All are descended from
the Mountain or Nomad Lapps.

The Sea Lapps are met along the wild coast of Nordland
and Finmarken, and are principally engaged in the cod-fisheries. They are daring and good sailors, and many are employed on the boats commanded by Norwegians. Some own
their own little craft; and I have not unfrequently seen such
commanded by the husband, while the wife and daughter, sisters, or hired women, formed the crew. The women are very
hardy, and excellent sailors. The dwellings of the Sea Lapps
are very primitive; they are called *gamme* (plural *gammer*),
and are very peculiar; they are constructed of earth, and vary
in shape; many are round, and some are conical, like summer
tents; the fireplace is in the centre, and the smoke finds its
way out through the aperture above; two or three of them
are sometimes together: these belong to the poorest Sea Lapps.
There are others of the shape of ordinary houses, built also entirely of turf, including the roof; walls of stone are occasionally placed outside, to protect the turf and make them more

durable. As many have no windows, the light comes only from above; when the fire is low the smoke-aperture is covered with a frame. Houses more pretentious are made entirely of logs; in the best districts they are not distinguishable from those of the Norwegian farmers.

To the occupation of fishing these Lapps add that of farming. Almost every one owns two or three cows, a few sheep, goats, and reindeer; patches of potatoes and grass often surround the gamme. Their principal labor, however, is fishing, which, when successful, is remunerative. The women take care of the barn and the household, often repairing the nets, putting bait on the lines, and splitting and drying the fish. In winter both sexes are clad in reindeer skins with the hair inside: their head-covering, like that of all the Lapps of the mountains, consists of an enormous square cap. The women wear an extraordinary head-dress, shaped somewhat like a cask; its form is owing to a hollow piece of wood. The summer garment of the women is a kind of long chemise, with sleeves to the wrist, often without a belt, made of woollen vadmal—very much the same material as is used for the tents of the Mountain Lapps; the color is usually blackish or gray, and rags and patches are very common. They have generally long, shaggy, dark or deep chestnut hair, with a reddish tinge, which they comb only on Sunday, and on this and their dirty garments vermin are abundant. The men are dressed in like manner, and on the head a cap of bright wool is worn. The women are so accustomed to hard work and exposure that, after a certain age, their features become so coarse as to make it difficult to distinguish a man from a woman; when young, it is hard to tell a girl from a boy.

One can judge of the standard of the Lapps by the number of families who live in houses or gammer. In Alten, Skjærvö, and Lyngen parishes the Lapps are greatly mixed by intermarriage with Norwegians and Finns, the offspring forming a good class of people. Many of them are as intelligent as the Norwegians, and are a valuable addition to the population of that country. The table on the following page gives the number of houses and gammer in different localities.

There are in Lyngen	264	log-houses to	13	gammer;
" " Skjærvö	225	" "	5	"
" " Indre Alten	38	" "	6	"
" " Kautokeino	18	" "	6	"
" " Trondenæs	1	" "	23	"
" " Maasö	1	" "	97	"
" " Lebesby	2	" "	50	"
" " Hammerfest	9	" "	129	"

By this it will be seen that the Lapps stand highest in the first parish, and lowest in the last named.

RIVER LAPPS.

Ascending the streams falling into the fjords, the River Lapps are found. These differ but little in their ways of living from the Sea Lapps, and many during the fishing-season go to sea; they are found in Norway, especially on the banks of the Tana, Karasjok, and Alten rivers, and their affluents. In summer their occupation is salmon-catching, or serving as sailors. Almost every family has a small farm, on which are kept cattle, horses, sheep, and goats; they cultivate the soil, and during the summer their reindeer are taken care of by the Mountain Lapps; they extend hospitality to their mountain brethren, and take care of them in sickness.

FOREST LAPPS.

Ascending the Lule, Pite, Byske, Skellefte, Ume, and other rivers, or near the lakes, the Forest Lapps are met here and there in the woods. Many of their dwellings are peculiar in shape; in some districts the lower part is square, built of three or four logs well joined together, the upper portion being pyramidal, of split trees covered with birch-bark, over which boards are put. A large flat stone is in the middle for fire, at the place where the cooking is done. There is the usual hole in the centre for the escape of smoke. In some the floor is covered with stone slabs, in others with young branches of the birch, and, as in the kåta, skins are spread for the family to sleep upon. Near the dwellings are large enclosures where, at a certain season of the year, the reindeer are penned every day. Many of the Forest Lapps own extensive herds,

LAPP GAMME, OR SOIL HUT.

which are milked two or three times a day. They have kâtas
built from distance to distance, for they are obliged to move
in order to pasture their herds.

In Herjeådalen the reindeer are sometimes allowed to roam
all summer; at the breeding-time, in October, they are collected again, and not let loose till spring. It is often necessary to make fires around the enclosures, that the smoke may
drive away the swarms of mosquitoes which otherwise would
set the herd frantic. In the southern part of Lapland the
reindeer (both in Norway and Sweden) do not go to the sea.

DWELLING-PLACE OF FOREST LAPPS BETWEEN SEUTNER AND JERFOJAUR, IN ARVIDSJAUR.
TO THE RIGHT A LUOPTE (LARDER): BUTCHERING OF REINDEER IN THE FOREGROUND.

The several herds are frequently mixed, but are easily separated when necessary, each owner knowing his own by distinctive marks. The Forest Lapps make a great deal of cheese,
and smoke reindeer meat and tongues, which are bought extensively by Swedes and Norwegians.

The Fishing Lapps are another class, derived, like the others,
from the Nomad or Mountain Lapps, who, becoming impov-
erished, and unwilling to serve, prefer to live independently.
By lonely lakes and on the banks of streams these Lapps build

DWELLING OF A FISHING LAPP FAMILY.

their habitations, surrounded generally by forests of fir, pine, or birch. A family may own several kåtor, and when the fishing ends at one place they go to another. During the summer they subsist on fish, and smoke and salt a large number for winter use, and for sale.

Besides fishing, they are engaged in several other industries—making wooden vessels, baskets, shoes, etc. Often at a place where the pasture is good and fish abundant, they improve the kåta, get a cow or two and a few reindeer, and become settled Laplanders. These little places during the winter are the rendezvous of the Mountain Lapps.

In the parish of Arvidsjaur, on the banks of Lake Jerfojaur (which forms the upper basin of

THE NJALLA.

the series of lakes of which Arvidsjaur is one) and of Byske River, which flows directly into the Bothnia above Skelleftea, is the picturesque dwelling-place of a Fisher Lapp, with two larders on posts: to the left is a frame for drying fish, and in the foreground a hässja for drying hay.

One sees now and then in some districts queer little houses (the njalla) built of logs, supported by a single post, or sometimes by four, so high above the ground that the winter snow will not cover them, nor can the wolves, foxes, or other wild animals get into them in summer. In these the Mountain Lapp keeps the stores which he does not wish to carry with him, such as cheese, skins, and pulverized milk. A ladder is necessary to reach the door, the njalla being used, in case of emergency, as a place of refuge for the night from storms.

We have also seen that Lapps live together in small hamlets. These are always situated on the shores of rivers or lakes. The church, parsonage, and school-house are the prominent buildings of the place. These Lapps are farmers. In many districts of Sweden their houses are of peculiar shape, and resemble those of the Forest Lapps. The following engraving shows a street in the village of Arvidsjaur, Pite Lappmark.

STREET IN THE VILLAGE OF ARVIDSJAUR, PITE LAPPMARK.

CHAPTER XV.

Departure from Varanger Fjord.—On the Way Southward.—Little Snow by the
Sea.—Meeting Laplanders.—No Reindeer.—Polmak.—The Tana River.—Good-
bye to the Lensmand of Nyborg.—Reindeer Coming.—Leave Polmak.—Sirma.—
Difficulties of Travelling in the Spring.—The Reindeer Weak.—Slow Speed.—A
Dangerous Start.—Upsetting.—Travelling on the Tana.—Utsjoki.—Dirty Quar-
ters on the Way.—Segelnæs.—The Karasjoki River.—Arrival at Karasjok.—Com-
fortable Quarters.—Friends in Need.—No Reindeer to be Had.—The Karasjok
Lapps.—Forests.—Variations of Temperature.—A Funeral.

THE journey from the Tana or Varanger fjord to the Gulf of
Bothnia is comparatively easy in winter. There are no steep
mountains to cross; the road is on the Tana River, which flows
in the valley, and is only a continuation of the fjord; after
the Glommen it is the largest river in Norway. The distance
to Karasjok is about 142 miles, from there to Kautokeino 126
miles, from Kautokeino to Karesuando 63 miles, and from the
latter place, by the route we have followed in summer, about
260 miles more—in all, from 590 to 600 miles.

Along the Varanger fjord the snow was only about three
inches in depth. Among false popular notions is one that the
farther north one goes the greater is the fall of snow. Ex-
plorers who have tried to penetrate towards the pole have
found less and less snow as they went in that direction. The
Swedish explorer, Nordenskiöld, and Dr. I. I. Hayes, whose
charming work many of us have read, state that in high latitudes the fall of one year was sixteen inches, and another year
two feet. The snowy tracts of Norway and Sweden are not
the farthest north; the great snow-belt is, as I have said, between lat. 61° and 64°.

From Nyborg to Polmak, on the Tana River, the distance is
about eighteen miles. We wended our way, after leaving the
fjord, through a wood chiefly of birch-trees, with here and there

a fine asp. There was no road, so we drove slowly. After a few miles the barking of dogs, which soon came in sight, warned us of the approach of Lapps, who shortly made their appearance, with ten loaded kerres, *en route* for Nyborg. They had been upon the mountains towards Nordkyn, and were going to join their people. The lensmand urged them to take me, promising good pay. They finally said they would stop at Polmak as they went south. The only way left for me was to pay well, for the tariff season was now over, and no reindeer were provided at any of the post-stations; and coaxing only could induce people to transport a traveller from one place to another. Farther on we came to a kâta, whose herd had also left; the inhabitants were waiting for those who were coming to carry the luggage and tent; the promise of good pay did not tempt them to undertake the trip.

Both sides of the river were lined with alluvial terraces showing the elevation of the land; here and there through the birches we could see the gammer and log-houses of the River Lapps. After a drive of a few hours we came to Polmak, situated at the junction of the river of that name with the Tana. The source of this little stream is a small lake, and the scenery about it is quite picturesque. The hostess and her daughter could hardly find words to express their admiration of the river. " You ought to come here in summer!" " How are the mosquitoes here in July?" "Very thick, very thick," was the answer; " but come after the mosquitoes are gone."

No reindeer could be procured. A gray sky warned the lensmand to leave, and, as we parted, he said, " We shall soon have the pleasure of meeting you in Nyborg again." He was mistaken; for early the next morning two of the Lapps we had met on our way, with three reindeer, were ready to convey me to Karasjok.

The Tana above Polmak forms for quite a distance the boundary between Russian Finland and Norway. The river flows through a fine hilly country clad with birch, and, higher up, with pines and fir; the dwellers on its shores are chiefly, if not altogether, River Lapps. Farms, generally two together, and sometimes small hamlets, far apart, were seen from time to time. The route was on the frozen river. We stopped at Sirma, about twenty-one miles from Polmak, where men had to go into the mountains for fresh animals—ours being exhausted—promising to return the following day. At this time of the year—the end of the season—the reindeer were very feeble, and it was the worst time to travel with them; they were shedding their coats and horns, and were lean and weak from their winter digging; they felt the heat of the sun, and seven or eight miles an hour was all they could travel in the softening snow. The place contained four or five farms; I was left at one where the wife could speak Norwegian. The accommodations were simple enough; there was a small room for strangers, having an open fireplace, with reindeer skins for a mattress on the bed, the wife's woollen dresses for a pillow, and skeepskins for blankets; but we found good coffee, reindeer meat, butter, and cow's milk. The people were comparatively rich: the farm had three buildings, and they owned three cows, an ox, several sheep, and a number of reindeer. Before my hostess was married she used to go on fishing-boats, and in that way learned to speak Norwegian. At this time of the year many of the men were on the coast engaged in the fisheries, so the man of the house was not at home.

The fresh reindeer, apparently not very well trained, appeared wild, and were harnessed with great care. Before reaching the river we had to pass through a birch wood. The young man who was to be my guide seemed distrustful even at the start; to guard against accident or a wild runaway our three kerres were tied together. I was the first seated, holding the rein of my courser. As the Laplander jumped in, and before he was fairly ready, the animal started at a furious speed, but the driver managed to hold on. The second one gained on the first, mine wanted to go faster than the other two, and the spare one, instead of keeping at the back of my sleigh, went ahead. We started, therefore, in the greatest disorder, bumping against the trees; from the rapidity of our course there was constant danger of being dashed against them. I immediately unfastened the rein around my wrist, so that if I upset I should not be dragged against a rock or tree. As we came near the banks of the river the reindeer became still wilder, and they went at a very rapid pace. Suddenly the first vehicle touched the stump of a tree, and all the dexterity of my Lapp could not prevent him from upsetting just as we reached the base of the river-bank. His leg became entangled in the rein, and his kerres ran over him. The second beast made a turn to the left, and the sleigh containing the baggage struck the first one, happily not touching the Laplander. Mine was coming double-quick against both; the spare reindeer behind rushed ahead, turning mine the wrong way, and I went broadside against one of the kerres, when, as if by magic, the animals came to a stand-still.

This took place in a great deal less time than I have taken to describe it, and was the only dangerous overturning I had experienced during the winter. My guide arose, angry at the mishap but not hurt. After this we were in no danger, as we were once more on the river, where there were no trees to be guarded against, and where, if our reindeer chose to go at railway speed, it was all the better for us.

After taking breath and adjusting the harness we jumped into our kerres. After a few miles the animals showed signs of getting tired, for the sun was warm, and the snow had become quite soft. We tarried at Utsjoki, the next important hamlet from Sirma, on the Finnish side; it has a church, situated by the river of that name at its junction with the Tana: it belongs to Russian Finland. Here we found Finn farmers, and one large dwelling-house; it was also the residence of a lensmand. The number of reindeer belonging to the district then amounted to over 40,000. In the afternoon it began to freeze, and after the snow had become crisp we started again. The track continued on the river, with short cuts overland to avoid the bends. Another accident happened here. As we were driving through a birch wood one of the kerres caught in a tree, and stopped suddenly, breaking the trace. The reindeer got loose and ran for some distance, and how to capture him was the question. My Laplander attempted to lasso him, but had to be exceedingly wary, for, as he approached, the animal quickly moved off. He stepped slyly and softly, appearing not to go specially for the beast, and finally succeeded in lassoing and re-harnessing him. A short time after, as we went down the steep bank of the river at great speed, a sudden curve threw me out of my sleigh with such violence that, notwithstanding the deep snow, I saw stars, and the granulated particles left their imprint on my forehead.

The traveller has great trouble in finding tolerably clean quarters, and even those in which he is finally obliged to stay are clean only by comparison. Many of the River Lapps are terribly dirty, but sheer exhaustion compels the traveller to stop in their abodes. In fair winter weather he knows exactly where he can stop and rest, free from such discomfort.

At midnight we came to a single house, where we found a man fast asleep, lying quite naked between two dirty black sheepskins. The filth of the place was such, and the vermin apparently so plentiful, that I could not remain. My Lapp, who was tired, did not seem to share my feelings, as he was accustomed to dirt, and wanted to stop. After a drive of about sixty miles from Sirma I reached Port, having been fifteen hours on the way, including four hours at Utsjoki and an hour of rest, on the river, for the reindeer. The principal room here was quite a sight, and another picture of filth. The dirty beds were filled with old hay: in one were three children, in another an old and young woman, and in the third were the husband, wife, and a child. None had clothes on; all were wrapped in unclean sheepskins. It was not easy to arouse the man, but at last, after a good deal of shaking, I succeeded. He put on a long woollen shirt, went through the entry into another room, and lighted a fire in a stove. I was glad to see the wooden bedstead bare. He took from a corner a clean reindeer skin; if this had ever contained vermin they had been frozen out of it. My companion offered to lie by my side, but I declined without offending him; he thought we might be warmer if we slept together.

Above Utsjoki, at a distance of perhaps seven miles, I had seen a solitary fir-tree, on the right bank of the river, in the forest of birch; I knew by that that the fir forests were not far distant. Farther on there were two groves, and others became more numerous on the left bank of the river. Farms were seen now and then along the way, till we came to the hamlet of Segelnæs, the last before reaching Karasjok. Here the house was comfortable; but the room for travellers presented a curious sight: a great number of empty beer and wine bottles were on the floor, with the remains of wax candles, tin plates, cups and saucers, knives and forks; a looking-glass and a few coarse colored pictures hung on the walls. Only an old woman and two young Lapp girls were at home; they were rather good-looking, though one was freckled, and both had dark-brown hair. This was a rich man's farm, for he owned a horse. He had gone into the forest to get the moss they had gathered during the summer for winter use. The old lady was very much delighted with a ring I gave her, and the girls with necklaces of large beads.

A short distance above Segelnæs the Karasjoki opens into the Tana. Ascending that river a few miles, we came to Karasjok, lat. 69° 35', and within a few miles of the longitude of North Cape—the distance by road from the Tana fjord or Nyborg being about 120 miles. Our arrival was announced by the furious barking of the dogs, and twice I was nearly overtaken by one more fierce than the others. The people had already retired, and not a soul was to be seen; but the smoke curling over the chimneys showed that they were not all asleep. My Lapp stopped before a large, well-built two-story log-house, the winter home of Herr F——, the merchant of the place. Nobody was at home, and there were no reindeer; Herr F——, with his daughter, had gone the day before to the Alten fjord with twenty-five of them. He generally went on the 1st of April, and returned by the 1st of December; but this year he had remained later than usual. A clerk was left in charge of the place, to whom I delivered the letter I had for his employer. The hospitality of the house was extended to me, and I became the sole occupant of the large comfortable building, enjoying the luxury of an excellent feather-bed, which, however disagreeable in summer, is very enjoyable in this climate in winter.

Karasjok is entirely a Norwegian Lapp village, with about 125 inhabitants; it derives its importance from being one of the chief centres for Nomad Lapps. It has a church with a parsonage, whose pastor remains only in the winter time, and a school that is open six months in the year; it is also the residence of a lensmand. The hamlet is composed of about twenty farms, having 20 horses, 60 cows, 12 oxen, over 150 sheep, and a large number of reindeer. From the south, horses are found as far north as Karesuando; from the north southward, as far as Karasjok—thus leaving about sixty miles of the inland country where the animal is not raised. Like man, horses seem to thrive in every climate. Here they are used to draw timber, and are fed on hay; but, for travelling, reindeer only are used. The tax from Karasjok to Bosekop was one specie dollar and one mark, or almost five kronor of the present money, for every reindeer. All the houses were built of logs. The people here live, as do the River Lapps, on the products of the dairy, by raising a few horses, fishing for salmon, and on the increase of their deer. It is the only place in Swedish or Norwegian Lapland where spirits are allowed to be sold, owing to an old patent-right owned by Herr F——. As in all small places, the arrival of a stranger created some excitement. The school-master and the under-lensmand, both of them Lapps, called upon me. I was particularly pleased with the latter, named Johnsen, for his honesty and kindness: he had received a good common-school education.

The lensmand, for whom I had a letter, was not at home; but his wife received me with true Norwegian kindness, and insisted that I should come and take my meals at her house. The plain log-house—some of the timbers forming the walls measured sixteen inches in diameter, and were from the surrounding forests—was a pattern of cleanliness, and, with that of the merchant, a shining example to the dirty population. In the parlor windows carnations and roses were in full bloom, and, as it were, looking down through the panes of glass at the snow, and in one corner of the room stood a piano. A family of tidy young children made the mistress forget her isolation.

MOUNTAIN LAPPS FROM KARASJOK.

To the Lapps the spring had come, and they were all dressed in their long woollen vadmal costumes, the women wearing no belts at home, and thus appearing as if they wore long night-gowns. The Karasjok Lapps, and those in their vicinity, are remarkable for their fine physique, and are the tallest among this strange people; the school-master was probably six feet high: the women also are tall and strongly built; they have high cheek-bones; few are fair, and most have dark hair; their eyes are generally gray or light-green, but numbers have dark eyes: blue eyes and fair hair are rare. Many of them are of mixed blood, and have the characteristics of the predominant race. The men wore square caps of bright red or blue flannel, lined with eider-down; the women put a wooden framework in their caps which make them appear odd. The summer dresses are generally blue; some wear white, with bright colored bands.

There were remarkably fine forests of fir on the banks of the Karasjok and on the Tana, some of the trees reaching eighteen to twenty inches in diameter; they grow on the alluvial terraces, gradually disappearing as the land rises, and reappearing on the other side of the slope towards Karesuando. Once cut, they do not grow again, as farther south, and hardly any young trees were to be seen; under favorable circumstances two to three hundred years are required for their full growth. The country at large is covered by glacial gravel, the bottom of the river-courses and valleys with stratified materials, in some places fine sand, in others with coarse gravel. We have before said that gold is found in these regions, but no attempt has been made to utilize the discovery. The forests here belong to the government, and special permission must be obtained to fell them, the trees to be cut being marked by the lensmand, and the people pay so much per tree. The regulations are so strict that the places for cutting are indicated, and even those to be used for fuel are marked every year. The summer is too short for the growth of cereals. The climate of Karasjok is warm in summer and exceedingly cold in winter, the thermometer falling sometimes to 45° and 48° below zero. At this time of the year, in these high latitudes, the daily variations of temperature are very great. On the 29th and 30th of April at Sirma the thermometer stood at 35° for several consecutive hours during the day; at ten P.M. it had fallen to 1° below zero—a difference of 36°. On May 2d the heat of the sun on a thermometer perfectly protected from the wind sent the mercury up to 86°, while it stood at 42° in the shade, and at night fell to 8°. These great changes were scarcely felt, as there was no wind, and the cold increased gradually and almost imperceptibly.

The sun was now so hot that travelling was impossible during the day, and had to be done at night. At five in the afternoon the snow would begin to freeze; then the reindeer could travel and the kerres would glide easily. Here at Karasjok, on the 2d of May, the twilight was not so bright as at Vardö on the 24th of April, it being farther south. The darkest part of the night was a little after eleven o'clock, but even then one could see to read. Jupiter and Venus were seen till about half-past one, but no other stars were visible.

One afternoon, just before sunset, a funeral *cortege* passed through Karasjok. A Laplander, who had come from a long distance, was leading a kerres, to which was attached a decked one—the coffin—and at some distance behind a young Lapp woman followed. These two people came from Gjusjavre, a farm about sixty-three miles distant, to bury an old man, who had died at the very ripe age of ninety-six. The next morning I followed the procession to the grave; three extra men, having cords and a saw, with the man and woman, composed the party. The winters are so severe in Lapland, and in many parts of Scandinavia, that the ground is frozen to a considerable depth, and is as hard as a rock; in the autumn, therefore, a deep common grave is dug, in which the dead are deposited until the spring, when they are removed to their respective family burial-places. As the cemetery was near by we walked slowly, talking until we came to the gate. The tops only of three wooden crosses could be seen above the snow; on one of these was written, in large coarse letters, M. I. D., which probably meant Marit, Ivor's daughter. The planks that covered the pit, to prevent the snow from filling it, had been removed, and at the bottom were seen four coffins; these were decked kerres, the extremities of which had been sawed off. They also sawed the ends off the one we had brought, lowered it down, and replaced the boards over the grave; but not before each of us had thrown a little earth on the coffin, and engaged in silent prayer.

CHAPTER XVI.

NILS PIERSEN GJUSJAVRE, who had come with the funeral
party, had agreed to take me to Kautokeino. Herr F——'s
clerk was as delighted at my getting out of my dilemma as if
he was to undertake the journey himself. "I know the man,"
said he, "and he is reliable. The price, ten dollars, is dear;
but when he reaches his farm he will be obliged to send far
to find the reindeer." I knew that I should have to pay
dearly all the way, as each would tell how much he had received; moreover, the season of the tariff had passed, and
travelling had become bad, and had to be done at night; why
should they not try to make a good bargain, so long as it
did not amount to extortion?

The distance to Bosekop is about 130 miles; and the fare,
during the post season, one dollar, and one krona for every
three reindeer. There are three *fjeldstuer* (houses of refuge),
two of which are inhabited. The distance to Kautokeino is
about the same.

The lensmand's wife would not let me go without two or
three loaves of bread she had baked specially for me; and before getting into my pulka insisted that I should take a cup
of chocolate. Nils Piersen was tall, but not full blooded;

there was something so pleasant about his face that I liked him at once. His maid, who had accompanied him, was a good specimen of the Mountain Lapp—small, wiry, and strong. The reindeer which Nils drove was a powerful and magnificent animal with superb horns, but it had been lately trained, and was still wild and unruly. The one the girl had and mine were also splendid creatures, and well broken to the harness. My luggage and the girl went in the same kerres; we had no spare animal. Nils led; his reindeer started wildly and at great speed, but would not follow the furrowed track. Two or three times he made a sudden turn back, and would then run across the river, and Nils had to get out and lead him for awhile. The wild course of the leader made our deer unruly, and as we could not proceed in that way, we decided to let the girl lead. We attached our kerres to each other, that of Nils being the last; his reindeer would not follow, but went ahead, knocking my kerres against the first one, the force of the contact often threatening to throw me over. Once or twice the legs of the deer came into my sleigh. I insisted on having the order changed, each vehicle being free. The unruly brute was harnessed to the girl's kerres, and Nils was to lead her reindeer. This way was no more successful, for the girl could not manage the creature, not being strong enough, and she was thrown over several times. Nils, who had now rested, took him in hand again, and finally his wild capers and the powerful hold of his driver tired him out, and he became manageable.

We glided swiftly over the frozen-crusted snow, our course being along a well-beaten track on the Karasjoki River; the banks were flanked with terraces, and the hills were clad with leafless birch and large fir trees. A few miles higher up the river was Assebagli, with its numerous hay-houses. Here many Lapps from the hamlet of Karasjok come in summer, on account of the fine hay which is kept for the horses. A stream, the outlet of the small lake Cejnojavre,* flowed into the river at this point. Farther up we left the Karasjoki

---

* Javre or järvi.

and ascended the Jesjoki, another of its affluents. The fir-trees had become scarcer, and looked like sentinels watching over the country and the forest of birches which they over-hung.

We stopped and allowed the animals to graze, making them fast by long cords, as we were afraid they would wander from the place in search of moss. Most of the reindeer belonging to Lapps will not eat moss that has been gathered, as they have not been trained to it. Nils and the girl were exhaust-ed, for they had hardly slept for three days. I covered my face with a mask and fell fast asleep on the snow, resting two or three hours.

No more furrows were seen, though now and then we could perceive the traces which Nils and his funeral *cortege* had made on their way to Karasjok. At times our track was near the icy banks of the river, and great care was necessary to pre-vent our sleighs from sliding and going down in the deep cracks of the ice, under which we could hear the water rush-ing. The numerous boulders in the stream and the rapids made the ice so uneven that we could not follow the river-bed. After a few miles we entered the Gjusjavre, a narrow lake of which the river is the outlet, on whose banks was the farm of Nils Piersen; it is about sixty-three miles from Karas-jok, and we had been seventeen hours on the way. The coun-try is undulating, and the scenery bleak and dismal; the snow was several feet deep, and over it appeared the leafless birches, among whose branches the wind sounded mournfully, and be-yond the frozen lake the farm looked very lonely. It was snowing when we arrived, but the few flakes that fell were fine and light, for it was 5° below zero.

There were fourteen old, weather-beaten, queer log-houses in the place, some supported by pillars several feet high, and all with earth-covered roofs. Several of them belonged to the Lapps, and were used as storehouses. Near the farm-house was the little Vuodasjoki. The dwelling-house was quite com-fortable, composed of two good-sized rooms, divided by a large hall, where firewood, shoes, fur garments, and other clothing were hung or laid at random. In one room the family and friends lived, and it presented a lively appearance all day long. A bright fire was burning in the open fireplace under a large kettle full of reindeer meat. Lapps were seated on the floor, dressed in fur and skins, some eating, others smoking. At night the guests slept anywhere on the floor.

Nils's wife was much older than himself, and apparently a half-breed between a Lapp and a Finn; he had also a tall, grown-up daughter, rather handsome; both were dressed in a loose, coarse, blue woollen garment of vadmal, described before. A woman nearly ninety years old, the widow of the man who had been buried, was living with the family.

I was under the impression, before visiting this part of the country, that the long-continuous daylight or dark short days must degenerate man; I found the contrary; the farther north I travelled in Norway or Sweden the more healthy seemed the people, the larger the families, and the greater the number of births according to the population; these reaching in Tromsö thirty-four and one-tenth, and in Finmarken thirty-six and three-tenths yearly, for every thousand inhabitants. It is not uncommon to see a family of fifteen and eighteen children by one wife, and sometimes, though rarely, twenty to twenty-four. Fish and milk are evidently good diet for the increase of the human race. I met many people living to a great age, showing them to be strong men and women.

On my arrival the mother and daughter made a general sweeping of the house, and the guest-room was thoroughly cleansed; the floor and the windows were also washed, the articles scattered about were put in their places, fresh reindeer skins from the storehouses and new hay were put on the bed, snowy white sheepskins were spread over it, and numerous nets hanging about were put in a pile in the corner. A very hot fire was kept up in the stove in order to dry the floor quickly. Four cows, ten sheep, an ox, and one calf composed the live-stock of the farm; Nils also possessed a herd of reindeer. Besides, he had a small store, and sold to the Lapps flour, coffee, sugar, salt, tobacco, and matches, and bought from them skins, shoes, and gloves. He was a wide-awake and energetic man. "There is good salmon-fishing and fine shooting here," said he; "there are plenty of ptarmigan, and I wish you would come and stay with me."

The clear water of the lake, the pretty little river Vuodas-joki, the grassy slopes, the beautiful foliage of the birches, and the long undulating hills were no doubt picturesque, but the mosquitoes would destroy all comfort in the summer. I could not drink sufficient milk or coffee, or eat reindeer meat, cheese, or butter enough to please this good-hearted, generous fellow. The Lapp visitors also had a lively time, for Nils had brought with him from Karasjok some spirits, and after a glass or two they seemed pleased with themselves and all the world.

This farm was a rendezvous for the Mountain Lapps, who liked to come and rest and smoke for a few days; they would bring their food with them, and at night sleep on the floor. Their wives and children would also come, and were sure to be welcomed at the farm. I did not wonder that Nils had a host of friends.

On the 4th of May I left Gjusjavre with Nils. The day was cloudy, the thermometer standing at 15° above zero, consequently a capital day for travelling. The dogs followed us in spite of the vociferous shouts of recall. Our course at first was on the Vuodasjoki, where the animals went very fast; then, leaving the stream, we skirted the Lappojavre, about 1200 feet above the sea-level, the ascent having been very gentle from the fjord. The snow was perforated everywhere with deep holes which the reindeer had made to get at the moss. The surface looked as if it had been roughly ploughed, the holes having been partly refilled by the wind. The heat of the sun had begun to tell on vegetation in spite of the depth of the snow, which was in that district about five or six feet, and yet the birches were in full blossom.

We had reached the top of the plateau dividing the watershed of the Alten and the Tana rivers. The Laplanders were wandering with their herds, walking on snow-shoes, the dogs keeping the reindeer together: they were moving to new pasture-grounds, where the snow had least depth, or where it had been partly blown away.

In one place we met a family on the march, some of the

women carrying their babies on their backs in the *kätkem* (cradle), and leading the luggage animal at the same time; then a family composed of an old man, three women, and several children, who had recently arrived, and had just put up their tent. Farther on I came to another encampment. The reindeer that had been drawing the luggage had been unharnessed, the children were walking around on their snow-shoes after juniper and dwarf birch for fuel, and near by was a large herd of deer, almost all of which were lying in the snow. They had come a long distance, and were evidently too tired to begin digging for moss. The dogs were crouching by the fire, apparently exhausted.

We were made welcome in the tent, and then coffee, which was clarified with dry fish-skin, and milk were immediately served, and the silver spoons were taken out of a little bag. I was astonished, as the milking-season had not yet come; The woman remarked that this was cow's milk, which her mother, living in Kautokeino, had given her the day before. "So your mother is not a Mountain Lapp," said I. "No," she replied; "but I have married a Mountain Lapp, and I have to follow the reindeer; but I often go to Kautokeino to see my people. I have a sister in America," said she. I thought I did not understand well. "Yes," said she again, "I have a sister in Chicago; her name is Ella. She married a man from Tromsö, and they have emigrated to Chicago. My mother will give you her address when you go to Kautokeino." I was much interested in the statement. While she talked she was busy washing the cups and spoons with water from snow which had been melted in an iron pot over the fire. Afterwards she took some sugar from a little chest for my especial use, cracked it with her teeth, and filled the cup to overflowing; this they always do, for they dislike to appear stingy. As I left she said, "Do not forget to go and see my sister, and tell her that we are all well, and that God is kind to us. God bless her! is often our prayer."

I saw her sister in Chicago in the winter of 1878. No one would ever think her to be a Lapp; her comely dress, her black eyes, dark hair, and high cheek-bones did not show it.

Her husband was a tailor, and they lived humbly but comfortably, and the piety of her northern home had followed her to her new one.   Several Finmarken Laplanders have migrated to America, where they call themselves Norwegians. Some have become rich ; one, especially, who lives in a brownstone house, and has a large store.   Many of the Lapps are well educated, and some are merchants and teachers in Norway ; they are very intelligent and successful in business, and are much respected by the Norwegians.

Coming to the steep hills which led to the river, Nils stopped and tied our kerres together, with two of the reindeer behind to act as a drag.   He gave me a short stick, the end of which I was to force into the snow, to steer by.   Everything being ready he jumped into his kerres, with his legs out behind, and off we started at great speed.   It would have been impossible to go directly down, for the snow was smooth and crusted, and the kerres would have run upon the legs of the reindeer ; we therefore descended in zigzag, I expecting at every sharp turn to be thrown out.

We stopped at a farm called Birki, on the left bank of the river, having travelled from Gjusjavre, nearly ninety-four English miles.   The farm was composed of four buildings. The dwelling-house was low and built of logs, with a roof heavily covered with earth.   The room was about nine or ten feet long and seven or eight wide ; a rough chimney in one corner ; a bed and a wooden chest to sit upon formed the furniture.   The annex was built of sod, and in the entry were wood, skins, and nets, while the other room was practically empty.   Another house was built entirely of turf, and consisted of three rooms ; one room contained a large quantity of moss for the cattle and reindeer, the central room was empty, and in the third were three cows, a calf, and five sheep ; a huge kettle, in which moss was softening for the cows, hung beneath a large aperture in the roof.   Two little log-houses, supported on wooden pillars, were the storehouses, and contained the flour, salt-fish, skins, clothing, and the worldly goods of the family.   The mother and daughter fished in the river, mowed the hay, collected their winter moss, went after wood, and worked as hard as any man; a faithful dog was their constant companion and protector.

It was late when we reached Kautokeino, and though it was the 7th of May the twilight was dimmer than at Vardö twelve days before. I did not recognize the Kautokeino of summer in the winter hamlet. I could not have come at a better season of the year; a week sooner or later would have been inopportune for my purpose. The beginning of May here is the moving season of the Laplanders. They were leaving their winter pasture-grounds, in the low lands by the rivers and woods, and were on their way to the higher lands and summer pastures near the fjords. It was important that they should leave before the thawing of the snow which floods the lower lands. Over sixty-five thousand reindeer are in the province of Finmarken alone.

Many reindeer passed before the hamlet. The sight of a large number moving on the vast snow-clad and trackless hills is very fine, especially when several herds are following each other. In the distance I often mistook them for black patches made by the tops of the birch-trees buried in the snow, and was undeceived only by discovering that the dark masses were moving forward. From the bluff overlooking the river, and 920 feet above the sea, I could see the Lapp girls and the men on snow-shoes urging on the herds, while the dogs brought the stragglers into the ranks, the mass gradually advancing till it appeared in the twilight like a black cloud on the horizon.

The hamlet was full of life. In summer, as we have seen, no one is at home. Every house was full of Laplanders, coming to see their friends and relatives, or to leave what they did not wish to transport, and to buy flour, coffee, sugar, ctc. They slept as usual on the floor, on skins: the houses at that time being very full, were particularly dirty, and could not be cleaned till the crowd had left. In each room half a score of people had quartered themselves with the family, where they cooked their meat and fish, the bones and refuse of which were often thrown on the floor; all were either smoking or snuffing (for they are great snuff-takers),

o 2

singing, playing cards, laughing, or talking. The welcome to their friends was hearty, because several months would elapse before they would meet again. On such visits the guests bring their own provisions. The hospitality of the host is unbounded concerning lodgings; he generally receives a large piece of reindeer meat, or a pair of gloves or shoes, when a friend goes away. During his stay the guest treats his host and family to coffee, and they return the compliment with the same beverage; when they are very good friends, the wife will bake bread for them: the principal food is reindeer meat, but bread, butter, and cheese are also used. The amount of coffee drank by the Laplanders is very great, the coffee-kettle being constantly on the fire. The great bustle in Kautokeino begins at Easter, and continues till the 10th or middle of May.

It always amused me to see the Lapp babies in their kätkem or komse. These are made of a single piece of wood, and are

LAPP CRADLE.

about two and a half feet long by fifteen or eighteen inches wide, and are slung around the mother's shoulders, who often endures fearful storms in her winter wanderings. In cold weather an extra skin is thrown over it. The infants are kept in these cradles most of the time till they begin to walk.

The Lapp babies were kept very clean, each being thoroughly washed every day. Entering one of the houses, I saw a youngster lying on a skin on the floor, crying furiously. His mother, a tall, rather handsome woman, with dark chestnut hair and deep blue eyes, was standing by his side, and making preparation for the little fellow's toilet before putting him to sleep in his cradle. The mother had before her a large wooden vase filled with warm water, in which she was dipping her hand to test its warmth, occasionally adding some that was cold. When all was ready she undressed the child, and, putting him in a long oval wooden basin or wash-tub, spread on it a cotton sheet; she then laid him in the sheet, the sturdy fellow yelling lustily all the time, when she sprinkled water over him, which acted like a charm, and he stopped crying at once; she washed him all over with her hand, and then rubbed him dry very gently. The cradle was covered at the bottom with fine, soft, well-dried lichens, over which a little cotton sheet was spread. The babe, stark naked, was laid in, the sheet turned down, with a coarse piece of vadmal and sheepskin over it; the whole was made fast by a cord laced through holes on each side of the cradle. This process did not entirely suit him, and he kept on crying till all was finished, and he was quieted by being nursed. Every day in summer the child went through the same process, which kept it free from vermin.

Late in April and early in May is the reindeers' calving season; the period of gestation is thirty-three weeks: the little ones are either carried or put into a sleigh. When the reindeer cows call for their young they utter a peculiar grunt, which is answered by the calves. Many of the animals had already dropped their horns. The large ones resembled those of stags, but they are smaller: the reindeer is clumsier than the deer, with stouter limbs, shorter head, and a larger and wider muzzle, more like that of a cow; the hoofs are broader and much larger. The hair is gray, very coarse and thick, especially in winter, and sometimes two inches in length; the color is much darker on the back, and almost white under the belly; the young are lighter-hued than the adults. The color often varies considerably among different herds, and frequently by this the ownership can be known.

The reindeer are never housed, for they like cold weather and snow. Food is never given them, and they will not touch the moss that has been gathered, unless brought up to do so.

NORWEGIAN LAPP.

They often will not even raise their heads as you approach them, and remain quiet when the Lapps pitch their tents, as we have seen. Some years prove unfavorable to their increase on account of the amount of snow, which prevents them from digging for food; the herd then becomes weak and emaciated, and many die. The spring is also a bad time for them; the snow melts during the day and a thick crust forms at night, so that their feet break through, causing lameness and disease. The horns of the males, which often weigh forty pounds, attain the full size at the age of five or six years, those of the cow at about four years. The time of dropping the horns in a herd varies from March to May; in the adult animal they attain their full size in September or at the beginning of October. After the age of eight years the branches gradually drop off. The shoulder-blades appear a little high, occasioning a slight hump or protuberance. Without the reindeer the Laplander could not exist in those northern regions: it is his horse, his beast of burden, his food, his clothing, his shoes, and his gloves.

Domestic reindeer are a curious admixture of wildness and tameness. In some respects they are greatly superior to other cattle; in a herd they are very easily managed; they usually keep close together, and in the winter season remain where they have been left to feed. When on the march, with the help of dogs, they go in a solid mass, and a herd does not scatter unless wolves are after them; but in summer they often wander a long distance when left by themselves, as is often the case. When harnessed they become uneasy and distrustful, and great caution has to be taken not to startle them. Often trained reindeer, like horses, become refractory or vicious and very difficult to manage, and then the Lapp shows his skill. In rutting time the meeting of two herds is very imposing, the bulls of each herd often advancing to charge each other.

The speed of the reindeer varies very much according to the time of the year, October, November, and December being the months in which they are fleetest, as then they are fresh from their summer pasture; the cold weather strengthens them, and they are not exhausted from digging the snow, not yet very deep, to procure their food. The rapidity of their gait depends much on the state of the surface. If this is well packed or crusted, and if previous furrows have been made, they go very fast. Much depends, too, upon the distance, and whether the country is hilly or not, with a long range of slopes. On the rivers, over well-packed snow and a good track, the animals can go twelve or fifteen miles the first hour, and down a long mountain slope twenty miles, and even more. They can travel five or six hours without stopping; the first hour rapidly, the second more slowly, and towards the fifth or sixth quite slowly, for by that time they require rest and food. Early in the winter, when they are in good condition, one can travel with a swift reindeer one hundred and fifty miles in a day, where the country is not very hilly and the way good, and easily enough one hundred miles; the colder the weather the greater is the speed: seventy or eighty miles is a good average, but they were slow at the season of which I write.

From Kautokeino to Karesuando the country I had crossed in summer was left to the eastward. Time was so precious that I did not dare to go and see old Adam Triumf, and Kristina his wife; besides, Henrik Pintha, my guide, was in a hurry, for he knew that no time should be lost. We crossed the plateau dividing the waters of the Alten from those of the Muonio, the hills being sparsely clad with birch; and again, as in the summer, we passed over that part of Finland which is wedged between Norway and Sweden. We came across hundreds of ptarmigan on the route; they were losing their white feathers and turning gray, as also were the hares.

The Lapp is naturally a hunter, and from his youth knows how to handle a gun. Often after a heavy fall of snow he pursues the wolf on his snow-shoes and overtakes it, as the animal cannot run fast through the soft mass, and it is either shot, speared, or clubbed. In the North are numerous foxes, of which there are several varieties—the red, the white, the blue, and the black; the latter becomes tipped with white, and is then commonly known as the silver fox, while the blue becomes white in winter. The bears are superb, and vary in the color of their fur, some being black, but generally of different shades of brown. Birds of prey are not uncommon— among them the celebrated hunting falcon (*Falco gyrfalco*); this bird is very rare; but the finest of all is the royal eagle (*Aquila chrysaëtos*). There are several varieties of owls, including the snow-owl (*Strix nyctea*). The Swedish statistics for the province of Norbotten alone show that during ten years the government paid a premium on 257 bears, 437 wolves, and 787 gluttons. These wild animals are quite common in Norway. There had been killed over 5000 reindeer, and a large number of cows and sheep.

Our reindeer were not in the least afraid of guns, remaining perfectly still while the birds were shot from our kerres. The air was so rarefied, and the firing of our pieces made so little noise, that I thought they had been scantily loaded, until I saw the game fired at, a good distance off, fall dead. The birds were so little frightened that they would allow us to approach to within a few yards of them. The number of ptarmigan within the arctic circle is enormous; in Kautokeino alone the Lapps often trap and carry to the coast over ten thousand. When the sun began to thaw the snow we stopped at one of the lonely farms found in these northern wastes, on the banks of a small lake called Suajärvi, and bought a few ermines that had been trapped the night before. As we descended the slopes towards the Muonio fir-trees once more made their appearance. We crossed the river, and after a journey of twenty-four hours without sleep we reached Karesuando.

On the 10th of May I left Karesuando for the south. The weather was very stormy, snow falling heavily. My pesh, or fur dress, too warm the day previous, was comfortable now. Large herds of reindeer were met on the Swedish side, and now and then Laplanders with their baggage. Like the men the women walked, some carrying babies, who were carefully protected from the cold. These were the last Laplanders I was to see on this winter trip. I had already met over 60,000 reindeer; in a short time they would be unable to draw sledges, and the luggage would have to be carried as the engraving (from a photograph) represents, and the animals led in the manner I have described in the first volume (pages 131, 132).

In the midst of the storm I reached Kuttainen. I had to stop at the farm of good Ephraim Person, who had helped me so much on the journey across the mountains from Karesuando to Norway. The reader may remember how he cared for me then—how he deprived himself of his own bear-skin for my sake, for he had an idea that I suffered in that great storm. I

had promised to make him a visit on my return, and I could
not pass the noble fellow's home without saying farewell.
The welcome was hearty, and nothing was too good for me.
The hamlet was composed of ten or twelve farms, with about
eighty head of cattle, six horses, and a large number of sheep.

REINDEER AND PACK, WITH LAPP DRIVER.

The ice cracks and breaks were already numerous, and in
many places the river was unsafe, though the snow was still
deep on the surface. The sun was warm, and melted the upper
crust, and the water filtered through. Numerous detours had
to be made to avoid the dangerous places. Ephraim's horse
often floundered in the soft mass, though at night the thermometer stood at 22°. As it now became hazardous to travel
with a horse, Ephraim and I had to part.

I stopped at Songamuodka, where fortunately the farmer
had reindeer at home. Here I had still another illustration
of the great honesty of the people. More than an hour after
I left the farm the next morning I heard loud shouts behind,
and saw a man coming towards us as fast as he could on snow-
shoes; he was in a dripping perspiration, for the surface was
in a condition to make walking very fatiguing. He brought

me my gold watch and chain, which I had left under my pillow; the honest fellow had come eight or ten miles to overtake me. I had some difficulty in making him accept a small sum of money for his trouble, and I succeeded only by showing that I paid him for his loss of time, and not because he returned what did not belong to him.

I journeyed south as far as I could, fearing every day the breaking of the ice on the river. We had for a short time stopped wearing our winter shoes, they being only good for cold dry weather, when the surface is crisp, otherwise the skin becomes wet and soft. The summer foot-covering is made of leather prepared against moisture, and is of the same shape as the others, having a band to fasten above the ankle.

On the 17th of May I crossed the Torne, and breathed freely when I reached Pajala and the high-road. There was at least four feet of snow in the surrounding forest, but it was fast disappearing at the time of my arrival; and near the hamlet the fields were already bare. During the day the mercury reached 45° and 48° in the shade, and 86° and 88° in the sun; the nights were still cold, the thermometer marking 20° above zero, but every day the weather became milder. On the 22d of May it snowed, but the flakes were large and damp. On the 23d it rained, the first rain of the year, a

LAPP SUMMER SHOES.

thick mist falling all day, with the thermometer at 42°. This day was the advent of spring, which comes on quickly.

I had about a month to spare before the first steamer of the season would come to Haparanda. I could now converse in Finnish, though not so fluently as I wished, and I accordingly wandered among the hamlets of the kind and hospitable Finlanders.   I was no longer a stranger among them, but was everywhere treated like a friend and brother, and I learned more of their ways and language in that month than I had during all my preceding journeys or visits to that part of the country.

CHAPTER XVII.

Primitive Customs.—"Evil to Him who Evil thinks."—An Arcadian People.—The Sauna or Badstuga.—The Custom of Bathing every Saturday.—My First Steam-bath.—A Remarkable Sight.—Running for the Badstuga.—Inside the Badstuga.—Terrible Heat.—Raising more Steam.—Cold Water.—Flagellating each other.—Leaving the Badstuga.—The Delightful Sensation in the Cold Air.—Rolling on the Snow.—Back to the Farm.—Visitors to my Room.—A Primitive Scene.

THE primitive customs described in this chapter exist in the most northern part of Sweden, Norway, and Finland, and are still met in some out-of-the-way places in other provinces, more especially in the region between the Gulf of Bothnia and North Cape, though formerly they were prevalent farther south, and probably all over Scandinavia. Some of them showed an innocent simplicity, which at first astonished me. What struck me most forcibly was that the people did not see the slightest immodesty in them, and there was an utter unconsciousness of any harm; which brought to my mind the English motto, *Honi soit qui mal y pense*—"Evil to him who evil thinks;" and on the principle of this motto the reader is requested to read this chapter. I am simply describing things I have seen during my travels. These customs, like many others, will disappear, and I wish to put on record what will soon be a thing of the past.

Had I been only once or twice on a visit to this country, unless staying very long each time, I should have been en tirely ignorant of many of its customs. What I here state is not from hearsay, but the result of my own personal observations, which verify the fact that the more removed people are from the great centres of civilization the more primitive they are, the more strange their habits, and the more honest and simple their ways. Wherever I went I was received with demonstrations of joy or shouts of gladness. "Welcome back,

Paulus, from among the Lapps!" were the first words that greeted me at the farms or hamlets where I had tarried several times before. My way of living among the people as if I were a native, had won their confidence and esteem. In various ways they had heard who I was, and if any fear had ever come into their minds it had been entirely banished. Only as a friend and brother can one enter the privacy of the household, and get an actual insight into their real life.

My usual experience ran thus: I express the wish to take a warm bath, and at once the preparation begins. The cow-house undergoes a complete transformation; the great iron pot, encased in solid masonry in a corner, used to cook food for the cattle, is thoroughly cleansed and filled with water; when this has become heated the fire is extinguished; everything has been thoroughly swept, and new straw is spread around for me to step upon, so I shall not soil my feet: I am just in the kettle when a stout girl of twenty summers, more or less, jumps in, dress and all, saying, "Paulus, I have come to help you." The words are hardly spoken before she begins to rub me with soap in a most forcible manner, and then to switch me with birch-twigs! The only thing to be done is to consider myself her little brother, and I submit in the meekest possible manner. I have been subjected to the same treatment, minus the switching, in Stockholm and other places, but by women old enough to be my grandmother.

One of the most characteristic institutions of the country is the *Sauna* (bath-house), called *Badstuga* in Swedish. It is a small log-house, built very tight, with no windows, having a single aperture above to let the smoke out; in the centre is an oven-like structure built of loose stones, under which a fire is kept burning till they are very hot; then the fire is extinguished, and the women clean the place thoroughly of ashes and soot, the smoke-hole having been in the mean time closed. A large vessel filled with water is placed within; a number of slender twigs, generally of young birch-trees, are put into it, to be used as switches. The bath-house stands by itself, and at some distance from the other buildings, for safety in case it should take fire. Every Saturday evening, summer

and winter, all over that northern country smoke is seen issuing from these structures. It is the invariable custom for all
the household, on that day, to take a bath, for the work of
the week is ended and the beginning of Sunday has come.
After washing, all put on clean linen and their best clothes.

The stranger, the passing inhabitant of the cities, does not
bathe with the people, for they are shy: he may have his bath,
but all alone. It was only when they had come to regard me
as one of themselves that I was allowed to accompany them;
then the neighbors, old and young, would often come to bathe
and keep company with Paulus. I remember well my first
bath *en famille*. One Saturday afternoon a couple of young
fellows, friends of mine, as the girls were giving the last
touches in cleaning the badstuga, shouted, "Paulus, take a
bath with us to-day!" "Yes, do," exclaimed the rest of the
company, among whom were the father and mother of the
large family. The weather was piercing cold, the ground
covered with snow, and I was glad that the bathing-place was
within a stone's-throw of the dwelling. From my window I
noticed several maidens wending their way with rapid steps
towards it, in a costume that reminded me of Africa, minus
the color. I did not wonder at their speed, for the thermometer stood below zero. Soon three rather elderly women took
the same route from a neighboring farm, but the two oldest
were clothed with old skirts around their waists; other young
women followed, and all were quickly lost to sight behind the
door, which they at once shut. They must be about to hold a
sort of levee in the bath, thought I. Several aged men then
made their appearance, followed in quick succession by younger ones, and children of all sizes; none had on any clothing
whatever, and they also joined the throng inside.

When I saw the field clear, I thought it was time to make
a rush for the building. I emerged from my room at a running pace, for I was dressed as scantily as those who had preceded me. I hastily pushed the door open, and was welcomed
by the voices of all the company as I closed it behind me. The
heat was so intense that I could hardly breathe, and I begged
them not to raise any more steam for awhile; the sudden

transition from twenty degrees below zero to such an atmosphere overpowered me. As my eyes became accustomed to
the darkness of the place, by the dim light which came
through the cracks of the door I began to recognize the faces
of my friends. There were more people than usual, for all the
neighbors had come to have a bath with Paulus. At first I
seated myself on one of the lower benches built around, after
awhile getting on the other above. More water was poured
on the hot stones, and such a volume of steam arose that I
could not endure it, so I jumped down again, and reclined in
a half seated posture in order to breathe more freely. In a
short time I was in a most profuse perspiration; again and
again steam was raised by pouring water on the stones, till at
last the hot air and steam became extremely oppressive.

Now and then we poured water on each other, which caused
a delightful sensation of relief; then with boughs every one's
back and loins were switched till they smarted severely. "Let
me give you a switching, Paulus," a fair-haired damsel or a
young fellow would say; "and after you get yours I want you
to give me one." This operation is beneficial, as it quickens
the circulation of the blood in the skin. In about half an hour
the people began to depart, first submitting to a final flagel-
lation, after which cold water was poured upon the body; then
all went home as naked as they came. As I emerged from
the hut the sensation was delightful, the breathing of the cold
air imparting fresh vigor and exhilarating my spirits; I rolled
myself in the snow, as did some others, and afterwards ran as
fast as I could to the farm-house. In some places the men
and women, as if by agreement, do not return together, and
the old women wear something around their loins as they go
to or come from the bath. I have gone out of the bath-house
with the mercury at thirty-two degrees below zero. It is not
dangerous to walk a short distance, as long as the perspiration
is not suddenly and entirely checked.

On returning one does not dress at once, for he must get
cool gradually and check the dripping perspiration. I had
hardly been fifteen minutes in my room, when suddenly the
door opened (the people here, as is the case in most parts

of Sweden, never knock at the door) and the wife, who had dressed herself, came in, and was not in the least abashed at my appearance; she talked with me as if I were in my morning-gown. The door opened again, and a grown daughter entered, and then another. I began to fear that all the neighbors were coming, as if to a reception. Though they did not seem in the least troubled, I was; I seated myself on a chair, however, and for a short time we carried on a rambling conversation; they then left, and I dressed myself and went into the stuga, or family room. At first I could hardly keep my countenance, for the sight was extremely ludicrous. There was a crowd of visitors, neighbors of different ages, and among them three old fellows—a grandfather, father, and an uncle—who were sitting upon one of the benches with legs crossed, minus a particle of clothing, shaving themselves without a looking-glass. Nobody seemed to mind them, for the women were knitting, weaving, and chatting. This was certainly a scene primitive enough. When the men had finished shaving clean shirts were brought, and they then dressed themselves while seated. The men usually shave once a week, oftener when courting, and always after the bath, for the beard then becomes soft.

These people are the only peasantry in Europe who take a bath every week, and they are very healthy. I never failed to bathe every Saturday. The custom described has come down from olden times; the Norsemen called Saturday *Laugadag* (washing-day), later *Lögadag*, and at present *Lördag*, but it is now chiefly observed in the regions of Scandinavia which we had crossed during the winter. Such habits can prevail only in a neighborhood remote from cities, where simplicity of manner has not been tampered with or modified by what are called higher types of civilization, and where a dissolute life is entirely unknown. From childhood the people have gone to the bath together, and their children are brought up in the same way; innocent of guile, they no more imagine harm in what they do while at the bath than if they sat down together at dinner in the customary way; still more, the statistics show no more moral a people in Europe   After the bath the women wear high-necked dresses, and are very particular in their deportment; no debased woman would be tolerated in any hamlet in that part of the country.

The custom of promiscuous bathing is a very ancient one in Europe, and prevailed extensively among our forefathers. Cæsar, in his Commentaries, speaks of the Germans of his time as follows: "Those who remain chaste the longest bear the highest reputation among them; this they consider insures stature to some, to others manliness and strength. * * * They all bathe promiscuously in rivers, without distinction of sex, and wear skins or slight coverings of deer hides, a large part of the body being nude;"* and Tacitus, Pomponius, and other Latin writers add their testimony to the chastity and purity of the people.

Here, as in many districts of Norway and Sweden, the family, including even the men-servants, sleep in the same room; the women wear garments with long sleeves, and rest with their skirts on, while the men remain partly dressed. A man-servant would feel himself greatly insulted, and believe the people of the farm thought him an unworthy person, if a special room were set apart for him, and no one would be willing to serve such a master. Servants, especially the girls, expect to be treated as members of the family. No farmer in those regions would venture to break through this long-established custom of equal rights, for it would raise a great outcry against him, and he would appear proud and haughty in the eyes of his neighbors. I asked the wife why she had not a special room for her working-man. He answered me himself: "Do you think I would remain in a family where I was treated like a dog, and sent to sleep in a room all alone, as if I were a villain? No, indeed; I will sleep only where the family does."

We must not be too hasty in condemning what we have

---

* "Qui diutissime impuberes permanserunt, maximam inter suos ferunt laudem: hoc ali staturam, ali hoc vires nervosque confirmari, putant. Intra annum vero vicesimum fœminæ notitiam habuisse, in turpissimis habent rebus: cujus rei nulla est occultatio, quod et promiscue in fluminibus perluuntur, et pellibus aut parvis rhenonum tegimentis utuntur, magna corporis parte nuda."

outgrown, or never known. Every day we witness customs which are not according to our ideas of propriety. We at times see a mother nursing her babe in public, but that certainly does not make her a woman deserving of reproach. In considering the subject we should bear in mind that if much has been gained by our advancing civilization, our ancestors were free from many of the vices which are the outgrowth of some civilized habits.

CHAPTER XVIII.

The Advent of Spring within the Polar Circle.—Rapid Transition.—Farmer's busy.
—Whit-Sunday.—Emotional Religion in Church.—At Sattajärvi once more.—
Whit-Monday.—A Warm Welcome.—Leave Sattajärvi.—Touching Parting.—
The Farm of Varra Perrai.—Welcome Back everywhere.—A Fine Singer.—End
of the Winter Journey.—Arrival at Haparanda.

THE spring was coming now with rapid strides, although
earlier than usual. On the 29th of May the highest temperature was 63° in the shade and 104° in the sun; on the 30th,
66° in the shade and 105° in the sun, with about the same
temperature on the 31st; and the last three nights had been
without white frost, which the people said was over. The
grass in sheltered spots by the rocks was green; swallows
made their appearance, and cuckoos were heard in the woods.
These were the forerunners of summer, and the people hailed
their appearance with joy. The birches were yet leafless, but
the buds were ready to burst forth, and the pines and firs
had already started with new life. People were busy everywhere, ploughing and manuring the fields. At the farm of
Varra Perrai, about nine miles south of Pajala, I saw on the
29th of May the men ploughing, and a mother, two daughters,
and myself sowed barley. The Varra Perrai farm was said
to be more forward than those around Haparanda. The last
week in May had been a hard one for the farmers. When
Saturday came all were well-nigh exhausted, and the day of
rest was waited for as the day of relief.

May 31st was *Pingst* (Whit-Sunday). I went to church at
Pajala, and witnessed there a striking scene of emotional religion. As the pastor was preaching a woman became greatly
excited; she wept, shouted, and fell into a sort of hysterical
fit; she thought her sins would never be forgiven, and that

she was doomed to everlasting punishment. Those near her tried to pacify and comfort her, but she only laid her head upon their shoulders and wept bitterly. During this time the clergyman was not in the least disturbed, but continued his sermon, in which there was nothing at all emotional or sensational. Even here persons sometimes become insane from religious excitement.

After the service I wended my way southward to the hamlet of Sattajärvi, where I was received with expressions of great joy. The natives of this place and myself had formed a mutual liking for each other from the first, and there is no village in the far North which has left more pleasant impressions of primitive simplicity and truthfulness on my mind than this one. These were the people who, in 1871, wanted Kristina to go to America with me, and who, this last winter, had brought Elsa Karolina to me as my interpreter and guide over the mountains to Norway. Father, mother, sons, and daughters were all very glad to see me again, and often would say, "Paulus, you are no more a stranger among us, and we think of you as one of ourselves." "Come dine with us to-day, Paulus," one would say, "for we have very nice fish, which we have just caught." (Enormous pike are found in those small lakes; they sometimes attain the size of four feet; there was a case in Kajana Lake where a man was bitten by one while swimming.) "Come and dine with us to-morrow," another exclaimed; and as I passed by, "Come in, Paulus, I have cooked a cup of coffee for you," would call some kind poor mother who could not afford more. Still others would bake fresh bread and make waffles, and the milk that had the thickest cream was sure to be for Paulus.

Monday was also kept as a holiday; no one was in the fields, and, as in many other hamlets, the young people enjoyed such innocent pastimes as blind-man's-buff, tag, singing in chorus, leaping, and a little flirting. I joined in the amusements, and was glad to find that none of the young farmers could leap as far as I did.

On the 4th of June there was quite a commotion in the place, for I was to leave that morning. They had come from far and near to say good-bye, and many were to accompany me along the road for some distance; this was, indeed, a great compliment, for at that time of the year every hour was precious and could hardly be spared. When the horse and cart were ready, I was greatly touched by their demonstrative friendship—the warm clasping of hands, and the tears flowing down the cheeks of several mothers. They were really sorry I was leaving, and I felt sorry also. As we started the people shouted, " Farewell, Paulus! farewell, Paulus!" "Happy journey to America!" "God be with you, Paulus!" "Come again to Sattajärvi—come again!" As I passed the farm of Varra Perrai, the farmer Johan and his wife Brita Kajsa, with Eva Mathilda, their daughter-in-law, and the two daughters, Brita Kajsa and Sophia Helena, were watching for me. " Come in, Paulus, come in!" they cried; " you cannot pass Varra Perrai without eating," and I had to tarry awhile; and so it went all the way. Wherever I was known I was requested to stop, either to take a meal or drink a cup of coffee, and was entreated to remain for the night, so that the journey of a couple of days took two weeks. Silver rings, buttons, scarf-pins, brooches, photographs, were given to me as mementos and keepsakes; and these, however humble they were, I have kept as souvenirs of this simple people.

Remains of heavy drifts were common on the hilly country between Kunsijärvi and Ruokojärvi. At Ruskola I was warmly welcomed by Grape and his wife. Farther on I spent a Sunday; in the afternoon we all met at one of the farms, and a young girl, eighteen years of age, delighted us with her sweet voice; she sang song after song, and I thought it was the sweetest and most pleasing uncultivated voice I had ever heard, which is saying a great deal for one who has travelled in Sweden.

The journey was drawing to a close. The last few days impressed me with the sudden change of the season; the heavy mass of snow disappeared very quickly, especially on the protected fields. Vegetation seemed to grow visibly; three days ago there were no leaves on the birches, now their buds had opened, the meadows were green almost all over, nature smiled everywhere, and one could hardly credit the sudden transformation. The spring burst into summer at once; and the birds heralded joyously the advent of the short and beautiful season of that northern land. The cattle were let loose in the woods by the roads, to feed on the dry old grass of the preceding year; insect life appeared, and I even heard the hissing sound of the snok (*Coluber lævis*) — a snake two or three feet long, of a grayish color, which I had never met but in summer—as it crawled from under the stones which still protected a little patch of snow.

On the 16th of June I was once more in Haparanda. My winter journey was ended. Only a few snow-drifts, protected by the rocks, were here to be seen; on many of the fields the barley had now germinated, and the birches, with their young leaves, presented a charming sight. We were but a few days in advance of the season I had spent here in 1871, when on my way north.

We have wandered together, dear reader, in summer and in winter in these high latitudes, and I have gained my object if I have been able to give you a correct idea of "The Land of the Midnight Sun."

CHAPTER XIX.

Dalecarlia.—Remarkable Characteristics of the Dalecarlians.—Independence of the People.—Their Beautiful Traits.—Their Simple Life.—Children Tolls.—Falun. —The Copper-mines.—Reception by the Governor.—A General Letter of Introduction to the People.—From Falun to Leksand.—Thrifty Small Farms.—The Crowded Inn at Leksand.—A Friend in Need.—A Cordial Reception at Bröms.— Superb Specimens of Manhood.—Costume of Leksand.

THERE is a beautiful province in Central Sweden, lying north of the great lakes, called Dalecarlia,* with nearly two hundred thousand inhabitants. The people are peculiar and primitive, adhering with great tenacity to their old customs and national costume, and are the handsomest of the peninsular population of Scandinavia. I know of no peasantry or people in Europe who present a prouder bearing or possess a more independent spirit. They are manly, honest, and kind-hearted; proud of their ancient history, and of the warlike deeds of their forefathers, who, under the lead of Engelbrekt the Stures, and later led by a Wasa, expelled the invaders under whose yoke Sweden groaned. They are fond of equality, addressing every one, even their king, by the prefix *du* (thou). Their representatives in the Diet come to Stockholm dressed in the costume of their parish, and go in like manner to the receptions of the court. Entailed estates are unheard of among them; the *torpare* of the south of Sweden and the *husmand* of Norway are not known. Perfect social equality has always prevailed. Every parish has its church, and each has a costume which distinguishes its people from all others; one of their peculiarities that struck me was that the people of one parish very seldom marry with those of another. They are imbued with a deep religious feeling, and from their earli-

---

* Called by the Swedes *Dalarne.*

est childhood are taught to do right because it is right, and to hate wrong because it is wrong; and as, in their poor country, there are no great temptations to pursue wealth, they follow the even tenor of a simple and virtuous life. Though shy of strangers, their confidence won, they are kind and warm-hearted. To gain their affections one must put aside all pride and presumption, and, in a word, be like one of them. Quick to appreciate a kindness, they are grateful for even the smallest token of friendship. When admitted to their intimacy and regard, a stranger is heartily welcomed to their homes; he has hardly entered before the wife or the daughter is busy arranging on the table a simple meal of the best they have, of which he is earnestly requested to partake, and entreated to eat more. I was constantly hearing such expressions as, "Paul, you must eat more; you must drink more; you must not be bashful." The best room and bed were invariably for me. They are not rich, for the farms are small and poor in most districts, and the families are large; but they are very thrifty and happy in their simple life, and merry when the hours of work are over. Often on a summer evening one hears in the distance the sound of music (an accordeon or a violin), for the young men are on their way from farm to farm to serenade the maidens. On Sunday morning crowds are seen driving or walking to the large parish churches; in the afternoon visits are made; and in the evening the young folks often indulge in innocent plays or in a dance.

One should visit the country between the middle of May and midsummer, for after that the hamlets and farms are deserted, and especially should one spend Sunday there. To the tourist the four most interesting parishes are Leksand, Rättvik, Mora, and Orsa, for in these the people have preserved a more Arcadian simplicity; I know of no other province in Scandinavia that has left on me a more delightful impression. The landscape in Dalecarlia is soft and sylvan; many of the hills are clad with woods, and streams and lakes abound; there are also large tracts of swamp-land covered with forests. As you drive through the charming and diversified district, and luxuriant fields dotted by farm-houses, you are suddenly arrested

by a gate built across the road to prevent the cattle from stray-
ing, and to protect the distant fields and meadows; as you approach, the children, who have been on the watch, are seen
coming to open the gate, and as you pass they range themselves in a line, trying to look unconcerned, but really greatly
excited. Their looks seem to say, "We have been here all
day long, and you have not been obliged to get out and open
the gate yourself." On giving them a few öre as a reward, an
amicable scramble occurs for their possession; but there is no
quarrelling, and an honest division takes place.

Three days before midsummer I found myself in the clean
little city of Falun, with a population of about six thousand;
it is the chief town of Dalecarlia, celebrated for its copper
mines, which have given the län the name of Stora Koppar-
berg (big copper hills). These mines are among the oldest in
Europe, and are known to have been worked for more than six
hundred years. In a document of King Magnus Smek, seen
in the Museum at Stockholm, dated 1347—which begins, "Magnus, King of Norway, Sweden, and Skåne"—these mines are
mentioned as very ancient, and certain privileges are granted
to the miners. In old times the master miners considered
themselves equal to the highest of the land, and were called
bergsadel (mining nobles); many of their properties were exempt from taxes, except in men or horses for the king's army.
At that period the miners came out early on Saturday, bathed
themselves, and on Sunday followed their bergsmän to the
church. It is said that at weddings or feasts each wealthy
noble came with his retinue of miners. Some of the mine-
masters were very rich, and their horses are said to have been
shod with silver.

The city of Falun is comparatively modern, and was founded by Queen Kristina in 1641. Charles XI. took great interest
in the well-being of the miners, and in their spiritual welfare.
He composed a prayer expressly for the mining population.
After his death, Charles XII. sent a number of texts, chosen
by his father, as the subjects most fit to be preached to them,
viz.: Gen. iii. 17–19; Deut. viii. 7–9; Deut. xxxiii. 19; Gen.
xlix. 25; Deut. xxxiii. 25; Job xxii. 23, 24, 25, 26, 27, 28;

Job xxviii. 1, 2, 3, 9, 10 ; Psa. xxiii. 4 ; Psa. lxvii. 6, 7, 8 ; Psa. xc. 17 ; Psa. xci. 11, 12 ; Psa. cvii. 21, 22.

A museum connected with the mines is well filled ; and the mines themselves are well worth visiting, as the most improved machinery is used. The fumes from the smelting-house destroyed for a considerable distance all kinds of vegetation ; but the same influence, as a compensation, has hitherto preserved this region from the cholera and other pestilences.

I tarried awhile in the city, in order to present my letter of introduction to Herr De Maré, the Governor of the province, who received me with the unpretending but none the less earnest Swedish manner, and expressed much pleasure at meeting me before his departure, on a vacation, for the southern part of the country. Like myself, the Governor was of French descent ; he was also of Huguenot extraction. His accomplished consort, like himself, spoke English and French. "When do you intend to start?" inquired he. "Immediately after my visit to you," said I. "We cannot let you go without taking a quiet Sunday dinner with us to-morrow," he said, adding, "it will give me time to write some letters of introduction for you ; and then we can talk quietly together, and I may perhaps give you some good advice." I gladly accepted the kind offer, saying that I should feel obliged if the letters were addressed chiefly to the Dalecarlian bönder, for I wanted very much to become acquainted with them. The next day I spent some delightful hours at his residence. Three friends had been invited to meet me, and I found, as I always did in Swedish gentlemen's homes, that affable simplicity of manner which refinement and good-breeding only can give, and which makes the stranger feel at ease at once. When I left, the Governor handed me five letters, explaining for whom they were ; and, besides, gave me a general letter of introduction to every one in the province :

As the bearer hereof, Mr. Du Chaillu, from New York, world-renowned both for his travels of exploration (undertaken especially into the interior of Africa), and as an author, has the intention of going through Dalecarlia and spending some time there, in order to acquire a knowledge of its nature, country, and people, it is therefore my friendly request to every one of its inhabitants, whom Mr. Du Chaillu

may solicit, to extend to him all the assistance and all the information he may require for the attainment of the object of his visit, and to make his sojourn in Dalecarlia an agreeable one to him.

De Maré,
Governor of Stora Kopparbergs Län.

Falun, *June* 22d.

The high-road to Leksand, just after leaving Falun, presents
for some distance a very barren aspect, because of the masses
of mineral refuse piled there for centuries, and the absence
of vegetation due to the fumes of sulphur; but after awhile
the landscape becomes cheerful, and all the more beautiful
from the sudden contrast.   The farms are numerous, their
buildings painted red with white borders; the houses are not
large, but look tidy and thrifty, being often surrounded by orchards of apple-trees, and little plantations of hops; luxuriant
fields of wheat, rye, barley, oats, potatoes, flax, and hemp, and
wooded hills gladdened the eye.   Many vehicles of all sorts
and carts loaded with goods were passing along the dusty road.
Hours had to be spent at the post-station by those who had
not ordered in advance a förbud, and even by some who had:
it was amusing to watch those who upon their arrival expected
to get a horse or two at once, and who with smiling faces
made the request: the sudden change of countenance when
told that they would have to wait six or eight hours, or perhaps till the following morning, seemed not to indicate satisfaction.

The perfume of that beautiful little flower, the *Linnœa borealis*, at this time filled the atmosphere; wild raspberries and
brambles lined the roads, and the yellow anemone and other
wild-flowers enlivened the landscape.   After driving through
a charming country for about thirty-five miles I crossed the
Österviken on a floating bridge, and alighted before the comfortable inn at Leksand.   The place was crowded by Swedish
tourists who had come to see the midsummer festival, and I
could obtain only a small room with two other travellers.
Knowing the dread Swedish people have of open windows and
draughts for ventilation, and being certain, as the weather was
very warm, that no fresh air would be allowed to enter at
night, I concluded that, as the choice of evils, I would rather

sleep under a tree, wrapped in a blanket, or in a hay-barn. I declined, therefore, the accommodations at the inn, and the landlord expressed himself as being very sorry not to be able to provide for me.

In my dilemma I suddenly remembered that one of my letters of introduction was to a farmer by the name of *Bröms* Olof Larson, who, I had been told, lived not far from the church. In Dalarne, as in Norway, every farm has a name, but here it is put before the name of the person. His house was near the bridge I had crossed; so, leaving my luggage at the inn, I inquired the way there. When I reached the place, I was shown up-stairs, and found myself in the midst of a gathering of Leksand farmers, who impressed me at once by their noble bearing; they seemed astonished at my sudden arrival, as they knew me at once to be a foreigner. "Is Bröms Olof Larson here?" I inquired. A handsome man came towards me, and said, "Here I am." I gave him the letter of the Governor, after reading which he shook hands cordially, and bade me welcome to Bröms, the name of his farm. "Welcome to Dalarne," they all said, after I had been presented to each. Swedish punch and wine were served, and in the course of conversation I mentioned that I could not get a room at the inn. "You shall have one here," said Bröms Olof. "Where is your baggage?" "At the gästifvaregård." "Wait a little," said he; "we will go with you; we have some business to transact relating to the affairs of our parish."

Such was my first acquaintance with Dalecarlia. I could not help admiring the men who surrounded me, as I was introduced to one after the other, for some of the handsomest specimens of Dalecarlian manhood were here represented. "I have a letter for the *riksdagsman* of the present Diet, Liss Olof Larson." "There he is," said my host, pointing to a man six feet three inches in height, and stout in proportion, with beautiful and expressive eyes, and honest face. Near him stood his father, who had formerly been riksdagsman, still taller—within a fraction of six feet four inches. Bröms Olof himself was of medium height, with regular features, bright eyes, and exceedingly intelligent expression of countenance.

Soon afterwards Bröms Olof, the riksdagsman, and I were on our way to the inn for my luggage; both insisted on carrying it themselves, and no others, not even myself, were allowed to touch it.

MORA WINTER COSTUME.

The holiday costume of the men of Leksand is sombre: they wear long dark-blue or black coats, falling below the knee, knee-breeches of the natural color of the hides, a waistcoat of the same material, or sometimes of cloth, thick white woollen stockings, shoes—many now wear the modern laced boots—and a woollen scarf around the neck; they part their hair in the middle, and wear round felt hats; as they leave the church on a Sunday in this costume they look very demure. On week-days they wear a long yellow leather apron, which hangs from the neck.

The Leksand woman's skirt, of a thick blue-black wool, nearly reaches the ankles, allowing the shoes and white stockings to be seen; the body of the dress is made either of leather, red wool, or silk, disclosing the white sleeves of the chemise; the apron is of a bright color, with longitudinal or transverse bands. The head-dress is ungraceful, as the cap fits closely to the head and hides all the hair in front and back; it is of a bright color, with a white border; on Sundays or festive days those of married women are of white linen. The children, both boys and girls, are most picturesquely dressed in canary-colored clothes, with little caps, from under which the hair hangs on the back. In winter the Dalecarlians of both sexes, of the four parishes I have mentioned, wear sheepskin coats with the wool inside.

I was not long in making friends in Leksand. The news spread that an American had come with letters from the Governor to Bröms Olof and the riksdagsman, and that he had been welcomed at the parsonage, and had dined there. Those who had relatives in America wished me to come and see them, and consequently it was natural that I should easily win the regard of these kindly people, and gain a hearty welcome during my different visits in their country; and if the many hundred letters I have received in America—some of them breathing most intense friendship, as the reader will see hereafter—are any proof of love and regard, I can truly say that I entirely succeeded in gaining their affections.

CHAPTER XX.

MIDSUMMER (24th of June) is, after Christmas, Sweden's most merry festival; the longest days have come, and the whole population seem to be bent on celebrating the advent of summer. At the seaports vessels are dressed with boughs of birch; in the towns the horses, driving-wagons, omnibuses, and other vehicles are clad with branches of trees; but it is in the country that the festival is most popular, and there the people flock in great numbers towards the *Majstång* (Maypole), which is raised in every hamlet and village. On midsummer-eve the maidens and lads adorn it with evergreens and garlands of flowers, and in some districts with colored eggshells, gilded hearts, and festoons of light paper.

On this occasion the traveller in the country sees everywhere signs of gladness; on the porches of the farm-houses, around the windows, at the gates leading to the lanes, green boughs and festoons are conspicuously displayed. He hears music in every direction, and sees crowds of merry dancers around the May-poles. There are no parts of Scandinavia where the midsummer-day is more interesting than on the shores of Lake Siljan, in the parishes of Leksand, Rättvik,

Mora, and Orsa, on account of the great number of people who crowd the large churches, and the stranger should not fail to be at one of these places for this festival.

All over Dalecarlia, on midsummer-eve, the *dalkulla* (young woman) comes with flowers, and the *dalkarl* (young man) with evergreens, to adorn the May-poles, amidst joyous shouts and merry-making. The fervid religious nature of the Scandinavian rural population leads them to celebrate all festivals by first going to church.

Early morning found me in a fir grove on a bluff overlooking Lake Siljan; the Leksand church, though near, being hidden from view. The weather was delightful, the water of the lake without a ripple, and like a sheet of glass. At five o'clock I was watching the boats from the hamlets rowing along the shore on their way to the church. Many were so distant that they appeared at first like black spots, which gradually became larger as they came nearer, and the number increased rapidly; then the moving of oars could be seen, and the shapes of the boats distinguished: the red bodices of the women's dresses shone brightly as their wearers also assisted in the pulling. As they came to the shore I saw that the boats were thirty-five to forty-five feet in length, and crowded, some containing as many as seventy persons. Now and then from a boat came a whole family, from grandfather to great-grandchildren, and babies in arms: all looked as demure as Quakers as they wended their way towards the church, whither I followed the crowd. By land, also, vehicle after vehicle discharged its load of people, the horses being hitched around the church. Many were seen coming on foot; every girl carried in one hand a little bouquet of wild-flowers, while in the other was her prayer-book, carefully wrapped in a handkerchief which she had herself embroidered; this handkerchief is thick, and frequently partakes somewhat of the character of a small table-cloth. From her apron hung a pouch, also adorned with embroidery, containing a lunch of bread, butter, cheese, and a few young onions, of which the people are very fond. The leather strings of the apron are sometimes worked with colored wools, ending in leather tassels or pieces of gaudy silk.

The church-yard was crowded with men and women, each sex by itself, waiting for the service to begin—some wandering among the tombs to place flowers on the grave of a relative or friend. On the shady side of the church, near one of the entrances, some people were busy reading their prayer-books while the children were playing. The scene was strikingly like that of the painting by Exner, of which I give a copy, and no sketch could be more truthful. The women who were to participate in the communion were especially solemn; they wore a peculiar broad white cap, somewhat similar in shape to those worn in Hardanger as a sign of mourning, to indicate that they were sorry for their sins. The young maidens are so particular at this time that their lovers for a week beforehand do not venture to visit them, and even a few days must elapse after the ceremony before they are allowed to continue their courtship.

The parish church at Leksand is in the shape of a Greek cross, and is an imposing structure; it is situated on the south-eastern side of Lake Siljan, near its outlet, where its white walls, embowered in shady trees, glisten in the rays of the sun. About five thousand persons were in the sacred edifice, which can seat nearly four thousand people, the women and the men apart. I was in the gallery facing the altar, in the pew of the old riksdagsman, who now and then showed me where I could follow the service in my book. The sight was very impressive; during the singing the whole congregation accompanied the organ with a fervor which could not be surpassed; and the colors of the dress of the women, with the sober costume of the men, made a scene picturesque in the extreme. The sermon was listened to with attention; even the shrill cries of several babies—of whom there were, perhaps, two hundred in the church—did not seem in the least to disturb the worthy pastor or his congregation, who evidently were accustomed to that accompaniment of the service. Mothers would often get up and go to the room which was built especially for their use, and which is entered from the church, to minister to the wants of the little creatures.

On account of the great extent of the parish, and the large

OUTSIDE THE CHURCH AT LEKSAND. FROM A PAINTING BY EXNER.

number of parishioners, the communion is administered every Sunday. A great many advance to the altar—an equal number of men and women—each sex taking half of the space at the railing, and after partaking of the bread and wine retiring, with bowed heads, to their seats. During the ceremony the whole congregation participates in chanting the old tunes used at the time of the Reformation. On some occasions only a very few people were seen at the communion-table, for those who partook of the sacrament could not engage in the festivities of the day. At the conclusion of the service the vast congregation retired, slowly and quietly, in a most demure and sober manner. Beyond the church-yard groups were formed, greeting each other, and many protected themselves from the sun beneath the shade of a very fine avenue of birch-trees. Others went to pay their respects to the pastor, who, with his wife, welcomed all with a pleasant smile, inquired about their families, congratulated some on their good fortune, or had a word of sympathy for those who were sorrowful, while two or three of the leading farmers were invited to remain for dinner. The parsonage was a fine building, surrounded by extensive grounds, and having an excellent view of the river. The living was considered one of the best in Sweden. As the parish is large, the pastor has two or three assistants to aid him in his duties.

The people of Leksand are among the most thrifty and prosperous in Dalecarlia ; their soil is pretty good, and the farmers are quite energetic ; some of the more far-seeing had succeeded in buying in various parishes (from their more simple brethren) large wooded tracts at comparatively small prices : this species of property had risen so much at one time that some had thereby become wealthy, much to the chagrin of those who disposed of their land and trees at a time when prices were lower. The farms are models of tidiness ; the houses are painted a bright red, with white borders around the windows, and porches have tiled or shingled roofs ; nearly all houses have a kitchen-garden, with gooseberries and currants, and often an apple-orchard. The people are exceedingly fond of onions, and every one cultivates a bed or two of these.

Q 2

Before going farther, let us wander awhile among the people of Leksand. On the other side of Södra Noret is the hamlet of Åkerö, and among its farms are Knubb, Lång, and Ersters. Knubb may be considered a typical farm of the parish. The buildings form a square, entered through a porch, on one side of which is a dwelling-house, with two rooms exclusively for guests; opposite is the hay-barn, used for threshing grain, etc.; here also is a porch.

The dwelling-house proper is entered by a small hall, from which a door near the front opens into the daughter's room. On the sides of the hall are two doors, leading into large rooms which form the rest of the house; that on the left is the *dagligstuga* (or family-room), in which is a large loom for weaving linen or wool and two or three spinning-wheels; in one corner is the open fireplace where the cooking is done; also a table of plain boards, with a few benches and chairs. In the chamber on the right, where the clothing of the family is kept, are some chests and a looking-glass; and on one wall, written on a piece of paper, "The congratulation of Erik to his wife," commemorative of one of her birthdays. On poles hang numerous woven skirts belonging to the wife, many of them new, with bodies of the dresses in bright colors or skin, and some belonging to the daughters, with stockings, under-garments, white bodices, aprons, and bright embroidered handkerchiefs in which to carry prayer-books to church. The girls had taken several years to weave these, and felt great pride in their wardrobes, the products of their own industry, which are always ready when they are about to be married, that they may have a trousseau worthy of their station and the wealth of the family. Several rolls of broadcloth, to be made into garments, the Sunday clothes of the husband and boys, and others for the daily use of the children, are distributed in an orderly manner; and winter garments of sheepskin, as soft as chamois, some trimmed with fur, have their appropriate places.

On the other side, opposite the porch, is a house, the lower floor of which is used as a store or larder; the upper part, reached by steep, ladder-like stairs, is the weaving-room in winter, and in summer serves for a bedroom, the beds being generally built one above another, like the berths on ships. Another building, which is used as stable and cow-house, completes the square.

Knubb Erik Andersson, the father, is a true type of the Dalecarlian; his wife is Anna Mattsdotter; the eldest daughter, called after her mother, Anna Ersdotter, is a bright, blue-eyed, good-hearted girl; Margareta and Karin and Maria, and the youngest of all, a fine lad, Anders Ersson, constitute the family.

At this time of the year the people were out in the woods getting hay, but many returned on Saturday evening to spend Sunday on the farm, to go to church, and to meet friends who, like themselves, came for the day.

Not far from Knubb dwelt Ersters Erik Mattsson and his wife, Karin Mattsdotter—a fine specimen of an old couple. Their daughter Karin had a husband in America, and two small children at home : Daniel was a cunning boy, dressed in canary-colored clothes; little Anna was a perfect beauty; no peach ever rivalled the color of her rosy cheeks, and she was as loving and confiding with me as if I were her papa; Kerstin, the other daughter, was a strong, rather masculine girl, but with as good a heart as one could wish to find.

A week after midsummer I was on my way to the fair which was to take place at Mora. I found myself, with several friends whom I had invited to go with me and be my guests, on board the small steamer which plies between Leksand and Mora, which is situated some thirty miles distant, on the extreme northern part of the Siljan Lake, a beautiful sheet of water, flanked with gently sloping hills, dotted here and there with hamlets and farms; four parish churches are found on its shores — Leksand, Rättvik, Sollerö, and Mora. The fair begins on the first of July, lasting three days.

The steamer was crowded with Dalecarlians of both sexes, and the deck was so encumbered with goods that it was with difficulty that one could move from one part to another. Among the passengers were a number of merchants who were going to the fair with their goods, and several Swedish tourists bound for the same place. Besides others with whom I became acquainted was a young lady from Stockholm, full of *naïveté*, who told me that she had been watching my doings with my peasant friends; then said, abruptly, " Herr Du Chaillu, I like you." I made a bow, and asked how I had created such a good impression upon her. She replied, " It is because you are so eccentric ;" and for this I made another bow.

Twice we passed vast numbers of logs, enclosed in floating triangular frames of beams, being towed by a steamer to the outlet of the lake ; we saw others at anchor, waiting for a tug. Everybody seemed bound to have a good time; and the hilarity became general, after a certain amount of refreshment had been taken by almost every one on board. One of the farmers from Mora, whom I treated to a glass of beer, was so much pleased that he insisted on my coming to stay at his farm, and offered me, in return, a pinch of snuff. The sail was delightful; and as the white church appeared nearer and nearer the young men combed their hair, and arranged it in what they considered the most attractive way. I did not wonder at these preparations, for the jetty was crowded with fair maidens who had come to witness the landing of the passengers. Numerous vehicles had already arrived, and the people were lodged at the hamlets near the fair grounds, whole families sleeping wherever there was space—even the barns were filled by the crowd. No room could be had at the comfortable inn of the place, the grounds of which were very pretty, with numerous summer-houses under the shade of which people could take their meals or refreshments ; and I was therefore delighted by the invitation of Johansson, with whom I found excellent quarters at Noret, receiving a hearty welcome from his old father and mother.

Not far from the landing stands the parish church, much less capacious than that of Leksand, with whitewashed walls shining in the sun. It contains some curious paintings, among which is a representation of the devil on a large scale, with a tremendous horn. This picture gives, I suppose, a good idea of what the people thought the monster was like at the time it was painted, and of the popular estimate of the prince of darkness.

At a short distance, on the other side of the river, is Utme-
land, so dear to the Swedish heart, for there the great Gustaf, founder of the Vasa dynasty, was hidden in a cellar by
Matts Larson's wife. When those who were seeking his life
arrived the wife was brewing the yule ale, and she placed a
vat over the trap-door leading below. The vault is the only
thing that remains of the old farm-house, but over it a shrine
has been built, enriched with historical paintings, one of which
is by Carl XV. It was with no little emotion that I descended into this small cellar, as I recollected the history of the
monarch and his descendants who have thrown such a halo of
glory around their country's name—not among the least the
great Gustavus Adolphus, the hero of the Thirty Years' War.

THE ORNÄSSTUGA.

Every place where Gustavus Vasa was sheltered or hidden
when he came to Dalecarlia is pointed out with pride. There
is a house in Ornäs, on Lake Runn, south of Falun, still standing, in which Gustavus slept overnight; but its owner, Arendt
Persson, an old friend of his, tried to betray him to the Danes,
when again he was saved by the traitor's wife, Barbro Stigs-
dotter, who provided him with conveyance to the pastor at
Svärdsjö, where he was safe for the time being.

The Mora costume is picturesque; the women wear red

instead of white stockings, and shorter dresses than those in Leksand, and evidently are not averse to showing the symmetry of their limbs. The skirt is of black homespun wool, often bordered with yellow, and the waist is red; the apron is generally of the color of the skirt, with two or three bright bands at the bottom. On the head they wear a neat handkerchief of calico, nicely ironed, and take great pride in properly tying the knot under the chin. The women part their hair on the back of the head, and the two locks thus formed are wrapped their whole length with ribbons—of a white color in the case of wives, and red for the maidens—and these are bound around the top of the head, forming a sort of crown. The men wear a bluish coat, shorter than that of Leksand, knee-breeches, dark-blue stockings instead of white, and on week-days the vest and long apron.

Very early in the morning the road was crowded with vehicles loaded with people, and with pedestrians on their way to the fair; by ten o'clock at least three thousand were on the ground, and the scene presented a most animated appearance, and very striking from the variety of costume. Over the doors hung skins, shoes, etc., as signs; there were also hardware and dry goods stores, the latter crowded with pretty girls in search of the printed head-kerchiefs worn in Mora and Orsa. Groceries, wool, and even salt pork from America, were bought and sold. The centre of greatest attraction was the jewellery booths, where thousands of silver rings, plain and ornamented, were displayed; for if there is anything a dalkulla likes it is to see her fingers well adorned with rings. A large assortment of brooches, thimbles, spoons, and fancy articles was a tempting sight. Few girls bought gold rings, as they were too expensive for their slender means. I gave away hundreds of silver rings to my fair friends. At the inn I kept open table, inviting many to partake of refreshment, and before the evening had over a hundred invitations to different farms. The heat of the sun was intense, and the cool places where lager and wines were sold were literally packed with people. A popular feature was a large tent, where a big bear was on exhibition.

During the afternoon, while among the horses and vehicles, where numerous groups of people were seated on the grass eating their dinners, my attention was drawn to a young couple commencing a flirtation; he ostensibly feeding his horse, she coming to her cart close by, apparently to get something that she had forgotten. Furtive glances were cast around to see if they were watched, for they would have no peace among their neighbors if they were suspected of courting: heretofore somebody had always been in the way, and their eyes only could meet, speaking tender messages; now they could have a little talk. When she said good-bye, the words *icke så brådtom* (not so hasty) made her tarry as long as she could without exciting suspicion. But he will come some Saturday evening (the lover's day) to her father's farm, and show the maiden that her beau of the fair has not forgotten her.

Spirits being sold at Mora, many men had gone to that place to fill their flasks or bottles to take home; but their good intentions were not carried out at the proper time, as the contents had disappeared during intercourse with friends, who in their turn thought themselves bound to return the compliment; the consequence was that soon they all began to feel the effects, and before the close of the day King Alcohol had most of the men as his subjects; but though exhilarated, and some even intoxicated, they were good-natured, and the younger men wanted to make love to all the girls they met, acting as if they were going to kiss them, and often walking with their arms around the maidens' waists. I noticed that none were so far gone as not to be able to distinguish the good-looking ones; but the dalkulla is no weak creature—she is fully equal to resisting approaches in a joking way, or suddenly disappearing among the crowd. It was a jovial and characteristic scene, with hardly any disagreeable features—certainly with none of the quarrelling, coarseness, and boisterousness usually accompanying such a festive occasion in more favored southern climes. There are only two fairs in a year, and every one wanted a good time. By seven o'clock the people began to leave, and by eleven the place was deserted. So passed the first and by far the more lively part of the fair.

CHAPTER XXI.

A Wedding in Dalecarlia.—Arrival at Westanor.—Welcome at Liss.—Preparations
   for a Wedding.—The Larder well stocked.—Drinkables abundant.—The Bride-
   groom and the Bride.—Great Number of Guests.—Lodging the Guests.—My
   Quarters.—Dressing the Bride.—Leaving for the Church.—The Procession.—
   Imposing Sight in the Church.—Many Bride'smaids.—The Nuptial Ceremony.—
   Return to Westanor.—Congratulating the Bride and Bridegroom.—The First
   Meal.—Dancing.—A Lull.—A Week of Festivities.—End of the Wedding-feast.
   —Giving Presents to the Bride.

ON a bright midsummer-eve I found myself again in Dalecarlia, and in the parish of Leksand, very weary, having travelled night and day from Umeå Lappmark, over a distance of
nearly six hundred miles. I arrived just in time for a wedding to which I had been invited, and which was to take place
the following day. Towards the close of a brilliant sunset I
entered the hamlet of Westanor, and alighted before the farm
of Liss. The tall forms of the old riksdagsman and his eldest
son appeared on the threshold, with warm words of welcome.
Carl, another son, and expectant groom, said, "Paul, I was
afraid that you would not be here for my wedding." I assured him that I should have been greatly disappointed had
I arrived too late for the ceremony.

I was no stranger at Westanor and the adjacent hamlet of
Smedby, and all my friends were glad to see me again. Not
the least among them were dear old Timgubb Ole Andersson
and his good wife Brita, with their young daughter Anna, and
the good people of Skaft, Olars, Nygård, and other farms.

A wedding in Dalarne, when the betrothed belong to the
families of wealthy bönder, is no small affair, especially if the
parents of the bride and bridegroom rank high socially among
their neighbors and in the parish. Invitations are extended
personally, by members of the respective families, about two

weeks before the ceremony, and each guest gives a small measure of malt to make ale for the feast.

For several weeks preparations had been made at the Liss and Olars farms for the coming festivities, and knäckebröd had been baked in large quantities; for the last two or three days several girls had busied themselves in making soft bread. Parties had been sent fishing, and returned with the results of their trip. Many sheep and an ox had been slaughtered; there was also an abundance of bacon, butter, and cheese: barrels after barrels of potatoes were lying in rows. Looking at the huge piles of bread and other provisions, I wondered if it would ever be possible for the guests to eat all. The drinkables, which constitute so important a part of a wedding-feast, had not been forgotten, and a large supply was on hand. A great deal of dark and strong ale had been brewed and was stored in barrels, near which were numerous kegs of bränvin, sherry, port-wine, and Swedish punch, and bottles without end. Though I knew from former experience how much would disappear, I felt sure that nothing would run short on this occasion. One of the ancient customs still prevalent is that called "förning." It consists of each guest bringing or sending a contribution in eatables or drinkables to help carry on the feast. Puddings and cakes of all kinds had been sent by neighbors and invited guests. A large arbor of branches of birch-trees had been erected in the yard of each farm, to protect the guests from the rays of the sun, and arches had been built over the gates and doors.

Liss Lars Olsson, the father of the bridegroom, was not only a wealthy farmer (said to be worth about twenty or thirty thousand dollars), but, as we have seen in a former chapter, had been for many years one of the riksdagsmen who represented Dalecarlia; his eldest son, Liss Olof Larsson, had now succeeded him, and was considered a very able man. He was a bank commissioner of the Diet—an office of great trust—and also *nämndeman* (juryman).* No two men were more re-

---

* In each härad (judicial district) there are twelve jurymen, elected by the landowners of the district, who, with the district judge, decide certain cases.

spected in Leksand. The father of the bride, Olars Anders Olsson, a neighbor, was also very much esteemed, and the owner of a large number of acres of good land and forests.

The wedding was particularly agreeable to the two families, for a sister of the bridegroom had married a brother of the bride. Generally the wedding-feast is given only by the father of the bridegroom; but in this case, as it was to be on a grand scale, and the father of the bride was a neighbor, the festivities were to be held at the two farms at the same time. One could hear continually the rattling of plates and dishes, the clatter of knives, forks, and spoons, and the tinkling of glasses sent by neighbors and friends, for no one household could furnish crockery enough for such an entertainment. Tailors and shoemakers had finished their work, especially for this occasion, and the last preparations were taking place.

It was no easy matter to lodge all the guests; but the neighbors came forward, and every dwelling in the hamlet was turned into a lodging-house. There is such pride in regard to hospitality shown to honored guests, that each family did its best; the finest linen sheets and pillow-cases were taken from the storehouse, for it would never do for people to return home with unpleasant remarks on the hospitality of Farmer So-and-so, or to be able to call him and his wife mean people. A small bright-red house, containing a single room, was assigned to me during the week of the festivities. The furniture consisted of two fixed beds, opposite each other, with a window between; but, on account of the great number of guests who had arrived from a distance, a temporary couch also had been put in.

I was the first to retire, and had hardly done so when the bride and the sister of the bridegroom came in, and said, "Paul, are you asleep?" On my saying no, each added, "I hope you will have a good time during the wedding;" and taking off their shoes, and partly dressed, they lay down to rest on the bed opposite mine. This was true Dalarne hospitality—a mark of honor and respect. I was trusted as if I were a Dalecarlian, for the girls said, "We come here to keep you company; we do not want you to feel lonely, for it is not pleasant to be all alone in a house." Soon after a dalkarl, and a handsome dalkulla to whom he was engaged, came in, and both lay, fully dressed, on the other couch, and fell asleep in each other's arms.

At three o'clock I was awakened by the bride, who had risen and was putting on her shoes; she was going to the house of her future father-in-law to begin her toilet, as several hours are required for this ceremony in Dalecarlia. I got up soon after and asked Carl, the bridegroom, and the old folks if I could go into the room where the bride was being dressed, and all at once said, "Certainly, Paul, you can go."

The girl was seated on a chair, surrounded by several of her companions, every one of whom was either making a suggestion or helping in her toilet. Then would come a pause, and a final judgment be rendered on what had been done. In front of the bride a looking-glass was held by an admiring friend. Now and then the old riksdagsman's wife would come in to see how things were progressing, and to remind the party that the hour for going to church was near at hand.

The wedding costume is like that ordinarily worn by the women of the parish, except that a large quantity of artificial flowers and beads are sewed on the body of the dress; all the brooches that have been given the bride are fastened in front, and for the first time she wears on her head the white close-fitting cap which designates the married state. The groom is distinguished only by a broad white collar falling over his coat; this, with the wedding-shirt, is the gift of the bride.

As the time to depart for the church approached I dressed myself, and for this especial occasion, in the costume worn by the men of the parish of Leksand: when I peeped into the glass to see myself a glow of satisfaction overspread my face, and, with a feeling of vanity natural to men on such an occasion, I really thought I was not ill-looking. When I appeared out-of-doors a shout of delight greeted me, and they said, "Look at Paul—he is not proud; he is now like one of us." I had no idea that this freak of mine would produce such a good effect on my Dalecarlian friends.

As the wedding-hour drew near cart after cart appeared.

A bridal party must be accompanied by a great number of
vehicles—the more there are of these, the greater the compliment to the families; every friend is expected to come on
wheels, so that the show on the way to and from church may
be worthy of the station of the bride.   The scene in the lane
and around Liss was of a most lively character.   A procession
was formed, the ex-riksdagsman with one of his married daughters taking the lead; the second carriage, drawn by two horses
—a very unusual thing—contained the bride (who held in her
hand the psalm-book, carefully wrapped in a large silk handkerchief, which, according to custom, had been given to her a
few days before by her intended husband), the groom, and
myself: more than one hundred vehicles followed, loaded
with people.   As we drove along the high-road and passed the
farm-houses many people were out to see the procession, and
I could hear them say, "Look at Paul in a dalkarl's dress."

The church of Leksand that day presented a most brilliant
appearance; it was literally packed, and there was hardly
standing-room; even the aisles were crowded, and over five
thousand people must have been there.   As the Midsummer-
day is a very popular one for weddings, six other couples were
to be united in the bonds of matrimony.   From the upper
gallery the view was very striking.   The couples were near
the altar, and the bride'smaids collectively numbered over one
hundred and fifty; they were scattered in different groups,
however, instead of being near the brides and bridegrooms.
They were easily recognized by the artificial flowers and beads
on the bodies of their dresses—although these were in lesser
quantity than on those of the brides—and by their red maiden
caps.   The service commenced with a hymn of praise, sung by
thousands of voices, accompanied by the great organ; after
this all couples to be married went under a red canopy before
the altar, where the marriage ceremony was performed with
the exchanging of rings.   When all was over, the bridal parties and guests got into their respective carriages, and, after a
little confusion, our procession started back, the newly-wedded
pair now taking the lead, the rest following in the same order
as before.

After arriving at Liss, the happy couple were congratulated by the guests, who shook hands with the bride, she receiving all with becoming modesty. In the mean time food had been cooked for more than five hundred persons by the respective parents of the newly-married pair, who were to keep open house the whole of the week. It being impossible for all to eat at once, the most honored guests and nearest relatives were first invited, and I among them. Then came the usual scenes characteristic of Scandinavia: all those specially invited kept themselves modestly in the yard, or in a corner of the room; when any name was called by the host or hostess, the person had to be dragged to the place assigned, often with some difficulty, each thinking the end of the table good enough for him: it is considered very rude to go at once. When my turn came, I imitated the natives—I resisted manfully, and it took five minutes to get me to my proper seat; which taken, I became as gentle as a lamb. The mothers and sisters were in the kitchen, surrounded by servants, serving up and sending in the dishes; the sons saw to it that the guests had enough to drink. Dishes after dishes were passed around, and all were constantly urged to eat more: it seemed to be firmly believed that on a wedding-day one can eat for hours without ceasing, and can drink at least four times as much as on ordinary occasions without feeling the effects.

Among the guests were a couple having a fine farm but no children; and as the fish was passed around I suggested that they should not let it go by, but help themselves, adding that I had come from the North, where the people eat much fish and have large families. This was taken up by the guests in the midst of uproarious laughter, and all shouted and urged them to help themselves, which they did bountifully, amidst general merriment.

I had hardly left the table, and was taking breath in the yard, when I was seized by the father of the bride, who insisted on my following him to his house to take another meal. In vain I expostulated and resisted—eat I must, and drink I must; they would not take no for an answer, and I soon had occasion to ask myself if I could continue this way of liv-

ing for six days more. By seven o'clock the hamlet was de-
cidedly exhilarated; everybody was happy—very happy—for
all had on this festive occasion drank many times to the health
of the bride. As it was vacation, the school-house, by permission, had been transformed into a ball-room; three musicians
played on violins in one corner, and here hundreds of guests
had been invited. Drinking was indulged in *ad libitum*, the
young men of the respective families being the bar-tenders, and
freely giving whatever was asked for. The dancing continued
all night, the bride having to dance with every man; but the
bridegroom, who was not in good health, was allowed to go
home, otherwise he would have been obliged to do likewise
with every woman. The second day dancing began in the afternoon, and again the bride had to be present and dance with
her friends. She had laid aside the flowers which adorned
her bridal-dress, and instead wore the silk handkerchief in
which was wrapped her psalm-book the day of the wedding.

On the third day there was a lull in the festivities for a
time, for many of the guests were very tired, some having
taken rest only now and then; others had violent headaches,
produced by want of sleep or excessive eating and drinking,
and were groaning under the pain. This peculiar headache is
called *kopparslagare*, as the throbbing pain in the region of
the temples is said to remind the sufferer of the thumps given
by a coppersmith on a vessel he is mending. I suffered some
discomfort from such promiscuous eating and drinking, for
with all my care I could not always refuse to skål with a
friend—here with a glass of wine, there with beer, then with
something else. I stole away to a neighboring farm with
friends who also felt exhausted. In one room was a bed
where the mother and father lay, and I threw myself upon
the other where the daughter was fast asleep.

On the fourth day there was a revival, and things went on
in the old way till Saturday noon; but nothing was wanting,
and food and drink were apparently as plentiful as on the first
day. In the afternoon the bride and bridegroom stood in the
main room of the largest dwelling-house of Liss, where the
guests, who had made preparations to return home, one after

another came to bid them good-bye, and thank them for the pleasant time they had had. Every one, as he left, put in the hands of the bride some bank-bills, which, without looking at, she dropped into the big linen pouch hung, on that occasion, at her side: this was the parting gift, and every guest, according to his means, gave money to the bride. The girls of the hamlet had held a meeting, and all had agreed that each should give exactly the same sum. A popular bride often gets a considerable amount in this manner, which enables her and her husband to begin life quite cheerfully. I thought the custom good, and most practical; so I made an offering, said good-bye, wishing the happy pair long life and happiness, and departed.

CHAPTER XXII.

ONE year had passed away since the wedding of the old
riksdagsman's son, and I found myself again in Dalecarlia.
The fair at Mora was over, and once more I was on my
way to Orsa—and to this day there are no parts of Scandinavia more pleasantly remembered by me. There was in the
vehicle Löf Kistin, Per's dotter, a poor widow with a small
farm, having more children than heads of cattle, who could by
working hard just get along; but, in spite of poverty, she was
kind-hearted, and her weather-beaten face was the image of
honesty. The other was Smids Kisti, from Stenberg, a pleasant girl, who was returning with the proceeds of a sucking-
pig, barely two weeks old, which she had sold at the fair for
six kronor—a pretty good price. She was delighted at the
thought of swelling the little sum by the proceeds of the fare
she was to receive for driving me: she had taken up poor
Kistin, who had come to the fair all the way on foot in the
morning.

We chatted merrily as we drove along; it was late, so the
road was not crowded, and we met only a few women—some
carrying their babies slung on their backs by leather bands—
or gayly-dressed girls, and young men on the way to their
farms. As I journeyed towards Orsa, to see my old friends, I

noticed everywhere the remains of midsummer festoons hanging over the porches, and the faded flowers on the May-poles. After a drive of eight miles we left Löf Kistin before her humble home; as we parted she said, " Paul, no cattle are on the farms now; but I have a milch cow at home, and the children to-morrow will bring you sweet milk and cream."

A little farther I entered the hamlet of Vångsgärde, where, on my former visit, I had been stopped on the highway, while passing his blacksmith shop, by Skrädder Anders Hansson, who owned a fine farm here. He shouted, "Amerikanare, stop your horse — sleep here! you will be welcome on my farm; I have caught some nice fish in the lake, and you will have a good supper. I have a brother in America, and I want you to stop with me. Please tarry, even if it is only for a night; I have a fine horse, and a good house close by, and I will take you to-morrow where you like; I will also give all the milk you can drink." I could not resist his earnest invitation, and my cart wheeled to his farm, amidst the joyous shouts of those around. I was treated royally by Anders and his wife Kirstin. Unfortunately, she spoke only the old *dalspråket* (language), and it was very hard for me to understand her. Anders was one of the best-hearted fellows I ever met. Soon we were quite intimate. There was nothing too good for me, and I passed the night in a little house by the porch leading to the lane. Skrädder was a fair farm; but, besides, my friend was an excellent blacksmith, and his trade yielded him a good living; he had the reputation of being one of the best fishermen, and also somewhat of a hunter. He invited me to come and visit him as often as I liked. "Paul," said he, "I will build an upper story, and there will be your rooms, and you will have a fine view over the Orsa Lake."

But this year the large gate leading into the yard of Skrädder was barred; nobody was at home. Continuing my way, I entered Holn, an adjacent hamlet, and alighted before Kaplans, where my friends, Per Persson and his good wife Kisten, Lars's dotter, received me with open arms, their faces beaming with joy, for they had been looking for me for some days, having heard that I was in Dalarne; little Kisten, a sweet, deli-

R 2

cate child, who was as fond of me as I was of her, soon climbed
into my lap, and their sons, Per and Hans, were asking me all
sorts of questions. Skrädder Anders had left word that he
was obliged to go to the meadows to mow the hay, and that
I must not fail to come and see him there.

In my turn I inquired for my friends: who had been married, and who had died since my last visit; what were the
prospects of the crop; while all the time little Kisten was
sitting on my lap, and showing me the photograph I had sent
to her parents. Meanwhile the mother was preparing a hearty
meal for me, and, as I was expected, they had dried some new
hay for my bed, which was to be in the loft of the barn.
Fresh sheepskins and homespun blankets had been spread
over, and when I retired they all said, "Paul, no fleas will
come and trouble you." Early the next morning Löf Kistin
arrived with a pail of sweet milk.

Many a farmer has a trade. Skrädder Anders, as we have
seen, was a blacksmith; Kaplans Per was a tailor, and had
earned quite a reputation for the making of leather knee-
breeches. His small house and farm were neat, and his wife
an excellent house-keeper; they were so fond of me that they
wanted me to take a meal at least every two hours. These
were, of course, very simple, for no cloth covered the plain
board; the frying-pan was often put on the table, the butter
was served in its pail, to make sure that I should have enough,
and there was bread for at least ten persons; they all seemed
delighted that they could give me milk, cream, wild raspberries, and other things they knew I liked.

Contiguous to Per Persson's farm was another of the same
name which belonged to Hans Olsson, whose family was composed of Anna, Lars's dotter, his wife, a son called Hans, two
daughters called Kirstin and Anna, and a young school-master.
Near by was Pålack. Here the husband was dead, and had
left a widow with six children—four girls and two boys; the
three eldest daughters, Anna, Kerstin, and Margit, were grown
up, and helped in the varied work of the farm; while the
younger children, Karin, Anders, and Lars, assisted in their
way. I admired the two little fellows: they never grumbled

at what they were told to do, and seemed always eager to help their mother and sisters.

Another farm, almost facing Kaplans, on the other side of the road, was Ullars, belonging to Per Hansson; and farther than Skrädder were the farms of Borbos, Bruks, Mångsa, Bogg, and others.

By the shores of Orsa Lake was the hamlet of Lunden. I was very fond of going there to visit Mårts, a poor farm, owned by a worthy widow, Anna Anders's dotter, dearly loved by my friends of Kaplans. Time had furrowed her bronzed but honest face, for she and her daughter Kerstin had to work hard, as the farm was small and its products were not always enough to support them; but they always insisted on my partaking of the best they had. Kerstin has since married a manly fellow, who I trust is worthy of her; but a letter I have received from them tells me that good old Anna is dead.

About two miles from Holn is Orsa Kyrkoby (The Church hamlet), a peculiarly ugly place, consisting of sixty or seventy farms or homesteads, close together, without fields between, and with very narrow streets. In summer the stables attract swarms of flies, which bite so persistently that after three in the morning one cannot sleep. The people do not take any measures to guard against them, and nets are unknown. Mosquitoes are also numerous, and fleas abundant, except at the station. Should a fire occur, with a high wind, the place would be entirely destroyed. The watchman constantly walks the streets while the people sleep, and cries the hours of the night. I was always amused by the old fellow, who had for his companion a young and handsome girl.

The inhabitants of this hamlet were far less hospitable than in others, on account of the crowd, and no milk or food were offered to the stranger. The inn was at that time much frequented; many had come to buy provisions before leaving for their farms. There were several stores, some being licensed to sell beer and wine. The place was a general rendezvous of purchasers, and many of the men rarely returned till they had indulged in several glasses of beer, or in a beverage called Norwegian wine, made of berries, containing so much alcohol that it took but little to make one tipsy. As the sale of spirits was forbidden, the wine had to be strong. One day the surroundings of the inn were more boisterous than usual. The young men of the beväring had come back, and were celebrating their return home by freely drinking with their friends either of the liquors they bought in the village or the bränvin they had brought with them. The beväring is a military organization, composed of young men between twenty-one and twenty-five years of age, and during that time they have to drill for three weeks the first two years.

On my first visit here I had discovered that the giving of a gold ring to a maiden meant a great deal. Among the many friends I had made at the fair at Mora was a kulla from one of the hamlets of the parish of Orsa, on whose engagement-finger, without knowing its significance, I had placed a ring. A few days afterwards, late one night, I came to that part of the parish near which her family lived; but the affair had entirely left my mind. At the early hour of four o'clock in the morning I was aroused from slumber by a knock at the door. Bidding the person enter—though grumbling at the same time at the disturbance—I recognized a friend at the fair and the father of the girl whose finger I had adorned. "Good-morning, Paul," said he, in a very friendly voice; "I am glad to see you in Orsa. You must come and see us; we live only half a mile from here." Approaching my bed he said, in a confidential voice, "Paul, there is a *stor språk* (big talk) in our village in regard to the ring you gave to my daughter; I come to ask you what is your meaning. Do you really think of marrying her?" I had no such intention, and no idea that I had created such an excitement. The girl was very pretty, and her fair complexion and unexceptional bearing had attracted my attention; from my giving her the ring the good people thought I had fallen desperately in love with her at first sight, and the family had no objection to the match, especially as many from that hamlet had emigrated to the United States. My answer was simply, "We do not marry so hastily in America, and do not bind ourselves in such a way. Your daughter is a very fine girl, and I gave her that ring simply as a token of friendship. I have given many such as souvenirs to remember me by." Nothing more was said, and the good fellow made me promise to come and see him. When I went to the farm I was received most cordially; but the excitement was great among the neighbors, who thought I had come to ask the hand of the fair Dalecarlian, notwithstanding my protestations to the contrary. Afterwards I was very particular when I gave a gold ring, and took the precaution to give several in the same hamlet, to prevent any gossiping.

The costume of Orsa is very unlike that of other parishes. The coats of the men are of white homespun cloth, and short; Generally two are worn, the under one being without sleeves; this is done for better fitting. Knee-breeches of white leather and dark-blue stockings are worn. All part their hair in the middle. The body of the dress of the women is of bright scarlet wool, allowing the long white sleeves of their chemises, which come to the wrist, to be seen. The skirt is of bluish-black thick woollen cloth, often ruffled in weaving, over which is a fine yellow leather apron, with a border of black cloth at the bottom, or one made of the same material as the dress. The stockings are of white wool; and often queer shoes, with the heel in the centre, are worn. They fasten the hair so tight that in the course of time it becomes very thin at the parting; their head-dress is a colored handkerchief, always smoothly ironed, the knot being tied with great care.

There are but very few names in Dalecarlia, as it is customary there, as well as in many other districts of Scandinavia, to call the children first after their father or mother, then after their grandparents and other relations. Among females Anna is by far the most common; then comes Kristina, Margaretha, Katharina, and Birgitta. These names, except Anna, are spelled in different ways by the Dalecarlians: Kirstin, Kirsten, Kestin, Kisten, Kistin, Stina, Margit, Marget, Margreta, Greta. No one is ever called Katharina—but Karen, Karin, Carin, Kari. Birgitta is always shortened into Brita or Britta. These four names, with few exceptions, are those of almost all the women; and the only way to distinguish one from another is by the name of the farm. The same may be said of the names given to men. Anders, Lars, Hans, Olof, Erik or Erick, Jöns, Per or Pehr, and Daniel constitute almost the entire list—the first five being very common.

The parish church, close to the village, and not far from Orsa Lake, is about ten miles distant from that of Mora, and is reached from the latter place by the picturesque highway passing through some of the hamlets we have mentioned. The edifice is of stone, plastered over, and is kept dazzling white inside and outside. The cemetery which surrounds it is also enclosed by a white wall. Sunday is the day on which the tourist can get the best idea of the physical development of the Dalecarlians.

The people of Orsa are, I think, the handsomest in Dalecarlia. The graceful costumes of the men show off their fair proportions. They are strong, tall, and active, as befits the hilly character of their parish. Many of their maidens have that peculiar Swedish complexion which, for clearness, fairness, and freshness, surpasses any I have seen elsewhere. The rose-tints which suffuse their cheeks are as delicate as those of the apple-blossom floating in milk. Add to this the deep-blue eyes, cherry lips, fine teeth—kept very white by chewing the *kåda* (gum from the fir-tree)—fair and silky hair, and you have what may be considered a type of beauty found only in Sweden. In no other countries where the blonde complexion predominates has the blush of the cheeks that exquisitely pink tinge, which gradually melts and diffuses itself into the extremely white skin. This complexion is probably produced by the peculiar climate.

But if the people are handsome their parish is poor, for the farms are small and the families large; very few of their houses are painted, and they are not kept as clean and tidy as those of Leksand, and have no gardens or orchards near them. Few farms have more than five cows—many have but two, with some goats, sheep, and a pig or two. Poor, indeed, is the family that does not own a horse; and the ambition of those who have none is to become so rich that they may buy one.

On the highway from Mora to Skattungen Lake branch many narrow, rough roads, leading to numerous hamlets, hidden from sight by intervening hills or woods. There the people are still more primitive and trusty. Among those I have visited are Sandbäck, Wiborg, Oljonsby, Torvol, Maggås, Kallmora, Stackmora, Orsbleck, and others. Even now methinks I hear the voices of welcome which greeted me at the threshold of every farm-house.

The first time I visited one of these was with Skrädder Anders, who wished to introduce me to one of his friends, Gubb Ole Andersson, the owner of a very good farm in Wiborg. What a welcome I received, and how great was the excitement of the neighbors who crowded around me when Anders gave the most minute details of his acquaintance with me—of what he heard the riksdagsman of Leksand and many others of that parish say of me at the fair of Mora. He also spoke of the special letters the governor had given me, among which was one for Mångs Hans Ersson, of their own parish, a well-known bonde of Stackmora; and, to crown all, he assured them that I was one of the best fellows in the world. Such were my credentials on my first acquaintance, and the warm welcome I received from all proved that his speech had the desired effect, and that his friends believed his words.

No introductions were now required in Orsa or anywhere near. Wherever I visited there was joy in the household; I was treated like one of their loved relatives, and the inner life of this warm-hearted people freely made known to me. The broad Atlantic divides us; months and years have rolled by, but the same warm Dalecarlian hearts beat; the old friends still think of me and love me. Often my thoughts wander back to the days gone by—to that pure and loving and trusting nature still found here and there in the midst of our restive and busy world, but especially in Scandinavia. If we cannot see each other we can at least write one to another: and how beautiful are their simple letters! There is no hiding of thoughts, no studied phrases; they come right out and say what they feel, and I never knew how much they loved me until we were parted. How endearing are their expressions!

so much so, that, if it were not for the signature, I would often mistake a letter from a man for that of a woman. I have received as many as three or four hundred letters a year from Scandinavia, many of which I have preserved, and sometimes I love to read them over again, as they bring back vividly to my mind friends that are far away, but who are not forgotten. All of them begin with some affectionate expression, of which I give a few examples:

"My good friend Paul Du Chaillu;" "Best friend Paul Du Chaillu;" "Good Paul;" "My dear friend Paul;" "My dear and kind Paul;" "My dear friend and brother Paul Du Chaillu;" "Best Paul;" "My best friend Paul;" "My kind and never-forgotten Paul, who has a heart which reaches as far as to Dalarne;" "My good friend Paul Du Chaillu;" "Kind Paul Du Chaillu;" "Beloved Paul Du Chaillu;" "My kind Paul;" "My kind friend Paul;" "Always remembered friend Paul;" "My beloved and kind friend Paul;" "Tenderly beloved Paul Du Chaillu;" "My unforgotten friend Paul;" "My beloved friend Paul;" "My dear and beloved friend Paul;" "My dear and kind friend Paul;" "My affectionate, tenderly-beloved friend Paul."

The letters are signed in the same loving spirit, showing the place which I still retain in their affection. I append a few signatures:

"To our beloved and much remembered friend Paul, for what we have received we sign our names;" "May God grant thee a happy voyage here. I never forget friend Paul;" "We never forget friend Paul;" "Be so kind as to accept this letter with friendly hand, sweet Paul;" "Faithfully and friendly I sign my name;" "Live well, friend Paul. Amen." "Farewell for this time. Signed by a humble friend;" "Many greetings from all thy friends;" "Live well, my dear Paul;" "Most hearty and dear greeting to my most humble and amiable Paul. Good-bye—live well;" "Do not forget thy friend;" "Signs with great friendship;" "Most friendly greeted from thy true friend;" "With friendship from thy true friend;" "Accept affectionate greetings from a humble friend;" "Good-bye for this time, my kind Paul, signs thy faithful and never-forgotten;" "A thousand, thousand thanks for the letter—it pleased me very much;" "I heard that thou hadst not forgotten me, and I had also not forgotten thee;" "Now I end my humble letter with a thousand-fold dear and frequent greeting from a true friend;" "Forget-me-not—I have certainly not forgotten thee, my friend;" "With great friendship signs thy—;" "Never forget thy friend;" "Most friendly I sign my name;" "I can never forget thee, but I often think of thee;" "I now must end my letter with a thousand-fold dear greeting to thee, Paul Du Chaillu, and all thy friends;" "And may God guard thee over the ocean, if thou wilt travel to us. Live well—be happy;" "Paul, thou hast promised us that if God gives us life and health we shall meet next summer;" "Live and feel well, my dear and beloved friend;" "Most faithful and affectionate friend Paul;" "Most sincere and dearest greetings to my heartiest and most amiable friend Paul. Good-bye—live well;" "Best friend Paul, I never forget thee. Live well;" "Now I send my humble letter with a thousand-fold dear and repeated greeting from a faithful friend."

From the perusal of the above the reader may imagine the friendly greetings I received when visiting Dalecarlia.

On a warm summer day I bade good-bye to Holn and Vångsgärde, and a pleasant walk brought me to the hamlets of Oljonsby and Wiborg, situated about two miles from the main road. The farms of these two places are scattered here and there, and a stranger does not know when he enters one and leaves the other.

In many parishes or judicial districts there is a public piece of land, like the English common, called *allmäning*, where the people of a hamlet have a right to pasture their flocks and herds. There are also forest commons (*skogsallmäning*). If any one in the parish, wishing to build a house, can show that he does not possess the forest required for his purpose, he makes an official request to the district judge, when he is holding court, who will then issue an order to the jägmästare and to two members of the communal council to have the wood cut for his use.

Almost all the farms were owned by friends of mine, and it would be difficult for me to say where I was the most welcome. I only remember that it was impossible for me to become hungry, for I could not call at any house without having a meal set before me, and to refuse to eat was out of the question; I could not have dared to do so without running the risk of incurring the displeasure of the family. I had eaten with a neighbor, and I had to do likewise with the next, no matter if the repast had been taken but one hour before. There seemed to be a rivalry among all to do the best they could, and outdo each other in kindness to me. When I called at a farm, immediately the husband and wife, the son and daughter, insisted that I should spend the night; and if I had promised some one else before, they insisted that I should not leave their hamlet without doing likewise with them. They wanted their dear friend Paul to be happy, for Paul was in *främmande land* (a foreign country), and they were afraid he would feel lonely and sad. Their love was returned by me, and I also tried my best to please them in a hundred little ways. The simple tokens of remembrance I gave them were appreciated the same as if they had been gifts of the greatest value; and often I think of the hamlets of Oljonsby, Wiborg, Torvol, Sandbäck, Maggås, and of the farms of Gubb, Jempters, Benjamin, Mikols, Ryttar, Bärtas, Guns, Hanser, Bäcker, Karins, Brätt, Lagger, Agdur, Nissa, Finspers, Jemt, and many others, where so many pleasant hours have been spent in the study of those primitive natures, in which I detected every day traits and characteristics which were entirely unknown to me before.

One peculiarity of the country was that whenever I met a dalkulla she would, as a sign of friendship, pull out of her pocket a piece of rock candy and give it to me, or insist that I should take at least a bite; or take out of her mouth a piece of the kåda she chewed, and give it to me to do likewise: to refuse the latter would have been a breach of etiquette.

Agdur Anders, Bärtas Hans, Benjamins Per and I were great chums, and when their work was over we would often meet and pay visits together; once or twice we went and serenaded the fair Dalecarlian damsels, whose parents, after awhile, would invite us to come in, and offer little glasses of spirits; and, a chat over, we would depart and visit another farm. At other times we would go to The Church hamlet to buy something, and then before returning would join in a glass of beer. Agdur Anders and Bärtas Hans are now married. Benjamins Per and friend Paul are still single.

I was struck while in Orsa by the great number of widows I knew. It was indeed sad to see so many large families under the care of poor mothers. "How is it?" I inquired. "Paul," they would answer, "money is hard to get; our farms are poor, our children are numerous, and our husbands are obliged to work at the quarries of grindstones; the dust breathed is very unhealthy, and brings on sickness and early death: that is the reason you see so many widows." The mother, in these cases, takes charge of the farm, and the children, always dutiful, help her to the best of their abilities.

Among my good friends, for whom I was full of sympathy, were those of the Guns. This farm was owned by Anna, who had been left with five daughters, who bore the names of Margit, Caren, Brita, Lispet (Elizabeth), and Kisten. Margit and Caren, the eldest, were respectively twenty and eighteen years of age, and, with the rest of the family, carried on all the work of the farm except ploughing and threshing. How hard the older ones labored during the summer, especially during the harvest and mowing time! how happy they seemed when I helped them to stack the hay!

The time to leave the hamlet finally came. The people had collected and dried the alder leaves, as shown by their stained hands; the fields had been weeded, and the furrows for potatoes had been ploughed; and every day many left for the *fäbodar* or sæters.

We will now wind our way among the hills, and spend a few weeks amidst the fragrance of the pines, visiting the Orsa and Rättvik fäbodar. Each of these has a name, and those we have visited are called Ecksjö, Skafåsen, Eskåsen, Hamråsen, Utengs Bleck, Höhes, Hjerpåsen, Grunneberg, Hörenberga, Spirisby, Tallhes, and Fjäsku.

CHAPTER XXIII.

The Fäbodar or Sæters of Sweden.—Wild Pastures of Dalecarlia.—The Dalecarlians's Fäbodar.—Girls following the Cattle.—Departure for a Fäbod.—On the Road.—Arrival at Hemråsen.—Life at the Fäbodar.—Life by the Swamp-meadows. —Åker Jonas Fäbod. —A Sunday at Rättvik. —Bright and Picturesque Costume of Rättvik.—Social Enjoyments.—Eskåsen.—Departure.

THE fäbodar (sæters) of Sweden occur in very few provinces, as the country is not mountainous, and only north of Stockholm. In Dalecarlia they are very numerous in the forest-clad hills, among which are rich pastures, chiefly in marsh or wet land, which dries up as the summer advances, and along the shores of lakes and ponds: as the water retires, the horse-tail (*Equisetum vulgare*) grows thickly, and of this the cattle are very fond, and are allowed to eat it, though it gives a disagreeable taste to the milk. In these lakelets cattle are sometimes fatally mired in the soft mud, and hence require constant watching by the girls. In many parts of Dalecarlia the forests are almost inaccessible on account of the swamps, and there the moose (*Alces malchis*) roams at will, being hunted for only six weeks in the year.

The fäbodar of Dalecarlia are in many respects unlike the Norwegian sæters, resembling rather hamlets in the forests surrounded by large fenced fields of grass and grain, the cattle often remaining with some of the family till after Christmas, to avoid the transporting of hay. The houses are comfortable and well built, with fireplaces, beds, and necessary outbuildings; in reality they are forest-farms.

During the day the cattle, sheep, and goats are taken to the pasture-land under the charge of a girl, who leads and guides them either by her voice or the sound of a horn (for dogs are not used either in Norway or Sweden at the sæters).

A pocket containing salt hangs from her waist; she knows every one by name, and if perchance one be missing, she calls the absent one by name, and rewards its coming by the gift of a little salt. As she walks along she knits a pair of stockings, for none of her time is idly spent. When a good pasture-ground is reached she seats herself on the trunk of a dead tree or upon a stone, in some dry spot in the shade, knitting as she sings a psalm or a love-ditty, and watches the sun, at whose setting she retraces her steps to the fäbod, where the cows are milked and the cattle housed for the night. To see from the hills a herd pasturing in the swamps and meadows, and hear the tinkling of their bells, brought vividly to mind the charms of pastoral life.

The farm property in Dalecarlia is very much divided; as it is distributed equally among all the children, the division is often so small that it is hardly worth having. With the inter-marriages which have taken place, it has become so mixed up, and each piece of land is so far away from the main farm, that much is wasted to secure a small crop. The government has taken the matter in hand, and is trying to make the farmers exchange properties, so as to unite them all in one. When a farm includes extensive marshes and meadows far away from the fäbodar, the only shelter for the hay-cutters is a shed of bark to protect them from the rain. Goats follow them and supply them with milk; and the hay is stacked, to be removed in winter on sleighs to the farm.

I saw in North-eastern Dalecarlia some fäbodar of a some-what different character. A fence enclosed a few acres of pasture-land, which often produces very fine hay; around this were several cattle-pens belonging to different farmers, who club to-gether and put their cattle, sheep, and goats under the care of girls, who on alternate days go to pasture the cows, or remain at the fäbod to make butter and cheese. The price is about one krona and fifty öre for each milch cow for the season, from June to the end of September; there is also a stipula-ted price for the care of dry cows, goats, and sheep.

Our party from Oljonsby consisted of Per, his wife Kirstin, and Karen and Margreta, her sisters. We had two horses loaded with bread, flour, cooking utensils, salt for the cattle, and blankets, ten goats and one pig—the latter proving the most troublesome of the party. Per took the lead with the horses, Margreta had charge of the goats, Karen of the pig, and Kirstin carried her baby. At about half way we stopped to eat our simple dinner and make a cup of coffee. The road, though very rough on account of numerous cobble-stones, was passable for carts used for transportation; rude bridges spanned the streams, and, where the ground was swampy, branches or trunks of trees had been laid close together across the road, as on our so-called corduroy roads. I found the weather in these forests very warm at mid-day, and was glad to rest awhile at Grunneberg, at the fäbod of my friend Agdur Anders; and, besides, it would have been a great slight to pass without partaking of the hospitality of his family. Before dark we reached Hemråsen, which has quite a number of houses scattered here and there, with hay-fields fenced around. Soon after our arrival the neighbors—all women—came and welcomed us. As my friends had to go to work the next day, we retired early to the barn, where we at once spread skins on a little hay, and slept in them; for, though the days were warm, the nights were cool.

The life at the fäbodar is a very laborious one. At daylight Per and the women were up and busy sharpening the hand-scythes, and after a meal taken in a hurry went out to mow a meadow about three miles distant, returning in the evening just at dusk. Often from early dawn till evening not a soul remained at Hemråsen, although every house was left open. One day, having lost myself in a swampy forest, and feeling exhausted on my return, I retired in one of the untenanted houses and fell into a long sleep. Great was my astonishment the next morning when I was roused from a profound slumber by Jemt Anna, Per's dotter, from Maggås. How she learned that I was there I could not tell. She said, "Paul, there will be no one here until night, and I did not wish to go before giving you something to eat."

There were days when a great number of people came to tarry only for the night, on the way to some grass-fields. One

A BÁTTYUK FÁBÓL.

day came friends Bäeker Anna and her brother Hans, with six
goats, on their way to a distant meadow, fairly loaded with
the food they had taken for the whole week and the scythes.
The goats, which were to provide them with milk, followed
like dogs. We agreed that in a few days we would meet at
Eskåsen.

Among the fäbodar was one belonging to Åker Jonas Andersson from Rättvik, who, at the time of my visit, was there
with Brita his wife; both of them spent their days in mowing grass. The cattle and dairy were under the care of two
kullor, one being a daughter and the other Dunkkol's Karin.
How pretty these maidens looked in the picturesque costume
of their parish—one busy at churning butter, and the other
standing before the hearth and attending to the making of
cheese, or roasting coffee, while the big brass kettle hung
above the fire. When Saturday evening came, Åker's Brita
suggested that Dunkkol's Karin, Finsper's Per and his wife,
with her two sisters and myself, should go to Rättvik and
spend Sunday at the farm of her father. This suggestion
was accepted at once by all of us, and at daylight on Sunday
morning we were on the way. After a tramp of several
hours, chiefly through swampy meadow-land and forests, we
reached a lovely tract of country and a good road, which
passed through an exceedingly rural and beautiful landscape
till we reached Åker in Gulleråsen, where we were received
with the usual warm-hearted Dalecarlian hospitality.

The costume of the women of Rättvik is the gayest and
the most picturesque of Dalecarlia. The skirt is of a bluish
color with a green border; the waist is dark; the woollen
apron is gorgeous with transverse bands of white, green, yellow, or blue. The dress is short, in order to display the stockings, or rather leggings, embroidered at the bottom in designs
of showy colors, like those worn in Norway at Thelemarken
and at Sæterdal. The cap is very graceful—black with red
trimmings, or sometimes of snowy-white linen, with two balls
falling on the back.

The afternoon was passed in social enjoyment; and I noticed here, as I have in many other parts of Scandinavia, the

fondness of the old folks for the young people. Often one sees a grandfather playing the fiddle for his small grandchildren, who enjoy a dance amazingly.

After leaving Rättvik I wandered from one fäbod to another; I went frequently all alone, surprised that I did not get lost every day in the forests, for many paths led only to swampy meadows. The silence of the woods was broken only by the shrill voices of maids in charge of the cattle, or now and then by the tapping of a woodpecker on a hollow tree.

One Saturday afternoon I found myself at the fäbod of Eskåsen; in the evening the people began to come in from every direction, from their week's work, and early on Sunday everybody was dressed, as if ready to go to church. Each friend insisted that I should come to his fäbod and partake of his cheer; and if anybody had told me the amount of milk and cream and buttermilk I could drink in a day, I could not have believed it.

I did not fail to go and see Skrädder Anders, and there I saw the plain wooden cradle in which he had been rocked, with his ancestors before him, with the date cut into the wood, showing it to be two hundred and fifty years old; after which I made visits to most all my friends.

It was, indeed, a great luxury to me to sleep in the barn on the newly gathered hay, and to feed on milk, cream, and the plain food of these hardy farmers, and I felt that my body and mind were strengthened by such a life.

As July drew to its close, many returned to their hamlets to mow the grass and harvest the grain; so, bidding good-bye to the Orsa and Rättvik fäbodar, I wended my way once more towards Orsa Kyrkoby, and thence over to Norway.

A HOME SCENE IN RÄTTVIK.

CHAPTER XXIV.

THE north-western part of Dalecarlia is covered with large forests, containing extensive swamps and bogs, which make this part of the country difficult of access. The Eastdal River, so called to distinguish it from the Westdal, flows through a very thinly settled country, falling into Lake Siljan, near Mora Church.

Leaving Orsa, I had for fellow-traveller a captain of the Swedish army, a most delightful companion, who was going a part of the way, and we had agreed to travel together to render the drive less tedious, as the country to be traversed was very uninteresting. At first the road was very sandy. We changed horses at the pretty hamlet of Garberg, with its red-painted houses scattered amidst verdant meadows, waving fields, and groves of trees, in the midst of which flowed a stream of clear water, running fast towards the river below. The next hamlet of importance is Elfdal, with an excellent inn, near which are celebrated porphyry works. The most common variety is of a dark-brown color, containing reddish crystals of felspar; other varieties of stones are also worked, especially hyperite and granite. The greatest production of

the place is the colossal vase before the royal summer country-seat of Rosendal. All the labor is done by the country
people living in the vicinity.

Here, as in many other parts of Sweden, the living of
the church is not in the gift of the Crown, but the pastor is
elected by the land-owners. I was there when an election
took place; three candidates for the office had preached on
the preceding Sundays, for the living was worth having. The
excitement was intense, and the church was crowded; the con-
test was so close between two of the aspirants, that the success
of either depended entirely on a gentleman who, being a large
property-owner, had several votes to cast, and whose preference
no one had been able to ascertain. Though I was not interested in the result, I was in the people assembled, for they certainly did not belong to the fine Dalecarlian stock. The difference was very striking, though only fifteen or twenty miles
separated them from the parishes of Orsa and Mora; they
showed evident signs of mixture with a Lapp ancestry, for they
were short of stature, particularly the women, with prominent
cheek-bones and the Lapp nose; there was hardly a good-looking
man, and not a handsome woman in the crowded congregation.

Beyond Elfdal the country became more thinly inhabited.
Ten miles farther up is Åsen, having a chapel where services
take place only a few times during the year, to allow the old
and infirm to go to communion.

Here I parted from my companion, who recommended me
to Soldaten Smed, owner of one of the best farms in the place.
From Åsen to Särna was a long stretch of six Swedish miles,
and there was no hamlet between the two places where a post-
station could be established. I travelled from there with the
soldat's son-in-law, his wife, and their little four-year-old daughter, Maria (who took a great fancy to me), and a deaf and
dumb girl, named Kirstin. We had two carts loaded with
scythes, food, and blankets, for the family were going to the
meadows for two or three weeks. After crossing the Elfdal
River at a ferry, and after a long drive, we left the road and
went through the forest till we came to a large meadow,
fenced all around with several hay-houses, one of which be-

longed to my friend. We arrived just in time to escape the rain, which soon fell in torrents. We all slept close together, on account of the cold and wet, for the roof was leaking badly. Mosquitoes were as abundant as within the arctic circle. Early in the morning we separated, man and wife going to mow in the meadows, while Kirstin and I went to a fäbod, where the goats had been left, to bring them back to give milk for the mowers. We found there a large enclosure with cattle-pen and houses, and perhaps one hundred head of cattle. All the girls at this place slept on the floor in one house, and Kirstin and I in the evening joined the throng and did the same. On our return with the goats we moved to a shelter roofed with bark, in a part of the forest not far from extensive swamp meadows. The mosquitoes were so numerous that we collected firewood and made as much smoke as we could, to drive them off. The following morning I was left entirely alone in the camp, but not before little Maria was put to sleep and left under my care. They were not gone one hour when she awoke. I succeeded for awhile in amusing her; but finally she began to cry for her mamma. In order to quiet her, I had to carry her and walk in the forest, making her believe that we were going after mamma, and, coming back, to play with her; but I was fast reaching my wit's end to amuse the child, when happily her mother came back, wondering that she did not find her asleep, and when I told her what had happened, she laughed and said, " Paul, you would make a good nurse."

Two days of this monotonous life was all I could bear; so, returning to the main road, I found Grund Olof Olsson, who had come that day from Åsen, according to our agreement, and was waiting for me with a vehicle to take me to Särna. I soon came to Nybodö, a fabod near the highway, in charge of two maids, called Kirstin and Charlotte, the first being old, and the last young and handsome. Olof recommended me to the care of these women, told them that they must show me the way to the farms, and left. Charlotte could play superbly on the horn, and when she followed the cattle the forest resounded with the airs she knew.

I remained a few days to visit the solitary farms of these woods, in order to study the effect of this secluded life on the character of man.   At some distance from Nybodö, on the other side of the road, I came to such a farm, called Räs, surrounded by a few fields and meadows.   I could not help thinking how lonely was the life of these people.   The old folks were not at home, but a daughter, an intelligent girl, received me very kindly, and prepared a meal for me; she was not afraid, as she had seen me before with Charlotte and Kirstin.   Two of her brothers were imbeciles.

Särna is prettily situated on the banks of the river, which here had widened into a lake.   It has a parish church, a good inn, and an excellent school, open from October to the end of June.   The pastor had been settled here for twenty-seven years, and visited the old church with me.   Ascending the pulpit, I saw near the Bible what resembled a policeman's club, at the end of which was a thick piece of leather, the whole reminding one of a martinet.   This had been used, until within a few years, to awake the sleepers, the parson striking the pulpit with it very forcibly, thus compelling attention.   Near the pulpit was a long pole, rounded at the end, with which the sexton, it appears, used to poke the ribs of sleepers.   These two implements, intended to keep the congregations awake, were used extensively in many out-of-the-way places in Sweden twenty or thirty years ago, and here till within a few years, but were discontinued by the present pastor.   Now pinches of strong snuff are often offered to the sleeper, who, after sneezing for a considerable time, finds his drowsiness entirely gone.

In one place, where I had been particularly well received, I got a good illustration of the fact that the young men' dislike to see the girls of their parish marry with the people of another. Asking my friend who had introduced me if he observed how charming the daughter was, he said, " No, indeed ! would you believe it, Paul, she is going to marry a man from Vermland, who came here to get his living, and made love to her on the sly.   It is a great shame that she should take for a husband a stranger; as if there were no fine fellows in our parish."

After traversing a distance of over three Swedish miles I came to Idre, a poor hamlet with a few farms scattered far apart. I found the clergyman mowing his field of hay, for he could not afford to pay a man three kronor a day to help him. Leaving his work, he invited me to his house, and presented me to his wife. I was urged to partake of his simple dinner, which I enjoyed very much. Here the carriage road ends, and the traveller wishing to go to Norway must follow the forest paths over the hills.

Wishing to cross the peninsula again from sea to sea, I concluded to go to Röros, a town noted for its copper-mines, and as being one of the coldest places in Central Norway. Swamps are numerous, and planed logs, often two or three abreast, are laid over the most boggy parts, for horses and people to go over. The first farm we reached was on the shore of a small lake, the *Elg-sjö* (Elk Lake). As a deep narrow stream had to be crossed in order to reach the house, my guide shouted for a boat, but apparently in vain, and I was about to cross on horseback, when a boat came in sight, rowed by an old woman over eighty, but strong and healthy; she had with her two great-grandchildren, who had been left in her care. I offered to row, but she said "no," and pulled both oars with a will and strength which astonished me. Arriving at the farm she shouted, and a girl soon came out of the wood, whom she sent for a horse. Here my guide from Idre left me, and accompanied by the girl, and with another horse, I continued my way through the forest, crossing many swamps. After two hours we came to the Storbo-sjö, whose flat banks are covered with reeds. She hailed a fisherman, who agreed to take me across in his boat, and bade me good-bye by a hearty shaking of the hand after she had received her pay. I was glad to land, for the boat was old, and leaked like a sieve. A few poor farms are scattered on the shores, in one of which I met two idiotic children, one having the goitre—the second case I had seen.

At the Flötning-sjö I experienced an attempt at extortion very uncommon in this country. I spent the night there, having for supper only a bowl of sour milk; on asking the price, old Jonas said, "one dollar." I declined to pay it; and when I asked him why he charged so much, he answered that he thought I had so much money that I did not know what to do with it, and he fell from one dollar to about twenty cents. It should be said that the owner of the farm was not at home.

I crossed the Norwegian frontier without knowing it, and came to the poor hamlet of Drevsjöhytte, whence there is a road to Fæmund-sjö. The Fæmund-sjö is 2150 feet above the sea, and thirty-five miles long; its outlet, the river Klar (clear), flows into Lake Wenern. This beautiful sheet has peculiar scenery, not possessed by any other Norwegian or Swedish lake; its shores are not abrupt, and in many places are thinly clad with fir and birch trees and fine reindeer-moss; the water is clear, contrasting singularly with that of the dark lakes we had passed, and swarms with fish. I saw several wild reindeer browsing upon its shores. About three miles from its southern extremity is a hamlet composed of four old farm-houses, one of which had been burned to the ground the winter before my arrival. The people were old-fashioned folks, who knew little of the outer world. Torbert Mikkelsen was the nabob of the place, and a fine old man he was; his ruddy face was surrounded by bushy whiskers gray with age; he was dressed in knee-breeches, white woollen stockings, double-breasted waistcoat with shining brass buttons, and a red Phrygian woollen cap. Berit, his wife, was as good as himself, and a true picture of an old matron; her white hair was partly hidden under a graceful peculiar little black cap, worn in that part of the country. The house was large and comfortable, the walls of the general room were painted green, and in one corner was the cheerful open fireplace. Old porcelain dishes and cups, heirlooms of the family, were on a sideboard, a lantern hung from one of the beams of the ceiling, and an old clock stood near the bed; poles adorned with good family linen; a table, two or three chairs, a couple of benches, a loom, and a spinning-wheel constituted the furniture. My bedroom was quaint. The walls were painted yellow (evidently old Torbert loved bright colors), with a red border about three feet from the

RÖROS.

floor, the ceiling yellowish white, and the cross-beams and my bedstead were red.

Torbert was a thrifty farmer, and took pride in having everything in perfect order; he owned eighteen cows, three horses, and thirty sheep; his land was good, and his summer pasture excellent. When I left he would take no money, for I had given a fine silk handkerchief to his wife, and was urged to come again.

A row of about twenty miles took me to the north shore of the lake, which was reached after passing through swamp meadows, and where I remained for a day.

The road to Röros went through a very picturesque country, and here and there we met a few farms. Röros, or Roraas, is a quiet little town of 1900 inhabitants, situated 2000 feet above the level of the sea, with many comfortable houses painted red, and clean streets. It derives its chief importance from the copper-mines, which were worked as far back as 1644. The Storvarts mines are at an elevation of 2800 feet. The Hitter River flows through the centre of the town, the two parts of which are connected by picturesque wooden bridges of construction peculiar to Norway. The logs are supported by the filling at the ends, and also by the braces, as the engraving shows.

From Röros I travelled leisurely down the Österdal valley, often along the shores of the Glommen—the largest river of Norway.

On the last day of August I entered the town of Hamar, on the shores of Lake Mjösen. It had a forlorn appearance; grass was growing in its wide streets; weeds clustered about the church, and the growth of the place seemed entirely checked. In former times it was of great importance, but was destroyed by the Swedes in 1567. Not far from it are interesting ruins—all that remains of its cathedral.

The Mjösen is the largest lake in Norway. It is four hundred feet above the sea, about sixty-six miles long, varying much in breadth, its widest part being ten miles. The greatest depth of water is two hundred and forty fathoms—much below the level of the sea. At the time of the great earthquake in

Lisbon, in 1755, it rose suddenly twenty feet, and fell back almost instantly to its level. In the spring it attains its largest volume, from which it falls eighteen to twenty feet. It has none of the weird aspect characteristic of Norwegian lakes, for the hills slope gently to the water, and are dotted with numerous farms and fields, churches and hamlets; the scenery is pastoral, but not remarkable. Passenger steamers, and others for freight or towing logs, ply upon its waters. In summer this trip is delightful. Its chief places of importance are the small towns of Hamar, Gjövik, and Lillehammer.

The old teacher of the free-school at Hamar reminded me of some old painting. He wore an old-fashioned frock-coat, a waistcoat buttoned to the neck, and queer-shaped high collar, surrounded by a thick white kerchief with a large clumsy knot. When we entered he was playing the violin. On the black-board the notes of the musical scale were chalked, with the words of a song below them, which the boys and girls were singing to his accompaniment.

The regions of the Mjösen and the Österdal are among the finest agricultural districts of Norway. Many of the people could hardly be called peasants; they had the air of American farmers. They had large, comfortable, well-painted houses, furnished with cushioned chairs, sofas, pianos, and books; surrounded by pleasure-grounds, gardens with summer-houses, and fine barns. They took pleasure in improving their herds of cattle, sheep, and swine; went every year with their families on a visit to Christiania, and set their tables in city fashion. Their linen was starched, and, in fact, many of them might be called gentlemen-farmers, fond of their horses, of fishing, and shooting, and only superintending the work done on their estates.

At the upper end of the lake, on a high hill, is the quiet village of Lillehammer, consisting of three streets, the principal one crossing the river Mesna by a bridge. It contains about 1700 inhabitants, and is a centre of trade, as it stands at the beginning of the high-road to Trondhjem, at the termination of the valley of Gudbrandsdal, of which the lake is a continuation; and there was a hospital—a well-built two-story log-house, with large rooms sixteen feet in height, with six beds in each. There were only two patients. It was free to those who were unable to pay, and was under the direction of the government doctor. The bath-rooms and the kitchen were very clean, and it was exceedingly creditable to those who had it in charge.

I was particularly fortunate in seeing the "Fall" of Lille-hammer, as the stream was much swollen by rains, and descended in magnificent cascades. The river Mesna, for several hundred yards, tumbled down from a height of hundreds of feet in a sheet of white foam, and in one place passed through a channel only ten feet wide; while the current of air sent the spray flying above the trees and meadows to a great distance. Though far more south than Trondhjem stift, the harvest in this part of Norway is more backward even than beyond the arctic circle. In the first week in September I saw a great deal of rye and barley still uncut; and in the garden of the doctor a few cherries were still on the trees; currants and gooseberries were ripe, and the apple-trees were loaded with fruit.

Once more I found myself driving towards the transverse valleys of the Gudbrandsdal. The weather was now beautiful. I was jolting along slowly, for at the end of the summer season the horses are completely worn out. I had one which, with all my coaxing, would hardly go more than three miles an hour. These station-horses, when there is so much travelling, are very cunning, and are trained to go but four or five miles an hour. They seem to laugh at the harmless whip which is given to the traveller, who gets tired before they do.

My main object in coming so late was to see the old farm-houses. In some of the narrow valleys the harvest was further advanced than in broader ones. The people were busy digging potatoes—men, women, and children being employed; these were assorted as they were gathered, the smaller being put aside for the swine, and the others spread out to dry before being stored in a dark cellar. Every farm had many extra hands, often employed only to help the poor neighbors; but the pay was very small—the men getting only twelve, and the women eight skillings per day, with food: many preferred being paid in potatoes. It was a busy time for the farmer's wife and her maid in the kitchen, for many extra mouths had to be fed. Bread was made in great quantity, the loaves being of such a size that one was given to each man for his allowance on bread-day. Ironing is done in a very particular manner: the articles are carefully wrapped around a wooden roller, about four inches in diameter and two and a half feet long, and smoothed by an implement called a mangle, of the same size, graceful in shape, elaborately carved, and somewhat resembling a carpenter's plane.

In the Gudbrandsdal valley the farms vary considerably in size; the houses were of one story, with covered porch, consisting of the main room, with two smaller ones, and of a guest-house. The people are poor indeed, some of them possessing neither land nor cows, and having to work by the day; but, I repeat, one never meets any emaciated from hunger; they are strong and healthy, though living on coarse bread, potatoes, sour milk, and now and then butter, but rarely tasting meat.

Leaving the highway just above Laurgaard, in the wild Rusten gorge, I followed a rude mountain-road along the Hövringdal, which led to the mountains where the sæters of that name were situated. The ascent was continuous; at a height of four thousand feet the firs were still fine; I do not know of any other part of Norway where these trees grow at such an elevation. My astonishment was still greater, after reaching the plateau, to see several fields where rye and barley had been harvested. The situation of the Hövring sæters is one of the finest in Norway; there were thirty-five of them, but most of these were deserted, with the doors of the houses strongly fastened. The silence which reigned over these places, and the faded color of the grass, plainly showed that the summer had departed, and that the winter storms would soon blow fiercely over the mountains. I know of no place in Norway so easy of access, and which combines so many advantages for invalids, as this sæter. Visitors can walk long distances without getting into bogs or ascending tiresome hills;

and horseback rides can be taken to a height of almost five thousand feet.

On the 13th of September we had a foretaste of the winter. The wind blew a gale at times, accompanied by heavy showers; but towards night the sky suddenly cleared, and the weather became quite cold; before sunset snow fell. Three men came here with two carts, loaded with ploughs, axes, and other implements of husbandry; they had been sent to plough some of the fields for the following year, and on their departure were to convey to the farm all the butter and cheese which had been produced during the season, and such articles as were not to be left at the sæter during the winter. They arrived just in time to cut a fresh supply of firewood for cheese-making; they wore their best clothes, for, of course, they wanted on their arrival to appear well to the girls of the sæter: one was desperately in love with Ingeborg, but she did not seem in the least to reciprocate it. They lost no time, but put on their working-garments; in the evening Ingeborg left them in possession of her sæter, and came to spend the night at ours.

In the morning the mercury stood at 23°. There was not a cloud in the sky, and the air was still; long icicles were hanging around the roofs of the houses, and the ice was nearly half an inch thick on the shores of the stream where the water was quiet. The following day the few occupants of the sæters were to return to their farms. I reluctantly bade farewell to Marit, Britte, and Ingeborg, and wended my way alone to the valley.

The number of lemmings (*Myodes lemmus*) I met on the road and in the mountains was enormous; many had been trampled by horses' feet or crushed by the wheels of vehicles; and, while walking, I stepped continually upon them. They resemble very much a field-mouse; are about five or six inches long, of reddish-brown color, with blackish stripes, thick bodies, and short legs. Twice during my travels in Scandinavia I had met them in untold numbers, covering vast tracts of country on their migration from north-west to south-east, on their way to the sea, in which multitudes are drowned. Their migra-

tion is periodical, and always from the north; they live in the
mountains, and nothing seems to stop them on their onward
march except insurmountable obstacles. They live in holes.
I have met them as far as 70° 30′ North. Where they have
passed, the country is bare; the grass, the moss, the leaves, and
even the branches of the dwarf-birch and willow are eaten up.

In the valley of Selsdal there are several farms near its
junction with Gudbrandsdal. Among the principal ones is
Ulsvold, which I had hardly entered when home-made beer
was brought to me in a solid silver tankard—an heirloom in
the family for several generations. While I was drinking,
the district doctor made his appearance, having travelled a
long distance in a drenching storm. His arrival caused a great
stir in the household. A pair of new thick stockings was
immediately handed to him to replace his wet ones, and a cup
of fresh coffee was prepared. It would have been a breach
of hospitality if he had been allowed to depart without having food or refreshment offered.

How primitive is the love-making in many of the regions
of Scandinavia! One evening while at a farm, the old folks,
the rest of the family, and myself were awakened by knockings at the door, and we heard a voice which we recognized as
that of one of the many suitors to the hand of the fair daughter of the house. The following dialogue took place: "Sigrid,
will you not open the door for me?" No sound was heard
from within; more gentle knockings and supplications; the
maiden still remained silent. "Sigrid," continued the lover,
"you are such a nice girl! you know that if I did not admire
you I would not come so far to see you! can you be so hard-
hearted as to send me away? There are no girls in the parish
I admire so much as yourself. Please, please open the door;
the wind is chilly; I am very tired; I come only to talk a little
while with you, then I will go away." Sigrid at last relented,
and he was admitted.

CHAPTER XXV.

THERE are no houses of Mediæval Europe that can rival in antiquity the farm-buildings of Norway; their log walls, which have stood the wear of centuries, have proved more durable than those of stone; they seem to defy the ravages of time. They were built of fir-trees from the primitive forests, and some of them date back before the year 1000, and from the seventh and eighth centuries; and some even are of older and unknown ages. The timber has become so hardened that the axe has hardly any effect upon it, for the resin has been absorbed by the fibres of the wood. The logs are often of great width, showing a size of trees not at present prevalent in Scandinavia. Several of these old houses are found with Runic inscriptions—among them one in Numedalen, on the farm Raudland, in Opdals parish, high up in the mountains: here the door-posts are ornamented with carvings like those seen on the stave churches; and in the timber over the door is written the name of the builder, with " Thorgaut built me."

Many of these old farms have remained in the possession of the same family from that remote period to this day, and in this respect exceeding in age any other landed estates in Europe. The reason why Norway can boast of so many

very old houses is that its inaccessible mountains have been
secured from the devastation of wars; and when these took
place, the conflicts were chiefly on the water or on the shores
of the sea. As there are, within the historic period at least,
no remains of buildings anterior to these of wood, it is prob-
able that the earlier inhabitants of Scandinavia lived in temporary structures; their houses were probably made of turf,
perhaps variously combined with wood or stone, which have
disappeared from decay or various disturbances of the surface.
As the people advanced in civilization — the country being
covered in most parts with forests—they began to build wood-
en dwellings.

Most all of those ancient houses are situated in valleys and
dales, which, but a few years ago, were accessible only by bridle-paths, and often in out-of-the-way places, chiefly inland—
in the Hedemarken, Hallingdal, Sætersdal, Hedal, Vaage, and
Lom, in Hardanger and in Jæderen. To this day the life of
the people of these regions is most primitive.

It was always a source of pleasure not only to study the inhabitants of the valleys, but also to look at the weather-beaten
houses, to see their interior arrangements, and to trace step
by step the improvements that have taken place in the art of
building.

The most ancient form was called the *ildhus* (house with a
fireplace), or *rögstue* (house without chimney, *rög* meaning
smoke). They are yet found, though very rarely, in different parts of the country. Another building, *bur*, *bod*, or *mat-
bod*, where the food and clothing were kept, stood near.

The ildhus contained only one room, with a stone hearth
in the centre of the floor; in the roof above was a large opening called *ljore* (light-hole), for the smoke to escape. In bad
weather, when the hole was partly shut, the smoke became almost unbearable.

The hearth is about six feet long and four feet wide; sometimes a high flat stone is put up endways on the side towards
the door, designed to prevent the gusts of wind from blowing
too hard on the fire. The cooking-pot or boiling-kettle hangs
from a swinging beam. In one house of this kind in Eken

parish this beam ends in a dragon's head as an ornament. The furniture in such a house was and is of the simplest description: a couple of fixed bedsteads, fastened to the wall; a long table, usually of a single board surrounded by benches, attached to the wall, and a few wooden chairs. These are very ancient, and made of the trunks of single trees (as shown in the engraving) of peculiar form, and are still used in many places.

FIRE-HOUSE, WITH AARE (HEARTH).

The next most primitive form of fireplace in the rögstue was called *rögovn.* In front of the hole is a projection of the masonry, and when the wood is burned out the embers are raked into a little recess on this shelf, thus allowing the heat to radiate into the room. The rögovn is a piece of stonework of the height of a man, and wide enough to admit of a bed being placed on the side of it.

When the rögovnstue is to be heated in the winter, it is done in the following manner:

In the morning a suitable quantity of wood is put into the oven—preferably branches, as they burn more fiercely, and throw out the heat quickest; the wood having been piled carefully, so as to give a good draught, the flame soon issues from the opening of the oven and runs up along the sooty roof in a manner to frighten any one not accustomed to it. When the

RÖGOVN (SMOKE-OVEN). FIREPLACE WITHOUT CHIMNEY.

fire has burned down the embers are raked out on the shelf, as above stated. These consumed less fuel, and were used near the coast, where wood was scarce — the first being more common inland.

The next improvement, and a great one, was the open fireplace with chimney. This form was called *peis, spis, ovn, grue, mur, sten,* and *skorsten,* in different parts of the country; it is open, with a flue for carrying off the smoke.

In the year 1493 an inspection was made on the king's farm in Jemtland, which at that time was a Norwegian province; and in the record from the same it is mentioned that the last tenant had built a new dwelling-house, with *skorsten* (chimney, or open fireplace) and all belonging to it. This skorsten was undoubtedly the same as the present peis— standing in the every-day room, and used both for cooking, warming, and lighting it; and this is the earliest information found of that kind of fireplace in Norway. The latter is placed at some distance from the wall, and is open on two sides, as shown in the engraving. Sometimes a peis is found in the room up-stairs, so that guests in winter could have a warm sleeping-room. This peis is the form of open fireplace still found everywhere. As is seen in some of the pictures of the book, it is almost always at the corner of a room. No other form will throw out such an amount of heat; but it consumes a great quantity of wood.

In many districts, as wood became scarce, stoves of tiles or iron were introduced. The tile-stove, of which we have spoken before, is of much more recent origin—probably by several hundred years—than the peis, and is now most extensively used in Sweden. Many of the iron stoves are beautiful, with figures representing religious subjects, and some of an age dating as far back as the year 1600, and used every winter.

In a description of Hallingdal it is stated that, about 1650, houses without chimneys, and with only a hearth, were in general use in that district. In the same is also described a table with rings in the side, by which it could be hung on the wall when not in use; for, when all were seated on the long benches, and the fireplace was in the middle of the room, there was hardly space for a fixed table: that this was so is shown by the saga relating how Asbjörn Selsbane came in and wounded Thore Sel as he stood in front of the high-seat table, waiting upon the king, St. Olaf. It is written in the saga of Olaf Kyrre, King of Norway, that in former times the high seat of the king was in the middle of the long bench, and the beer was handed over the fire burning on the hearth in the middle of the floor; but that he was the first one who had his high seat made on the bench which ran across the room, and that he introduced the rö-govn, as well as the custom of having cup-bearers standing by the table. Former-ly it had been customary, when the king wished to honor any one by drinking with him, for the horn to be ex-tended across the fire to the person thus honored.

OLD PEIS IN A HOUSE IN SOGNE.

As time went on another house was built, called *nystue*, or *storstue* (new house, or large house), while the older one was named *gammelstue*, or *dagligstue* (old, or every-day house). Then the family had a separate room, and the old large house was used only for cooking, and for servants, etc.; then the fashion came, in many districts, of constructing a large number of buildings for the different uses of the farms. The mat-bod (larder) was originally a room where all kinds of provisions and clothing were kept—the latter being hung under the roof—and was probably the first of the buildings to receive a second story. Corridors or covered piazzas extended along three sides, and the two stories communicated with each other by steep, ladder-like staircases, as seen farther on in the engravings. These had to be preserved as long as possible as a protection for the door; and as no windows could be put on this side, they were placed in the gable walls. The windows in the ends prevented the house from being extended longitudinally. Afterwards the stairs to the loft were put in the porch, and thereupon followed the arrangement of an upper piazza, with its openings and pierced work, as seen by the engraving in the next chapter. These gave the house a strange appearance. The loft was built expressly for the clothes, that they might be by themselves, and hang high, free from any dampness from the ground. It was important to take great pains to preserve the clothing, as in those times most of their personal property consisted in garments—either wearing-apparel, or for beds. Originally built for these, the upper story soon came to be used also, as it is to this day, as a sleeping-room for guests, and thus got the name bedloft: even during the time of St. Olaf (1016–1030) lofts were in use for this purpose, and from the old sagas it appears that guests, especially the principal ones, slept in them. In a saga it is stated that he had a large *utebur* (outside larder), where he kept all kinds of goods, large chests, many sorts of meat, dried fish, cheese, and all necessary food: he there had his bed, where he and his wife slept. He also arranged in this room beds for his guests, and places for their arms—everything in the best manner; and even to this day, in many districts, the same arrangements are seen. The one store-house was soon changed into two—a larder and a separate bed-house. The larder for a long time retained its simple form, but sometimes it was built larger, with two rooms, each with a door on the gable-end. Great care was taken in the construction of these buildings, and there was always provision for a draught of dry and fresh air under the floors. To prevent the entrance of rats and mice they were sometimes built on posts, hence the names *stolpebod* and *stabbur:* these required outside stairs. The stabburs of Southern Norway are unlike those of other parts of the country; their peculiar shape attracts at once the attention of the stranger, and their dark and hardened weather-beaten walls tell of their antiquity.

STABBUR IN RINGERIKE, WITH GALLERIES.

With time improvements began to take place, and additions were made to the primitive fire-house, and the extension was called *ramloft,* from which the houses now existing take their name. This ramloft goes up in a tower-like fashion at one end, with the stairs on the outside which lead to a door opening into the loft, which is a bedroom constructed with peculiar care and of the same size as one in the story below; the primitive, and large, and lofty fire-house remained open up to the roof. There are a number of these in different parts of the country, but they are more common, though even there but sparsely found, in Lom, where I will take the reader in a following chapter.

In Hedemarken, on the old crown farm Huseby, in Stange, is an old ramloft house, which, however, now has many recent additions. The ramloft here was divided by partitions into two apartments, in one of which was a small fireplace; in the other, the walls were ornamented by paintings representing tapestry, in imitation of a custom of hanging tapestry on the walls on festive occasions. The paintings give a very good idea of the manner of this ornamentation: above are shown small bars, and from these are hanging gay-colored aaklæder in folds, fastened with cords in the upper corner; there is not much art in the painting, but it is an interesting relic of antiquity. One is reminded by this ramloftsal of the first chapter of Sverre's saga about the "fine loftsal" of which his mother dreamed, or of Snorre's story of Asta's love and eagerness, when she was told that her son Olaf (the saint) was every moment expected to return from foreign countries: she rose up immediately, and ordered men and women to get everything arranged in the best manner; she had her women bring ornaments into the house and decorated it, as well as the benches, with tapestry.

Another ramloft house is seen on the farm of Stemsrud, in Grue parish, at Solör, in the valley of Glommen; in one of the timbers is cut the year 1324; it has for several generations been in the family of Kolbjörnsen, who keep it in good condition.

In Northern Österdal is found a peculiar kind of buildings called *barfrö*. This form is also very old, and should the tower be taken away the house would remain intact—a primitive type, with the fireplace in the centre. In front of the door is a square porch, sometimes of horizontal timbers, but oftener of posts, with plank walls; a flight of stairs leads up to a small square room used for clothing, but also as a sleeping-room: this front part is called barfrö. The origin can be traced to the ancient Germanic language, now known only by old manuscripts, where its name was berevrit, which reads berkfrit. The first syllable is related to the Norwegian *bjerge* (to preserve, to keep), the last is the same as *fred* (peace). In France it is called to-day berfroit or berfroi, hence the English name belfry. The use of this kind of tower spread to

ÖSTERDAL BARFRÖ STUE.

Denmark, and finally to Norway, where it at present is found only in Österdal.

The *opstugu* is the oldest kind of building in Trondhjem stift; next to the rögstuer is the opstugu still found in Opdal. The opstugu is the little room above the porch, and the lower

AN OPSTUGU.

bedroom is very like the ramloft, only that the stairs are inside the porch. This arrangement is now seen only on the older houses and on the smaller farms. Two of these houses can be seen on the high-road from Christiania to Trondhjem, at the post-stations Drivstuen and Rise. The porch wall, where the entrance-door is, is generally panelled with open pillars over and on each side of the door, giving light and air to the hall.

From the engraving it will be seen that the opstugu is similar to the ramloft, the difference being that the stairs on the latter are outside; from which cause again the former had to be divided into a hall and the room: both are built at the transverse end of the house, while the barfrö is a tower entirely outside, and built in the middle of the house—besides, the ramloft has corridors and piazzas. The picture shows the exterior appearance of the opstugu. Properly the little chamber is called opstugu, situated over the small bedroom underneath. The stairway is built in the hall; it leads into a smaller one above, from which one comes to a small sleeping apartment.

On an old stave-church in Tins parish, in Thelemarken, was found in 1822 a Runic inscription—showing, beyond doubt, that the church was inaugurated between 1180 and 1190. The building has been torn down, but the plank in which these runes were inscribed is preserved in the antiquarian collection of the University, and looks as if it could withstand the tooth of time for centuries to come. Næsland's stave-church, taken down 1850, had a similar inscription, showing it to have been inaugurated in 1242.

The farm Korterud, in Eidsberg parish, of the province of Smaalenene, is noted for the very old spar-house building found there. The two entrances on the partition wall are so low that one has to stoop in entering; each is surmounted by a wooden arch, cut out of a single piece, one foot thick; on these arches are carved ornaments with some undecipherable letters; each door consists of hewn boards or planks, and the ornamented iron rings extend over its entire width. Beyond the threshold one has to step down nearly one and a half feet into the house, the floor of which consists of rough logs. Along the three sides were formerly benches of timber, between which and the walls earth was filled in to keep out the wind. Opposite the doors are two windows, and on that part the floor was one foot higher than the rest, and held a long table made of thick planks; in the middle of the lower division was formerly the stone hearth, traces of which are still seen. In the corner of the room, near one of the doors, is a small closed fireplace, provided with a narrow baking-oven, but it is not now in use; a porcelain stove has later been added. But the sign showing the great age of the house is the hearth in the middle of the room, and with only a hole in the roof, now closed, but which still can be traced by the smoky, and in some places half-charred appearance of the timbers.

In Valders, on the farm Hande, in West Slidre parish, is a large building which has for a long time attracted attention

BEDLOFT HOUSE IN VALDERS.

for its antiquity; it shows remarkably good timber-work, though there is not much ornamentation or carving. The doors in the lower story open into two low dark rooms (as shown in engraving) without windows, evidently used for provisions; in the floor is a trap-door connecting with the cellar. The principal part of the building is the upper story, divided into two apartments; the larger with fireplace and three windows, but quite dark from being partly surrounded by corridors, suitable for a bedroom, or in the daytime used as a feast hall. The date of its erection is not known; but it is evidently of the same form as another house described on the farm Skjelbred, in Annebo parish, in Jarlsberg, which even in 1751, when a drawing of it was made, was considered as very old, having been the residence of Count Alf, and known to have been standing at the end of the thirteenth century.

Other old buildings of the same kind may be seen on the

farm Finne, at Voss, in Bergen stift; at Oroug, in Askim; and on Lang sæter, in Thrykstad; in Smaalenene (jutul stuer, as they were called by the peasants); at Sorknaes, near the Glommen; at Hofnord, near Hole, in Ringerike; Gavelstad, in Lardal, above the town of Laurvik. These houses were probably identical with the höieloft and jomfrubur of the sagas, also known under the name of skemme.

A good specimen of the jutul stue is found on the farm Uv, in Rennebo, Örkedalen, Trondhjem stift. The saga says that *jutuls* (giants) built the house, bringing the immense timbers on their shoulders from the forests; it is probably over six hundred years old. These logs are among the largest found in old Scandinavian houses.

The Jæderen type (a district near Stavanger) is exceedingly

FIG. 1.—FRONT.

interesting, and possesses characteristics very peculiar. Fig. 1 shows the front, Fig. 2 the back, and Fig. 3 the end of such a one. The window above lights the loft where the provisions

FIG. 2.—BACK.

are kept. Such houses often show the planks and timbers of stranded vessels, timber being very scarce in that district; turf and stone are also used extensively on this account. They are large and comfortable inside. The room proper is built

of wood, with high seat, fixed bench, long table, the master's
bed, oven; porch partitioned off, with stairs to the left; kitchen
also divided, with back-door and window
by its side; in the kitchen the fireplace,
from which the oven in the house is
filled: there is a bedroom for guests, in
which is the clothes chest. This room,
as well as the principal one, is built of
timbers exclusively. There are additions
at both ends of the house, used for pre-
serving turf; there is also a small room on the back of the
house, with the wall partly of stone and partly of wood, communicating with the kitchen, and used as a larder.

FIG. 3.—END.

The Mandal form of stue (house) presents features quite
different from those of any other. The original was a rög
stue, with the hearth in the middle of the floor, and a hole in
the roof for the smoke. The old house is still left standing,
and is used as a kitchen, bakehouse, etc., while between that

ARRANGEMENT OF BEDS IN THE STUE (HOUSE) AT MANDAL.

and the new one is a hall, with stairs for the upper story. The
inner arrangements of this new addition are made after the
type of the old house; the difference being caused by the
substitution of an iron stove for the hearth. The placing of

the beds is peculiar, as shown in the engraving; between them is a closet, generally with fine carvings.

On many an old farm are found chests of different shapes and sizes, made centuries ago, long before closets were built; and in many districts they are still in use. Cupboards and movable closets occur, which are also interesting on account of their age and elaborate carvings.

One often meets with a kind of coverlet called *aaklœder*, sometimes also used as a curtain for hiding shelves and the like. They are made on a loom called *upstadsgogn*, and by a process more like plaiting than weaving. Many of the coverlets, often in very bright colours, have scenes on biblical subjects woven into them. Some of them are seen with figures showing that they were made about 1600. They are from Bergen stift, where the manufacture of them is still prevalent.

CHAPTER XXVI.

WE will journey towards a district where some of the oldest farm-buildings are to be found.

On a pleasant afternoon I crossed on a wooden bridge the turbulent Logen, and soon after entered the Hedal, one of the transverse valleys of the Gudbrandsdal. The leaves of the aspen had already turned, and the bright crimson contrasted finely with the dark coniferous foliage. After a drive of a few miles I alighted before Slette, and, passing a quaint gate, found myself in a yard formed by eight houses of somewhat peculiar architecture. On the left of the enclosure was the dwelling-house, entered by a porch with a pointed pinnacle; a closed piazza protected the upper story; the roof was of earth, upon which the grass grew; it was built of rough logs, darkened and hardened by age. On the lower floor was a large room about twenty-eight feet square, with ceiling ten feet high, supported by eight stout beams, underneath which another beam served as a brace, indicating the strength of construction. In one corner was the common open fireplace: the furniture consisted of a long table, an antique buffet, a few wooden benches, an old-fashioned closet, and a bed. The floor was very clean, and some of the planks were from twenty to twenty-three inches in width; four low windows gave light to the room, and in them stood pots filled with flowers; the walls were painted of a bright yellow, and the ceiling white. A widow, the owner of the farm, was spinning; by her side was her only child, a fair-haired girl of nine years. Two ser-

vant-maids were sewing some garments. I excused myself
for coming without invitation, but said that her place appeared so strange that I could not resist the temptation of aligbt-
ing and looking at the house. I was invited to spend the
night, but declined, as I was going to a farm farther up.
Upon which I was told that I could not leave before partaking of a cup of coffee, which was preceded by a small glass of
spirits, given as a token of welcome.

Beyond Slette the farms were numerous. Many of them occupied the summits of rounded hills formed of alluvial soil, all
of the same height, and appearing in the distance like a continuation of the terraces. Each one looked like a small village, on account of the number of its buildings. Near the
church was the old farm of Heringstad, with its peculiar stabbur and upper piazzas.

A little farther on was Björstad, a very old farm, owned by
the Tofte family from time immemorial. It was late when
I reached its yard : the dim light of the moon made the buildings appear still more fantastic. I thought, as I looked at
those silent walls with piazzas, of the scenes which, in former times, must have taken place within. On our left, after entering the gate, was the stue or dwelling-house seen in the engraving, built of logs, rough on the outside and inside, and set
upon a thick stone foundation. This house was about forty
feet long and thirty wide, and along three sides of the upper
story ran a piazza partly enclosed by boards ; the entrance, as
at Slette, was through a fine old porch (*dörsval*) with elaborate
carvings, from which a steep staircase led to the piazza above.
Here was a room occupying almost the whole breadth of the
house, its dimensions being fifteen feet in depth and twenty-
six in width. It contained a bed, but no antique furniture ;
the hall was hung with winter fur-coats, robes, blankets, and
other articles of apparel.

In the yard two houses formed one side of the square;
these were more odd, and more antique in appearance than
the one we had left, especially the belfry, dark piazzas, porches, and ladder-like stairs—the hard logs seeming to defy the
ravages of time. Their stone foundations were high, and in

BJÖLSTAD.

the first house the basement was used for keeping the milk, cheese, and butter. Firm stairs led to a sort of porch, with carved wood-work, and thence to the rooms of the first story; by a staircase like the one before mentioned I reached the gallery above, which was enclosed by boards, with an opening above, seven feet long by eighteen inches wide, to admit light and air. Some of the rooms on the upper floor contained beds, but others had no furniture whatever; in one of them eight working-men slept. This house had formerly evidently stood alone; but it has long been the custom in Gudbrandsdal to add new houses to the old ones, and join them in some way or other. The piazza of the second house was reached by very steep stairs. In one of the rooms the panes of glass were very small, and the frames which held them were of lead. Two other old houses formed the opposite side of the square; the lower part of one was used as a stable, and contained eighteen stalls; this was thirty feet long, and had three doors, the centre one leading to a passage where the hay was placed in the mangers on each side. The next one was a quaint building containing two rooms on the first floor, in one of which the flour provided for the use of the family was stored in leather bags, each of which was numbered; there were in the same apartment huge piles of flat bread. A staircase led to the upper story, which contained one large room, in which the meat was kept—a large supply of which had been left over from the previous year; the killing-season for the next winter had not yet arrived. Among these stores were a great number of sausages, twenty-two halves of pigs, blood-puddings, sides of bacon, and several dried shoulders of sheep and goats, besides a lot of cheese. To complete the square was the guest-house, of more modern date, about sixty-five feet long and forty wide; a wide hall, lighted by a window at the end, ran through its centre, and on each side were two comfortable bedrooms; a steep flight of stairs led to the upper story, where the arrangements were the same as below. Everything was scrupulously clean; not the smallest spot could be seen upon the white pine floor, and the polished wood of the logs inside appeared so new that one might have fancied they had been laid but a few years before, although the house was finished in the year 1818. This building was erected upon a strong stone foundation, and its cellars were spacious. These walls were of the heaviest kind, and proved to last, as we have seen, for centuries. The beams supporting floors and ceilings were of great strength, and the logs of the sides were joined with great care, as were the posts supporting the piazzas; the birch-bark on the roof was carefully laid, and on this the earth covering had been placed.

Near the yard was an old house which was used as a granary, the grain being stored in large wooden compartments. There was a large building for the cows, on the declivity of a hill, and also constructed on a stone foundation: in this were housed eighty-eight cows. Close by was another, with twenty-eight. It would be tedious to go through a catalogue of the numerous houses upon this farm; for, besides those forming the yard, twenty others were scattered about, used for the storage of hay, sleighs, wagons, carts, and for black-smithing, etc.

Among the interesting and useful structures found on every farm is that where the grain is dried before being stored (the kiln); an oven, used also for baking, is built in the centre, and on each side were long troughs, about three feet wide and a few inches deep, in which grain is placed to dry by the hot air. If not thus treated it would mould, on account of its humidity.

Wherever I went on this farm tokens of past centuries met me on every side. Here was a spot where once stood a cemetery and a church; the latter, one of the first erected in Norway, had disappeared, no trace of it remaining except one of the old doors. Now and then are seen relics of former times; among them two crosses, like those of Gotland, which once stood over tombs, their Runic characters, partly obliterated, attesting their antiquity. I saw a piece of a wooden cross, kept under the house, with the letters and date, "T. T. S., 1735," meaning "Tord Thord's son;" this cross had been placed above the grave of one of the Tofte family.

Bjölstad, besides being the largest farm in Hedalen, was also a sort of post-station. It was of great extent, comprising within its boundaries large tracts of mountain-land which, though not of much value, had extensive forests of birch and good grazing-lands; several sæters belonged to it. The land under cultivation for grain, as on almost all these mountain farms, was not very great. Tofte planted about seventy-five acres with grain, and his farmers the same number. Butter and cheese were the chief products of the farm, and large quantities of hay were required for the stock during the long winters; in harvest-time, forty or fifty extra hands were employed; in winter, nine girls, twenty men, and four lads composed the household. Machinery is very little used, and cannot be at all in many districts, on account of the rough and stony character of the soil. The richer farmers are therefore under the necessity of helping their poorer neighbors, and of employing their daughters and sons for awhile; otherwise their reputation would be injured, and a good name is precious to them.

My host did not know the exact dimensions of his estate, but said it extended far back into·the mountains. He raised horses, and among the thirty-three he had in his stables pointed with pride to one of a chestnut color, which had won the first prize at the fair in Christiania; some of his ponies were very fine animals. There were several husmænd, who either paid a stipulated sum each year, or performed labor for a certain number of days.

Bjölstad and other farms have been for centuries in the possession of the Toftes. The cause of these estates remaining for so long a period in the same families is due to two laws, which are so ancient that the time of their enactment is lost. These are the *Åsædesret* (homestead right), and the *Odalsret* (allodial right). The first is the right of the eldest son to inherit the farm after his father; he, however, being obliged to pay the other heirs their share of the estate, the value of which is given by the father, or else it is estimated far below its valuation. If the former be dead, his eldest son takes it, and so on. If the first named has left no son, his eldest daughter inherits, etc. If a farm is of such a size that several families can exist on it, the father is allowed to divide it among his children, under such conditions, however, that the eldest son or daughter shall not receive less than one-half of the farm. The second (the Odalsret) is the right, when a farm is to be sold, of any member of the family to buy it—or, if sold to a stranger, their right within ten years to redeem it at the price paid, with the additional cost of the improvements; if there is any controversy, appraisers are appointed. A later law has modified this, so that an owner selling his farm may determine whether he renounces for himself and heirs this right.

This fine old farm narrowly escaped a transfer to other hands two or three years before my visit; but Ivor was able to buy it by asserting his Odalsret. These two rights are held on to very tenaciously by the Norwegian bönder as safeguards, as many have told me, against the absorption of their land by the rich people of the cities, or capitalists, who in time would destroy their small homesteads, and unite them into vast landed estates.

An unpretending man was the actual owner of Bjölstad; he was forty-six years of age, and a bachelor. He was dressed in a bluish-black frock-coat, of homespun material, with high-necked waistcoat, and pantaloons of the same material, and a bright-red woollen Phrygian cap. He wore the same garments all the year round, except that on Sunday he had a newer suit. At meals Ivor Tofte presided at the head of the large table, as the chief of the household, eating at the plain red-painted board with his men and maid servants, in the honest, simple, and patriarchal way of the olden time. This primitive custom exercised a beneficial influence, and banished the disparities of social distinction. His orders were always conveyed in a quiet way, without show of authority, which made them the more pleasant to those who received them.

On these large Norwegian farms everything goes on like clock-work. There is a rule about food—certain days having fish, meat, sausage, etc., etc. The supper is very simple, and invariably consists of the thick porridge called *gröd*, made of meal or grits boiled in water, and served in wooden dishes, with several bowls of sour milk. The people eat with wooden spoons, and help themselves from the same dish. In summer, during harvest-time, home-brewed ale is given to the men. There are two dinners a week with meat, the others with fish—potatoes always being served with these.

In the Hedal Valley, and at Björstad, each girl employed by the year received two pairs of shoes, one dress, two bodices, one skirt, three other undergarments, and three or four dollars in money, with wool enough to make two pairs of stockings. A man received one coat, two pairs of shoes, two shirts, one pair of pantaloons, one pair of stockings, two pairs of socks, and ten dollars a year. The male day-laborer had in summer eighteen skillings, or a mark; in winter, twelve skillings with food; and the girls received from eight to twelve skillings. Money has great value with these mountain people, and in the districts remote from the sea is not easily obtained; they have generally little to sell, but enough to eat. The house-keeper here was paid eighteen dollars, but had to provide herself with clothing and shoes. Saturday is house-cleaning day, for everything must be in order for Sunday. The floors are washed, the tables scrubbed, and everything made tidy. The girls make their toilets and change their clothes. About four o'clock the men stop work, shave themselves, put on clean linen—looking forward with impatience for the evening, as Saturday is the lover's day. As soon as it is dark they start to visit their sweethearts, often having to go a long distance; they take great care lest the neighbors know what girl they are courting, for gossip is then let loose, and the girl becomes shy: this is not always easy, as the boys are watching, and there are many prying eyes and busy tongues among the villagers.

On Sunday, immediately after breakfast, every one is attired in holiday clothes. Here many of the men, even the lads, wear swallow-tailed dress-coats, made like the rest of homespun cloth, their heads being covered with a long woollen cap. The shoes are particularly well-polished and greased. In the evening there is a dance. I was much amused by observing that, whenever one of the girls wanted to go out, she would call two or three others to accompany her—being

u 2

afraid the company would suspect she was seeking a chance to talk with a lover—for the girls and the men in this quiet place were continually on the watch to discover love affairs. The dancing ended at ten o'clock, for there was much work to be done on Monday.

From the old farm of Bjölstad the narrow road continued on the left bank of the Trykja—upon whose shores were several little grist-mills; the hills were clad with coniferous trees, but a thick fog prevented me from seeing the summits of the mountains. We kept ascending till we came to the little Bjölstad Lake, which we passed on our left, and soon reached the summit of the ridge which divides the Hedal from the Ottadal.

The descent was very abrupt and picturesque, and the Otta River was crossed on an old bridge supported by piers of logs filled up with stone.

COURT-YARD AT SANDBO, IN VAAGE.

CHAPTER XXVII.

The Ottadal.—A Region with Old Farm-houses.—Old Buildings on the Farm of
Sandbo.—A Kind-hearted Doctor and his Wife.—The Vaage Lake.—The Tesse
Falls. — The Farm of Haakenstad. — Ascending the Valley. — The Church of
Gardmo—its Antiquity.—King St. Olaf and Thorgeir.—Why Thorgeir built the
Church.—St. Olaf's Iron Bracelet.—Old Paintings.—One of the Descendants of
Thorgeir.—The Church of Lom.—A very hospitable Dean.—The Loms Eggen.—
The Hard Winter of 1868.—Snow Avalanches.—Loss of Life.—An Historical Re-
gion.—The Olaf Saga.—How St. Olaf converted the People to Christianity.—The
Ramloft House on the Farm of Lökkre.

FROM the Gudbrandsdal there is a grand valley, the Ottadal,
which extends westward in a straight line, and would join the
southern branch of the Nord fjord if it were not shut off by
the mountains. In that valley are many of the oldest farm
buildings of Norway.

The Ottadal at its opening lies between the Hedal and Selsdal, from which it is separated by mountain ranges. Crossing
the Logen, one is struck at once by the difference in the aspect of the two streams—the Otta being of that peculiar color
which showed its glacial origin, while the other is perfectly
clear. The drive from the farm of Aasor, which takes its
name from the mountains on the other side, is very fine.
We changed horses at Snerle, where the river becomes a lake;
on approaching the church of Vaage the mountain scenery is
truly grand as Kopfjeld and Kvitingskjölen burst into view,
with their large patches of snow. In the neighborhood of the
church of Vaage are a number of very old farms, and among
these is Sandbo. As one enters the yard, the dark color of all
the buildings impresses him at once with the antiquity of the
place. On the left is the matbod or larder, with a reindeer
horn. Two high step-ladders lead to the piazza of the next
house, while beyond is the most ancient building, the old Ild
house, which has been improved, and there the family resides.

The engraving shows a house on one of the farms of Sandbo. What is especially to be pointed out is its being a kind
of transition from the old to the new. The principal entrance-
door is not situated on the wall of the room itself, but first
opens into a hall. This hall has several advantages; it better
protects the room-door than a corridor, so that rain and wind
do not strike in every time the door is opened, and it also

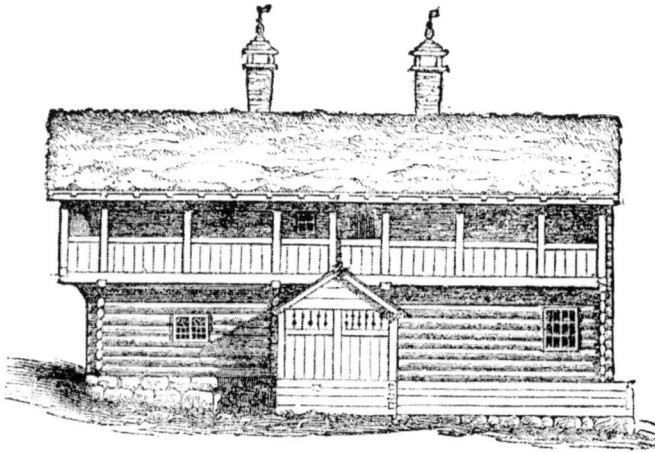

HOUSE AT SANDBO.

makes a nearer connection between the different parts of the
house; one does not need to go out in the corridor to pass
from the old part to the new, or to the stairway leading to
the loft.

At the relay-station of Sve I made the acquaintance of Dr.
R—— and his young and accomplished wife; they were not
yet settled, and had been there but a short time. I could not
leave without partaking of their hospitality. The doctor insisted that I should take his cariole, which had springs, while
mine had none. It was in vain that I expostulated, and before
I knew it he was himself loading the vehicle, his wife helping
him; if I had been their brother they could not have been
more in earnest for my comfort.

At Vaage the Findal Valley joins the Ottadal; the road
here branches, one fork going northward to Lesje, in Roms-

dalen. A little above the church the river is crossed by a
bridge, and the road follows the left shore of the Vaage Vand,
1120 feet above the level of the sea. Farther on the country
becomes more barren, and the Thesse River, coming from the
Thesse Vand, 2700 feet above the sea, tumbles down in a series of beautiful falls—the last one from a flat surface. Just
beyond is the Storvik farm.

SIDE VIEW OF HOUSE AT SANDBO.

In Findalen, not far from the church of Vaage, is Haakenstad, one of the largest farms in the parish. This farm has, like
Bjölstad, a very large number of houses, amounting to thirty-
three. Among them are a grist-mill, three stables for horses,
others for cattle and sheep, two wagon-sheds, two granaries,
smoke-house, kiln, houses for warming water for feeding the
cattle and for a laundry, several barns with even three stories,
and a dwelling for male and female servants.

A drive of about four hours from Vaage brought me to
Gardmo, an old farm, not far from which, on a tongue of land
issuing into the Vaage Vand, stood the old church of Gardmo,
or Garmo. Opposite the same rose the mountains of Skardhö,
with a few farms at their bases; while behind, on the other
side of the lake, a huge mass of hills culminated in the Kvitingskjölen and its glacier, rising to a height of 6276 feet.

This old church was erected in the time of St. Olaf, is built of logs, and surrounded by a walled cemetery; the sight of the logs, hardened by age, carries one back to the time when Christianity dawned upon the land.

King Olaf went across these waters to Thorgeir (the old) at Gardmo, in Lom, and the latter, as a token of gratitude, built a church to the saint's memory on his place; the oldest parts of the present Gardmo church are the remains of that one. The church was small, and the additions made to it from time to time had given it the shape of a cross: remains of the Roman Catholic symbols formerly in use were still visible. Among the interesting relics I saw an iron bracelet, said to have belonged to St. Olaf: above the altar hung a painting of the Lord's Supper, inscribed with the words the Saviour uttered when he broke the bread and poured the wine; under that painting was written "Henning Garmo, Tore Siversdatter, 1735," in common letters. Above it was a picture of the Crucifixion.

STORVIK, NEAR VAAGE LAKE.

The ceiling above the altar was painted in gorgeous colors, and the walls were decorated with twenty-two paintings illustrating different scenes in the life of Christ. The dates of these pictures ranged from the year 1710 to 1735, and one was inscribed 1746; all were gifts from different persons.

The most interesting portion of the building was that built in 1130: there was a sort of box high up on the left, entrance to which was gained by a ladder outside of the church. In the graveyard lay the remains of some of the ancestors of the families I had visited, their line of descent dating back to a time long before this place of Christian worship had been built. The old and historical Gardmo farm is owned by one of the descendants of old Thorgeir, and dates still farther back. The owner received me kindly, but the house was far from clean.

Leaving Gardmo, the road winds along the valley towards the church of Lom, some ten miles farther. The view was superb. The bottom of the valley was quite flat, and at times presented a pretty broad expanse: numerous sand-banks were seen in the lake. In the distance, on the left bank of the lake, Loms Horungen rose to 5500 feet, with numerous farms at its base; still farther up, on the right, was Loms Eggen, 6570 feet. It is not so much the height of these mountains, as their massive grandeur and the sombre colors, which impress the observer.

At the foot of Loms Eggen, on an exceedingly well-formed terrace, stands the church of Lom, at the junction of the Bæverdal with the Ottadal. This church is built of logs, and is of great strength; it contains several paintings—one of 1608, another of 1650, and others from 1710 to 1740.

Near the parsonage, which was a large and commodious dwelling, was a pleasure-ground, with walks winding among rocks and groves of birch-trees; and the river Bæver formed a fall through its narrow rocky channel on its way to the lake.

I was received warmly by the *provst* (dean), who was quite a learned man, and spoke English fluently. Several friends were on a visit. Our host produced enormous pipes, and passed them around among the guests, who seemed to enjoy smoking very much. The weather being very cold, toddy was also served. The ladies were busy with their needle-work while we were talking, and did not seem to dislike in the least the clouds of tobacco smoke.

The Loms Eggen rises like a huge promontory to a height of 6570 feet, and 5314 feet above the Lom church. On its northern side is the Ottadal, which is merely a continuation of the Vaage and Lom valleys westward, while the Bæverdal, starting from the same point, takes a southerly course.

The weather had suddenly become cold, and heavy over-coats were very comfortable while driving. In the Skeaker Valley, but not far from the church, my attention was drawn to a part of the mountain-side which was perfectly bare, and the provst gave me with great emotion the following explanation:

"In 1868 there was a very hard winter, and in this district snow fell almost incessantly for three or four weeks, until on the sides and tops of the mountains it attained an enormous depth, and cut off all communication. On the 8th of February, the weather having suddenly cleared and turned very cold, a huge avalanche came down the mountains, carrying everything before it—earth, trees, rocks—and leaving all behind it bare." Then he pointed to a pile of stones which marked the site of a little farm which had been swept away; the whole family, father, mother, and two children, had been crushed by the mass of snow, and only this heap of rocks had been left to tell the story. Then he added: "I heard of the accident a few hours after it occurred; I called all the male population of the district together, and mustered all the horses on the farms, and we went to digging while the other people were watching, for fear of more avalanches. We dug all day on Saturday and a part of Sunday, before we came to the ruins, but the people and the cattle were all dead."

Continuing on our way, the provst again pointed to some other ruins—the remains of another farm swept away by the avalanche; the father of the family had gone to Trondhjem, leaving his wife and three children, but when he came back he could find neither family nor home; an avalanche had overwhelmed all except his mother, who had escaped as by a miracle. I saw a new house near the ruins, in which the bereaved man was living alone, mourning for the dead. The provst also told me that in Bæverdal two persons had been buried by the snow; and he added, with feeling, "It was a dark winter for us; sorrow came to the door of many a household."

There is also another road along the lake where one can drive as far as Skeaker, going eastward through the Ottadal, following the lake. Farms are found as far as the Juran lake. There is also a bridle-path going to Stryn, in Sogne. Several exceedingly wild valleys open into the Otta, the most interesting being the Lunderdal and Tundradal. The lakes of the Otta valley are encased between the Loms Horungen and Loms Eggen.

This region is full of historical reminiscences: here the inhabitants were Christianized by St. Olaf. The visit of that king to Lom is described in the Olaf saga: "The king stopped overnight on the farm Bö, near Lesje, where he ordained priests for that district; he then went over the Loradal and came to Stava Brækken ridge, and remained there awhile; below this ridge lies a farm called Bö or Böje, a river called Otta running through the valley; and the neighborhood on both sides is called Lom. The king could see along the valley, and said, "It would be a great pity if one should be forced to burn this beautiful country." Then he passed down into it with his men, and stayed overnight on the farm *Næs*, and lodged in a loft, where he slept. It is said that the king remained there during five nights, and summoned before him the people of Lom, Vaage, and Hedalen, and sent messages that either they would have to come and be baptized, and abjure heathendom, or else see their farms burned, or try their luck in arms against him; and in the former case they must give him their sons as hostages, which they, however, ought to consider as an honor, and not as a compulsion. And it is related that nearly all the bönder came to the king and were reconciled with him, but those that did not fled."

On the farm of Næs is found the house in which St. Olaf slept more than 860 years ago, but unfortunately it was changed some forty years since; before this it was a ramloft, like that at Lökkre. It is to this day known as St. Olaf's house.

At the head of the Ottadal, here called the Lom Valley, the country is very thickly settled. Among the many old farms is that of Lökkre, which has the latest ramloft house that has been built in that region. Here the stairs leading to it are on the outside, from which a door opens into a bedroom of the

FRONT OF RAMLOFT HOUSE AT LÖKKRE.

same size as the one below. The drawing shows the covered corridor-like piazza peculiar to all the houses on the Gudbrandsdal, concealing the walls, but here the lower gallery is entirely closed. On the transverse side the building is also enclosed by a piazza in two stories, and there are stairs leading to the ramloft. The picture represents the length of the structure, but the log-wall of the lower story is hidden by an outside corridor with parallel wall, having only an opening in the middle, through which is seen the door of the house — this being one of the most striking traits of the Gudbrandsdal houses; but generally they are more or less open, and not with a closed wall like this one.

The house proper, or every-day room, is large and lofty, without ceiling. On the crown cross-beam is marked in the wood, E. R. S. (Esland Rolf's son), 1769. The whole house is twenty-nine feet long, not including the piazza. The large room is twenty feet long and twenty-three wide, and the height from the floor to the crown of the roof is thirteen feet.

To the left of the entrance is a large closet, used by the mistress as a cupboard; along-side of it is the high seat of honor, with a smaller closet to the left and above it, in which the master keeps his papers under lock and key. The space on the wall above the high seat is occupied by book-shelves, which on festive occasions, according to old custom, are covered by an aaklede (described in Chapter XXV.), a kind of bed-spread woven in bright colors. In Lom five of these, with biblical figures, are still used for the purpose. One has the year 1620 woven into it. Next to the small closet is a long

REAR OF RAMLOFT HOUSE AT LÖKKRE.

bench fastened to the wall, and in front of it the large table with another bench running the length of it opposite the first one. In the left-hand back-corner is the master's bed, with a fixed seat next to it. In the inner right-hand corner is the fireplace, and on the other side of the bedroom door a stationary bench; and in the room below the ramloft stands a bed, with a few steps leading up to it. As a general rule, the beds in the houses are fastened to the walls. Often there are separate sleeping-houses for guests, containing a larder or storehouse in the lower story, and bedrooms above.

CHAPTER XXVIII.

The Wildest and Highest Mountain Region in Norway.—Height of some of the
Peaks.—Difference between Swiss and Norwegian Mountains.—To Jotun Moun-
tain.—The Bæverdal. — Protection against Avalanches.—From the Visdal to
Galdhöpiggen.—View from Galdhöpiggen.—The Leiradal.—The Lang Lake.—
The Gjendin Lake.—Its Scenery.—The Bes and Rus Lakes.—The Bygdin Lake.
—A Hunting Region.—Lake Tyen.—A Snow-storm.—In a Predicament.—Ap-
pearance of Fishermen.—Deserted Sæters.—End of the Journey.

THE wildest and highest mountains of Norway are the
Jotun, known also under the name of Jotunheim, "the home
of the giants," between Lom and the great Sogne fjord, culmi-
nating in Galdhöpiggen, 8300 feet above the sea.

Among other high peaks of this range are Glittertinden,
7860 feet; Leirhö, 7400; Heilstuguhö, 7550; Tykningssuen,
7550; Tjærnhultinden, 7530, and Beshö, 7400 feet. In the
Horungerne, which are included in the Jotun, the highest
peak, Skagastöltinderne, rises to 7860 feet. Besides these there
are a large number of peaks of hardly less altitude. The
peculiarity of the Jotun is that several of its mountains are
pointed. In this superb group, which covers over sixty square
miles, are found many fields of perpetual snow, deep valleys
with immense glaciers falling into or overhanging them, and
lakes several thousand feet above the sea. This region affords
some of the grandest pictures of Norwegian scenery.

The difference between the mountains of Switzerland and
Norway is this: those of the former are much higher, more
bold and pointed, and sharp in the outlines of their thousand
fantastic forms. On the other hand, the Norwegian mountains have a grave and sombre character, appearing like a
gigantic stony wave, with a peak here and there, impressing
more by their vastness than their height and ruggedness. In
Norway the valleys are less numerous, and separated by broad

masses of mountains, generally excavated by ice. In Switzerland narrow ridges divide one valley from another.

Let us now wander awhile in the Jotun mountains and the Visdal and Leiradal valleys.

In order to reach them from Lom, one must ascend the Bæverdal by a rough carriage-road as far as the farm of Rösheim, situated on the shore of the furious Bævra, 1559 feet above the sea, and 300 above the Vaage Lake. This valley is enclosed on the north by the mountain ridge called *Loms Eggen*, and on the south by the *Galdhöerne*. The lower parts of the surrounding slopes are covered with birches interspersed with firs.

Looking at the incline of the mountains, the stranger can realize the dangers to the inhabitants of that district from avalanches or snow-slides, which are not uncommon. Little stone huts, hardly peeping out of the ground, and protected by hillocks or by the configuration of the ground, with sometimes a little window for light, have been built as places of refuge.

Rösheim is near the Visdal. This valley is flanked on both sides by grand mountains, snow-fields, and glaciers; on the east the Glittertinden peak rises proudly above the sea; on the west is the majestic Galdhöpiggen, divided by two chasms into three peaks, almost surrounded by dark, insurmountable walls, around which is a sea of snow.

From the Visdal the ascent to the top of the Galdhö is comparatively easy. A number of sæters are met at about four English miles, at a height of 2775 feet above the sea, the path ascending all the time till the common birch vegetation ceases, and wild birch and willows take its place. These disappear as the snow boundary is neared. The mean altitude of the Galdhö plateau is between 6000 and 7000 feet.

After a tiresome tramp over snow, ice, and rocks, the Galdhöpiggen is reached, several hundred feet above all other peaks. At its base is a sea of snow glaciers. There are terrible precipices towards the Styggebræen, and chasms and fissures are seen in the masses of ice. Galdhöpiggen stands like a round snow cupola, overlooking all, bounded by precipices almost on every side.

The view is superb; about the horizon is spread a panorama not to be forgotten—to the north range after range, and
the Romsdalshorn, the mountains of Dovre and Snehætten; towards the east, the Runderne and Österdal mountains; in the
west, the Horung; and across the Visdal the shining Glittertinden, with snow-fields and glaciers in every direction; in
the south the Jotun, with their wild, sharp, pyramidal peaks.

The entrance to Leiradal is a few miles west of Rösheim,
by the Bæverdal Valley. In the east it is flanked by the
Galdhöpiggen, and in the west by the Veslefjelds, rising 6366
feet. At the entrance of the valley are found some sæters,
2900 feet above the sea, at the base of the dark mountains.
Near the top is a small lake surrounded by rocky shores. Not
far distant is Kirken, a queer-shaped mountain, which seemed
to have a girdle round it towards the summit. Below is Leira
Vand, a charming lake 4736 feet above the sea; we skirt its
borders, where one of the glaciers of Smörstab Peaks meet its
water. Leira Vand forms the top of the water-shed of Leiradal; crossing a ridge, which divides the water-shed, one
comes to two lakelets, which flowed towards the Gjendin
Vand. Here was presented a wild scene—masses of rocks of
every size and shape being piled upon each other on the left,
while on the other towering mountains clad with snow and
glaciers were seen.

Soon after we came to the Lang Lake, about five miles long.
On the left side were fine pastures, where the cattle of the sæters come to feed, while on the other were the Skarvdal mountains with their glaciers, rising to a height of 6140 feet. The
murmur of the wind, water-falls, and torrents, and the dash
of the waves as they strike against the shore, sound mournfully enough when heard under a gloomy sky. Nature is still
and solemn, and only now and then during the short summer
is the voice of the lonely maiden of the sæter heard to break
the silence of these solitudes.

The Lang Vand falls into another lake—the last link in the
chain, with wilder surroundings—in a cascade from seventy-
five to one hundred feet in height. Far below is the Aadal
Valley, the descent to which is rapid, over diluvial soil, passing

some sæters; and here grass, the dwarf birch, juniper, and wild willow are seen once more; and at last the Gjendin Lake is reached. In this lonely place is a poor solitary sæter, built of rough stone; quite near is a log-house, owned by the Turistförening Society, where the members can find shelter. This lake is 3155 feet above the sea; it is eleven miles long and one mile wide, running east and west, and is surrounded by snow-clad mountains, in the midst of which are several glaciers. The mountains flanking its northern point, covered with perpetual snow and ice, present magnificent scenery; at the foot of these lies the Rusvand. Wild, indeed, is nature there. The Beshö, a mass of rocks, lies between the Bes and the Rus lakes; the latter is separated from the Gjendin by a narrow strip of rock, which might be called a saddle, from which can be seen at a glance the Gjendin, lying 2000 feet below on one side, and the Bes, 800 feet on the other. From these heights one can go down to Bes sæter, 3110 feet above the sea, and then follow the Sjödal—one of the beauties of Norway—and reach Hedal, which we have visited before.

A few miles from Gjendin is Lake Bygdin, 3520 feet above the sea, and about fifteen miles long. It was late in the season when I found myself there; the first two weeks of September had gone, the sæters were deserted, and the narrow stone huts built for the men who roam with cattle were empty. The stillness of the place was disturbed only by the cries of a few gulls: even these would soon leave, for winter was at hand, and, though the sky was bright and the grass green, a snow-storm might come any day. This region is much frequented as a hunting-tract by the people of Valders, but no sportsmen were to be seen.

Still farther is Lake Tyen, 3596 feet above the sea: lonely enough was this region with its deserted sæters. Coming to a small house built by the Tourist Society, I being one of the members, my guide and myself prepared ourselves to take shelter under its roof for the night. We hobbled our horse, and after a simple meal lay down on the hay, covering ourselves with our overcoats; the air was cold and still (30° F.). At three o'clock we were awakened by a high wind, which we could hear whistling fiercely around our dwelling. The panes of glass in our hut were covered with snow, and we were in the midst of a great snow-storm. Erik jumped up from his bed to look after the horse, but the animal was gone. He tried to find him, but in vain—for, on account of the thick snow falling, he could not see, and when he returned he said, in a desponding way, "The horse has gone home." "Gone home!" said I; "how does he know the way?" "Yes," he said, "he has gone." The poor fellow was dejected enough, for his horse could not go fast with his hobbles, and in the darkness might have lost his way in the mountains. The horse was part of his fortune, and he no doubt thought it would have been difficult to raise the money to buy another one. As I was the cause of the trouble, and had come here contrary to his advice, I made up my mind to buy another horse for him if his was lost, and told him to write to me in Christiania, if he did not find the animal. The drifts grew higher and higher, and I began to wonder how long the storm would last; he at once consoled me by saying that it was too early in the season for a heavy fall. He was right, for towards noon it cleared. I fired gun after gun to call the fishermen, and increased the charges to make the detonation louder, but no boat was in sight. At last one came, and it was agreed that the two fishermen should take me to the road which crosses from Lærdalsören over the Filefjeld.

Erik was to go in search of his horse, and take his family and the cattle back to the farm, and I was going in the opposite direction. As we shook hands, I told him to remember me kindly to his wife, and recommended him again not to fail to write in case he had lost his horse. I knew the good fellow was too honest to write a lie, and that, if he found the animal, he would not tell me he had not.

The distance from the southern extremity of the lake to the high-road was about three miles. Wending our way through the deep snow, it had become cold, the mercury standing at 22°, and after awhile I saw with joy the telegraph-poles along the road: several paths leading to pastures branched off in various directions, and birch-trees became abundant. We passed by the Hagesæt sæters, consisting of several stone huts and houses overlooking the valley. Here, too, the dwellings were deserted, the doors were made fast, and a dead silence reigned; the busy life of the sæter was over, and the merry laugh of the dairy-maid was heard no more. From there a short walk brought me to the high-road, near the base of the Filefjeld. It was the 19th of September, and my summer rambles over the mountains were ended for that year; I found myself again on the shores of the Great Sogne fjord, having crossed once more from the Baltic to the North Sea, between the sixty-first and sixty-third parallels of latitude.

CHAPTER XXIX.

STRANGERS travelling in Sweden, unless they make it a special object, have but a faint idea of the great number of large landed estates, castles (*slott*), chateaux, and fine country-seats which are entailed in the families of the old nobility, many of whom bear names illustrious in the history of Scandinavia and of Europe. These estates are found in the midst of fertile tracts, and not farther north than the province of Upland; they become more numerous from Lake Mälar southward, while in the southern part of the peninsula they dot the country everywhere.

Many of these ancestral homes, built in the fourteenth century, are picturesquely beautiful, surrounded by superb woods, meadows, fields, and clear lakes and streams. Within their walls the halls are filled with art treasures; paintings by the old masters of the Italian, Dutch, Flemish, French, and other schools are abundant. One meets gems by Raphael, Rubens, Rembrandt, Hobbimas, Guido, Vandyck, Claude, Correggio, Salvator Rosa, Poussin, Snyders, Ruysdäel, Wouverman, Lely, Ehrenstrahl, Paul Veronese, Wertmüller, Velasquez, Pietro di Cortona, Zucchero, Leandro Bassano, Backhuysen, Paul Potter, Mignard, Domenichino, Jordäens, and Camphuysen; besides several Swedish artists, among whom are Pilo, Lauræus Martin, Sandberg, Lundberg, Taraval, Claude Lorraine, Pash, Breda, Roslin (portrait-painter), Borgognone, Zorg, Vanloo, Chardin, Boucher, Loutherbourg, D'Oudry, De Raoul, David Kraft, Adam Behn, Bremmer, etc., etc. The noble historical portraits bring up vivid pictures of by-gone centuries with kings, queens, princes, statesmen, warriors—men of great repute; old ladies, sweet and beautiful women, whose faces appear to smile upon those who look at them, with tints as fresh as if their likenesses had been painted yesterday.

Many of these portraits were presented by the persons themselves to some member of the families whose walls they now adorn. Besides valuable paintings, the halls are often filled with many gems, cabinets, old furniture, clocks, arms, shields, and curiosities of all sorts — the spoils of the Thirty Years' War, and other famous campaigns, brought or sent home by the victorious generals of the Swedish army.

Some of these chateaux contain a Riddarsal (knight's hall), often of great magnificence. There, in olden times, the armor of the knights was kept, and on the walls there are niches or compartments, where the harness of mail was kept bright and shining; in them are also often large and valuable libraries. Not unfrequently they are built with several towers and pinnacled roofs, and surrounded by a moat, with stately avenues of linden, elm, horse-chestnut, or other trees leading to them; while flower-gardens and greenhouses add their charms to the scene.

I have noticed a growing opinion throughout the country in favor of abolishing the *Fideikommiss* (entailed estate), and allowing the children to divide equally the property of their parents. I have but little doubt, unless there is a revulsion of feeling on this subject, that the law of entail will be abolished, and indeed no estate can now be entailed.

If fortunate enough to be invited as a guest, the stranger is surprised at the simplicity of life, and the unostentatious manners of the family; the hostess quietly superintending the house, and a friendly feeling existing between the landlord and his tenant, or the laborer on the estate. The urbanity of the superior towards his inferior is delightful to see, and could be imitated with advantage in many other countries.

I have been in no country where its inhabitants did not believe themselves, for one reason or another, more religious or moral than the rest of mankind; the same may be said of different religious sects. I have also remarked that the nobility everywhere think themselves—in blood, antiquity, or deeds of valor—superior to those of other lands. They of course do not declare this in words; but their manner and actions in speaking of foreign lands indicate, unmistakably, such an idea.

Any one who has studied the history of Scandinavia sees indubitable proof of the remote ancestry of many Swedish families, and in no country can there be found a more brilliant record of deeds of valor and consummate generalship.

We will now wander awhile by the Mälar. There are no lakes in Scandinavia around whose shores are clustered so many historical reminiscences, so many mementos of the past, from the Stone Age to that brightest epoch of Swedish history, the period of the Wasa Dynasty—under which Sweden rose to the rank of a great power, and exerted a governing influence in the councils of Europe. Sailing by the shores of lovely islands, the traveller passes a spot once celebrated as a heathen site, or sees a town whose church or cathedral recalls the palmy days of the Roman Catholic power in mediæval times, when the monks owned the best of the land in almost every country.

At a distance of about seven miles from Stockholm is the island of Lofö, one of the largest and most beautiful found in the Mälar; on its shores is built Drottningholm, a handsome royal residence. The foundation of the present castle was laid by Queen Hedvig Eleonora, of Holstein, the widow of Charles X., who was the first king who dared to cross with his army on the ice between the Danish islands, and who led it victorious into the heart of Poland, and it was finished during the reign of her son, Charles XI., 1660–'97. The builders of this noble structure were Nicodemus Tessin, the elder and the younger. The palace is an imposing edifice, built near the water, and commands a fine view of the lake and

of its rocky and wooded shores. Avenues of lindens diverge
in different directions towards charming spots. The grounds
are laid out either in the old French, Dutch, or English style.
From the terrace a flight of steps leads to a garden—which reminds one of France—ornamented with vases and groups in
bronze and marble of considerable merit, with several foun-
tains, artificial ponds, and water-avenues where swans live and
breed. There is a Theatre de Verdure (the French name has
been kept), a most unique and charming structure, built by
Gustavus III., with stage and room of clipped trees and turf,
where that sovereign loved to act French plays—for the language of France was then and is still the one spoken at court
and used in official documents. There is also a maze of com-
plicated walks, hidden by trees and bushes; a Swiss cottage;
Flora's hill, with the statue of the goddess; the Kina slott, or
Chinese castle—a sort of plaything—built in 1752 by King
Adolf Frederick, and presented by him to his queen, Lovisa
Ulrika, on her birthday. This building is filled with Chinese
curiosities. And near the so-called Canton Village, composed
of a number of villas, was a factory hamlet, where the manufacture of steel and iron ware was carried on—conducted by
that king himself, probably then the most skilled locksmith
and turner in Sweden.

Ascending wide steps leading to the palace, one enters a
hall recognized at a first glance by its decorations as the work
of Tessin. A noble staircase leads to the rooms above, where
several hours can be pleasantly spent in looking over the
paintings, tapestry, collections of china, and portraits of King
Adolph Frederick (1751-'71) and his beautiful blue-eyed
wife, Queen Louisa Ulrika, sister of Frederick the Great
of Prussia. Her letters to her "très chère maman," the
Queen of Prussia, which are numerous and written in French,
teem with the love this remarkable woman had for the arts,
and show also the great interest she took in Drottningholm.

The "Salle des Contemporains" contains the pictures of
recent sovereigns, among them good Queen Victoria in her
youth, Napoleon III., the Empress Eugenie, etc.

One pauses before the fine portrait of Peter Olsson, a remarkable man in his day, when Sweden had a Parliament composed of the four estates of the realm—the nobles, the clergy, the merchants, and the peasants.

Farther westward from Drottningholm is the island of Björkö, a famous port in the later centuries of the pagan era. On the northern extremity are still seen numerous remains of the old *Birka*. The earth there is filled with coal and ashes, among which are sometimes found household utensils, ornaments, and arms, with immense numbers of animal bones; thus, to a certain extent, making these heaps correspond to the so-called "Kjökkenmöddinger" of older periods.

As the inhabitants of the town were often exposed to the attacks of Vikings, and could not meet force with force, they had tried by fillings to render the entrance to the harbor difficult. On the east side is still seen a rampart with openings for entrances, and which no doubt also surrounded the town on the south side, but has long been obliterated, and given room for arable land.

The hill on the west end of the town was similarly enclosed except on one side, where it was so steep that fortifications were considered unnecessary. This wall differs from those of similar forts in the Mälar Valley, in that it is not made of loose stones piled upon each other, but of a stone wall covered with earth. This place offered perhaps the last refuge for the inhabitants; in spite of this, however, it was finally destroyed. This event must have happened after the year 936, when Bishop Unne, of Bremen, died there, and before 1070, when it is related that it was so nearly annihilated that its site could hardly be distinguished.

It is said that there, in the year 829, Christianity was preached for the first time to the Swedes by Ansgarius. A stone cross was erected in 1834 on the shore to commemorate the event.

In the biography of Ansgarius—a monk sent from Corbey, France, to Hamburg, where he became archbishop of the city, and made an Englishman named Simon the first bishop in Björkö—written by Rimbert, probably a contemporary of his, Birka is mentioned as an important port, situated in the

GRIPSHOLM.

land of the Svear, where many rich merchants dwelt, and where there was an abundance of all the good things of this life, and enormous treasures. He further relates that the inhabitants, at the time of an unexpected attack by the deposed King Anund, who came with the Danes, took refuge in a fort lying close by the town; as, however, the fort was not very strong, and the defenders few, they entered into negotiations with Anund, and he promised them peace in consideration of 2000 pounds of silver, which were without difficulty collected and weighed out to him.

Adam, another chronicler of this time, says that Birka is a town situated not far from Upsala, the most renowned heathen temple of the Svear.

On the shores of the Gripsholm fjord, near the village of Mariefred, stands the old and stately palace of that name. The former structure was built in the beginning of the fourteenth century, and was destroyed in 1434. The estate afterwards came into the possession of Sten Sture the elder, then regent of the kingdom, who afterwards gave it to the cloister of Mariefred, from which it was taken by King Gustaf Erikson Wasa I., who erected the present building, which was finished in 1537. The four towers were named after the four sons— Erik, Johan, Magnus, and Karl.

In the outer court-yard lie two large cannons of beautiful workmanship, called by the people the boar and the sow, taken by Count Jacob de la Gardie at Ivanogorod, in Russia, in the year 1612.

To the lover of history a pilgrimage to Gripsholm, which may be called the pantheon of the Wasa family and of their contemporaries, is of great interest. This collection of portraits, numbering about two thousand, is of its kind, I think, the finest and most valuable in Europe, for it includes a wide range of sovereigns, and men and women of note unrivalled in number. Some of these are even anterior to the Wasa family, and are five hundred years old. Here are found the portraits of Gustavus Adolphus, of the diplomatists of the Peace of Westphalia, the councillors of Charles XI. and Charles XII., the sovereigns who reigned at the time of Gustavus III., many distinguished persons, both Swedish and foreign statesmen, kings, queens, beautiful and ugly women, etc; besides there are numerous curiosities—old furniture, precious wall-papers, rich silver vessels, etc.

There are portraits of the Stures, once regents of Sweden. On the 1st of May, 1471, a general Diet met in Arboga, where Sten Sture the elder was with acclamation chosen to be regent and chief of the kingdom, mainly because the Swedes were unable to agree upon a native king, and also because a large, and for the time being omnipotent, party would under no conditions have a continuation of the union with Denmark and Norway.

On November 11th, 1497, King Johan of Denmark and Norway was also accepted as King of Sweden, on account of the ascendency of the Union party in Sweden. In 1501 he was again deposed, and Svante Sture elected regent. He was not related to Sten Sture the elder, but of another family. He died in 1512, and was succeeded by his son, Sten Sture the younger, who was, however, not chosen at any general Diet, but only by the chiefs of the then all-powerful native party. He died in January, 1520.

There are several portraits of Gustaf Erikson Wasa, who reigned 1521 to 1560—a man of uncommon ability, energy, and of undaunted courage, the founder of the Wasa Dynasty. He was the progenitor of a line of warlike kings, during whose reigns appeared a succession of generals of most brilliant military genius, which perhaps has not been equalled before or since. Grandfather of the great Gustavus Adolphus, his life is most remarkable and romantic. He was in early manhood a fugitive from the Danes, who oppressed his country and who sought his life—often not knowing where to lay his head—going here and there, trying to make the people rise and throw off the yoke of the foreigner—meeting with disappointments, but never despairing, and dying full of honor. In an interesting likeness painted by his son Erik he is represented clad in the steel armor, inlaid with gold, which he wore at the battle of Brunkeberg. In another he is represented with a white flowing beard.

Sigrid Eskilsdotter Banér, married in 1475 to Magnus Karls-
son Wasa, grandmother of the founder of the dynasty, is represented as a young and beautiful girl.

We notice the three queens of Gustaf Wasa—Catherine (his
first), daughter of Duke Magnus of Saxe-Lauenburg, mother
of his eldest son, the unfortunate Erik; Margaret Lejonhufvud,
mother of ten children; Catherine Stenbock, two portraits,
one representing her as young and beautiful, another in her
old age.

The Knights' Hall is one of the most interesting in the
palace, for there the visitor sees the contemporaries of the
first Wasa. Among the most prominent portraits are those
of Francis I. of France, Henry VIII. of England, Charles V.,
Emperor of Germany, Queen Isabella of Denmark, wife of
Christian I., daughter of Archduke Philip of Austria and
Johanna of Castile, and sister of the Emperor Charles V.
Among the French are Henry IV. and his great minister
Sully, Marie de Medicis, Anne of Austria, Louis XIV. and
XV., the Duchess of Orleans, the Prince of Conti, Princess
Mazarin, the great Condé, Henrietta of England, the Countess
of Soissons, La Valliere, Cardinal Fleury, and many others.
One pauses before Charles IX. and his first wife, Maria de
Pfalz, and Kristina of Holstein, his second, the mother of
Gustavus Adolphus.

Here are the faces of many of the contemporaries of Gustavus Adolphus, the last male direct of the Wasa. On the 25th
of November, 1620, Gustavus Adolphus II. was married in
Stockholm to Princess Maria Eleonora of Brandenburg. Her
father was Electoral Prince Johan Sigismund of Brandenburg,
and her mother was Anna of Prussia. The young queen was
distinguished by an uncommon beauty; her hair was dark,
forehead, nose, and eyebrows highly arched, the eyes large
and deep blue, the figure petite, the temper lively and con-
descending. Also the sweet Ebba Brahe, the first love of
the great hero, and who reciprocated his affection, but who,
through the queen-mother, married Jacob de la Gardie while
Adolphus was waging war against Poland. Oxenstjerna, the
famous chancellor, has two portraits; the generals of the

Thirty Years' War; Charles X., the successor of Gustaf Adolphus, also a great warrior; his queen, Hedvig Eleonora of Holstein-Gottorp, whom he married in October, 1654; Charles XI. and his wife, Ulrika Eleonora of Denmark; Charles XII., Adolphus Frederick, Louisa Ulrika.

England is well represented. Not the least interesting are the portraits of Henry VIII., Mary Stuart, Elizabeth, and of the Georges, etc., etc. Erik XIV., the son of Gustaf Wasa, in one of his love-letters to Queen Elizabeth, states that she is wrong in supposing that he wished the hand of Mary Stuart.

One sees Frederick II. of Prussia, the Emperor Joseph of Austria, Charles of Spain, Stanislas, the last King of Poland, Sigismund of Poland, Christian IV. of Denmark, Philip IV. of Spain, and the seventy Ministers of the Peace of Westphalia, which terminated the great Thirty Years' War.

In a large hall are portraits of celebrities of the period of Gustaf III. (1771–1792). These paintings are the presents of the sovereigns of that time to their dear brother: among them are Maria of Portugal, who founded the Brazilian empire, and Maria Theresa of Austria. The great Catherine, in one picture—sent by her to Gustaf—is represented as a fine old dame. In another she is a young woman, with her infant Paul, and Peter the Great by her side. One stands thoughtfully before a beautiful likeness of Marie Antoinette, by Wertmüller, a portrait and historical painter, born in Stockholm in 1751. In 1770 he went to Paris, where he created quite a sensation, and among other things painted the unfortunate queen and her children, about which Madame Campan in her memoirs says that it was the most striking likeness of this queen she had seen. After having remained in Paris some twenty years he returned to his native country; but in 1800 again went to Paris, and thence to Philadelphia, where he married, and died in 1811. No doubt many gems of the great artist are to be found in America. A sincere friendship existed between Marie Antoinette and Gustaf III., and in the Gustavean collection are found several of her letters. The landgraves of Hesse, and other German princes, now entirely forgotten, are numerous; also Catherine Opaluska, queen of Stanislas Leczinski, a beautiful woman; William of Orange, Queen Anne, and a most ridiculous portrait of six court-ladies of Queen Ulrika's court, represented with heads over the bodies of hens.

At the death of Gustaf Wasa, Gripsholm came into the possession of his son Charles, who afterwards ascended the throne under the title of Charles IX. The old castle has many sad tales to tell. From the Knights' Hall, descending through a narrow staircase, you enter a vaulted cell where the victims of the blood-bath of Linköping were once incarcerated. In one of the towers is a room with three windows overlooking the lake; here Johan, one of the sons of Gustaf Wasa II., was imprisoned by his brother Erik—who had previously gone to England—for rebellion, and remained there three years. Queen Elizabeth wrote to the latter in 1565, inquiring the cause of his brother's imprisonment, and saying that she would be glad to see him again reinstated in the favor of his king.

The four sons of Gustaf Wasa were violent in their disposition; Erik was subject to terrible fits of ungovernable passion. Dissatisfaction having arisen in the country on account of the imprisonment of Duke Johan, King Erik, of a very suspicious mind, feared the hate of the nobility, and especially the jealousy of the Sture family. A report was spread that a conspiracy, at the head of which these nobles were said to be, was soon to break out. Svante Sture and his sons, together with Erik Stenbock, Sten Erikson Lejonhufvud, and others were put in prison in the castle of Upsala. Soon after Göran Persson, the evil-minded adviser of the king, whispered into his ear that Johan had escaped from prison, and at the head of his supporters was on the way to Upsala, then the royal residence, and that he came with the intention of revenging himself. Erik then lost all control over himself, and ordered the execution of the prisoners. With his own hand he gave Nils Sture several thrusts with his poniard; he did not even spare his former teacher, Dionysius Beurreus, who was warmly attached to him, and sought to calm his excited mind. Thereupon came repentance and despair: he fled, disguised in the garb of a peasant, and avoided all the people he met. After having in some measure regained his senses, he sought to appease the relatives of the murdered nobles by valuable presents; and these also announced that they would not revenge themselves on the king, because they laid the blame on his adviser, Göran Persson. During this state of mind he had been

ASPÖ CHURCH, ON THE ISLAND OF TOSTERÖ.

persuaded to set his prisoner at liberty. Johan received back his duchy (Finland), and a reconciliation between the two brothers took place. But Erik soon gave new causes for dissatisfaction, and Göran Persson regained the confidence of the king, who demanded back the presents he had given to the families of the murdered nobles. He married Katarina Månsdotter, who was of low birth, and publicly crowned her as queen: this caused great dissatisfaction among the nobility. Around Johan the disaffected assembled, and Duke Charles also joined them, whereupon Erik, deserted by all, was captured in 1568, and adjudged guilty of high crimes, and kept a prisoner for nine years, until he, in 1577, was poisoned upon the order of Johan at Örbyhus. Several years of his captivity was passed at Gripsholm.

After leaving Gripsholm, following the indented shores of the Mälar, one comes to the old historical town of Strengnäs, now, however, of little importance. The cathedral is a fine building, dating from 1291, and has a length of 300 feet. Charles IX. is buried there, and many other renowned personages, among them Sten Sture the elder. Opposite the town is the island of Tosterö, with the old church of Aspö.

Farther on from Strengnäs is the well-known old chateau of Fiholm, once belonging to Axel Oxenstjerna, the great adviser of Gustavus Adolphus. At a short distance is the Jäder church, in which are numerous mementos of the Thirty Years' War, and the tomb of the chancellor.

SEAL OF TORSHÄLLA.—ST. OLAF IN A BOAT.

Beyond, a short distance up the the Eskilstuna River, is situated the little town of Torshälla, and that of Eskilstuna—the latter being the most important and populous of those on

and near the southern shore of the Mälar. It has considerable
manufactures of arms, cutlery, etc. Near the western extremity of the lake are the small towns of Köping and Arboga,
situated on the rivers which bear their names.

ARBOGA CHURCH.

From the Arboga River a canal runs to Lake Hjelmar.
A couple of miles from the western end of this lake is the
old city of Örebro, with a population of over 10,000 inhabitants, situated on a plain which is divided by the Svartå
River, here forming several small islands. Örebro has in the
older history of Sweden played quite an important part. Of
ancient buildings the most remarkable is the castle, on an
island in the river. It is built in a square with four towers,
of which one still has some of its loop-holes left. The City
Hall is a fine new stone building in the Gothic style, and nota-

ble for a small tower. The church was built in the fourteenth century, and contains the remains of Engelbrekt Engelbrektsson, a famous man, born in Dalecarlia, whose statue adorns the open place near the church.

During the reign of Erik XIII. (1397–1439) his bailiffs com-

ÖREBRO CHURCH.

mitted the most lawless and cruel acts; among them Jösse Eriksson was especially distinguished for his many revolting cruelties: he resided at the castle of Vesterås, and his district comprised a part of Vestmanland and Dalarne. By enormous and unjust taxes he robbed the peasants of their property; and, when thus their horses and oxen had been taken from them, he harnessed the peasants to the plough, and their wives, even the pregnant ones, to the hay-loads. Unprotected women were kidnapped, and forced to submit to his infamous passions; and many wealthy men were imprisoned on false accusations, and then sentenced, to enable him to confiscate their property. When the peasants came to him and made their complaints, he had their ears cut off, or had them lashed, or hung up in smoke until they were smothered.

At this time lived near Falun copper-mine Engelbrekt Engelbrektsson; he was a noble, though not a very high one. Although small of stature, he was, however, of dauntless courage, and was besides eloquent, and well versed in the arts and sciences of his time, as he had in his youth resided at the courts of some of the great men. He felt pity for the Dalecarlians on account of the oppression under which they suffered, and promised to appear before the king and try to have their wrongs righted, as well as to have Jösse called away. Engelbrekt therefore went to Copenhagen. Erik XIII. would not at first believe him; but as he offered to answer therefor with his life, his majesty referred him to the council, who went to Dalecarlia and examined into the matter, and found it to be true, and so reported to the king. When Engelbrekt appeared before the latter, he said, in great anger, "Thou always dost complain. Go away, and never show thyself again before my eyes!" He obeyed and went away saying, in leaving, "Once more I will come back!" When he returned home with this answer to the peasants, they turned out from every house, and resolved to die rather than longer endure such oppression. They therefore arose, and under Engelbrekt's command marched to Vesterås, where they were met by the council, who promised to see that their grievances were remedied, and they at once departed satisfied. But nothing was done towards the fulfilment of these promises, and Jösse soon again sent his armed men to force them to pay taxes. They therefore rose a second time, but instead of going down to Vesterås, where they had been sent away with fine promises, they went to the castle of Borganäs, by the Dala

River, south-west of Falun, and burned it on midsummer-day, 1434. The rebellion soon assumed great proportions, and within a short time the Danes were driven away from the whole kingdom; an armistice was then closed, and Engelbrekt chosen regent of the kingdom; and at the conclusion of peace he was also made commander of Örebro Castle. King Erik did not keep his word; a second rebellion broke out, also under the leadership of Engelbrekt, who had now become very eminent, and thus was an object of the envy of the great nobles of the kingdom. One of these, Bengt Stensson Natt och Dag (night and day), of Göksholm, a castle by Lake Hjelmar, had a quarrel with our hero, which, however, was settled in Örebro, April, 1436; and when the latter, on the 3d of May, 1436, was on his way to Stockholm, he encamped for the night on an islet in the Hjelmar, close to Göksholm. Hither came the son of Bengt and killed Engelbrekt, who expected no harm from his late adversary, after the reconciliation. As soon as the news of this treacherous murder spread, the peasants assembled and tried to avenge it, but the murderer had fled. Therefore they went to the islet, where they picked up the mangled body of their beloved chieftain, and with tears carried it to Mellösa church, where they buried him who had been their only protection and help in their oppression.

About twenty miles from Örebro lies the pretty town of Nora, which is the centre of a very important mining region, among which the ore-fields Striberg, Dalkarlsberg, Pershytte, and Klacka are the most remarkable. Nora parish is the one in which more iron ore is mined than in any other of Sweden.

The northern shores are also very interesting. Vesterås, at the mouth of the Svartå River, with a population of 5448, in mediæval times was an important place; it had four churches and a Dominican monastery. The cathedral now standing near the water was built during the twelfth century, and has a spire of 320 feet, the highest in Sweden, and a length of 306. In it are the tombs of Svante Sture, Erik XIV., and Chancellor Magnus Brahe. The elementary school has a fine library of 12,000 volumes, which includes that of the Electoral Prince of Mayence, given by Axel Oxenstjerna.

The castle of Strömsholm was built by Gustavus I., and was formerly used as a summer residence by the Swedish kings. Here is also the largest stud of Sweden, and a riding-school for the officers of the army.

At Strömsholm begins a canal more than seventy miles in length, of which only about seven miles are dug, while the rest are formed by natural watercourses. This route offers one of the most beautiful water-ways of Sweden. The most northerly end terminates at the village of Smedjebacken, in Dalecarlia. Numerous iron-works are met with along the journey.

On the northern shore, some twenty-five miles from Stockholm, is the Sigtuna fjord, from which one can journey all the way by water to Upsala. Near the water is the royal castle of Rosersberg, with beautiful surroundings. Here is the village of Sigtuna, often mentioned in the old sagas, and in those days a rich and populous city.

In the middle and end of the twelfth century the coasts of the Baltic were constantly harassed by the attacks of the heathen fleets of countries to the east. Such a fleet, under the Esthonians, entered the Mälar in 1187 and destroyed Sigtuna, which, after the destruction of Birka, was then the most important trading town. They carried away two large church doors of massive silver, which are still in the church of Novgorod in Russia. Of the former churches only a few ruins remain, and one cannot but wonder how the immense boulders of which they are constructed were put in their places.

Farther up the fjord, after passing the narrow strait of Erikssund, one enters the bay of Sko, in the midst of dark forests. Near the shore loom up the towers of the castle of Skokloster. This cloister was founded in the latter part of the thirteenth century, and was destroyed by fire. Not far from the castle the monastery church still stands, well preserved.

Karl Gustaf Wrangel was one of the most renowned generals of Gustavus Adolphus, but his great achievements were made after the death of his king; he was chief commander of the armies at the Peace of Westphalia.

In the church are several paintings of artistic value, taken from Oliva monastery, near Dantzic, Karl Gustaf Wrangel's equestrian statue, erected in his chapel, the walls of which are ornamented with half-raised representations from his campaigns, and the grave-stone of the holy Holmgeir. The pulpit, the altar, and other ornaments are spoils from Germany.

Gustavus Adolphus gave Skokloster to the Field-marshal Herman Wrangel, whose son, the still more renowned Karl Gustaf Wrangel, erected the present edifice.

The only child of Admiral Wrangel, a daughter, married a Brahe, and thus the estate came entailed in that illustrious family. The chateau is one of the handsomest private ones in Sweden. It forms an exact square; it encloses a court, has four stories, and is flanked by four towers, which are a story higher than the rest of the edifice. The principal entrance towards the lake is marked by a frontispiece, with the Wrangel coat-of-arms. The arch of the vestibule is supported by eight Ionic pillars of marble, a gift of Queen Christina to Karl Gustaf Wrangel, but which Count Nils Brahe, during the "reduction" of Charles XI., had to redeem at an immense sum of money. The reduction during the reign of Charles XI. embraced the restitution of such crown estates as had, during the preceding reigns, especially during that of Queen Christina, been given to nobles for real or pretended services. The interior of the castle is a museum of curiosities; stairways and corridors are ornamented with paintings, mostly portraits of Wrangel's Scottish companions in arms. Room after room is filled with portraits, including other comrades of Field-marshal Herman Wrangel, and dating back to 1623. As we looked at them our thoughts turned to that fierce struggle marked by the military genius of Gustavus Adolphus and his generals.

One is almost bewildered in the rooms containing the collections of arms—which number about twelve hundred—comprising fire-arms of all kinds, and a great number of sabres, swords, poniards, and bows, some inlaid with gold and precious stones; others of historic value, such as the sword of the Hussite chief Ziska; and armor taken by Marshal Wrangel and other victorious generals. Not the least interesting is the beautiful shield of the great emperor Charles V., which was taken in Prague when that city was sacked by the Swedes. The state apartments are hung with old tapestry—the gift of Louis XIV. of France; others are hung with gilt skins. A great delight is the old-fashioned chimney, reaching to the ceiling, with beautifully-carved armorial designs. The walls are adorned with portraits, Venetian mirrors, cabinets inlaid with ivory, amber, and blood-stone; china and great

KNUTBY CHURCH, IN UPLAND.

numbers of objects of art are arranged in huge cabinets in the so-called King's Hall, the ceiling of which is a masterpiece of the plasterer's art.

In historical paintings Skokloster ranks next to Gripsholm. The collection of portraits here also is very fine, including the families of Wrangel, Brahe, Königsmark, and Bjelke. There is a splendid library, containing over 30,000 volumes, and many valuable manuscripts and letters, among which is one of Erik XIV., in which he orders negotiations for a marriage with Mary Stuart, which he denied when he wished to wed the English queen, Elizabeth. One is never wearied in looking at the wonderful treasures : nearly every object has a tale to tell. From the paintings we return to the cabinets, and back again to the paintings, being loath to part from this most fascinating collection, which it is hoped will never leave the country.

We will bid adieu to the Mälar, upon whose shores we have lingered many a day dreaming of the past.

From the Mälar some time may be spent pleasantly in visiting the castles, chateaux, and churches of Upland, many of which are full of interest.

The province of Södermanland is bounded on the north by the southern shores of the Mälar, and partly on the west by Lake Hjelmar. The landscape is in many districts well wooded and picturesque, with lakes and streams in every direction ; the coniferous forests of the north are often replaced by trees of a greater variety, the foliage of which adds to the beauty of the country. The linden, the elm, and the horse-chestnut attain large growth, while the oaks are often of superb size ; many of the hills and dales are clad with those pre-eminently Scandinavian trees, the birch and the fir. In the western part of the province—Wingåker—most of the people still adhere to their national costume, which is for the men composed of a long woollen white homespun coat, coming down to the ankle, with crimson bar lining, blue cuffs, leather knee-breeches, and short waistcoats. The women's head-dress is a high red roll, which on Sunday is covered with a ruffled cap of varied colors and forms, according as the wearer is maiden, betrothed, wife, or mother.

Numerous estates are scattered here and there, with fine old chateaux situated in lovely retired spots. On the eastern end of the Hjelmaren is the magnificent estate of Stora Sundby, belonging to the family of De Geer. The castle is imposing, with turrets ; the apartments are of royal splendor.

Near Wingåker is Säfstaholm, entailed in the family of
Bonde.   The chateau is surrounded by rural scenery; its
apartments are adorned with Italian and Dutch paintings, and
others of great merit; the library is very valuable, and some
of the archives date back to 1300.

STORA SUNDBY, IN SÖDERMANLAND.

The finest estate, not only in regard to size, but on account
also of its beautiful situation, and grand ancestral home, is
Eriksberg, which is entailed in another branch of the family of
Bonde.   The castle, which is about two hundred years old,
occupies a commanding position on a hill overlooking the
charming little Eriksberg Lake.   The main building, showing
unmistakable traces of the master-hand of Tessin, is of stone,
three stories high, with ground-floor and four wings.   Its
rooms contain choice objects of art from the period during
which it was built.   The south-western wing includes a richly
and tastefully decorated chapel.   The elegant halls are ornamented with valuable portraits and paintings.   The former

ERIKSBERG.

so-called audience-hall is now occupied by a library of 10,000 volumes—as regards Scandinavian history, one of the most complete in Sweden. The grounds are in harmony with the whole. Between the two southern wings rises the castle terrace, ornamented with statues, and directly in front of this is a bronze fountain. Bounded on two sides by shady old linden alleys, a spacious lawn stretches in front of the castle with flower groups, *bosques*, and *parterres*.

One of the most prettily-situated estates of this province is that of Sparreholm, on the shores of the charming little Lake Båfven. Its mansion, although it cannot compare in grandeur with some others, presents to the visitor a most cheerful and inviting appearance. It has a fine library, a collection of coins, and also some good paintings of native and foreign masters.

A few miles distant is the interesting old chateau of Stenhammar. It lies by Lake Valdemaren, surrounded by extensive parks, in which may be seen stately old oaks and other deciduous trees. The beauty of the place is greatly enhanced by the ever-changing panorama of the lake, with its maze of islets and winding passages. The estate is mentioned as early as the year 1300. The whole neighborhood is one of the most charming in Södermanland, and is rich in memorials from by-gone days.

CHAPTER XXX.

A CHARMING summer journey is that of crossing the peninsula, from sea to sea, by the Göta Canal and the lakes connecting the Baltic with the North Sea. Linger here and there in the midst of the romantic scenery found on the banks of some lonely river, or on the shores of lovely lakes; tarry awhile in some clean, quiet, thrifty town, with castle, cathedral, or church dating from mediæval times; visit some spot where remains of the stone and bronze age are to be found; and stop at some old chateau which brings recollections of the by-gone centuries.

This beautiful water-way, crossing the central part of Sweden, is about 259 miles long, with 74 locks; the highest level reached is 308 feet 2 inches, on the Lake Viken, between the Wettern and the Wenern. The canal is 10 feet deep, generally 48 feet wide at the bottom and 88 feet at the surface; the locks are 123 feet in length and 24 feet in width; there are more than 30 bridges over its course. The traffic is considerable, the number of vessels cleared from the North Sea to the Wenern averaging yearly between six and seven thousand, and between the lake and the Baltic about three

thousand. This superb work shows in several instances great
engineering skill; in many places locks after locks are cut
out of solid granite hills. The construction is made to last,
and the banks have been so built that they are secured against
dangers from steam navigation. Comfortable steamers make
the journey direct, and are generally two or three days on the
way, according to the number of stoppages to discharge or
take cargoes; others ply on their respective lakes from one
city to another, stopping at intermediate places.

From Stockholm the steamer follows the southern shore of
the Mälar to Telge-viken, and ere long enters the Södertelge
Canal, which connects the lake with the Baltic. Down the

SHIP CARRYING ST. ERIK TO FINLAND.

fjord, and not far from the shore, about sixteen miles south
of Södertelge, is the old and interesting church of Östmo,
which possesses many very old and grotesque paintings; one
of them represents the devil as the people believed him to be
in those days. Beyond is the royal chateau of *Tullgarn*, an
imposing edifice, surrounded by parks and gardens, luxuriously
decorated by the Swedish artist Hillerström. The estate, which
formerly belonged to some of Sweden's most famous noble
families, such as Brahe, Bonde, Sture, Oxenstjerna, and De la
Gardie, was in 1772 sold to the Crown, and has since been
used as a summer residence for members of the royal family.
To the south, one enters the Slätbaken fjord, and soon after

looms up the tower of Stegeborg, a fine ruin by the sea. The former castle was mentioned in the thirteenth century, when King Birger used it as his residence. In its early history it was many times besieged—taken and retaken by Swedes and Danes. The tower is the only portion remaining.

About ten miles from Stegeborg the entrance to the Göta Canal is reached. Three miles beyond is the small town of Söderköping, once a place of considerable importance, and boasting in olden times of a castle, four churches, and two monasteries; of its churches only two remain, St. Lars and St. Drothems. Continuing the journey, at about fifteen miles from the sea the boat enters the charming Roxen, with its wooded and hilly shores. The lake is 109 feet above the Baltic, has a length of about 15 and a breadth of between 6 and 7 miles. It has three considerable streams—the Motala, the outlet of Lake Wettern, the Svartån, and the Stångån.

Along its shores are a number of large estates. Among the historical ruins are those of Stjernarp, formerly the dwelling of the Scotch earl, Robert Douglas, who entered Gustavus Adolphus's service in 1631, and by his military genius rose to great distinction. The castle was built in 1654, and withstood the ravages of time well, until a fire in May, 1789, laid it in ashes. It lies in a magnificent situation overlooking the lake and surrounded by trees. The two wings escaped destruction; in one of them is the chapel, and the other is still occupied. The court-yard is apparently square. On the north side the ruin is four stories in height, with nine windows in width, and the middle part, with three windows, rises two stories higher. In the portal one can see traces of the beauty of the old building.

On the eastern shore of the lake, at the port of Berg, the canal is continued, and sixteen locks have to be passed, which makes the ascent tedious. Overlooking the lake near Berg is the Wreta church, built on the ruins of the old monastery which belonged to the Benedictines, and later to the Bernardines, who sent out nuns all over the country. Here are the tombs of Inge the younger, who reigned between 1118 and 1130, and his queen, Helena; of King Ragwald Knaphöfde (1130–1133), belonging to the Stenkil, and King Valdemar Birgersson, of the Folkunga dynasties, besides other men great in their day, but now forgotten.

In the Folkunga family was a renowned chieftain, Folke Digre (the stout), who died about 1100; his posterity became very powerful. One of his great-grandsons was Birger Jarl, who for a long time governed Sweden with a strong hand, and was the founder of Stockholm. His son Valdemar, who in 1250 became first King of Sweden through his father, was so only in name. The descendants occupied the Swedish throne until 1389.

The canal skirts the shores of the Kungs Norrby Lake, which is below, and beyond this enters the Boren Lake, 245 feet above the sea, and 136 above the Roxen, which we have left behind. This charming sheet of water is about nine miles long, clear as crystal, and with beautiful shores. In Ekbyborna church-tower is seen the chamber where St. Birgitta dwelt. Near by is the old estate of Ulfåsa, which belonged to the Folkunga family in the twelfth century. Among the historical facts connected with them is one that is most pleasantly remembered, as follows:

Bengt, a brother of the powerful Birger Jarl, was *lagman* (judge) of Östergötland, and lived at Ulfåsa. All the other brothers of the family had married women of the highest nobility, and thus satisfied the pride of Birger Jarl. Bengt, however, had fallen in love with a young girl of a family of much less repute, but of such uncommon beauty that she was generally called Sigrid the Fair. He had also married her clandestinely, which greatly angered the proud Jarl. He therefore sent Sigrid, as a wedding present, a cloak, half of which was made of gold cloth, while the other half was of coarse woollen material (vadmal), in order to thereby signify how little suitable was a union between two persons of such unequal stations, as was the case with Sigrid and Bengt. As an answer Bengt returned the cloak to the Jarl, after first having had the vadmal portion covered with gold, pearls, and precious stones, so that this part of the cloak became much more valuable than the other. Birger, still further enraged by this constancy of his brother, promised to come and have a talk with Bengt himself, and soon after journeyed to Ulfåsa. When Bengt heard of his coming he went away from home, and told Sigrid to receive the Jarl. She therefore dressed herself in a manner to heighten her great charms. On the arrival of Birger, Sigrid met him, greeted him most reverently, and bade him welcome. When the Jarl saw her, he was so enchanted by her beauty, and modest though dignified demeanor, that he forgot all his anger, embraced and then kissed her, saying that if his brother had left this undone, he would have to do it himself. Bengt was now sent for, and the brothers were reconciled. Bengt had by Sigrid a daughter, called Ingeborg, who was married to Birger Persson Brahe of Finsta, lagman of Upland. Their daughter was Birgitta, who afterwards became a seeress and prophetess, and founded the cloister of Vadstena, and finally was made a saint: people even from foreign lands came in pilgrimage to her tomb.

In the cathedral of Upsala is shown to this day the slab under which Birger Persson and Ingeborg were buried. The inscription, which commences at the left foot of Birger, reads: "Here lie the noble knight Sir Birger Persson, Upland's lagman, and his wife, Lady Ingeborg, with their children; whose souls may rest in peace. Pray for us." On the shield is seen the coat-of-arms of Birger (two down-turned wings), and on the sides of the stone his seven children, with their names. Sir Birger died in 1328, and his wife, Lady Ingeborg, in 1314.

During the oldest times the people were their own judges in their Things, their lagman explaining the laws to them. Later, this lagman, who was chosen by the people, but whose office often descended from father to son, acted as judge, as well as speaker in the Things within the provinces; and for his decision were submitted a multitude of questions, not only judicial, but also purely economical. Gradually the kings assumed the right of appointing the lagman, and the functions of his office changed, until they became purely judicial, corresponding with those of the present *häradshöfdings* (district judges).

The royal jury (*kungsnämnd*), similar to the present *häradsnämnd* (district jury), formerly in some instances judged cases in place of the king, without his presence or that of any one in his stead. Their number was twelve in each judicial district. The ruler during those times travelled around in the different provinces, and personally heard and judged cases submitted to him. Every province then was an independent

SLAB OVER THE GRAVE OF LAGMAN BIRGER PERSSON AND HIS WIFE, INGEBORG.

state, which had its own laws and its separate taxation; and the king on his accession to the throne had to go to every one of them separately, and there receive the oath of allegiance of their different populations. Just as the kingdom was a union of independent states or provinces, every province was a union of smaller districts; while the district was a union of several families, who joined together for mutual protection. The members of the family not only had a common origin, but also were joined together for mutual assistance and responsibility. If one member was killed, the whole kindred was obliged to avenge his death, and had the right to receive an indemnity in lieu thereof, which in the latter case was distributed equally between the members.

The land was divided in the same manner; but in case of a sale the relatives of the seller had the first right of bidding in the property. These free owners of the land were the safeguards of society; over them stood at the end of the heathen age only the *jarlar* (earls) and the king. It is the general idea that the inhabitants of Sweden in olden times enjoyed a complete political equality; this is, however, a mistake; for among them, as other nations, only the free possessor of the soil, who had not entered the military service of any one, had complete political rights.

Leaving the Boren, the ascent is by five connecting locks. The distance between the lake and the Vettern is about two miles, and presents most charming views. On the south of the water-way runs the outlet of Vettern, the Motala River forming occasionally small falls, which set mills and forges in motion. Motala is near the mouth of the Göta Canal on Lake Vettern, and is a village of some 1800 inhabitants, not counting the employés of the iron works a little higher up in its course. These works have the largest machine-shops in Sweden, and are of great importance to the country; they employ about 1700 people; for whom are established schools, dwelling-houses, hospitals, etc. Twelve miles north of Motala are, in an exceedingly pretty neighborhood, the mineral springs of Medevi. These waters were known as early as the first periods of Christianity, but did not attract general notice until 1674, when they were opened for the public. Medevi resembles a little town, with church, post-office, hospital, a large number of dwellings for patients, fine parks, promenades, etc.

The Vettern is the second largest lake in Scandinavia; it has a length of 84 miles, and in its widest part a breadth of over 20; its level is 297 feet above the Baltic, and its greatest depth is 427 feet, showing its bottom to be much below the sea-line. It is fed by a large number of small streams. It is so clear and blue that when smooth it looks like a mirror of blue glass. But the mariner at times dreads its surface, which is very sensitive, and without warning is often stirred up without any apparent cause. It is also noted for its eddies, whirlpools, and mirages. It is encircled by four provinces—Nerike, Östergötland, Småland, and Vestergötland. It has but few islands, the largest being Visingsö. Upon the shores are five towns—Vadstena, Grenna, Jönköping, Askersund, and Hjo.

On the eastern shore, a few miles south, is the famous town of Vadstena, with 2500 inhabitants; it exports grain, lumber, iron, and spirits. The place, celebrated in old Catholic times, had a cloister in the eleventh century. In 1383 a fine monastery was founded by St. Birgitta (St. Birgit), and consecrated with great ceremony. This establishment was then the richest one in Sweden, receiving gifts of money and land from all parts of the country. To be buried within its precincts insured the entrance into heaven, and large offerings were given for that object.

The convent of Vadstena was in constant communication with Italy. The house in Rome in which Birgitta had dwelt had been given to these monks, and was often used by them and their people during their visits to the holy city. But the intercourse was not limited to travels by its monks. From Florence came, in 1405, a request that it should send some one to the latter city to found a Birgittine cloister, which later was called Paradise. Pilgrimages were made to the shrine from foreign countries; and these pious devotees, who always left some token of their visit, greatly increased the wealth of the fathers. The Swedish clergy and monks during these times consisted mostly of sons from the families of common people, or at least not from the higher strata of society. Among the nuns it was, however, quite different; for many of the sisters

were daughters of the high nobility. The nuns of Vadstena
convent were, however, not of Swedish birth only, but many

SLAB OVER THE GRAVE OF QUEEN PHILIPPA.

were from Denmark, Norway, and surrounding countries. The
noble families showed their concern for the place by acquir-
ing the right of having their remains buried within the holy

precincts of its church. It was not the intention that the cloister should become rich in silver and gold; but presents were nevertheless not refused. Queen Philippa gave to the church two golden crowns, ornamented with precious stones, the value of which was 1771 marks, a golden necklace, a golden girdle, and a golden tablet worth 1080 marks. In 1412 it received from the two brothers, Sten and Ture Bjelke, a shrine for preserving the bones of St. Birgitta, made out of pure silver, weighing 428⅘ marks, worth at that time about $40,000 of our present money—a very large sum.

The wealth of the nobles at that period must have been enormous, for it is mentioned that Karl Knutsson at a feast had on his table 1400 silver plates, besides innumerable other ornaments of gold and silver.

The monks and nuns lived well in those days. It is recorded that twenty-five monks and one hundred and sixty nuns consumed yearly 480 bushels of rye, 96 bushels of wheat, 1152 bushels of malt, 192 bushels of barley, 26 barrels of butter, 120 oxen, 300 sheep, 3600 pounds of pork, 2000 pounds of cheese, a large amount of fish, and other things in proportion.

Among the interesting remains of the cloister is the church of St. Birgitta—built of cut blue stone, and in good order—begun in 1395 and finished in 1424. It is 220 feet long, 110 wide, and 55 high, and had formerly a square chancel to the west, and entrances to the east. To this day, in spite of the many changes it has undergone, the greater part of the floor of the church is composed of slabs engraved with the coat-of-arms of the nobles who had their places of burial there. Here are the remains of Queen Philippa of England and the beautiful Katarina, the first the queen of Erik XIII., who reigned 1396–1439, and the last of Charles VIII., 1448–1457. The inscription on Queen Philippa's gravestone is the following in Latin: " Here rests her Highness Queen Philippa, wife of Erik, formerly King of Sweden, Götaland, Denmark, and Norway, and Duke of Pomerania—daughter of Henry IV., King of England, France, and Ireland—who died on the 5th of January, 1430."

Formerly St. Birgitta and her daughter, St. Katarina, were

laid in a heavy silver shrine, but King John III. melted it for coining money; now these are preserved in a casket covered with red velvet.   Great men of their day, Gustaf Olofson Stenbock, Jösse Eriksson, and others are here buried.   Prince Magnus, the insane son of Gustaf Wasa, lies under a fine monument, supported by fourteen Corinthian pillars.

VADSTENA CHURCH.

Among the notable persons here entombed is Bo Jonsson Grip, who died in 1386, and left the greatest fortune ever owned by any man in Sweden.   At his death he possessed Nyköpings Castle with South-eastern Södermanland; Stockholm Castle, and South-eastern Upland; a part of Vestmanland, with the mining districts and Dalarne; Kalmar Castle, and the greater part of the present Kalmar län; Åby, Viborg, Raseborg, Tavastehus, and Korsholms castles, with the whole of Finland; Öresten and Opensten castles — also Mark and Kind districts of Vestergötland; Forsholms Castle, and part of the southern shore of the Wennern.   He further owned the whole of Norrland (in which at that time was not reckoned Gestrickland), Ringstadholm, and other castles, with a large part of Östergötland; Stäkeholm Castle, with Tjust district in

Småland; Ydre and Kind districts in Östergötland; and Rum-
laborg Castle, with Northern Småland and Jönköping. Besides
these were large estates all over the kingdom, partly inherited,

INTERIOR OF VADSTENA CHURCH.

partly acquired; and one may imagine the extent of his wealth
in personal property when told that he willed away 57,500
ounces of silver, which at that time was a fabulous fortune;

and also an immense amount of ready money. He also
owned Gripsholm, which got its name from him. No private
man ever had so much land in Europe. There was not
much of the country left for the king, and of this great slices
were in the hands of other men. The reputation of Bo Jonsson reached even outside of Sweden. Once he declared war
on the powerful Hanseatic town of Dantzic, and Lübeck's
burghers advised its council to make peace with him.

REFECTORY IN VADSTENA CLOISTER.

In 1383 this extraordinary man made his will, wherein he left
all his fiefs and a part of his estates in trust to ten persons, who
should manage all this until the debts which he had incurred
on behalf of the kingdom were paid. With these fiefs his lawful heirs should have nothing to do. He was so anxious that
this provision should be enforced, that he selected alternates,
who should serve in case any of the original trustees died.

Though he had inherited great wealth, he during his life
used all sorts of means for increasing the same. When his
first wife, Margaretha Porse, died pregnant, he caused her to

be opened in the presence of witnesses to show that her child
was still alive; and he, according to Swedish law, inherited her
property through her child, which had, however, never been
born. The clergy considered this act a great sin, and Bishop
Nils, of Linköping, sharply took him to task therefor. To
appease him, Bo Jonsson gave to Vadstena cloister twelve
farms and two hundred and fifty marks in money.

CRUCIFIX, CARVED IN WOOD, IN VADSTENA CHURCH.

Bo Jonsson had raised and educated a poor young nobleman, Karl Niklasson, and also had him knighted on account
of his prowess, and manly and noble qualities. He also gave
him the estate of Färla, and many others in Östergötland and

other provinces. This youth was betrothed to a beautiful young girl by the name of Margaretha, her father being a nobleman by the name of Lambert Eriksson, living on his estate of Rimstad, on the shores of Lake Roxen.

One day Bo Jonsson happened to see her, and at once became enamored, and demanded her in marriage from her parents; they did not dare to refuse the all-powerful *Riksdrots* (chancellor of the realm), who sent the lover away on business, and married the girl during his absence. When the young knight returned and found he had been robbed of his most precious treasure by his benefactor, his wrath knew no bounds, and he went up to Bo Jonsson's residence in Stockholm, and, appearing before his former betrothed, accused her of having betrayed him. She, however, pleaded with him most earnestly, and showed him that she could have acted in no other way, and at the same time exacted of him a promise that he never would draw sword against Bo Jonsson. After having done this she gave him her hand, and he kneeled, covering it with most fervent kisses. At this moment Bo Jonsson entered, and seeing the young knight in such a position, accused him of trying to seduce his wife, and drew his sword, calling upon Karl to defend himself. But the latter, true to his promise, refused to draw against his former protector, and retired through the door into the hall-way and thence into the street, followed by the enraged chancellor. Thinking he would be safe in the church, he ran into the cloister of the Gray friars—the present Riddarholms church—closely pursued by Bo Jonsson, who, beside himself with rage, forgot the respect due to the sanctity of the place. At the high altar he came up to Karl, and gave the latter thrust after thrust, until he fell a corpse on the floor beside the sanctuary. This sacrilegious murder caused the deepest indignation; and in order to gain the pardon of the Church, Bo Jonsson had to give 1200 marks to Upsala Cathedral, 600 to Linköping, 500 to Strengnäs, 500 to Vesterås, and 600 to Åbo; he gave, also, five marks to the church in every parish where he had estates, besides five marks to the parish priest. During his time he used to meet the people on the Boslätten (Boplain), when he talked to the multitude from the so-called Bostone, which still exists. Then, when the mighty nobles were nearly exclusively the governing power, the masses, who most felt the consequences of every measure, had the greatest need of knowing what in the future they must hope or fear. Except on such occasions, the common people had little or no chance of learning what was taking place on the heights of the social structure. The name of Bo Jonsson was a power not only among the nobles, but still more so among the people. The knowledge that not only the highest authorities, but the king himself, were forced to obey his will, drew the masses towards him. Around those who dared to speak out their meaning, the oppressed people of mediæval times always rallied. Bo Jonsson kept up the Swedish custom of sometimes calling out the populace for a consultation about measures of importance — to talk with them and let them give their opinion. Although he well knew how to lead their judgments and resolutions to his own ends, he made them believe that they participated therein, and were valued accordingly. Probably no Swede either before or since has wielded a greater power than he did; and, although about five hundred years have disappeared since he lived, his name is still upon the lips of the people.

BO JONSSON'S COAT-OF-ARMS.

Säby, on the Stångån River, was one of his favorite castles. The island upon which it was built is still called Bosholmen. Formerly, from the northern side of this place, a road led to a meadow a short distance from the river, and there stands to this day a high stone, somewhat resembling a chair, called Bo's stone, now surrounded by three grand old oaks. Here Bo Jonsson held his meetings with the people, and addressed them. It is worthy of note that, although the meadow is now cultivated, and a ditch ought to pass where the above

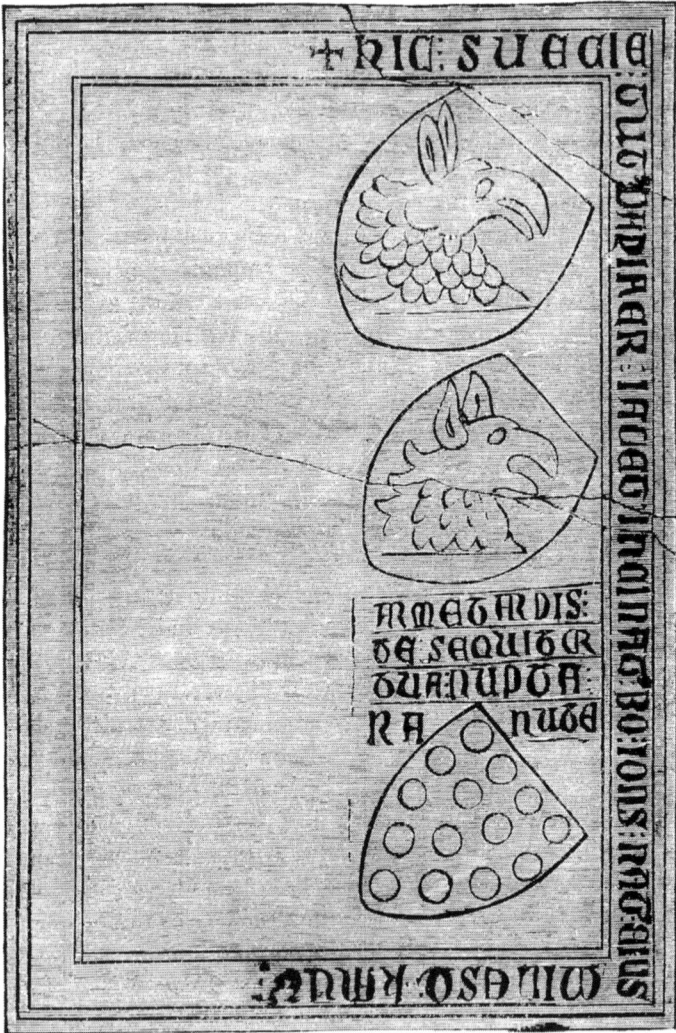

SLAB OVER THE GRAVE OF BO JONSSON AND HIS SON.

Bo Jonsson's road runs, the people on the estate could not be persuaded to open the former—such is the reverence for the memory of the great Bo. He owned, among others, the castle and estate of Gripsholm, built and named by him;

there he resided in royal splendor, holding diets and meetings of nobles. In Östergötland he had the castles of Brokind, Säby, and Vesterby, besides many more of greater or less importance. On the slab under which he was buried in the church the inscription, in Latin, reads as follows:

HERE LIE

THE SWEDISH CHANCELLOR, BO JONSSON,

IN SAFETY BURIED,

AND HIS SON, SIR CANUTE.

ARMAGARD, THY WIFE, FOLLOWS THEE, CANUTE.

Here is also the tomb of his son-in-law and daughter, Sir Algot Magnusson and Margareta, with the following inscription, with the date of the latter incomplete:

UNDER THIS STONE ARE HIDDEN THE BODIES OF THE NOBLE PERSONS,

SIR ALGOT MAGNUSSON,

AND HIS BELOVED WIFE,

LADY MARGARETA BOSDOTTER,

WHO DIED IN 1414, AT EASTER, WHILE HE DIED IN 14—.

The castle of Vadstena consists of an oblong square main building, enclosed in a rectangular court, and flanked by four round towers. The middle part rises like a high tower, surmounted by a lofty spire. The whole is surrounded by the Wettern, and the moats which are filled by its water. The neighborhood has been much changed, but the old castle has been kept in repair, and stands pretty much the same as during the days of Gustaf Wasa I. It was begun in 1545, and finished in 1552. In it the old king celebrated his third wedding, with Catharina Stenbock.

Here also Prince Magnus, in an attack of insanity, threw himself from one of the palace windows into the Wettern, tempted by the siren-song of the water-nymph; and here, after a separation of sixteen years, Charles XII. again met his sister, Ulrika Eleonora. Little remains to tell of the great splendor of this fine castle; the Knights' Hall must have been in its day a magnificent room. After the death of Gustaf Wasa, Vadstena came into the possession of his son Magnus.

About ten miles from Vadstena is Omberg hill, 574 feet above Lake Wettern, and 871 above the ocean. On the sloping

VADSTENA CASTLE—LAND SIDE.

side grows a luxuriant forest, through which streams of limpid water find their way to the lake. At the foot of Omberg,

VADSTENA CASTLE—LAKE SIDE.

about seventeen miles from Vadstena, is Alvastra, the finest ruin of Sweden. The cloister, the oldest and one of the largest and most renowned, was built in the middle of the twelfth century, probably by Alfhild, queen of King Sverker (therefore Alfhilstad, Alvastra); it was in the possession of Bernardine monks, and finally was given up to nuns. Here rest the remains of the kings Sverker I., Karl VII., Sverker II., and Johan I., all of the Sverker Dynasty; and also Birger Brosa, Ulf Gudmarson, the husband of St. Birgitta, with others. At the Reformation the cloister came into the possession of the Crown, and part of the buildings unfortunately have been taken down and used in the construction of the castles of Vadstena and Visingsborg. One of the oldest churches standing is Heda Church, not far from the rocky side of the Omberg towards the

KÄLLSTAD CHURCH, ABOUT SIX MILES SOUTH OF VADSTENA.

Wettern Lake, which is called the red gable, and from which the stone for the church is said to have been taken.

At the southern end of the lake is the city of Jönköping, with a population of 15,000, and a commodious harbor, protected by a regular breakwater. Its communications with different parts of the country are excellent, the railroads of the State here forming a net-work whose terminal points are Malmö, Göteborg, Christiania, and Stockholm, and through branch roads to several of the coast towns of Southern Sweden. Water communication with Stockholm is effected by three or four steamers, which go and return every week; with Göteborg by three others, and with the ports on the Wettern by a smaller one.

The industrial establishments are numerous, embracing paper and linen mills, steam dyeing works, manufactories of snuff, cigars, wall-papers, and chemicals, machine shop, iron-foundery, and match factory. The situation of the city is very pretty, being chiefly between the Wettern and two lakes, a canal communicating with one of them. At a distance of about ten miles is Taberg, 1129 feet above the sea, an iron-mountain which, with a few others found in Lapland, are the only ones in Europe where the ore is broken or blasted above ground. A few miles east of the city lies the factory of Husqvarna, where rifles and sewing-machines are made; its employés number about one thousand.

To the south, a short distance from the shore of the Wettern, and between Alvastra and the foot of a mountain range, embosomed in luxurious fruit-groves, is the town of Grenna, with about 1500 inhabitants, who export grain and potatoes. It was built in 1652, by Count Pehr Brahe the younger, and is especially noted for its beautiful site. One mile from Grenna is Visingsö, Wettern's largest island, about ten miles long and two wide, the property of the State, and rich in relics belonging to the iron age. On the south side are the ruins of Näsbo, an ancient castle, still seen under the water. Here have been found graves in great numbers from different periods, whence it has been concluded that the island was employed as a burial-ground by the tribes around it; before the founding of Stockholm Visingsö was often used as a residence for the kings. Here lived and died Karl VII., who reigned 1160–1168, Erik X., Johan I., and Magnus Ladulås.

In 1561 the island came into the possession of the Brahe family, who built the splendid fortified castle of Visingborg, completed in 1657. At the "reduction" it became the property of the Crown. The structure was burned in 1718, and nothing of its former splendor remains but ruins. The church, of cut stone, finished in 1636, has a fine portal, and is ornamented by numerous paintings, among which a couple on copper are said to have been done by Catharina Stenbock, the third queen of Gustaf Wasa. Highly gilt silver tablets shine on the walls, and the church contains other curiosities. In its chancel are the marble statues of Pehr Brahe the younger and his countess. Under the church are the burial-vaults of the Brahe family.

Crossing the Wettern from Vadstena to Carlsborg, a fortified place intended as a base for the defence of the country, one enters the Bottensjö, which may be considered a bay, and, sailing through this, reaches Forsvik, where the canal is again continued, and, by means of a lock, an ascent of eleven feet takes place; after which Lake Viken is entered. This is the highest water on the route, being 308 feet above the Baltic, and 160 above the Wenern. The Ymsen is a lake midway between the Wenern and Wettern, with pretty (formerly oak-clad) shores. On the top of a promontory are still seen ruins of the eight-feet-thick walls of a castle, the remnants of a well cut through the rock in its central part, and, surrounding all this, remains of breastworks and ditches. Gold chains and rings have been found in the ground around these old ruins, which date from 1229. From Viken the canal runs in a north-westerly direction towards the Wenern, and for several miles is perfectly level, in one place being carried through the rocks. The steamer wends its way slowly on account of the locks, and finally reaches Sjötorp on the Wenern, with its spacious basins, docks for repairs, and workshops.

The Wenern is the largest lake of Scandinavia, its length being ninety-three miles, and its widest part forty-seven; its greatest depth, 359 feet, is found north of a group of islands called Lurö; its level varies sometimes ten feet, according to the amount of water poured into it in the spring by the rivers. It has but few large islands, the most important being Kollandsö, near the southern shore; Hammeron and Amon on the north, and Forsö and Bromö on the south. The banks of this inland fresh-water sea are beautiful and picturesque, with its bays, fjords, archipelago of islands, wooded hills, cities, hamlets, churches, farms, and historical castles. It is supplied by more than thirty rivers. Sailing-vessels and steamers plough its surface in every direction; more than forty light-houses have been erected, to warn the mariner of danger, or show him the approaches to his port of destination. Along its rivers and shores are numerous saw-mills and iron-foundries. In its north-eastern corner is the town of Kristinehamn, with a population of over 4000; it is connected by railways and canals with Filipstad, and other mining districts of the province of Vermland; it exports bar and cast iron, and ores, timber, and grain. Every year, in April, is held the fair, when contracts for iron and timber are made between producers and exporters. It has a match factory, tanneries, machine shops, etc. Filipstad was founded by Charles IX., and has a mining-school supported by the iron-masters' association.

In its neighborhood, especially north of it, are situated a large number of iron mines, smelting furnaces and works, making it one of the most important places in Sweden. All these are connected with the new railroad, either by tram-ways or lake transportation, thus getting their products to the sea.

In the southern part of Vermland, on the Skagen, about sixteen miles from Kristinehamn, stands the church of Råda, one of the oldest wooden ones of Scandinavia, built in the beginning of the fourteenth century. The outside of the edifice presents no special features, but the interior is very interesting. Odd paintings illustrate the Scriptures; those of the chancel dating from 1323, and of the nave from 1495. There is one porch, which in olden times was used as a depository for weapons during the services; for at that period men came armed, as if ready for a fray.

West of Kristinehamn is the town of Karlstad, on the shores of the lake and of the Klar River, with a population of 7000. In 1865 a fire laid almost the whole city in ashes; it is now entirely rebuilt, and looks handsomer than before, with wide streets, boulevards planted with several rows of trees, large squares, stately buildings, and fine stores. Quite a number of manufactories have a permanent exhibition of the products of the province, near the city park. Along the river, north of the city, are a number of iron-founderies, saw-mills, and other factories, among which the Uddeholms works are the most important. These consist of seven iron-works and four smelting-furnaces, the estate embracing an area of nearly half a million acres, and employing more than 10,000 workmen. The forests are exceedingly well managed, so that their new growth is properly cared for.

The next valley west of the Klar River is Fryksdal, with Lake Fryken, skirted on both sides by ranges of hills. This, as well as that of the Klar River, constitutes one of the large arteries in which the industrial life of the province of Vermland pulsates; but the former is in a higher degree than the latter distinguished for its beauty. Steamers ascend the By River

INTERIOR OF RÅDA CHURCH, VERMLAND.

and the Seffle Canal, and far into the interior of West Vermland. There is another and most charming route by the Dalsland Canal, and a series of lakes which bring one to the frontier of Norway. The scenery is at times extremely beautiful, and the canal in many places displays great engineering skill, especially near Håfverud. Hemmed in on either side by perpendicular rocks, there is a cataract, beyond which the vessels must be carried. To build this canal and locks on the left side was always considered impossible, as there was no safe bottom; to lay them on the right was also exceedingly difficult, the rocks above the cataracts being of such a nature that a cutting could not be made through them without enormous expense. The engineer overcame these obstacles by placing the lower part of the canal and the locks on the right side, but carrying the upper part first over the cataract in a colossal hanging aqueduct of iron, 122 feet long and 15½ feet wide; and then, in an obtuse angle, following the left bank of the stream, against which one wall was built, while the other was blasted out of the rock. When the vessels are in the aqueduct, they seem, as it were, to swing in the air.

Among the most lovely spots on the lake are the hills of Kinnekulle, rising several hundred feet, from which a magnificent view of the Kinne Bay and the surrounding country can be had. At the base is Hellekis—a large estate, with a fine mansion. In the southern part of the bay is the town of Lidköping, where the Lidan River empties itself into the lake: it has a population of over 4000.

A few miles south of the entrance to the canal is the chateau of Börstorp, built by Baron Falkenberg: iron letters show the name of the builder, and the date of its construction, 1646. In one room hangs a remarkable little painting, representing the daughter of King Magnus Ladulås, named Elna. In the border of this picture, which is an original portrait, is written: "Elna des Königes Magni Ladlos Tochter zu Schweden, ihr herr Vater hat sie in St. Clara gegeben. Anno 1288 da sie nicht ihr 7te Jahre erreichtet ist ge-Contre—fait. Anno 1299." A royal shield with three crowns rests by the foot of the princess, who is ornamented with two chains, which she got from her father, and which she always carried while a nun in St. Clara convent. From her these chains descended, and were worn by the abbesses in the convent, and when this was abolished by Gustavus I., they remained in the possession of the last abbess, Anna Reinholdsdotter Leuhusen, in whose family the estate fell. One of the chains is composed of 98 rings of pure gold, and weighs about 400 pennyweights; the other is a rosary, consisting of 101 little balls of silver, seven of gold, all of filigree work, 45 still smaller

VIEW ON DAISLANDS CANAL.

BÖRSTORP, IN VESTERGÖTLAND.

golden balls, and an ornament of the same with a few small
images of apostles—altogether weighing about three ounces.
The ornament is completed by two very finely-worked ear-
pendants of gold; in each of which there is a pair of scissors,
and a knife and fork, all of steel. They have been in the
Leuhusen family three hundred years, and are carefully kept
in a large case, and are, with the very rich library, entailed
to the eldest son. If to these three centuries, during which
these valuables belonged to the pious abbesses of St. Clara
convent, are added those in which they have been in possession of the Leuhusen family, we have an aggregate of six
hundred years, during which they have descended regularly
from hand to hand.

2 A 2

There is no country in Europe where so many old stone churches of the eleventh, twelfth, and thirteenth centuries are found as in Sweden; they are abundant from the central part to its southern extremity. Their spires and towers, rounded and pointed arches, present most graceful proportions; many are perfect specimens of the architecture of those periods, with doors of exquisite design. A few are peculiar, and no doubt were parts of heathen temples, to which additions have been made. These often appear when least expected, as they are embosomed in groves. In them are found

RELIC SHRINE OF WOOD, COVERED WITH EMBOSSED AND GILDED COPPER, FROM THE END OF THE TWELFTH CENTURY—ERIKSBERGA CHURCH.

many mementos of those days, in the shape of crude paintings illustrating the Scriptures, or wooden carvings on the same subject; baptismal fonts of stone, with odd sculptured figures or designs, surrounded by Latin or Runic inscriptions;

embroideries of remarkable pattern, shrines chased and covered with enamelled copper, or of solid silver, wood-carvings, old altars, and other relics too numerous to mention, many of which are now kept in the museum of the State. Here

REPRESENTATION OF THE CRUCIFIXION ON A CABINET, FROM ÖSTERÅKER CHURCH, UPLAND.

and there one sees a *skampallen* (shame stool); persons convicted of crime or misdemeanor, against either Church or State, were formerly condemned to stand upon it in front of the high altar, so that the delinquent might be seen by the whole congregation. The reason why these structures have remained untouched is that, even during their intestine wars, the churches and tombs of former enemies were always respected ; and when the Reformation took place there were few Vandals willing to burn and destroy them. The accompanying illustrations are representations of some of these relics, and a volume might be filled with them :

The relic shrine is from Eriksberga church, in Vestergötland, near Falköping ; the inscription, two lines on all four sides, enumerates the relics kept therein : of St. Andrew, Holy Cross, St. Pancratius, blood of St. Vincent, etc.

BAPTISMAL FONT OF STONE FROM NORUM CHURCH.

The baptismal font is from Norum church, in Bohuslän, now in the historical museum of the State. The Runic inscription reads : Svän Kärthe (Swain made the font) ; the signification of the last five characters is not known. Below the inscription is seen a man surrounded by four snakes, who seems to rest with his feet on a harp, or something similar. Probably this is meant to represent Gunnar in the snake-pit, a scene from the Eddaic sagas of the Völsungar and Gjukungar. The wooden door with iron mountings is in the church of Versås, in Vestergötland. The inscription in Runic characters on a strip of iron reads : Asmunter gärthi dyr (Åsmund made the door). The same name also occurs on similar doors in the

churches of Visingsö, on the island of that name in the Wettern Lake, and Väfversunda in Östergötland, on the shore of
the Wettern, about eight miles south of Vadstena.

Near the southern border of the bay of Kinne is Husaby church, one of the most historical and the oldest of Sweden, situated at the foot of the hills, on the southerly side,
about twenty-five miles from the town of Mariestad. The
ancient graves, the stones with Runic inscriptions, and other
relics bear testimony to the antiquity of the place, which dates
from the dawn of Christian-
ity upon the land. It was
here that Olaf Skötkonung,
born about 965, and who died
in 1024 (the first Christian
King of Sweden), was bap-
tized by Sigfrid, sent by King
Ethelred about the year 1001.

The castles of the kings in
olden times were called *hus*
(house), and after his conver-
sion Olaf Skötkonung established his court in Husaby,
which was long before his
time a king's farm; for he
would not live among his
subjects in the province of
Upland, who clung with great
tenacity to the religion of
their forefathers. A few
years later he gave this farm
as a residence to the first
Bishop of Vestergötland, and
it became chiefly the abode
of his successors, while the

WOODEN DOOR OF VERSÅS CHURCH.

cathedral of Skara was being erected on the site of a great
heathen temple.

From the king's house rose the Husaby church, which
still possesses the original three towers belonging to the old

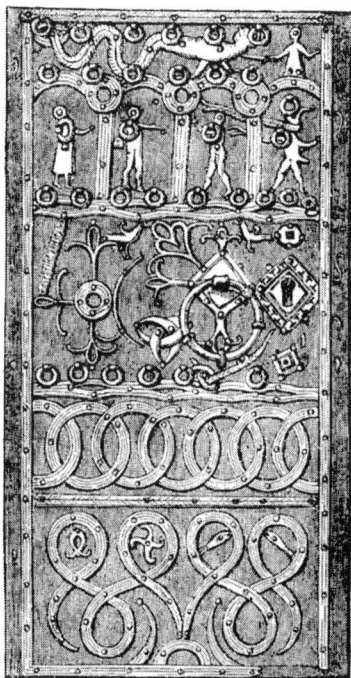

Kungshus. This edifice is about thirty-two feet wide, and, with the chancel, 105 feet long, and was the cathedral of the bishops for nearly one hundred and forty years, and until the Cathedral of Skara was inaugurated. The towers are three, one beside

HUSABY CHURCH.

the other, on the west end of the church, and are seen with their spiral stairways, from which there are doors opening to four stories; the two side towers were the entrances to the castle, of which the middle tower then was a part. The old stone sculptured baptismal font, the stakes to which torches were fastened at bridal-parties, the altars, the bishop's chair, and other relics of the Catholic Church remain. There are queer epitaphs on the old slabs over the tombs inside and outside the edifice. Among the most remarkable tombs are

TOMB OF OLAF SKÖTKONUNG.

those of King Olaf Skötkonung, and of his queen Astrid, just outside the west end, and nearly nine centuries old.

One of these is wholly without inscription, while the other has on the east end two animals, which seem to meet in anything but a friendly mood; on the west end two others, which

HUSABY CHURCH-YARD, WITH TOMBS OF KING OLAF SKÖTKONUNG AND QUEEN ASTRID.

appear to devour a human head; on one side two persons
holding a chalice and a balance, a bishop with a cross and
a fish, another who with one hand receives a key from a
hand extended from above, and in the other holds a bishop's
staff—two children sitting on the border of a well-house, near
which is an altar on which a chalice is put, and a person with
outstretched arms; on the north side two dragons, against
which two men armed with swords and shields are battling—

END VIEW OF THE TOMB OF KING OLAF SKÖTKONUNG.

one with a short dress seeming to be a layman, whose foot a
dragon has taken hold of, while the other, with a long wide
robe (an ecclesiastic), thrusts his sword into the mouth of the
monster. These are symbols of the Law, the Gospel, the Bap-
tism, the Lord's Supper, and the battle between Christendom
and Heathendom. Tradition indicates that Olaf Skötkonung
was baptized in St. Sigfrid's spring, which is situated east of
the church; and several places in the vicinity bear the name
of Sigfrid.

Olaf was called lap-king, because he was chosen a king while a child in his mother's lap. He, with King Sven Tveskägg of Denmark, defeated Olaf Tryggvason of Norway at the famous naval battle of Svolder.

After this battle Sven Tveskägg's hands were free to renew his expedition to England, where he had been twice before. An occasion soon arose, giving him a pretext for going. On the 13th of November, 1002, the English had agreed to the general destruction of all the Northmen then living in the country; this resolve they put into execution, killing the greater portion of them; even Gunhild, the sister of Sven, who was married to the English earl Paling, was also murdered. Angered in a high degree by this treachery, Sven equipped a large army and landed on the English coast, continuing his ravages until 1007, when the weak King Ethelred paid 36,000 pounds to obtain peace from the invaders; but the desired peace he did not gain, for other chiefs continued to plunder the country. Sven died the 2d of February, 1014, and Ethelred thought it a good chance to recover his entire kingdom; and after having bought the assistance of the Danish chief, Thorkil the High, for 21,000 pounds, he managed to expel the young Canute, the son of Sven. But he did not long enjoy this state of peace, for, in the latter part of 1015, Canute returned with a large army and a splendid fleet, and soon drove Ethelred away; and, finally, after many hard-fought battles, Canute was, at the end of the year 1017, in sole possession of the kingdom, which he kept till his death, November 12th, 1042. He reigned over England, Denmark, Norway, and the southern part of Sweden.

One of the most interesting places between the Wettern and the Wenern is the town of Skara, an ancient trading and offering centre on the Vestgöta plain. This place was, before Christianity, the centre of heathendom in Götaland, just as Upsala was in Svealand. The cathedral, next to that of Husaby the oldest in Sweden, was consecrated in 1151 by Bishop Ödgrim; of its many towers only two are left. The town has a fine elementary school-building, and a new library with 20,000 volumes. There is also a seminary for female teachers of the folkskolor, and a veterinary college; it has about 3000 inhabitants. Between Skara and Falköping is Gudhem, during the heathen age a great sacrificing place, later a cloister for nuns, of which, however, now only a few ruins are left. About six miles east of Skara stretches Axevalla heath, now used as a field of manœuvring or drill for the military; but in olden times a great burial-place, to which numerous passage-graves and other reminiscences bear witness. Not quite three miles east of Axevalla, near the base of Billingen, is the old cloister-church of Varnhem, originally built in 1150 by King Sverker the elder; the structure, in which several kings rest, was burned by the Danes in 1566, but was restored to its original state by Count Magnus Gabriel de la Gardie, 1668–1671. It is in shape a Gothic-cross with three towers, and is one of the handsomest in Sweden. The old royal tombs were restored by the above-mentioned art-loving magnate, who in the church built a magnificent mausoleum for his family.

Near Kinnekulle is the historic island of Kollandsö, which forms part of the bay, and is almost contiguous to the shore, upon which stands the interesting castle of Leckö, commenced in 1298 by Bishop Brynolf of Skara. The structure is on a high cliff on the north-eastern corner of the island. It was occupied by the Catholic bishops of Skara, and Brynolf Gerlachsson at the end of the fifteenth century extended and strongly fortified it. From one of these bishops, Didrick Slaghök, it was captured by Gustaf Wasa I.; afterwards, in 1527, it was confiscated by the Crown from Bishop Magnus Sommar, and was, in 1615, with three districts, made a county for Jakob Pontusson de la Gardie. Not only the latter, but also his son, Magnus Gabriel de la Gardie, greatly improved the castle, which had been burned by the Danes in 1566; scarcely more than the foundation and a wall of the original structure were remaining; finally it had as many as seven towers: it was seized for the Crown by Charles XI. Although with all its irregular additions presenting a certain disorder, it is still a stately square building with four towers, and surrounded by a garden, and a moat blasted out of the rock separates it from the island.

From Leckö the channel runs through the rocky passage north of Kollandsö, and then out into the open Wenern, or rather that part of it called Dalbo Lake, and thence in a south-westerly direction. To the right are seen the shores of Dals-land, and to the left Hinna light-house. The Wenern now gets more and more narrow towards the end. Soon comes in sight the hill Halleberg (290 feet above the lake), and beyond the Hunneberg, both with perpendicular walls, after which is shortly reached the port of Wenersborg.

From Wenersborg the journey westward continues to be very interesting. First the vessel enters Lake Vassbotten, and from this through a canal into the Göta River, thus avoiding the cascade of Rönnum, 19 feet in height. At last the fa-mous Trollhättan (witches' caps) falls are reached; these are 111 feet in height, but are divided into four large cascades and rapids called Gullö, Toppö, Stampeströms, and Helvetes, extending altogether nearly a mile. First comes the Gullö, with a height of 26 feet; then the Toppö, where the river, which here attains a considerable width, throws itself down 44 feet on both sides of the islet of Toppö, which can be reached by a frail bridge, and from which a very good view of the scene can be had. Here is also situated the so-called "King's Grotto," an excavation in the rock, where many royal person-ages — Gustaf III., and Gustaf Adolf, Karl Johan, Desideria, Oscar, and Josefina—have had their names cut. Next after the Toppö fall comes that of the Stampeström, nine feet high, and immediately east thereof the water is seen to rush through the Polhems lock, 64 feet deep, with the assistance of which it was the intention to pass both the Toppö and Stampeström; it therefore had to be of colossal dimensions, with floodgates of not less than 53 feet in height. Below Stampeström the river forms a still-water, called Håjumsvarp; but it soon again gets narrower; and then follow each other with terrific speed the three Helvetes falls (falls of hell), together, however, only 28 feet in height. Finally, 1000 feet farther, the river forms another cascade near Flottbergsströmmen four feet high. The canal, most of which is blasted out of the rock, first runs 6600 feet to Åkersjö (129 feet above the sea), and then through eleven locks of 24 feet in width and 10 feet in depth, down to Åkersvass, where it ends. These are the new locks, the old ones, eight in number, which are still used for smaller vessels, lying close by the new; they were opened in 1800. The journey is then continued on the quiet river, which here is only 19 feet above the sea, past Skärsbo down to Åkerström, where a fall of three and a half feet necessitates another lock; then past Torpa, remarkable for a salt spring—one of the very few in Sweden—until the village of Little Edet is reached. Here the river gets narrower, and forms a fall of 10 feet, to avoid which, near the fine estate of Ström, commences the so-called Ströms Canal, 4000 feet long, with two locks; beyond this the stream runs along smoothly until it empties into the North Sea. Upon its shores many historic events have occurred. Near Foxerna church two battles took place between Inge the elder, King of Sweden, and Magnus Barefoot of Norway.

Not far from the fall of Little Edet is the ancient town of Liodhus or Lödöse, once powerful, rich, and strongly fortified, several times besieged and plundered, but now an insignificant hamlet with a ship-wharf. A little beyond is the village of Kongelf, with about 900 inhabitants, remarkable for the historic memories which cluster around it. In Northern history it is often mentioned as the proud and mighty Konghäll, formerly Konungahälla, *i. e.*, the Kings' Hall, so called on account of the many meetings of kings held there. By reason of its situation on the former boundary between Norway and Sweden, it constantly was the scene of remarkable events. Here was held the fatal meeting between King Olaf Tryggvason and Sigrid the Proud; here Inge the elder met the kings of Denmark and Norway. In the beginning of the twelfth century Sigurd Jorsalafar intended to make Konghäll, which was then the most powerful town of Norway, and whose fleets sailed to the Mediterranean, his permanent residence; but in 1135, five years after the death of this king, the place, although strong, was completely destroyed by the Vandalians, and never afterwards regained its former greatness. On an island opposite are the remains of the old fort of Bohus.

CHAPTER XXXI.

The Provinces of Halland and Bohuslän.—Rivers abounding with Salmon.—Halmstad.—Bohuslän.—An Ancient Viking Place.—Its numerous Relics of the Stone, Bronze, and Viking Ages.—Extensive Fishing.—Bathing-places on the Coast.— Särö.—Life at Särö.—Marstrand.—A Fashionable Bathing Resort.

On its west coast Sweden has two provinces, Halland and Bohuslän; the latter in olden times belonged to Norway. They were ceded to Sweden by Denmark in 1658, by the Peace of Roeskilde, between Charles X. and Frederick III. Before this the only territory owned by Sweden on the North Sea was a narrow tract of land belonging to Westergötland, lying between the two provinces.

The shores of Halland are bathed by the Skagerrack and Kattegat; its rivers abound in salmon, said to be superior in flavor to those of the other rivers of Sweden, especially those caught on the Nissa. Most of the fish are smoked by a peculiar process, giving to them a flavor much relished by the Swedes. Numerous fishing-villages are found on the coast.

The seaport of Halmstad, on the shores of the Nissa, with 8000 inhabitants, is the capital of the province. Here, in 1062, a fierce naval fight took place between the Danes, led by Sven, a grandson of Canute the Great, and the Norwegians under King Harald Hårdråde, in which the latter were victorious. The church was built about 1400, and ruins of old cloisters and of the fortifications still exist.

Bohuslän was, in ancient times, a province where many a Viking resided, and well chosen was their abode. The shore is indented everywhere by deep fjords; innumerable islands of all sizes guard the coast, the most dangerous in Sweden; these hide from view the rivers and bays, where the pirate chiefs assembled their fleets unknown to their enemies, or from which they sailed for distant lands in search of booty. There is no part of Scandinavia where so many tombs of the stone, bronze, and iron ages, with their relics, are to be found, and weeks and months can be spent in their examination. I have given an account of some of them in the chapters on these graves (Vol. I.). How thoughtfully I have stood before these tokens of the past, which so well illustrate the littleness of

HIGH CHANCEL, HALMSTAD CHURCH.

man, and show how quickly he is forgotten when the usages and manners of his time have passed away! His remains, once buried with great honor and deep religious feeling, are disturbed and taken away as objects of curiosity for the people of distant lands, who care nothing for, and know little of, his deeds.

The bare rounded hills contrast singularly in summer with

the blue sky above; while in winter the waves dashed by the tempests seem to sing a sad, long wail on the dark gray coast, which then partakes of the color of the clouds. The islands act as reefs, guarding the shores and giving safe anchorage. Some of them are inhabited; and in protected places there are green meadows and fields of grain, with now and then a windmill, a red-painted farm-house, or a fisherman's cottage, roofed with red tiles. Fishing is carried on extensively, especially that of herrings and sprats; lobsters and oysters are abundant.

From Bohuslän northward the bleak shores of Norway come into view; the scenery increases in grandeur and ruggedness, and presents the character before described. On the frontier is Fredrikshald, at the siege of whose fortress Charles XII. met his death. The most important town of the province, after Göteborg, is Uddevalla, with 6000 inhabitants, at the end of the By fjord, which is fifty miles long.

On the coast there are a number of very pleasant bathing resorts, among which is the village of Grebbestad, in whose vicinity is the large battle-field of Greby, studded with a great variety of grave-stones, raised, according to the saga, over the remains of Scots who, after a plundering expedition to the Bullar lakes, were here overtaken by their pursuers and slain. Strömstad is the most northerly town on the Swedish coast, with a population of about 2000. Lysekil is another fishing and bathing village. Gustafsberg is a charming spot.

The two most fashionable resorts of Sweden are Särö and Marstrand. On a warm July day I sailed from the river Göta towards Särö, the islands rapidly increasing in number southward; seals were basking in the sun upon the rocks, and wild ducks swimming quietly, surrounded by their broods; gulls were flying above our heads or resting upon the water, while here and there on some deserted islands were sheep left to browse for the summer. In August and September there is capital sport here in seal-hunting.

A whistle from the steamer announced to the inhabitants its approach, though there was nothing but rocks in sight. Trees soon after made their appearance, and in a short time

we came to the wharf of Särö. A few ladies, dressed in the
height of summer fashion, with their children queerly accou-
tred in sea-side costumes, were waiting to meet their husbands
or friends. Särö is an island connected with the main-land by
a causeway, and is a peculiar sea-bathing place, no house overlooking the water. Less than a hundred yards from the shore
groves of large oak-trees, often from ten to twelve feet in
circumference, with long spreading branches, and other trees,
formed a park, in which were scattered charming villas of
different sizes, some containing only two rooms, surrounded
by gardens. Paths led in different directions, every rock and
bit of ground being used to advantage. Life was very quiet,
there being no bustle, and very little driving; the cottages
were rented for the season, and chiefly occupied by the inhabitants of Göteborg. In Sweden ladies and gentlemen do
not bathe in company, and here do not get sight of each
other, the respective places being separated by a promontory.
The beach for men is in the hollow of a rocky cove, where
the sea is so clear that one can see the bottom at a great
depth. The people wear no bathing-costume. The water was
73° Fahrenheit, and I found it too warm to be refreshing.

Marstrand is on an island of the Kattegat, and at the entrance of the By fjord. It looms up in the distance, with its
castles of Gustafsborg, Fredriksborg, and Carlsten, which were
considered formidable before the invention of modern artillery. The town was founded in 1220 by the Norwegian king,
Hakon Hakonson; during the sixteenth century it became one
of the most flourishing places of the north on account of its
herring fisheries, but now depends for its support on the summer visitors. About 2000 persons come to spend the summer
here, ladies being in greater number than gentlemen. I noticed that the former were attired more fashionably than at
any of the other watering-places; the dresses, in warm weather, were chiefly of white or light-colored muslin, with long
and broad silk scarfs around their waists. Graceful hats partly hid their blue eyes and smiling faces; no one wore a silk
robe, for the sea-shore was not the place, according to Swedish
notions, to wear costly fabrics, the salt air ruining them. The

gentlemen were clad in summer suits, and everybody had an appearance of refinement.

The bathing season lasts from the 1st of June to the end of August. There were restaurants and hotels, and houses were rented for the season. There was also a small ball and concert room, in which was dancing twice a week, on Wednesday and Sunday evenings, besides concerts and other entertainments given by actors or artists. Almost all the visitors rented rooms and took their meals at the restaurants, of which there were two. There was no driving, and the people amused themselves by walking, boating, and fishing, while flirtations by the seaside took place here as well as elsewhere.

The bathing-place was peculiar, being enclosed with a fence in a sandy spot where the sea was as quiet as a pond, and where the bathers could not be seen from the outside. There were several rooms for the use of gentlemen, but no bathing costumes were worn. The ladies had their own place also, and as I saw no wet garments drying, I suppose they bathe in the same fashion as the sterner sex. The water was 71½°, and consequently a little cooler than at Särö. Among the bathers were a few Russians, Norwegians, Danes, and Finlanders.

The arrival of the steamer was always an event, and all Marstrand was out. The Swedish ladies looked very pretty, and many of the men were really handsome; I was especially attracted by their pleasant manners.

There is a church in the village, and a shaded promenade of fine trees. Among the curiosities are so-called "giant holes," which were, no doubt, made by water. I fared well, for the friends who had received me so kindly on my arrival in Sweden had made known to their wives my intended visit, and their reception was most affable. With great trouble they had been able to secure a room for me at the hotel; for in the height of the season, unless one has done this in advance, the chances are that he will spend the first night walking through the streets or contemplating the sea.

CHAPTER XXXII.

The Province of Östergötland.—Risinge Church.—An Historical Battle-field.—The City of Norrköping.—The largest Manufacturing Town in Sweden.—How the Artisans live.—Comfortable Dwellings.—The Iron-works of Finspong.—Laws concerning the Employment of the Young.—Intelligent Citizens.—Fine Schools. —Interesting Ceremony at the closing of Schools.—A Teachers' Sociable.

SOUTH of Södermanland we enter Östergötland, one of the most fertile provinces of Sweden, whose territory lies chiefly between Lake Wettern and the Baltic. From the north the traveller on his way to Norrköping passes near the ancient Risinge church, remarkable for its wood-carving and painted ceilings of mediæval times. As he nears the coast, and approaches the Bråviken fjord, he comes to Bråvalla heath, the scene in pagan history of the bloody battle which took place, about the year 740, between Harald Hildetand and Sigurd Ring.

The city of Norrköping, with a population of 27,000, near the head of the Bråviken fjord, is built on both sides of the Motala River, whose rapids furnish apparently an almost unlimited water-power to the numerous manufactories located on its banks. Vessels ascend the stream as far as the lower bridge, and quays are erected on both sides; the streets are wide, and some are far superior to those of Stockholm, large slabs forming the pavement of the sidewalks. The town is clean. Most of the houses are of wood, painted, and not more than two stories in height.

This city is the principal manufacturing centre on the peninsula of Scandinavia. There are paper-mills, lithographic establishments, machine shops, tobacco, soap, and match factories, tanneries, breweries, sugar refineries, chemical, hosiery, and starch manufactories; three ship-building docks, one of which belongs to the Motala iron-works; extensive woollen and cotton mills — some employing from five to seven or eight hundred hands. The manufacturers have discovered

INTERIOR OF RISINGE CHURCH.

that the greater the power of production the cheaper is the cost of the goods; they have awakened to the importance of adopting the latest improvements in machinery devised in England, America, France, and Germany. There is a great deal of enterprise, which I have no doubt will in time greatly enlarge the industries of the place.

The working population is thrifty, and their houses exceedingly clean; indeed, cleanliness is one of the characteristics of the Swedish artisans. They live generally in flats, of three to five rooms. In some cases the owners of the mills have houses which they rent for a stipulated sum to their hands. I met no beggars; and altogether was delighted with this little Manchester of Sweden. I was particularly pleased, in visiting the manufacturing establishments, to see the order, and, as a rule, the tidiness of the women; and only in the lithographic works did I notice a few girls twelve years of age.

Eighteen miles north-west of Norrköping is the magnificent estate of Finspong, with iron-works and a cannon-foundry. It has a very fine castle, erected in 1668, with a chapel, and it also contains a valuable library, a theatre, and a number of paintings, among them some by Titian, Guido Reni, Rubens, and other masters. The parks are beautiful; the iron-works and foundry are near the castle. The works, established during the sixteenth century by the Crown, were, in 1641, sold to the renowned Louis de Geer; in 1685, during the "reduction" of Charles XI., the estate was again taken by the State, but it was the year after given back to Louis de Geer the younger and his heirs or assigns, in consideration of certain yearly contributions which are still in force. The property, which by late purchases has been greatly increased, now covers an area of over 96,000 acres.

The laws concerning the employment of the young are rigorously enforced; no child, male or female, being engaged in a store or factory, or in any handicraft, unless over twelve years of age. In manufacturing establishments or workshops, no one under eighteen years is employed between nine o'clock in the evening and five o'clock in the morning. No labor may interfere with the school, and the children who work during the day must attend the evening classes. But the statutes, however beneficent, compared with those of other countries, are capable of improvement. Children above twelve years have often to work here ten hours a day in close rooms; this is entirely too long a time, especially as they have besides to attend the evening school.

The merchants have their country-seats in the suburbs. Some of these retreats are beautiful, hidden in glens and shaded nooks. The villa of the gentleman to whom I am indebted for much of the pleasure I enjoyed in Norrköping is situated in a romantic spot, in the midst of fine groves of birches, firs, and pines, by the side of a narrow dale, with meadows flanked on either side by a ridge of granite. The citizens are most intelligent and liberal in their views. The schools are among the finest in Sweden, and this is saying much. There is a technological institute, also an excellent high-school standing in the midst of open ground, and commanding a grand view; this is an ornament and a credit to the town, and would compare favorably with any in the United States. One of the rooms is 80 feet long, 40 wide, and 25 high; there is plenty of light, and the ventilation is good; the scholars meet there daily before the hours of study. A chapter of the Bible is read at the opening of the school, and one of the scholars reads the prayer for the day. This room is also used for musical entertainments, for there is a musical society belonging to the school. There is a small museum, furnished with zoological and mineralogical specimens, skeletons and skulls, shells, eggs, corals, fish, turtles, etc.; also a library stored with scientific works and books of reference. French, English, and German literature are well represented by the works of Thackeray and Dickens, Napier's "History of the Peninsular War," Thiers's "Consulate and Empire," the works of St. Beuve, Lamartine, Balzac, and Jules Janin, and even those of Voltaire, and the "Biographie Universelle." The school also possesses a good laboratory for the study of chemistry; and one room is used for the instruction of classes in drawing. The number of teachers and professors is between twenty and twenty-four. The gymnasium hall stands at some distance from the main building.

There are several free-schools, all occupying good buildings, showing the intelligence of the people and the interest taken in education. There are also one or two private schools.

By Herr E——, director of one of the banks, to whom I had a letter of introduction, I was received most kindly. "You have come just in time to see the closing of the free-school; would you like to go with me?" I assented, and went. The children had gathered in a large hall, and numbered about 1500 girls and boys belonging to the working-class. All were dressed in their best; and if I had not known I was in Sweden, I might have thought myself in one of the large school-rooms in an American city.

I found that Herr E—— was a man of large and extended views. He thought it might prove advantageous to educate boys and girls together, and he also believed that there should be more female teachers; that women ought to be paid the same price as men for the same work; and that the high-school should be as free to young women as to their brothers. I was presented to the superintendent, who was on the platform with two clergymen, members of the Board of Education, and several ladies; the children sang Swedish hymns and songs; and a few prizes, consisting of books, were given to the best scholars in the different classes. Then one of the clergymen made an address, directing his remarks especially to the girls who had finished the course of study prescribed by law, and who would not return the following term. He exhorted them to remain pure in thought, to love and fear God, to cultivate virtue, and to believe in the atonement of the Lord and Saviour Jesus Christ. The superintendent kindly invited me to attend a little sociable given by him to all the teachers. The party was held in one of the Folkskolor, and there were thirty lady and eight gentlemen teachers present. Most of the former were young, and all were attractive in appearance, and modest, and some of them quite handsome. I began to feel after awhile that the place might prove dangerous to a bachelor like myself; perhaps I might not be able to resist the smiles of so many pretty Swedes. Several of the gentlemen present were married, and their wives were teachers also—a step in the right direction, which might be imitated elsewhere with great advantage to the comfort of the household. I could not at first induce the superintendent to talk in any foreign language; and, in order to draw him out, I said, " I find that the students in Upsala can speak foreign languages better than in Lund." The Doctor was a graduate of Lund, and this was a little too much for him. My remark had the desired effect, and he replied in English that the graduates of Lund could speak other tongues as well as those of Upsala, and then laughed heartily over my subterfuge.

CHAPTER XXXIII.

The Schools of Sweden.—Fine Buildings.—Regulations.—Teaching considered a High Calling.—How Teachers are regarded.—Respect shown to Governesses.—Compulsory Education since 1842.—Large Attendance of Children in Schools.—Number of School-houses.—Studies in the different Grades of Schools.—Gymnastic and Military Exercises.—Standard of Studies before entering some of the Schools.—A Small Fee required for some Schools.—How Schools are supported.—Ambulatory Schools.—Supervision over Schools.—Professional and Trade Schools.—Seminaries to prepare Male and Female Teachers.—Industrial Schools.—Technical Schools.—Institutions for the Deaf, Dumb, and Blind.—The Agricultural Colleges.—The Schools of Norway.—Universities of Sweden and Norway.—Scientific Institution of Learning.

WHAT most forcibly strikes a stranger travelling in Sweden is to see the fine school-buildings scattered all over the kingdom, even to the farthest north. Entering a town or village, almost invariably the structure that is the most conspicuous is the school-house, in which the people take great pride. When he gains a better acquaintance with the country, he is astonished at the number of institutions of learning it contains. He wonders that in that far away and barren corner of Europe the people, though poor, have such a love of knowledge; that the study of the sciences and foreign languages is very common, and that the inhabitants strive to root out ignorance from their land. Visiting the schools, he is surprised to see how well managed they are, and that a gymnastic hall, fully equipped, is attached to each one, showing that the body is as well taken care of as the mind. He finds that, among the regulations, the younger children have to go out of the building every hour for an airing, and play in the yard for about ten minutes. Every school has a library, provided from a fund, and additions of books are made at each term. I have seen in some more than 30,000 volumes. Many besides have museums, with zoological, geological, and botanical collections. The smaller scholars learn from the black-board to read music. The children of the poor are neatly dressed, for the parents feel that it would be a shame to send them otherwise.

It has always been a cause of sorrow to me, while travelling in Europe, to come in contact with communities where the great

SCHOOL-HOUSE AT HAPARANDA.

mass of the people did not care for education until quite recently, preferring to see their government or their cities spend in the construction of theatres enormous sums of money, which could have built thousands of school-houses in the midst of a vast population that could neither read nor write. I am not speaking here against theatres, for I myself attend them, nor against amusements, for they are necessary for the health of the body as well as of the mind; only I would have the school-house first, and should prefer to live in the poorest town provided with one, where children can be well educated, rather than in a beautiful city without any. No country can thoroughly love education unless the people sincerely respect those who instruct its youth; and I was particularly glad to notice in Scandinavia how much the teachers were esteemed, their calling being considered a high one: the educating of the future generation is fully appreciated. This is partly due to the fact that the school-teachers are unusually proficient, most of them being graduates of the universities. In districts where the population is sparse, the country school-master, a peasant himself, not a graduate, nor knowing enough to enable him to teach the studies the law requires, is nevertheless held in high regard by the good farmers, and is always welcome in the family circle. I was specially pleased to see the consideration shown by parents to the governesses of their children. They are generally highly educated, and regarded as part of the family, and, as well as tutors, are treated by all with a great deal of respect.

Compulsory education has been enforced for a long time in Scandinavia. A law was passed by the Swedish Diet in 1842, requiring every child to attend a school, or to receive instruction at home, from the ninth year to the time of confirmation at home, from the ninth year to the time of confirmation. Norway followed the lead of her consort in 1848, making education compulsory between the ages of eight and fifteen.

By the census of 1873 the population of Sweden was 4,297,972;* of which, according to the latest statistics, the whole number of children of school age was 734,165, or 17 per cent. Of this number 371,622 were boys, and 362,543 girls. Nearly 83 per cent., or 607,986 children, attended the primary and people's schools: of these, 239,517 the stationary, 149,565 the ambulatory, 218,616 the primary, and only 288 the högre folkskolor. In other public schools 9293 were instructed; in private ones 29,405; at home, 68,682; altogether, nearly 15 per cent. of the children of school age. The grand total, therefore, was 715,366, or over 97 per cent. of all the children of that age. Those who, for one cause or another, did not attend school, were 18,799. The number of people's schools was 3973, of which 2805 were stationary, and 1168 ambulatory, besides 4143 nursery, and 10 higher people's

---

* In 1879 it was 4,578,901.

schools, making a total of 8126, or about one for every 529 inhabitants.

The teachers numbered 5039 males and 2776 females. Of the former 3444, and of the latter 564, were employed in the people's schools; 1585 males and 2212 females in the primary; and at the higher people's schools, 10 males. Of the male teachers 3215, and of females 485, had graduated at a seminary of learning.

The population of Norway in 1875 was 1,817,000, and the whole number of school children was 267,000, of whom 211,000 were instructed in the stationary; in ambulatory, 30,000; in private schools of the same scope as the almueskolor (people's schools), 4000; in the higher ones and under private teachers, 17,000; while 5000, from various causes, received no instruction. The instruction was given by 3900 teachers, male and female. The whole number of stationary people's schools was 4470, with 2266 teachers. The ambulatory numbered 1911, with 999 teachers. Of higher people's schools there were 19, with 467 pupils, besides 20 people's high-schools, with about 400 pupils. The lower schools of the towns were attended by 33,200 children, with 638 teachers. The average salary of a Norwegian or Swedish country teacher is about 500 kronor, besides which he gets a house and a piece of land to cultivate.

The educational system of Sweden, as well as that of Norway, is worthy of great praise. The free-schools include Småbarnsskolor, or primaries, which instruct children under the school age in the rudiments of religion, reading, writing, mental arithmetic, and singing. The folkskolor (people's schools) are of two kinds, the stationary and the ambulatory; the latter being under the care of teachers, as we have seen in the course of these volumes, who go from place to place at stated periods.

The instruction in the folkskolor is reading, religion, and Biblical history, Bible reading, and the memorizing of hymns and selected pieces out of a Reader, combining natural history, the elements of natural sciences, and the history of the country, besides singing, writing, reading, written arithmetic, and, if circumstances allow, gymnastics and military exercises. The School Board can, if so disposed, extend this curriculum also to grammar, geography, history, natural sciences, drawing, surveying—and, for girls, needle-work—and, in the country districts, horticulture or gardening. These schools are generally open for eight months in the year in the southern part of the country, and nine or ten months elsewhere. In most places instruction is given every week-day, but in others only on five days; and in the ambulatory schools the pupils are examined on the sixth day. The daily period of attendance is from five to six hours.

The folkhögskolor (people's high-schools) have only lately come into existence; their object being to instruct young men and women of the working-classes, who have already attained an age far beyond that required by law for attending school. The studies here pursued comprise a more extended course of the subjects taught in the free-schools, besides the elements of useful sciences and their application. There are fourteen of them. For the instruction a small fee is charged, the schools mainly deriving their support from private subscriptions, and from appropriations by the county or the State.

The nation is continually progressing, and the högre folkskolor, or higher people's schools, which were established in 1858, in 1875 numbered ten, with ten teachers. They are open only during the winter months, and their purpose is to give to such children of the working-classes as are endowed with greater capacities and desire for learning an opportunity to acquire a higher degree of knowledge, without detriment to their occupation. The course of instruction is the same as in the folkskolor, book-keeping and free-hand drawing being added, but the studies are extended. The teachers are required to be graduates from one of the universities. The State considers itself bound to give free education only so far as is provided by these institutions.

The elementary schools are divided into two grades, the lower and higher; the smaller towns having only the former, which has five classes or less; the higher, seven. In both, the studies are the same in the corresponding sections, but scholars of the lower grade have to go through the course of study of the last two classes of the higher school to enter one of the universities. The course requires five years for the first five classes, and four years for the last two, the scholastic year being divided into two terms of eighteen weeks each. The number of these schools amounts to 98, with 967 teachers. The object of these institutions, which also receive support from the State, is to impart a general education, and knowledge of the sciences higher than that of the people's schools.

The morning exercises begin with prayer, the reading of the Bible, and the singing of hymns, which occupy half an hour. The studies are in religion, in the Swedish language, mathematics, geometry, writing, natural philosophy, history, geography, singing, drawing, Latin, French, German, and English; but those who study Latin cannot be instructed in English. The tasks of the two higher classes embrace a more extended consideration of the same subjects, with the addition of Greek, philosophy, natural history, physics, chemistry, mineralogy, and geology, Hebrew being optional. Instruction in gymnastics and military exercises is given to all the seven classes for half an hour every day; besides which the fifth class is instructed for one hour, and the sixth and seventh for two hours each week, in the use of arms. At the beginning and end of each school year a more extended course of training is given in drill, target-shooting, and field manœuvres, for eight or ten weeks, to the scholars of the sixth and seventh classes. These elementary schools are so situated that the people who desire that their children shall receive a good education are not compelled to travel very far; for example, in the far North, Luleå has a complete institution of this kind, with seven classes. To be accepted as a pupil in this grade of schools a boy must be not more than ten years of age, and shall pass an examination in the reading of the Swedish language, both in the Gothic and Roman characters, and be able to repeat any passage read to him, write a plain hand, spell tolerably, know the simple rules of arithmetic, practise mental calculation, and possess a knowledge of the geography of Norway, Sweden, and Denmark. The degrees of progress in study and standing in the class are recorded daily, ten being the highest mark in each subject; and every year the pupils are examined. Every scholar has to pay an entrance fee of 6 kronor, and 12 kronor 50 öre per term; so that for the modest sum of 25 kronor, or about six dollars a year, a young man can prepare himself for the University. He has, however, to pay for his books.

At the suggestion of the faculty of the school, the superintendent may exempt a poor scholar from a part or the whole of the fees required. In order to become an instructor in an elementary school, it is necessary to have taken the degree of doctor of philosophy, to have taught on trial for one year, and to have passed a competitive examination.

Neglect to send a child of the prescribed age to school, or in some other manner to provide the instruction required by law, is punishable by fine in Norway; and, in case of opposition from the parents, the child can be taken away and be left at their expense with another family. In Sweden no fine is exacted. Factory owners, who employ children, regulate their work so as not to interfere with their education.

The folkskolor are supported by the districts, but also receive aid from the State, and are governed by a school board chosen by the people, whose president is the pastor of the parish, or, in the towns, a minister selected by the bishop. In the country, if farms are situated near enough together to enable thirty scholars to attend school every day, a house is erected or rented for such a purpose. Where the farms are far apart the school is ambulatory, and it is the duty of the farmers to provide rooms for the pupils and teacher, as well as board for the latter during the time the instruction lasts. In this are also embraced such holidays as may fall within this period.

In Sweden the board consists of at least four members besides the president, elected by the voters of the parish for four years. The bishop and consistory of the bishopric have general supervision of school affairs, and are obliged to report every third year to the ecclesiastical department, which has supreme control of the schools. The supervision of the folkskolor is exercised by a school inspector appointed by the head of the same department. The inspectors are appointed for five years. In Norway there is one in every stift or bishopric. Their salaries are paid by the State, and are proportionate to the size of the district. They are also allowed travelling expenses.

The private schools are under the general supervision of the public board, which, if the instruction does not come up to the standard prescribed by law, can order the children to be transferred to some other institution.

The cost of the school is defrayed as follows: for the erection of school-houses it is procured in the same manner as for the building of churches, by taxing the real estate; and for the pay of the teachers and necessary expenses, by an individual tax, which cannot exceed eighteen öre for each taxpayer; and, if this is not sufficient, and there are no other means of obtaining the amount, then the contributions are made over again in the same manner as the communal assessments. Under certain conditions, when the cost of the schools exceeds the limits of taxation, the government grants a subvention, which is principally invested to pay the teachers, who advance by a system of promotion which prevents favoritism. The highest salary is attained after twenty years of faithful service, an increase being made every five years.

Once a year, in Norway and Sweden, all the boys of the free-schools are collected, and go through a great military parade. Each school has its place; some of them even have a band of music, and show the public on drill day what they have learned. They are cheered by the people, who prepare a feast for them, for great interest is taken in the evolutions, especially the exercises with wooden guns.

Besides the public schools there are some private schools in the towns, the graduates from a few of which have the right of admission to the universities. There are also a large number of public and private professional and trades schools, in some of which fees are charged for instruction, while in others it is free. There are also seminaries for the education of male and female teachers, to which a primary school is generally attached, where the future instructor has an opportunity of learning his art, and in which the tuition is free. For girls there are, besides the national schools, a large number of private elementary, and also public and private industrial schools.

There are in the country eleven free *folkskollärare-seminarier*, which are seminaries for teachers of folkskolor—seven for males and four for females. These seminaries have three classes, and the course in each class is one year; the year consisting of 36 weeks, divided into two terms, with 36 hours of instruction weekly. The studies include religion, the Swedish language, arithmetic, geometry, geography, history, natural philosophy, the science of teaching writing, drawing, music, singing, gymnastics, the manual of arms, horticulture, and cultivation of trees. The number of students in 1875 was 780, of whom 588 were males and 192 females; and the number of graduates was 193, of whom 146 were males and 47 females. In the new female seminaries there are special classes to prepare instructors for the primary schools.

The "Seminarium for bildande of lärarinnor" (seminary for the education of female teachers) was established in 1861, and has a corps of instructors 18 in number. In this the pupils have to go through a course of three years, but no charge is made. Instruction is given in religion, Church history, the Swedish language, including the mythology of the North, Icelandic, French, German, and English, the history of the North, universal history, geography, natural science, hygiene, mathematics, and the art of teaching, besides singing, drawing, and gymnastics; and, at the option of the pupils, botany, zoology, and chemistry, natural philosophy, physiology, geometry, algebra, and English and German speaking exercises, etc. This institution has connected with it a normal school for girls.

In the industrial schools, which are found only in the towns, instruction in different trades is given; and in that for girls there are regular lessons in needle-work, etc. In some of the larger cities the girls also learn the common household arts of baking, washing, ironing, mending, etc.

There are technical elementary schools, where young men intending to learn a trade receive, without charge, a theoretical and practical education. The course lasts three years, and comprises instruction in mathematics, linear and free-hand drawing, modelling, mechanics, mechanical technology, engineering, natural philosophy, chemistry, botany, zoology, modern languages, book-keeping, and commerce. The number of teachers in these is from six to nine, and of pupils exceeds a thousand.

There are in several towns free evening and Sunday classes, where the pupils are taught mechanical trades, and two higher technical schools, where a tuition fee is charged. The Teknologiska Institutet (Polytechnic Institute) at Stockholm, founded in 1798, was established to give scientific education to young men intending to follow some technical business as a profession. The studies are mathematics, geodesy and topography, theoretical and practical mechanics, descriptive geometry, physics, elementary chemistry, chemical and mechanical technology, geology, road and canal construction, drawing, mining, metallurgy, and smelting. The course continues for three years. In 1875 there were 17 professors and tutors, and 218 students pursuing the entire course, while 52 were studying only certain branches.

The Chalmerska Slöjdskolan (Chalmer Polytechnic School) in Gothenburg, founded in 1811, has the same course of studies, except those belonging to the branch of mining. It had, in 1875, 10 teachers, one of whom was the principal. The number of scholars was 149.

Two elementary mining schools are established at Falun and Filipstad, which are, properly speaking, private enterprises, being supported either by the society of miners or by the Ironmasters' Association (Jernkontoret).

As I have before mentioned, there are 27 agricultural schools and 2 agricultural colleges. I have given an account of the former in the first volume, with the studies required. Of the latter, one is situated at Ultuna, near Upsala, and the other at Alnarp, near Lund, in the southern part of Sweden. The first I have visited. In the colleges the studies are agriculture and rural economy, cattle-raising, anatomy and physiology, diseases of domestic animals, geology, chemistry, natural philosophy, forestry, gardening, land laws, book-keeping, farm architecture, practical mechanics, machinery and map-drawings, surveying, and management of the dairy. The students also have to participate in actual farm-work. The number of pupils in 1875 was 63, with 20 teachers. The charge for board and tuition is 600 kronor per annum, and at each college there are four free scholarships. The course is for two years. There are large tracts of land connected with Ultuna. This institution sends out some of the very best practical farmers in the country. Distinguished professors and teachers deliver lectures to the students; a veterinary surgeon instructs them in the diseases of cattle, and a museum, stocked with skeletons and other specimens, illustrates their lectures. Numerous scientific works on chemistry and agriculture are in the library; and there is a fine laboratory, in which chemistry applied to agriculture is thoroughly taught. There is also a botanical garden, where cereals of different countries are grown, and where experiments with fertilizers are made, besides a vegetable and fruit garden; but the fruit-trees seemed to be neglected, it is said, on account of the poor ground. Special care is taken in the breeding and crossing of stock, and fine horses and cows are raised, many of which are sold. There is also a dairy, where great attention is paid to the making of butter and cheese.

A prerequisite of admission is that the applicant must have passed the examination necessary for matriculation at the universities, or a similar one at the college. The colleges are supported exclusively by the State. There are two dairy-schools for women, where they receive theoretical and practical instruction.

Good care is taken of the deaf, dumb, and blind. In Sweden there is a very fine institution, the Manilla, in Stockholm, with 208 pupils; besides 13 smaller ones, situated in different parts of the country, with 398 inmates. In Norway there is a special institution for the blind, and four for the deaf and dumb.

In Norway the scope and regulations of the Almueskolor (common people's schools) are about the same as those in Sweden. The School Board also can establish sewing and other industrial schools, as well as others for children under the legal school age. The higher people's schools and people's high-schools are similar to those of Sweden, except that the latter are free, although supported by private means. In the mountain districts, where, in consequence of the sparsity of the population, even ambulatory teaching cannot be arranged, the Board is empowered to provide for the instruction of the children in some other manner.

The Norwegian high-schools correspond very nearly to the Swedish elementary schools, the studies and the time of instruction being the same. They, however, differ in the fact that the separate branches generally have independent schools. Of State high-schools there are 16, with 195 teachers and 2122 pupils. Of private high-schools there are 4, with 1266 scholars. There are 14 seminaries for the training of male teachers, with 343 students; but for female teachers there is only one, situated in Christiania. In the country districts there are 400 free evening classes, most of which receive support from the State. In the towns there are 35 communal middle schools, with 173 teachers and 26,345 scholars; and 126 private middle schools, with 5592 pupils. Of private high-schools only a comparatively small number are established, owing, no doubt, to the excellence of the public schools, and these are found mostly in the largest towns.

For girls there are no public schools corresponding to the elementary schools, but a considerable number of private institutions, supported principally by the fees paid by the scholars, only a few of whom receive aid from the State. From these the graduates have the privilege of admission to the universities.

The yearly school time of Norway is far too short to give a practical education; and in this respect it falls far behind that of Sweden. The Norwegian school year in the rural districts must be at least 12 weeks per annum, or, where the school is divided into classes getting instruction at different times, 9 weeks—each week being reckoned at 6 days, and every day at 6 hours, thus giving instruction for 432—or 324 hours yearly. It is also required that in every factory employing on an average 30 men or more in steady labor, as well as in a collection of smaller works lying near each other, which together have that number of workmen, there shall be constructed and organized classes for the children of the laborers, if the owners of the works cannot agree with the School Board in regard to the use of the schools already in existence. In the larger towns one or more classes are organized with separate departments for boys and girls, and they have to be kept open daily —each child receiving at least 12 hours' instruction each week. As a rule, no teacher may instruct more than 60 pupils at one time. A yearly examination is held in presence of the pastor of the parish and the members of the School Board. At visitations of bishop or pastor the children are examined in their religious knowledge.

Refractory children receive marks for bad conduct; after which they are warned by the principal of the school twice, and if they then do not improve, they receive corporal punishment.

Sweden has two universities: that of Upsala was inaugurated September 21st, 1477, and of Lund, January 28th, 1668. The former was already a seat of learning in 1249. At that time there was a college where the studies of theology, philosophy, and medicine were pursued. In 1875 the number of professors and students at Upsala were as follows:

	Professors.	Students.
Theological Faculty	10	332
Law "	9	142
Medical "	14	151
Philosophical "	71	855
Total	104	1480

The University of Lund in the same year had the following:

	Professors.	Students.
Theological Faculty	7	112
Law "	6	54
Medical "	9	44
Philosophical "	47	313
Total	69	523

Norway has one university at Christiania, inaugurated in 1811, before which time Norwegians who desired a higher education had to go to the University of Copenhagen, that city having been for centuries the common capital of the two countries. There are 46 professors and 831 students.

The whole number of university students in the two countries amounted to 2834, with 219 professors.

There are numerous scientific and other institutions, some of which have been described in these volumes—schools of midwifery for women, colleges of medicine, veterinary surgery, pharmacy, and forestry, etc., etc.

Teachers, after thirty years of service, receive a pension. In Sweden each school district is bound to pay to the pension fund four per cent. of the salary of every teacher. In Norway they are pensioned by the State. The system of education is so perfect that there are no private boarding-schools in either country.

I have dwelt particularly upon the educational system, because I consider that it has been developed to meet the requirements of the people in an extraordinary degree; and, as I leave the subject, I cannot refrain from the expression of an opinion that the example so well set might be followed with favorable results by other countries which make much greater pretensions in this direction without producing so substantial an effect.

CHAPTER XXXIV.

Linköping.—Its Cathedral.—A Water-way through South Östergötland.—Superb Trees.—Åtvidaberg.—A Night Watchman.—The Estate of Adelsnäs.—A Pleasant Welcome.—The Manor of Adelsnäs.—Unpretending Life.—Our Host and Hostess.—The Copper-mines of Åtvidaberg.—Wages of Miners.—The Miners' Homes.—Kindly Manners towards the Artisans.—Politeness to Inferiors.—The Village Dancing-place.—Good Feelings.—A School for the Miners' Children.

From Norrköping* one of the highways leads to Linköping, an inland and very old town on the shores of the Stångån River, with a population of about 8000. The cathedral, begun about 1150, has a length of 329 feet; Roman in style, with twenty large pillars in two rows to support the roof. Another church, St. Lawrence (St. Lars), also dates from the twelfth century. The castle, built between 1470 and 1500, is a massive but not handsome building. In the old elementary school is a library of over 30,000 volumes, together with coins, portraits, and antiquities.

From Linköping an interesting trip is by water south, through the remaining part of Östergötland, a distance of over one hundred miles. A canal connects the lakes with each other, and steamers make the passage every alternate day. On the way are seen some large estates with fine chateaux— among them Sturefors, one of the largest of the province; Säby, on the Rängen Lake; Brokind, with its fine collection of paintings and library, and whose park occupies several islands.

Taking one of the highways which leads south of Norrköping, I saw, a few miles from that city, the chateau of Löfsta, on a hill overlooking the road and a small lake, with its fine and shaded grounds. Farther on, after passing Fil-

---

* In one part of Sweden the names of quite a number of towns end in *köping* —as Malmköping, Nyköping, Norrköping (norr, north), Söderköping (*söder* meaning south), Linköping, Lidköping, Falköping, and Jönköping.

linge, I entered a splendid wood of pines and firs, among the finest in Sweden, and as yet untouched by the axe. A picturesque scene suddenly came into view. The fields of wheat and rye were bright with poppies, while buttercups and dandelions relieved the green of the meadows. The weather was quite warm, and the time passed so rapidly among these beauties of nature that before I knew it I reached the station of Örsäter, where we stopped to allow the horse to rest.

As we approached the copper-mines and smelting-furnaces of Åtvidaberg the distant hills looked dark and desolate, for the sulphurous smoke, carried day after day by the wind, had destroyed vegetation. I saw on a hill the family vault in which the barons of Adelswärd are buried. Soon afterwards I came to Åtvidaberg, a small hamlet consisting of a row of white-plastered houses, with vegetable gardens attached. It had a comfortable hotel, which, like all the other houses of the place, belonged to the estate. In the valley were the smelting-furnaces, around which clustered the dwellings of the operatives—the whole forming a street of red-painted log-houses, roofed with red tiles, with a public square, and a pond with a bathing-house for the people. At some distance was a brickyard, a foundry where iron pipes were made, and a blacksmith's shop where the tools were mended. The village was silent, for its inhabitants had gone to rest. The night was beautiful; the rays of the moon mirrored themselves in the pond; the music of the water, as it plashed down from the mill, added its charm; the smoke from the high chimneys rested among the hills in bluish streaks. The blowing of the horn of the watchman—an officer who is found in every Swedish village—warned me that the clock had just struck, and I heard him sing,

> "God keep
> Houses and the land
> From fire and burning,
> The hour of eleven has struck.
> God keep
> The house and the land
> From fire and burning,
> The hour of eleven has struck."

Åtvidaberg is part of the large estate of Adelsnäs, which is entailed in the family of the Baron of Adelswärd, and embraces nine parishes; that part which is in Östergötland alone contains over 41,000 acres, and is one of the largest and most valuable properties in the country, on account of its copper-mines. The family dwelling is about two miles from the hamlet, on the farther shore of a small lake. On my approaching the water, a young girl, thirteen or fourteen years of age, rowed towards me. She was tidy and clean, her complexion fair, and thoroughly northern, her hair blonde, braided and twisted back of her head, and she was barefooted. The child ferried me over to the house. Two ladies and two gentlemen were playing croquet on the lawn, while another gentleman was seated on the piazza. With him I exchanged salutations, and presenting my letter of introduction, was welcomed in excellent English. He said his father was not at home, but received me with the air of a polished man of the world; as I afterwards discovered, he had been in America for nine months, besides having travelled in England and in many other parts of Europe, often "roughing it," as many English noblemen do. The game of croquet seemed to be disturbed for awhile by my arrival. I was presented to the guests and the members of the family; and refreshments having been brought in, we kept up a pleasant conversation. The charming hostess, a model of simplicity, was attired in a pretty calico dress, fitting like a glove, with a plain white collar, and a ribbon fastened with a simple brooch. The other ladies were dressed in the same unostentatious fashion.

An atmosphere of repose surrounded this unpretending abode. The view of the lake, a shady walk under a row of tall trees, beds of flowers, large spreading oaks, and white-trunked birch and other trees, and the green grass, gave a great charm to the place. Near the mansion were the graperies and hot-houses, which, among other things, contained apricots and peaches on trellises; also forced strawberries, cherries, and raspberries. A long white house, with only one story and roofed with tiles, contained bedrooms for guests.

At the manor the life was simple and unostentatious. During the warm days the drawing-room windows were open, to let in the balmy air, and to enable the mother or attendants to watch the children playing upon the lawn; their school-days were now over, vacation had come, and the tutor of the boys and the governess of the girls were soon to leave on a visit to their friends. The merry laugh of the young people fell pleasantly upon the ear, and now and then the half-hidden smile of the mother showed that she could hear and was enjoying the happiness of her little ones.

Industry is part of a lady's education in Sweden, and idle habits are very seldom indulged in, even by members of the aristocracy. The duties of house-keeping are not considered below the dignity of the high-born or of the wealthy. They are often busy with their needle-work, which does not prevent their taking part in agreeable conversation.

Dinner was social, and the table was adorned with a beautiful silver vase—given by Gustaf III. to the family of the baron—in which was a large bouquet of fresh flowers. There was no formality; the conversation was pleasant and varied; and nothing was wanting that could make the repast agreeable. The governess was also at the table. After coffee, a drive or walk wound up the day. The hostess and myself occupied one carriage. The good lady, as I learned, always provided herself with a bag of new pennies for the little children who were watching at the gates on the road to open them for travellers.

The largest of the Åtvidaberg mines is that at Bersbo, with a depth of 1286 feet, while that of Mormorsgrufvan attains a depth of 1360 feet, the greatest in Sweden. These are the most important, but there are several smaller ones.

According to appointment, the baron in his carriage drove me to the copper-mines of Bersbo, six English miles from the smelting-furnaces, the ore being transported by a railway. I declined the invitation to go 1200 feet underground, and wind my way through the dark galleries and narrow passages. The mine employed from 400 to 500 persons, whose wages ranged that year from 40 to 60 kronor a month each. Women, girls, and boys were also employed to assort and treat the ore preparatory to smelting, making from four to six kronor weekly. The women were working, while their children played around; some of the mothers had left their babies under the care of elder sisters. None appeared coarse or dirty. Some two hundred females and quite a number of children were employed; for among the poorer classes of the Swedes, as with the thrifty French and Germans, every member of a household helps in its support. Besides their pay, each family received every year ten cords of wood and lodging free. The rooms in the cottages were about 18 feet long by 14 or 15 wide; a spacious hall ran through each dwelling, and each had an upper story, with a detached store-house for wood and provisions. The floors in all I visited were very neat, and everything about the houses was exceedingly tidy. Sewing-machines were quite common: the furniture was plain; a few wooden chairs, a clock, simple pictures, a bed or two, and a stove, made up the frugal appointments. Many of the houses contained looms, with which the mother or the elder daughter wove cloth for the family, when they had time to spare. On the walls of some of the rooms hung tin boxes, used to keep leaves or flowers collected by the miners' children on their botanical excursions, for the love of botany is extensively cultivated in Sweden. In one cottage a poor widow was quietly weaving, and by her side a bright-looking lad was studying, in preparation for entering the high-school in Linköping: a part of the little money left by the father was appropriated to the education of this lad. I was struck with the kindly manner with which everybody was treated. Now and then a poor barefooted working-woman came to the superintendent to make some inquiries; as soon as he was addressed he at once uncovered his head, notwithstanding a very warm sun, and listened to her, paying attention to her remarks, and showing no sign of impatience; his answers were made in a quiet and polite way. It would be well if the higher classes everywhere should give the example of good-breeding to the humble. The baron never entered a miner's cottage without uncovering and remaining so while he was under the roof of his workman.

When the miners or their families fell ill, they were cared for at the expense of the baron; and if a man was killed, a pension was given to his family. When I asked the superintendent, "Do you not turn away the wife and children of a deceased miner, and leave them to shift for themselves?" his answer was, "No, indeed!" with a look of disgust, as if the very thought of such a selfish act had never been entertained by the owner of the estate, and would be considered wicked by himself and the community.

Now what are the results of the support of schools, and of a certain degree of education among the working-people? To what does this politeness of all classes towards each other tend? Simply this: to bring about a better state of feeling in all the different elements of society, and to produce mutual consideration. A few strikes have taken place in Sweden, but only within late years; ordinarily, a disagreement and the causes of a dispute are talked over by employer and employed as among intelligent rational beings; there are no threats of intimidation, no arson, no carrying of arms, no murder, no lying in ambush, and beating of those who do not wish to join the strike; no armed bands parading streets and districts with looks of anger and hate; no hooting, no vulgar language, no oaths debasing the children who hear them, and brutalizing still more those who utter them.

There is a pleasant spot near the church, shaded by fine old oak-trees, under the branches of which the workmen, their wives, and the village people meet, and, seated on the grass, listen to the music. All the musicians are either miners or workmen. A circular dancing-floor had also been built on this place by the baron's father especially for the use of the people—an act which showed the kindly feeling that existed. The baron and his family rarely failed to come to the social meeting. I noticed the politeness, and at the same time the manliness of the villagers, of the miners, and working-men who were present; there was none of that extreme obsequiousness from the humble to their superiors which one so often meets in many countries; while at the same time there was not the slightest show of authority or display of pride on the part of the latter, who, by their position, might have thought themselves entitled to receive homage from those they employed.

A visit to the public school showed the beneficial influence it exerted morally, socially, and intellectually. These miners' children were all very attentive to their studies, and tidy in their persons. Each girl had a colored calico handkerchief over her head, in true Swedish fashion, with the hair nicely combed, and face and hands clean; they attended the classes for three days in the week, and none of them seemed to be overworked. The boys were all barefooted, but their feet were clean, being washed often during the day; they all looked happy, and evidently enjoyed the exercises of the hour: the marching and countermarching was regulated by the stroke of a bell. In one of the rooms music was written on a blackboard, and the children sang from these notes, the teacher pointing with a wand from bar to bar; in this way they learned to read music at sight. One class was composed of girls and boys, the girls occupying all the front seats and the boys the rear. Some children of seven years of age wrote sentences on their slates for me, and their bright eyes shone merrily as I read them.

It was with regret that I parted from this Arcadian spot, where the wealthy and the mining population were so friendly. I do not know of any place in any part of the world, either in a mining or manufacturing district, where the feeling is so cordial between employer and employés. It left a deep impression upon my mind, and reflects great credit on the noble rich family of Adelswärd: may their descendants follow their example.

CHAPTER XXXV.

The Province of Småland.—A Thrifty Population.—Vexiö.—Poor Stations.—Gamleby.—Westervik.—Visits at the Parsonage.—A Festive Occasion.—A Concert
by Ladies.—Oscarshamn.—Kalmar.—A Holiday.—Bad Temper of the People.—
A Beautiful Highway.—Grand Beech and Oak Trees.—Great Variety of Mush-
rooms.—Poor Food at the Stations.—The Churches of Hagby and Voxtorp.—
Nearing Blekinge.

A FEW miles east from Åtvidaberg one enters Småland, a
large but a very poor province of Sweden. Many parts are
either barren or covered with moorland, forests, and also numerous lakes—of which the chief is the Åsnen, whose shores
are extremely picturesque. The people are so frugal that it is
a saying among the Swedes, "Put a Smålander on a barren
rock in the sea, and he will manage to make his living."

There are a number of seaports, among them Westervik,
Oscarshamn, Mönsterås, and Kalmar. There is only one inland
town of importance, Vexiö, with a population of a little over
4000 inhabitants. The place is prettily situated on the shores
of a lake, and a small rivulet runs through it. It has an excellent elementary school. Its cathedral was built about 1300,
and contains the grave of St. Sigfried, one of the apostles of
the North. In the church-yard is a monument over the grave
of the poet Tegnér, who was bishop of Vexiö. Near the
town are the episcopal residence and the central hospital. On
an island in the lake are the ruins of the castle of Kronoberg.
The town is connected by a short railway with the trunk line
which traverses the country from Malmö in the south to
Stockholm.

The morning of my departure from Åtvidaberg was clear
and bracing; the country was the more beautiful for the rain
of the day before; everything looked fresh, though some of

the rye, which here grows very high, was prostrated. Travelling was very pleasant, as the roads were not dusty.

Beyond, a chain of small lakes ran towards the Baltic in a south-easterly direction. At a short distance from the village a cross-country road, with a post station, led from the main highway through a charming country as far as the village of Gamleby, on the sea. The cross-roads increase largely in number towards the south, and often pass in so many directions that the

VEXIÖ CATHEDRAL, FROM THE SOUTH-WEST.

traveller is at a loss which to choose when desirous of getting out of the more direct highway. The landscape continued to become more picturesque; the rocky hills were covered with trees, the fields were in fine condition, and the banks of the lakes were dotted with small thriving farms. At Öfverum there was a large manufactory of agricultural implements; mowing and threshing-machines and ploughs were made here, the machinery being moved by water-power.

It was late in the afternoon when I entered Gamleby. The

situation of this village is quite picturesque, at the head of a narrow fjord; a small stream runs through it, upon the banks of which a saw and two other mills are kept busy during the summer months. There was a Tingshus, or court-house, built of stone, which was used partly as a hotel; the station was good. Some of the houses were painted white or light green, but the greatest number were red, and roofed with red tiles; numerous pots with flowers in bloom ornamented the windows. From here one can go to Westervik either by land or water; but in order to take the road it is necessary to be ferried over the fjord. A small steamer runs daily between the two places, leaving every morning at half-past six o'clock. After a pleasant sail of an hour and a half we came alongside the quay of Westervik, a town of 5500 inhabitants, and possessing two ship-yards and some factories. The streets are paved with very small cobble-stones put close together, and walking is difficult and fatiguing to those unaccustomed to such pavements, unless they wear thick-soled shoes. The houses are spacious and airy, with large yards. If relay-stations are bad as regards food, one is sure to find in a town a comfortable hotel where the table is good, and this place was no exception to the rule.

At Åtvidaberg a letter of introduction had been kindly given me to Dr. B——, a learned professor living in Westervik, who did all he could to make my stay agreeable. I was invited by the pastor to join a party of gentlemen at dinner, and was received very warmly and hospitably by him and his wife. The entertainment was given in honor of the School Board of Examiners; thirty gentlemen were present, nearly all of whom could speak French, German, and English; and the sociable and pleasant manners of the company were very agreeable. According to the custom, where so great a number of guests are assembled together, we helped ourselves, and took seats at little tables in the different rooms. A toast was proposed by the pastor in honor of the School Board of Examiners, and we all exchanged bows with them before sipping the wine. Afterwards the host kindly proposed my health, and paid me the high compliment of saying that I was known in Sweden, and was welcome in the country. I felt uncomfortable at such pointed remarks, but again we all bowed to each other. Coffee was served under the trees in the garden, and then we separated. During the summer months musicians and theatrical bands travel through the country, and on this evening a concert was given in the high-school building, which began at seven o'clock. The performers were three ladies, one of whom played on the violin, another on the violoncello, and the third on the piano; they were excellent musicians, and one sang finely. The audience was large, for Westervik seemed to have turned out in a body on this occasion.

From Westervik the sail along the shore is pleasant, as it generally is in summer on the tranquil waters of the Baltic; for at this season the sea is seldom rough.

Either by land or by steamer one may reach Oscarshamn, on a small bay protected by numerous islands, with a population of 5500 inhabitants; it has ship-yards, a machine-shop, and a foundry. Farther south is the port of Kalmar, the most important in Småland, with a population of about 10,000. The situation of the city is very picturesque. The streets are wide and clean, and paved with cobble-stones; the houses are generally two stories in height, with large rooms; and on the public square is the church, a fine, spacious building. The streets extend at right angles from the square, and lead to every part of the town and to the old fortifications. At intervals you see some queer old-fashioned pumps, which supply the people with water. The old ramparts are the pride of the place. Upon them a park-like garden has been created; the ample ground being tastefully laid out with beautiful lawns, groves, hedges ten feet high, and chestnut, elm, maple, apple, and other trees, and a flower-garden. From this can be seen the Baltic, the island of Öland, and the vessels at anchor.

The ancient Kalmar during heathen times was a great market-place, and afterwards was known by the expedition, the so-called Kalmare Ledung, of Sigurd Jorsalafar to Småland. It was long the greatest city of Southern Sweden, and for centuries was considered the key to the country, being strongly fortified. Among the many historical events which have taken place within its walls was the Diet of 1332, when Skåne, Halland, and Blekinge submitted to the Swedish Crown; but a sum of 70,000 marks had to be paid to the Duke of Holstein and others, who held these provinces as pledges for money loaned to the King of Denmark. In 1397 there was a Diet, when the so-called Kalmar Union was concluded. It contained the following provisions: 1. That all three kingdoms should always be united, and have one and the same king. 2. A new king should be chosen by the councils of the three united kingdoms, together and unanimously, but not by each kingdom separately. 3. Each kingdom should be governed by its own laws and customs. Besides these, there were several similar articles. This covenant was written on parchment in duplicates, which are preserved.

COAT-OF-ARMS OF KING CHRISTIAN I. OF DENMARK, SWEDEN, AND NORWAY, DURING THE TIME OF THE KALMAR UNION.

Often since has the city been exposed to attacks of the enemy. The old castle, built shortly before the year 1200, is still standing, and its interior has for many years been undergoing a restoration to its original appearance. The great object of attraction is the octagon bedroom of Erik XIV., in one of the turrets. The ornamentation of the ceiling and inlaid floor, and other adornments of the apartment, were the work of the king's own hand. This castle was once changed into a still; then into a granary; and was left at last to perish, until Oscar, father of the present monarch, interposed for the preservation of this historic pile; but, with the exception of the ramparts and castle, nothing remains to indicate the antiquity of the town, for it has suffered greatly from fires.

The Kalmar Union was substantially in existence from 1389 to 1521, though several times interrupted by jealous wars. In 1521 the first Wasa appeared, and the Danish power was broken.

COAT-OF-ARMS OF THE NIPERTZ FAMILY, NOW EXTINCT.

One midsummer day found me in Kalmar, when the ringing of the morning bells called the faithful to the church; the edifice was large, but the congregation was small, and composed principally of women. The city had a gala appearance; the people were dressed in their holiday garb, and steamers were crowded with them going to Öland to spend the day. Good-looking girls were diligently taking passengers in their boats from one place to another, reaping a good harvest of cash. On this part of the coast the midsummer dance is often marred by scenes of drunkenness, and the May-pole festival ends in a general fight. I was present at one, and was startled by the evident specimen of rowdyism, and the use of the knife.

The people around Kalmar are among the worst characters I met in Scandinavia; and, with those of Blekinge, are noted for their fiery tempers. It was common in former days for women of the latter province, when they went to these dances, to take linen with them in case their husbands or brothers were wounded; people not unfrequently were killed, especially in the frontier towns. They used to wrestle with knives, the men divesting themselves of their garments, and putting a belt around their waists which encircled both; then each holding a knife in his right hand, and with the other clasping the wrist of his opponent's knife-hand, they tried to cut each other.

Among the highways leading out of the city of Kalmar the one running parallel with the shores of the Baltic southward is very charming, and passes in the midst of the most romantic part of Småland, and for about thirty or forty miles presents a constant and ever-changing panorama, with tracts of lovely landscape; views of the sea and the shores of Öland, with its windmills; grand old beeches (*Fagus sylvatica*) and oaks, with their long, spreading branches, appear here and there. The beech-trees were among the finest I had seen in this or any other country; they began to make their appearance on the coast only about thirty miles north of Kalmar.

The great variety of the mushroom found in the forests is wonderful, the species numbering about two thousand. Of these several hundred are not only a useful article of diet, but a great many are exceedingly palatable; of late years they have come into general use. They are most abundant in the northern forests, especially during the autumn; though this seems incredible, the data are furnished by the eminent botanist, Professor Andersson, of the Royal Swedish Academy of Sciences.

The stations are poor, and the fare reminded me forcibly of the Swedish proverb that, "At the Småland stations one dines sumptuously if he has a good knapsack with him."

HAGBY CHURCH.

This saying can justly be applied to many other provinces than Småland, for, as a general rule, except in cities and large villages, the food is of the plainest kind. As I had no knapsack, and preferred to live poorly to taking one, I was content with eggs and a piece of cold pork and coffee; as for fresh bread, it is generally out of the question. Near one of the stations a bell was suspended to a wooden framework, above which was a cross; close by was the court-house, surrounded by a fine garden; there was also a small prison, which at that time contained no prisoners.

About nine miles south of Kalmar, near the road, is the quaint and interesting church of Hagby, and, a short distance beyond, that of Voxtorp. These are very old. The middle parts or circular towers are thought to have been heathen temples, which on the introduction of Christianity were altered into churches. The loop-holes in the walls were probably used to shoot arrows against enemies. The Solna church, near Stockholm, is of the same style and period of architecture, and its

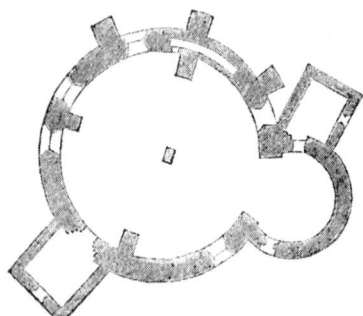

PLAN OF HAGBY CHURCH.

tower is built of large boulders. The earliest Swedish churches were nearly all of this shape, like the heathen temples, the priest standing in the middle, and the hearers around him; in the same way they were accustomed to have their *lagman* (lawman, judge) stand in their midst and read the law to them, the people closing about him in circles as near as they could get. The church-yards were also round, and the stones enclosing graves and mounds were generally laid in circles. These walls are still called ring-walls, although they now are square. When high-mass was held, the people gathered to the church from long distances; tradesmen also came thither with the intention of selling their wares; they had their booths erected outside of the ring-wall, which was called *Bodgårdsmur* (Boothyard-wall). Among churches of circular shape there is now left only Dimbo, in Vestergötland; but existing foundations and remnants of others show that they formerly were common.

About twenty miles south of Kalmar is the estate of Vär-
nanäs, which was in ancient times the seat of a jarl; later it
belonged to Gustaf Wasa, and afterwards to Axel Oxenstjerna,
the chancellor of Gustavus Adolphus: at present it is owned

VOXTORP CHURCH AND BELFRY.

by the family of Mannerskantz. There is a fine avenue of
trees, about two miles long, leading to the sea. From a thick
forest of pines and firs we emerged into a picturesque rolling
country, and a few miles beyond entered the hamlet of Söder-
åkra. On approaching Blekinge, the soil becomes poorer and
more sandy, erratic boulders are numerous, and the fine trees
begin to disappear.

CHAPTER XXXVI.

The Island of Öland.—The Church of Albōke.—Relics of Ancient Times.—The Village of Borgholm.—Imposing Ruins of Borgholm Castle.—Karl Gustaf.—The Queen's Farm.—Proud Karin.—Celebrating the Advent of Spring.—Song welcoming the Spring.

At a short distance from the Swedish coast, near the province of Småland, is an island called Öland, about eighty miles long and six to ten miles broad, which, with the main-land, forms a beautiful sound. A ridge with wooded slopes runs along its western shore, upon whose summit are found a great number of windmills, which add to the picturesqueness of the scene. The ridge, like the island, is of limestone, and this in the south rests on a stratum of Silurian alum slate. Often the red limestone comes to the surface, and there the soil is barren. Besides a home supply for a population of 40,000 inhabitants, the island exports from 300,000 to 350,000 bushels of grain, principally wheat, every year; is rich in apples, pears, etc., and has good hunting-grounds; it exports also lime and limestone. Formerly it was celebrated for a breed of ponies, now extinct, smaller than those of Shetland; and it was the favorite hunting resort of the Swedish king, Karl Gustaf. Few of its once superb forests of oak now remain. Some of its churches are very ancient, being of the so-called klöfsadels form (saddle shape). One of these is that of Albōke. A passage from the roof connects the two towers, in one of which are rooms with the open primitive fireplace, with no chimney for the escape of smoke. In old Catholic times, when the Church owned immense tracts of land, Öland belonged to the convents of Vadstena and Alvastra.

The island is rich in antiquities. Several ship-forms of upraised stone are models of the vessels of the Vikings, or perhaps of more ancient inhabitants; there are also many graves, and numerous valuable finds, containing bronze and gold ornaments of the Roman period, some of which have been mentioned in the chapter devoted to this subject. Ruins of old castles are found, the most remarkable of which is Ismanstorp, which is mentioned in Vol. I. It is certain that Vikings dwelt on this island.

The village and port of Borgholm, having a population of 800, is the most important place on the island of Öland. Entering the harbor, we were soon moored along-side a jetty, which also acted as a breakwater. There were no vessels; the place was quiet, and only a few persons were walking in the broad streets, in which grass was growing. The old church rose above the surrounding buildings. The houses appeared comfortable, and now and then a dame or damsel looked out to see what strangers were passing by. Near the village, on the brink of a ridge clad with bush-trees sloping rather abruptly to the sea, and where the limestone comes to the surface supporting a few stunted oaks, rise the ruins of the castle of Borgholm. The square court-yard is flanked by dark walls pierced with numerous windows to the third story, still intact; but its chambers are roofless. It is a sad picture of the past. This great place once resounded with the hum of life—mighty men and beautiful women dwelt in its now deserted and crumbling remains. The ruins consist of two distinct parts. The old castle is mentioned as early as 1280, and the foundations are still extant. About the year 1312 it was occupied by Duke Waldemar of Sweden and his consort, Ingeborg of Norway, daughter of King Erik (priest-hater), who married Isabel, the sister of the Scottish hero, Robert Bruce. The present castle was built by King Johan, who reigned 1568–1592. It was several times besieged and taken by the Danes—the last time in 1612—and its possession was often an object of contention between Sweden and Denmark. Upon the walls and windows overhanging trees were growing, giving to the majestic pile an aspect of desolation and silence broken only by the croak of the ravens nestling there. The view from the upper part was fine, and the beautiful day made the ruins less gloomy.

Between the village and the castle was the queen's farm. It was a combination of garden and park; the walks were lined with high hedges, formed of trees so trimmed that they resembled walls. Birds were hiding in the thick foliage, especially nightingales; although we were in latitude 56° 52', they were in every bush, and the air was filled with their melodies in the twilight and moonlight.

Borgholm was the favorite residence of Karl Gustaf, eldest son of Johan Casimir, the Duke of Pfalz-Zweibrück, and Catherina, daughter of Charles IX. He was at one time engaged to be married to his cousin Kristina, the only child of Gustavus Adolphus; but when she abandoned her intention of marrying, she selected him as her successor to the throne. Before his accession to the crown he spent most of his time at this castle, which during his residence attained the height of its glory. Karl Gustaf loved Öland, which at that time was clad with oak forests filled with deer; and at his coronation Öland ale was served, as a compliment to his beloved island.

There is an old song which still lives in the memory of the people in the neighborhood of Ismanstorp and Långlöte. There formerly lived a famous man, whose fair daughter was called "Proud Karin." She once went out with her maids— fourteen young girls, but she the fairest of them all—to enjoy themselves with songs and plays. Suddenly there came in from the sea a ship carrying a son of the Danish king. He went ashore and listened to the voice of Karin, which seemed to him like the music of a golden harp; but when he came into the grove he was still more charmed by her beauty. He invited her to drink with him (the manner of courtship of those times), and won her assent and good-will. He then took her in his arms, carried her on board his ship, and sailed away.

Proud Karin was Jarl Asbjörn's daughter, who was married to Harald, son of the Danish king, Sven Estridson, a nephew of Canute the Great. Harald, against the last wish of his father, by the cunning and power of his father-in-law, Asbjörn, excluded his brother Canute from the kingdom, who thereupon fled to the court of the Swedish king, Hallstan, and re-

mained there in peace until the death of his brother Harald in
1080. Canute had many friends in Sweden and Scania, but
was not liked by the Danes. When he came to reign in Denmark he fostered Christianity in every way; but the worldly
power and distinction he gave to the clergy, calling them into
his councils in preference to jarls and others of high rank,
awakened against him the enmity of the most powerful men
of his kingdom. This, however, would not have caused him
much trouble, for the people in general were easily persuaded
that it was right that the servants of God, and those who took
care of souls, ought in worldly matters to be treated with
more regard than the king's servants and those who had
charge simply of the material affairs of the country; but
when he imposed tithes, and collected them with great severi-
ty, then the peasants arose, and a rebellion was soon in full
blast. The king retired to Odense, whither Jarl Asbjörn
went, assuring him of his friendship. Canute did not suspect any wrong, and easily agreed that Asbjörn should go
to the rebels and sue for peace; but no sooner had he met
them than he urged an attack on the king at once, as the latter had only a small force: which they did. Asbjörn led the
forces, and came upon the king as he was praying at the altar of St. Alban's Church, where he killed him. Asbjörn had
red hair, and since that time red hair is in the North considered indicative of a treacherous mind.

One of the ancient customs preserved in some parts of Sweden is that of welcoming the advent of spring. The evening
before the first of May is called Valborg Mass-eve: in mediæval
times mass was celebrated. Even before darkness has come, in
many districts lads of neighboring farms are seen engaged in
collecting material for bonfires, and to stack it on the top of
the highest and nearest hill; generally each hamlet has its separate fire, and they vie with each other in having the brightest;
often from an eminence may be seen at once twenty or thirty
of these blazing piles. The old folks remain at home, and pay
special attention to the number of fires—if it is odd or even,
if the sparks fly northward or southward: if odd, with a north
wind, the spring will be cold; with a southern one it will be

warm. When the well-fed flames are at the highest, a ring is formed by the young men and women; or, if the crowd is large, two or three, and the släng polka, a very pretty and graceful dance, which varies according to the different provinces, is enjoyed by those who participate in the frolic; the dancing is accompanied by singing,

> So did we go out on Valborg Mass-eve
> For to dance;
> So did we upon the highest mountain go.
> Oh hey! Let us be merry.

> I have played on Valborg Mass-eve,
> Tralle-ralle-ralle-rej;
> Out did I go with both hat and gloves,
> Hey tralle-ralle-ralle-rej.

> Hey, how merry it is to dance!
> We as others.
> We all join in a ring,
> We all dance around;
> The fire burns on the rock.
> Hey, how merry it is to dance!

Another spring custom is also observed in the South, though fast disappearing. The young men of the hamlets assemble on Valborg Mass-eve at dusk, and go around among the farms carrying birch-twigs with newly opened leaves, and sing the May song before every door; whereupon, in case they meet with a good reception, they put twigs over the porch. Baskets are also brought along, in which are collected the gifts received, consisting mostly of a liberal supply of eggs; these are used at a feast which takes place on Whit-Sunday, when, between plays and dances, abundance of pancakes and other good things are served.

The May song is as follows:

> Good evening, if home ye are,
> May is welcome!
> Excuse us if we wake you up.
> Summer is sweet for young folks.

Now we come to your farm,
May is welcome!
And ask if you will let us sing.
Summer is sweet for young folks.

For now we carry May into hamlet,
May is welcome!
And praise it with songs new.
Summer is sweet for young folks.

The little lark's sweet song,
May is welcome!
Goes up to the skies with May song.
Be glad now for such a sweet summer.

For winter's constraint now has left the land,
May is welcome!
For leaves and grass now are green.
Be glad now for such a sweet summer.

Welcome is the month of May,
May is welcome!
God bless this summer mild!
Be glad now for such a sweet summer.

Give us an abundant year,
May is welcome!
Guard both house and farm.
Be glad now for such a sweet summer.

Hop-vines yield on the poles,
May is welcome!
Then bitter wormwood in the meadows.
Be glad now for such a sweet summer.

Give milk and cheese so sweet,
May is welcome!
Buckweat also for mush.
Be glad now for such a sweet summer.

Give the beeswax and honey sweet,
May is welcome!
For healing, food, and candles, and mead.
Be glad now for such a sweet summer.

Let the hen lay eggs on plates,
May is welcome!
For pancakes and egg-cakes.
Be glad now for such a sweet summer.

Now we put sprigs on your porch,
May is welcome!
That you can see to-morrow by day.
Be glad now for such a sweet summer.

Good-night, and thanks to you,
May is welcome!
For the gift was very good.
Be glad now for such a sweet summer.

In case the song should not awaken any attention in the party for whom it is intended, the following end verse is sung:

Then lie and lie, thou lazy ox,
Till crows and ravens shall drive thee out!

This festival is a remnant of the religion of the Scandinavians in heathen times. On that day it was the custom to sacrifice children on the top of the stendösar or cromlech (which is represented in Vol. I.), and the people danced until the sun rose.

CHAPTER XXXVII.

From Småland I entered Blekinge, one of Sweden's most picturesque provinces, celebrated all over the country for the beauty of its women. Its landscape scenes are very diversified; here the soil is barren and stony; there the country becomes fruitful, and presents rural scenery of great loveliness. Though the province is not more than seventy miles in length and about twenty-five miles in its greatest breadth, more than three hundred lakes and lakelets are scattered over its surface. Luxuriant woods and groves greet the eye everywhere; colossal oaks, with gigantic spreading branches, which are among the largest in Sweden, and the finest in Europe for grace and beauty, and magnificent beech-trees, excite the astonishment of the stranger.

The coast makes a sudden sweep, running east and west, and its shores are indented by numerous bays, and lined with superb trees growing even to the edge of the sea. Here and there are hamlets or farms, with tiled and thatch-roofed houses painted red.

In some districts the farms are large; often the roads leading to the towns are lined with trees, and the fields protected by stone walls, while others are ditched instead of being fenced. Now and then on a bare granite hill or on some charming spot stands the windmill, the sails of which move briskly to grind the grain. The house of the miller is always close at hand, and there is generally a faithful dog watching while the farmers with their carts are waiting for their grist.

Here, as in Dalecarlia, of which we have spoken, and other places, the roads are often barred by a fence to keep the cattle within bounds, and children are looking for travellers. As soon as one makes his appearance there is a general scramble, each anxious to be the first to open the gate, and earn the coppers which they hope to receive.

OPENING THE GATE.

There is perhaps no province where the love of flowers is greater than in Blekinge. In summer the garden surrounding even the poorest house is usually gorgeous with bright colors; while in many a window, through snowy muslin curtains, can be seen an array of plants loaded with blossoms, belonging to the female members of the family. It is considered a great compliment when one of these flowers is given to a friend. The poorest of the people know how to make their rooms cheerful with Nature's bounties. Under glass tumblers shoots or cuttings are raised, which, when large enough, are transplanted with great care.

On one of the latter days of June I was jolting on my way towards the road that skirts the shores of the Baltic on the eastern part of the province. My horse was going slowly, for the day was warm; many of the wild flowers were drooping under the powerful rays of the sun. The poppies displayed their gorgeous tints among the tall, waving fields of rye and wheat in bloom, and the bright blue of the *Centaurea cyanus* was beautiful. The air was perfumed with the fragrance of the red and white clover; farm-houses were scattered about; cows and horses were grazing in the fields, with children watching them. Now and then I met peculiar carts drawn by two oxen, or long kärra, on their way to a farm or a hamlet.

The majority even of the humblest cottages are spotlessly clean, for the peasants of Central and Southern Sweden are neat; the floors by their whiteness attract the attention of the stranger. Everything is in place, and in summer wild flowers are displayed in cups and saucers to create a cheerful aspect. Old matrons and blooming girls are spinning, weaving, knitting, or doing needle-work; and bareheaded and barefooted, blue-eyed and flaxen-haired, children are playing around their humble home, their rosy cheeks and happy faces reminding one very forcibly that wealth is not essential to bring health and content. As I was going along I saw a woman put carefully on a stone a piece of bread which she had been eating; the Swede or Norwegian never throws bread on the ground, but, when on the road, after they have satisfied their hunger, they lay the remainder carefully on a spot where the passer-by, if hungry, may find and eat it. They think it sinful to cast away the gift of God. I have even seen persons when a piece of bread fell down pick it up and kiss it. Farther on I met a strapping fellow of twenty-two years of age, with a happy face, who was coming from the parsonage with a paper in his hand which he showed me with great pride.

Every Swede, male or female, leaving his village or city for some other part of the country, is obliged by law to have a certificate of character, called prestbetyg (clergyman's certificate). This document contains the name of the person as numbered on the register of the parish church, his vocation, date of birth, whether married or single, if vaccinated, and his qualifications in reading and writing. There are three degrees or classes in education, and the class to which each belongs is indicated in the certificate, as is also the rank in Christian knowledge—whether the individual has attended the husför-hör, a meeting where all the people of a parish are examined in Scripture once a year by the pastor, whether confirmed or not, and has attended communion, and the general moral character. If one has been in prison, or had an illegitimate child, it is so stated.

Among the customs of the Swedes, showing their horror of perjury, is the värjemålsed, or "oath of defence." When the evidence against an accused person is insufficient to convict, though there is a strong presumption of guilt, the judge gives him a chance to clear himself by the above oath. Before this can be taken, however, he is sent to his pastor, who solemnly instructs him on the nature and responsibility of an oath, and who gives him a certificate that he has been thus instructed, which he must produce to the court before he can be sworn. This may be required in cases where there is only one witness, or one unworthy of belief, or where witnesses contradict each other.

Many women were busy in the fields, weeding potatoes, beets, turnips, and carrots. The meadows were being mown, and the cut-grass filled the atmosphere with its fragrance. The maidens were superb specimens of womanhood, the embodiment of health and strength, and often were beautiful, with that exquisite Swedish complexion already described, and which, strange as it may appear, is not burned by the sun. In consequence of the warmth, they wore only their white linen chemises, made fast with a scarf around the waist, and a picturesque red head-dress. Their bare legs were as white as milk, and they moved gracefully about, in simple unconsciousness of their odd attire, as they busily raked the hay.

A gay crowd of damsels and lads in their holiday dress were on their way to a neighboring farm, where a feast given in honor of a betrothal was to take place. A betrothal in Scandinavia is celebrated in a festive manner. In the country districts the engaged couple often go before the clergy-

man, who, in presence of the respective families, says : " Before
God the All-knowing, and in presence of these witnesses, I ask
thee if thou wilt have him (or her) for thy betrothed?" After
an affirmative answer from both, rings are exchanged as a
pledge; these are worn on the ring-finger of the left hand.

BLEKINGE MAIDEN RAKING HAY.

The custom of going before the parson is dying out. In the
cities, or among the educated classes, after a gentleman and a
lady have become engaged, both their names are written on a
single visiting card and sent to all their acquaintances, this
being a notice of the betrothal; it is also published in the
newspapers. The lady, after her engagement is announced, is
allowed to go alone with her affianced, and they are often seen

together without their families at balls or places of amusement. But even in Scandinavia engagements are sometimes broken. Nothing but a plain gold ring is given, even among the most wealthy. The wedding-token is of the same character. When a woman has a family she wears three rings as a mark of distinction, of which many feel very proud, though this last fashion is going somewhat into disuse. It is only in the country that weddings are interesting, for in the cities the ceremony is the same as in other lands.

On Sunday afternoons, in every hamlet, on the grass under the trees were groups of peasants — hard - working men during the week—quietly amusing themselves; fiddlers were playing while the people were dancing, and all were in holiday attire. I thought that in no country had I met with a more happy and contented population.

One evening after sunset the singular condensed vapor called by the peasants *Elfdans*—a " dance of the elves "—a soft mist, not heavy like a fog, but white and transparent, hung over the plain, forming a sort of veil through which the meadows, fields, and groves were visible in shadowy outlines. It was like a fairy cloud, making the whole landscape a scene of perfect loveliness; I could see through it every flower and every blade of grass. People who were working in the fields looked like phantoms, and, though they were near, appeared to be far away. The white veil seemed to form a stratum only ten or twelve feet in height, apparently hanging in the air, gradually thickening towards the ground. We had emerged from this one when I drove into another precisely like it, and was startled by a new phase of the phenomenon. Fairy-like figures were apparently intent upon preventing my farther progress. The sight seemed supernatural but lovely. Yet these angels were only a group of flaxen-haired maidens partly shadowed by the mist; I saw only their heads and shoulders as in a haze, their bodies being wholly hidden by the thick lower strata. I felt like apostrophizing them : "Are you the daughters of Blekinge, so famed in Sweden for their beauty, or are you their spirits ?" My horse stopped, and I said, " Beautiful maidens! are you the Scandinavian valkyries who travel through

THE DANCE OF THE ELVES. FROM AN ORIGINAL DRAWING BY G. E. FISCHER.

the air, or their spirits flying before me ?" but no answer came. The heads drew nearer and nearer, when suddenly on the other side of the road I saw other forms advancing. It seemed as if I were in another world; the whole was like a vision; I might have fancied myself in space, surrounded by the disembodied.

Such scenes are often observed in some districts of Sweden in summer.* These phenomena are caused by the sudden contact of cold air with the warm surface of the earth, and the transparency is occasioned by the dryness of the atmosphere. Farther on a gentle zephyr came, and the vapor took a thousand fantastic shapes, which at times seemed to represent human figures, and "the dance of the elves" began. In old times the people said that this dance always took place over the spots where good people had been buried, and where their spirits dwelt.

The elves were gentle beings—the friends and assistants of the gods. They were divided into two classes—the light, or elves proper, which dwelt above-ground in *Alfheim* (elves' homes), and were fairer than the sun, and the dark elves, or dwarfs, which lived underground, beneath stones or in mountain caves, and were blacker than pitch. The former were held in such esteem that offerings were made to them as to the gods. The dwarfs could not bear daylight, and during the day hid in their holes: none could make such arms and ornaments as they did, for they were the finest smiths in the world, and as such continually executed work for the deities. These spirits, whose name is derived from the beautiful clear rivers, are the forces of nature which work for the good of mankind, either above or under ground—in the plant life that spreads over fertile plains, or the precious wealth of the mines. It is, however, natural that the light-winged, beautiful elves stood nearer to the empire of the gods than the heavy, clumsy, and ugly dwarfs; the popular tales have also preserved the distinction between them.

---

* There is a painting in the royal palace in Stockholm which portrays the fairy-like scene with marked effect.

The elves are well-known under the names of *Ellefolk* or *Elfvefolk* (elve people), the small beings who dwell on the elf-mounds. The elf-maiden is extremely beautiful, like a snow-white lily; her voice is silver-toned, and no one can withstand her charms and her speech. She sometimes glides with the sun's rays through an opening in a house, but she may disappear very suddenly; she is not to be depended on—often infatuating the mind of youth with love; but when he tries to embrace her, she becomes an empty form or a tree. One must be careful not to sleep by an elf-mound; but happy is he who is privileged to hear their beautiful harps and songs on a summer eve, to watch them dance in the moonlight, and to see them, swan-like, sporting or bathing in the waters.

The dwarfs of the sagas were small and ill-shaped, delighting to deceive human beings, and steal from them things they like. They did, however, show gratitude; and when their women at childbirth asked their earthly sisters for help, they often gave the latter great treasures, for in their caves they possessed immense riches. On Yule-eve the stones which closed the mouth of their abodes were raised, as if by magic, upon four glowing pillars, and glimpses of their sumptuous homes appeared within; one was then careful not to enter, for it was very difficult to return. It was especially maidens they wished, and those whom they had enticed were called "mountain-taken."

Gradually the twilight became very dim; but far away towards the north the pale glow from the sun shone like the light of day fading away high up in the heavens. The night was so beautiful that I kept travelling. The aspens (*Populus tremula*) were scattered here and there in groves, and, as I gazed, there seemed to come a carnival of joy among them; their leaves quivered and danced like merry maids, as the breeze from the hills touched and kissed them on its journey to an adjacent lake. This was the ball of the trees; the blue canopy of heaven was their banqueting-hall; the thousand stars were the lights; the murmur of the wind among the branches was the music; the wild flowers scattered in the meadows were the spectators, and the still night presided over all.

The dim outlines of an old mansion rose in the distance like a spectral castle, while oaks near by looked on as silent witnesses of the past and the present. The ball of the trees drew towards its close; the lights gradually disappeared, and the rustling of the leaves became fainter and fainter, for the wind was dying away with the expiring night. Darkness slowly merged into the twilight of morning, and the birds began to sing as harbingers of the coming day; then clouds took on a golden hue, which was reflected in the lake; the flowers raised their heads refreshed, after the heat of the preceding afternoon. Then the great orb rose full of majesty and glory above the hills, and in the sunlight the dew-drops shone like precious gems. One by one the tillers of the soil appeared in the fields; the songs of the lads and maidens, the hum of insects, the warbling of birds, the lowing of the cows, and the neighing of the horses, were mingled together. Another morn was come, and nature took on new life, and only as one can behold it in the North.

Approaching a cheerful little house with a flower-garden in front, I was startled by a sweet voice, fresh and clear; I stood still, and beheld, unseen, a beautiful girl doing her morning work. I listened with delight to her song, as follows:

> When fourteen years I was, I believe,
> A little girl so merry and so gay,
> No woe I ever heard of,
> None either thought upon.
> > Tra, la, la, la.

> Indeed, when seventeen I became,
> The sun shone, the cuckoo sang, and it was spring;
> All was fair, the earth green, the heavens blue,
> But I, however, was wanting something
> > Tra, la, la, la.

> Yes, now it is no more as it was—
> Sometimes I am so sad, sometimes so merry,
> Sometimes I am so white, sometimes so red,
> And I want neither to live nor die.
> > Tra, la, la, la.

This was followed by another old folk-song full of sentiment:

THE BRIDE'S QUESTION.

Lovest thou for beauty's sake?
Love me not then!
Love the sun! See, in gold
Luxuriously do her curls glow in the blue.

Lovest thou for my youth's sake?
Love me not then!
Love the spring! It is full
Always of fresh roses.   Mine will soon vanish.

Lovest thou for treasures' sake?
Love me not then!
Love the Sea-queen! Pearls, gold,
Forests of corals does she offer thee.

Lovest thou for love's own sake?
Oh, do then love me!
Love have I. Faithfully
It has long been, and will eternally be thine.

She had hardly finished this song when she began another
folk-song of Southern Sweden.

LITEN KARIN (LITTLE KARIN).

And little Karin served
On the young king's farm;
She shone as a star
Among the gentle maidens all.

She shone as a star
All among the maidens small,
And the young king spake
To little Karin thus:

"And hear thou, little Karin!
Say, wilt thou be mine?
The gray horse and the golden saddle,
Them I will give thee."

"The gray horse and the golden saddle,
Them I do not suit.
Give them to thy young queen;
Let me with honor go."

"And hear thou, little Karin!
Say, wilt thou be mine?
My red gold crown,
That I will give thee."

" Thy red golden crown,
That I do not suit.
Give that to thy young queen,
And let me with honor go."

'·And hear thou, little Karin!
Say, wilt thou be mine?
Half my kingdom,
That I will give thee."

'' Half thy kingdom,
That I do not suit.
Give that to thy young queen,
And let me with honor go."

"And hear thou, little Karin!
Wilt thou not be mine?
Then I will have thee put
Into the spiked barrel."

"And wilt thou have me put
Into the spiked barrel?
God's little angels, they will see
That I am innocent."

They put little Karin
Into the spiked barrel,
And the pages of the king
Then rolled it around.

Then there came from the heavens
Two white doves down;
They took little Karin,
And instantly they were three.

Then came two black ravens
Up there from hell;
They took the young king,
And instantly they were three.

Little Karin was followed by another song:

THE ALUNDA SONG.

My boy he lives in Alunda hamlet,
Alo—Alunda, Alundalej !
Eyes has he blue as heaven's clear sky.
Alunda—lunda, Alo.

Goes with his scythe light as a wind,
Alo—Alunda, Alundalej !
Little burnt by the sun, but fresh and red on his cheek.
Alunda—lunda, Alo.

Just he rode his horses to pasture,
Alo—Alunda, Alundalej !
Never saw I colt better tended in stall.
Alunda—lunda, Alo.

He goes in to dance—modest and shy,
Alo—Alunda, Alundalej !
Looks he at a girl, it is just done on the sly.
Alunda—lunda, Alo.

Whit-Sunday-eve came he to me,
Alo—Alunda, Alundalej !
"Rosa little, hear what I will say to thee!"
Alunda—lunda, Alo.

"Rosa, my Rosa, lovest thou me?"
"Oh no!" Alunda, Alundalej !
"Thou will get some one else—meet thy fate so quiet!"
Alunda—lunda, Alo.

So he came to me on midsummer-eve,
Alo—Alunda, Alundalej !
Went with me in the dance, light, swift, and quick.
Alunda—lunda, Alo.

Girls, only hush! but own it I will,
Alo—Alunda, Alundalej !
How it was, but a kiss he forced upon me.
Alunda—lunda, Alo.

"Rosa," he said, "shall I die of grief?"
"Oh no!" Alunda, Alundalej !
"Here thou hast my hand, I take back what I said."
Alunda—lunda, Alo.

Evidently the singer's *repertoire* was extensive, and she loved both lively and sentimental lays. Suddenly she sang again:

> High up in the heavens
> There sit little stars;
> The friend I loved
> I can never get.
> > Oh! oh! oh! oh!

> He fell into my mind—
> That I cannot help;
> He swore to be to me true
> Unto the bleak death.
> > Oh! oh! oh! oh!

> And then he went away from mé,
> And soon I got another;
> I got the one I did not want,
> And Sorrow was his name.
> > Oh! oh! oh! oh!

Here the maiden stopped, for she had seen me listening, and her cheeks flushed. Bowing to her, I continued on my way.

On a warm afternoon I neared Karlskrona, the chief town in Blekinge; the wind was high, and the dust flew in thick clouds, as it had not rained for many a day. The drive was dreary, the soil in many places poor and stony, and trees scarce. At Jemjö a tomb was pointed out to me as that of the former sheriff, who, on a dark evening, as he was seated in the station-room, was shot from the outside in cold blood; his assassin escaped in the darkness, and has never been identified, although the authorities made great efforts to discover him. The murder was supposed to have been committed for revenge. The station-keeper was arrested on suspicion, but soon released, his innocence being established. Approaching the city of Karlskrona, the country became more pleasant, and the highways lively.

The people, where there are many small seaports, were not so good as those inland. The prisons were not empty: they talked of thieves, and doors were carefully locked: two or three times I had detected attempts at overcharging; and on

my way from Kalmar I saw a revolver hanging by the bed-
side of a landlord, and drinking had become a vice. Karlskrona (lat. 56° 10′) is a naval station, the most important of
Sweden, and has a population of 18,000. The town is built
on several islands, the largest of which is Trossö, connected
by floating and other bridges, the one communicating with
the main-land being of stone. The streets are very broad and
regular; the dwelling-houses are large, and there are many
squares, and a shaded garden or park, called Hogland, crowded every afternoon. Along the quays were boats laden with
vegetables and fruits from the main-land, and in the early
morning with fish. One is soon reminded of the military importance of the town from its geographical position: barracks,
fortifications, dismantled men-of-war, piles of cannon-balls, etc.,
give a warlike appearance to the place. Numerous islands
protect the approaches to the harbor, which are strongly fortified.

The Swedish navy is recruited like the army, by enlistment.
Certain estates and hamlets are obliged to furnish a stated
number of men for the service; and these sailors, when on
duty, are treated like the soldiers, and while ashore are permitted to cultivate their little farms. There are no conscrip-
tions, and the regular sailors voluntarily engage themselves.
One branch of the service is that to which is assigned the defence of the coast lakes. The sailors, while on shore, are kept
under strict discipline. They live here in large, clean, and
well-ventilated barracks. There is a library, accessible to all.

Among the fine estates of the suburbs is Johannishus, famous for its oak-trees. At a short distance the little Nettraby
empties into the Baltic. Small steamers ascend the stream
several times a day. The shores are lined by meadows, fields,
and groves; the sail is sometimes under a perfect canopy of
branches overhanging the water. Steam navigation is stopped
by a stone bridge, below which, on the river brink, is the ancient parish church of Nettraby, with its shaded graveyard
and old tombs. The grand trees, grassy banks, and beautiful
lilies floating on the water added to the beauty of the place,
while the hum of human voices contrasted with the stillness

of the scene. The surrounding country is so charming that one might fancy himself driving in a park. About midway between Karlskrona and the seaport of Karlshamn is the celebrated Spa of Ronneby, situated a distance of about fifteen miles from Karlskrona. The high-road thence traverses a fruitful country; some of the views are exquisitely beautiful, but very few large farms are met. Most of the dwelling-houses are small, and contrast greatly with the buildings found in the northern provinces.

CHAPTER XXXVIII.

RONNEBY, in lat. 56° 13′, has a population of about 1600;
and from its protected situation in a fertile valley and proximity to the sea enjoys a mild climate, which in summer is
quite warm. This village is celebrated for its mineral springs.
The waters are especially beneficial in anæmia, scrofula, chron-
ic and intermittent fevers, rheumatism, diseases of the diges-
tive and nervous systems, when accompanied by general or
local weakness. The mud-baths have been found especially
advantageous in rheumatism, and are very much frequented.
The charge for each patient of the first class is 10 kronor,
which includes contributions for the chaplain, service of
water, music, and the poor. The fee to the doctor is optional.
Patients of the second class pay 4.50 kronor to the establishment and 2 kronor to the doctor, and, when circumstances
make it necessary, these charges are lessened to 2.50 kronor
and 1 kronor respectively.

The village is about three miles from the sea, on the banks
of the Ronneby River. Above the bridge navigation is interrupted by a fall, while below a small steamer goes as far as
the Baltic, so that visitors can enjoy the sea-bathing or boating.
The same steamer takes the people to the springs and back
every morning.

The old church well deserves a visit. The paintings are

odd, and sometimes excite a smile. The candlesticks, with double-headed eagles, are probably spoils of the Thirty Years' War.

The place was burned in 1864 or 1865, and has been completely rebuilt since. It would require a large hotel to accommodate the travellers who come to the springs. Patients board in the different houses; and in the height of the season, unless lodgings are secured in advance, one may not find accommodations. The cost of living is three to four kronor per day. Every one here retires early, and at five in the morning the town is full of people on their way to the springs.

The grounds are pleasant, and the trees furnish a grateful protection from the sun. Around the spring the visitors await patiently their turn to drink the water. A band of six musicians plays lively airs. At eight o'clock the music ceases, the crowds draw together, and the pastor of Ronneby offers thanks to the Almighty for his goodness, beseeching him to bless those who have come in search of health. No one thinks of leaving the spring before this act of devotion. This custom prevails at all the Swedish spas.

The Swedes are very methodical when they go to a spa in search of health. The resident physician was on the ground from six to eight o'clock, and was surrounded by those who wished to consult him. The doctor had a smile and a pleasant word for every patient, and, however foolish their questions or insignificant their ailments, examined into their cases. He kept a register of the invalids. The usual duration of the treatment was from three to four weeks. In one part of the grounds there was a hospital for the poor, and those who could not afford to pay drank the water and procured advice without charge, the doctor receiving a given sum from the parish for this duty. The amounts paid by patients are devoted to the support of the hospital, the improvement of the grounds and buildings, and of the bathing establishment; but the last was still burdened with a debt at the time of my visit.

The doctor was also the health officer of the parish or district, which contained a population of 13,000. He had been in office for seven years, but had lately been promoted to that

position in the province of Blekinge; his duty being to trav.
el, to attend to sanitary precautions, and to hold autopsies.
The governor of the province and five leading citizens were
charged with the direction. When a vacancy occurs in the
health department the medical college in Stockholm is informed of the fact. The name of a doctor whom the local
authorities would like to see appointed is called for, and the
person chosen is generally accepted. There is a health officer
for each province, besides one for each parish or district, all of
whom have to attend to the poor gratuitously and watch over
the health of the people, and take precautions necessary to
avoid the spread of epidemic diseases.

For curiosity's sake I took a mud-bath. An old woman was
in attendance, who smeared and rubbed my body with mud,
and afterwards with a soft brush; after being washed I received a cold douche, producing a delightful sensation; finally I was enveloped in a warm linen wrapper, and over this a
thick blanket, and stretched myself on a sofa to rest. The
bath caused a temporary prickly sensation in the skin, but the
after effect was pleasant. This water is so strongly impreg-
nated with iron that it is only used in baths, and is heated to
92° Fahrenheit. In this quiet watering-place there was no
show, and no rivalry in dress. There was a committee of
amusements, composed of three ladies and three gentlemen,
who every day chose a spot where coffee was served, and at
the foot of the stairway to the springs the name of the place
selected was displayed upon a placard. The servants preceded
the guests, and when the company had been gathered together
innocent games and plays were indulged in. No Swedish
punch, spirits, or wine was allowed to be sold on the spot chosen, and no gambling was permitted.

In the square of the village music was played until 9 P.M.,
and up to that time the place was crowded. At 9.30 P.M. everybody was in bed. There was very little driving, the people generally preferring to walk. There was a club, where those who
chose could obtain their meals—a privilege of which nearly all
the guests availed themselves. Three meals were served daily.
The fare was simple but excellent, and calculated to produce

good hygienic effects. The prices at this restaurant were wonderfully cheap—the breakfast costing about 35 öre; the dinner, consisting of two dishes with soup, or three dishes without soup, 1 krona; and the supper about 70 öre. Wines were not generally used. A good room could be procured for 1 krona and 50 öre or 2 kronor a day. The doctor presided at one of the tables—all standing for a moment in a silent and prayerful attitude before taking their seats. The want of ventilation in the restaurant, however, was oppressive to one not accustomed to a stifling atmosphere. We have already noticed the great dislike of the Swedes for fresh air; they seem to be in constant dread of draughts and rheumatism. The windows were kept closed, and at dinner every opening in the dining-rooms, which communicated with each other, was shut, though the weather was exceedingly warm—the thermometer standing at 86° Fahrenheit. If one window remained partly open by mistake, it was immediately closed. The universal trust in the honesty of people is prevalent here. When one is ready to depart, he goes to the club and pays his bill, and not before: nothing would be easier than to leave without paying. I should think the visitor would be glad to get out of the place, for its life is certainly very monotonous.

At Djupadal, the country-seat of Baron Wrede, I went to see one of the mills which had lately sprung up in Sweden and Norway for the manufacture of the wood-pulp used in the production of paper. As this invention unfortunately causes the destruction of millions of young white-pine-trees every year, the lovers of nature, who dread the demolition of forests, regard this new industry with alarm. Taken together with the requisition for timber for mines, the increasing demand will eventually destroy the forests, unless a law is made to restrict the cutting down of the trees of less than a certain diameter.*

In pursuance of an old custom, every year on the first

---

* The wood used for the manufacture of paper is white pine; the red pine, on account of its resinous quality, being unavailable. The logs are broken and ground, and the mass is passed between heavy rollers until it forms a perfect pulp, which is then dried and sent to England, where it is converted into paper.

Sunday in July crowds of country-people make their way to Ronneby. A large part sleep on the way at different farms. In the suburbs many groups of maidens, sheltered under the trees, were engaged in removing the dust of travel and combing their hair, so that they might make their entrance in a becoming and tidy manner; hundreds arranged their toilets in this fashion, afterwards putting on their heads silk handkerchiefs which they had carefully protected on the road. More than 5000 peasants had arrived, and in the church to which they had flocked there was not even standing-room.

It is considered a kind of betrothal-day: men and girls arrived with bunches of flowers; the people came to meet their friends: if one of the men saw among the girls one whom he wished to marry, he proposed by offering to the chosen one a bouquet; if she accepted it, her act signified an affirmative; but the custom is getting into disuse. Men seen with flowers are afraid of ridicule, and this assembly of marriageable persons may be said to be virtually a thing of the past, and is now only the occasion of a merry gathering. During the day long wagons, arched over with branches of birch-trees, were packed with people bent upon a frolic—a custom which reminded me of the "straw ride" parties common in the rural districts of the United States.

The only unpleasant feature in the quiet life of Ronneby is the Saturdays, when the peasants and laborers come to the village to get their supply of bränvin, and drunkenness is prevalent. The right of granting licenses for the sale of spirituous liquors is left with the communal councils, which in most cities dispose of the privilege to companies or individuals at a stated sum per year, these again subletting this right to retailers. In some cities, however, companies have been formed consisting of some of the most prominent inhabitants, who, wishing to diminish the evils of drunkenness, take the sales of spirits into their own hands, paying for the licenses, and, after getting a fair interest—generally six per cent.—turn the surplus into the city treasury, to be used for the benefit of the poor, hospital, or other good object. It is forbidden by law to sell spirits to intoxicated persons or minors. It has been found that this system has been the means of diminishing intemperance to a considerable degree, as the licenses are limited. In Norway retailers of bränvin are not allowed to sell from 5 o'clock P.M. on Saturday to Monday, at 8 A.M.: the same regulation applies to religious holidays. In Sweden bränvin is made from potatoes and grain, and before coming into the market must be free of fusel-oil. The yearly consumption of bränvin per head is in Sweden about three gallons; in Norway, one and three quarter gallons.

One of the favorite drives or walks is towards Djupadal, above which the Ronne River rushes through a channel about 120 feet long—in one place only 5 to 6 wide; the walls are smooth, and the water 100 feet deep. Below the mill the river breaks. Lodged between the walls is a huge rock of granite, which, according to tradition, was brought there in the following manner: " In the days of old there were two giants, Ronne and Mörrum, who resolved to force a passage to the sea for the water from the upper lakes. The one who first brought the water to the sea was to have his river full of fish; while in that of the other a human being would be drowned every year. They worked away, each at his own river; but when Ronne reached the rocks at Djupadal the work was so hard that he rested and lay down to sleep. In the mean time Mörrum got the road open to the sea for his stream. That river is now called Mörrum, and it empties into the sea about seven miles from Karlshamn. When he had finished his task he sent a woman to tickle Ronne on his head to awaken him. When Ronne awoke he flew into a rage, and dashed the woman against the rocks; and some hundreds of years ago the mark of the place where she struck was pointed out. At the same time he took a huge stone and threw it with such force against the obstruction that it split open, and the water found its way to the sea, the rock remaining where it was," for tradition says it is the very one that did the work. Great abundance of salmon are found in the Mörrum River, while the Ronne has none, and every year there are some people getting drowned in the latter.

The province of Blekinge is very rich in antiquities, espe-

2 F 2

cially old graves or bautastenar. Half-way between Karlskrona and Ronneby is Hjortshammar, on a small promontory running into the sea. Here are found nearly one hundred memorial stones and ship-markings: some of these bautastenar are of considerable size. The place was evidently a Viking burial-ground, and the spot a fitting resting-place for these heroes of the deep. A little farther west, north of the road, are three fine bautastenar, one of which has a Runic inscription. These brave men appear always to have chosen for their final resting-places some romantic spot in the neighborhood of the sea.

On the way to Karlshamn I passed the church of Hoby. Karlshamn has a population of about 6000; it is a thriving town, with ship-yards and factories of various kinds. It has a large square surrounded by a row of shady trees, and in the centre an old-fashioned pump, to which the people come for water. One side is flanked by the white wall of the churchyard, and comfortable houses adorn the three other sides. A shaded square lies at the mouth of the river on the bay. There is a park just outside of the town, on a hill called Bellevue, adorned by superb trees, among which are very fine oaks and beeches.

Swedish towns are very quiet except on market-days; as is usual on such occasions, many on their way home feel rather exhilarated, and have entirely lost the demure countenance they had on their arrival.

One of the primitive sights which amused me was an antiquated dredge in operation, moved by two poor-looking cows, which wearily went round and round.

Walking through the streets I came to a house before which fir twigs were scattered. This is an old Norwegian and Swedish custom, observed on the day of burial. Often in small villages or towns these are spread from the house to the church. In the cities, in the room where the dead lies, the mirrors, as well as the front windows of the house, are covered with a white sheet. The announcements of death are published in the newspapers with a black border around them, specimens of which are appended:

That the ever-merciful God, in his supreme and impenetrable wisdom, has called to himself our beloved little daughter, HANNA YRA EBBA AGNES, who, born on midsummer-night's-eve, 1878, after only a few hours of suffering, calmly and peacefully expired at Askaröd, Tuesday, March 11th, 1879, at 1.37 o'clock A.M., mourned, regretted, and bewailed by parents, a little sister, grandfather, and relations, is only in this way announced to relations and sympathizing friends. Sw. Ps. No. 477, v. 8.

AGARINE PEHRSSON,
WILHELM PEHRSSON.

Askaröd, March 11th, 1879.

That the grand chamberlain, commander of the Order of Vasa, knight of the Order of Nordstjernan, COUNT AXEL JACOB DE LA GARDIE, born April 4th, 1819, died calmly and peacefully at Maltesholm, January 16th, 1879, at 1.50 A.M., deeply mourned by the surviving wife, brothers and sisters, relations and numerous friends, is only announced in this manner. Sw. Ps. No. 91, v. 5.

That it has to-day at 9 A.M. pleased God to call away by a calm and peaceable death my dearly-beloved wife, ELNA NILSDOTTER, after a life of thirty-seven years six months and nineteen days, mourned and regretted by me and five little children, parents, brothers, and sisters, is only in this way announced to relations and friends. Sw. Ps. No. 478, v. 4, No. 344, v. 4.   NILS PERSON.

Vestra Kattarp, February 28th, 1879.

That the servant-girl CAROLINA PERSSON died calmly and peacefully in Klintarp, March 14th, 1879, at an age of fifty-five years nine months and eight days, mourned by sisters and their children, is only in this manner announced to relations and friends. Sw. Ps. 478, v. 1.

Huge boulders in some parts of Blekinge are common. Near Karlshamn there are some of very great size, almost square, with rounded corners. Upon one of these are marks resembling impressions of feet, knees, and fingers which in olden times were supposed to have been made by the giants.

At a short distance from the town is the hamlet of Asarum, where there is a spring called the offering spring (offerkillan). On All-hallow-eve the boys and maidens from far and wide come to make their offerings at this place, consisting of small pieces of money, bread-crusts, egg-shells, etc. This old custom was originally designed to gain the favor of the fairies, who were thought to have their homes around this spring, and who would assist them in getting sweethearts.

A few miles from Karlshamn there is a beautiful spot called Valhall, made of gigantic boulders piled one upon another, which form in one part a grotto. It is so steep that its summit

is accessible only on two sides. This was in heathen times an
ättestupa, that is, a place from which the people, when old and
infirm, used to throw themselves, it being considered shameful
to die in bed or of old age, as men ought to have died before
on the battle-field, from which they were carried by the
Valkyries to Odin's hall, Valhall. Of all the religions invent-
ed by man, none ever taught a more utter disregard of death,
or led to more reckless deeds of bravery, than that of the
Northmen.

On the way south is the estate of Elleholm, from whose
grounds one has a most beautiful view of land and sea; and
near by is the now quiet town of Sölvesborg, the ancient residence of the great Viking Sölve.

Not far from the boundary-line between Blekinge and the
province of Skåne, at a short distance from Sölvesborg, and
near the Baltic, is the country-seat of Valsjö, entailed in the
family of Count Trolle Wachtmeister, a descendant of one
of the old and famous families of Sweden. From the road, as
is often the case in this country, one does not dream that such
a beautiful place is hidden from view. Having a letter of introduction to the owner, I directed my steps towards the mansion, which was embosomed in trees. I was received with a
courtesy that was the more gratefully appreciated as I was a
stranger to all. The countess expressed her regret at the absence of her husband.

Near the porch stood a post-chaise ready to start; but my
unexpected arrival delayed the departure of the guests, a
gentleman and two young ladies, his daughters; a cousin of
the host, bearing the same name and title, who was governor
of Karlskrona län (province of Blekinge). During the short
time of our acquaintance I was invited to visit them at their
estate of Johannishus. The mansion at Valsjö is unpretending and small; indeed, a large building would seem out of
place; but no wealth could give the spot its exquisite natural
surroundings. It is a gem, and may be ranked as one of the
prettiest places on the shores of the Baltic. There are no extended lawns or majestic avenues of trees; but these, in such
close proximity to the sea, would spoil the effect of the land-

scape. The woods grow down to the very edge of the water, and when the sun is powerful one enjoys the shade of the superb beeches, the long branches of which spread widely from the trunks. One of these trees measured between six and seven feet in diameter. The ground was carpeted with ferns, and large boulders were covered with a thick, green, velvet-like moss, forming natural cushions several inches deep, adding greatly to the beauty of the view. At times one skirts the Baltic, upon the shores of which lay large bare masses of granite, brought down by glaciers. The countess was an admirer of nature, and loved Valsjö for its beautiful scenery, and a great deal more than her more pretentious chateau of Ljungby. We sat for awhile at a favorite place where the members of the family often stopped to rest, and whence we had an extended view of the coast. Soon after we came to another point, from which the sea, the islands, and the mansion could be seen, and then plunged again into the midst of a grove of splendid beech-trees, and among moss-covered rocks, until we reached a promontory of bare granite, upon which we seated ourselves to enjoy the view of the bay, studded with rocky and barren islands, with a background of dark forest. Two or three fishing-smacks, with sails shining white as the sun struck upon them, were slowly moving, for it was almost calm, and not a ripple disturbed the still waters. The scenery was peculiarly Swedish, and can only be seen on the southern shores of the Baltic. We continued our ramble under beautiful trees until we came to groves of white-trunked birches, two of which were centuries old, with crooked limbs and hollow trunks, covered with thick moss. Meadows and fields of winter rye lay between this grove and another wood of magnificent birches, and as we approached the house, which looked home-like, the fragrance of roses in full bloom perfumed the air. The cherries in the kitchen-garden were getting ripe as early as July 1st, and their bright red color could be seen.

When I thought that the time allowed by etiquette for my visit had been exhausted, I rose to bid good-bye to the family; but the hostess said, "Be so good as not to go yet; do not be in a hurry;" and then delicious strawberries and melons from the garden were served to us outside the house, after which the countess insisted that I should remain, and upon sending for my trunk at Sölvesborg. My engagements were such that I could not accept, but I could not leave before taking tea with the family. There was no ostentatious display, but a sense of home-like comfort pervaded everything. The daughter of the house, a charming young lady, poured the tea, which with the cups had been placed on a separate table, after which she came to join us, while the servant waited upon the guests.

When the hour came to say farewell, two members of the family prepared to accompany me back to the village, and all came out to see me safely in their own carriage. I have not forgotten my kind reception at Valsjö, nor the pleasant walk under the old trees.

CHAPTER XXXIX.

The Province of Skåne, or Scania.—The Garden of the Peninsula of Scandinavia.
—Chateaux.—Ancestral Homes.—Mild Climate.—Fine Farms.—Peculiar Construction of the Houses.—Character of the Scanians.—Diet of Farmers.—Names
given to Females and Males. — Trolle Ljungby. — An Old Drinking-horn and
Whistle.—Interesting Legends.—Lake Ifö.—Its Chateaux.—Åhus.—Christianstad.—The Estate of Råbelöf.—A Fruitful Garden.—Great Numbers of Birds.—
How Farm-hands are Paid.—Law concerning Master and Servant.—Home Life
on a Large Estate.—Estates in the Neighborhood of Christianstad.—Ystad.—
Chateaux around Ystad.

SKÅNE or Scania is the most southern province of Sweden,
covering a space of 4300 square miles, and is justly called the
Garden of Scandinavia. Large estates under high cultivation,
belonging to the old nobility of Sweden, are met in every direction, and numerous chateaux, many of which are surrounded by moats. Often their ancient walls are green with ivy,
honeysuckle, or fruit-trees growing in espaliers; while a garden in the French style, resplendent with the bright colors of
many flowers, contrasts singularly with the greensward, and
the majestic trees or parks which are around them. A view
of the sea, sometimes seen afar over the plain, or of a neighboring lake, may add to the charm of those lovely homes.
Graperies, hot-houses filled with flowers and exotics, are close
by, perhaps hidden from sight by shrubbery or trees. The
owners of many of these remain all the year round, enjoying
the life of country gentlemen, and, possessing fine studs, take
great interest in the improvement of stock and horses. Shooting and fishing are the principal pastime.*

---

* Among the game are *Tetrao tetrix* (black grouse), *Perdix cinerea* (partridge),
Gallinula chloropus (moor-hen), *Scolopax rusticola* (woodcock), *Gallinago media*
(common snipe), *Gallinago major* (double snipe). *Capreolus capræa* (roebuck), *Cervus
elaphus* (stag).

Many of these ancestral homes were erected in the beginning or middle of the fourteenth century, when Skåne belonged to Denmark. Their structure reminds one of the mode of building of that period, and of the intense religious feeling of the people at that time; over the gate-way, or under a stone arch, are often seen sculptured representations of the Trinity. The owners bear names known in the annals of history; within their walls are libraries and archives, which are valuable to the student, and in their halls hang portraits of famous men and women of their days. The climate is comparatively mild, as the province is surrounded by the sea on three sides; the summers are warm, the thermometer reaching 90° in the shade, and I found the rays of the sun more powerful than in England: the winters may compare with those of the State of New York, but the summers have not its intense heat. In the most southern part, at the latter end of April or beginning of May, the horse-chestnuts unfold their leaves; and a little later the oaks are full leafed. Apple, pear, plum, mulberry, walnut, and chestnut trees flourish, while peaches, apricots, and grapes do well in espaliers in many places.

The landscape of the province has characteristics of its own; the large forests are missed, except in the northern part, the country is not so well watered, lakes are few, and mostly shallow. In the south the country is flat, and hamlets with their red-tiled roofs, the spires of churches, and farms embosomed in trees, can be seen from a long distance in the midst of waving fields. The farms vary in size from 20 to 300 acres, and the people raise grain, cattle, and horses. There are several kinds of properties in Sweden :

Frälse..........A farm or estate upon which no direct tax to the State is levied.
Frälseskatte..⎫ Free from direct tax to the state, but pay an annual tax to
Skattefrälse..⎰ some other party.
Skatte..........Pay direct taxes to the State.
Krono..........Crown estates are leased generally for twenty years.
Rusthåll.......One or several farms supporting a horseman.
Rotehåll.......One or several farms supporting a foot-soldier, or marine.

Skåne is celebrated for its fine farms belonging to the peasantry, many of whom are quite wealthy, and independent in their politics. The mode of construction is peculiar. The farm-buildings along the roads form a perfect square, often more than 100 feet in front, with a single entrance or gate, through which the carts enter; there are no windows on the side towards the road. The dwelling-houses stand back, and often front towards the fields; most of these are thatched—a mode of roofing almost unknown in other parts of Sweden. Generally such places have no trees around them.

The smaller farms, of less pretensions, occupied by the poorer people, are so arranged that the buildings form only two sides of a square, presenting an odd appearance. On one side is the dwelling-house, of a white color, often built of bricks plastered over, and sometimes of wood, with lathwork covered with mortar, while on the other is a long structure, generally of wood, painted red, used for the cattle, for stable and cart-house, the storage of wood, and other purposes. The people here have much less capacious buildings than in the far North. On account of the scarcity of timber, they have a peculiar kind of house called "korsverkshus;" the frame is of wood, filled in with bricks, with the outside plastered. There are others besides, which are built in the following manner: the timber frame is first set up, on which boards are nailed inside and outside to a height of about three feet; then a carefully prepared mixture of clay and straw, three-quarters of the former and one quarter of the latter, is rammed in as tightly as possible; then another height of board is put on, and the same process is repeated till the eaves are reached; when the boards are taken off, the walls are left to dry, and the outside is further protected by mortar. These buildings are very comfortable, and some are to be found over two centuries old.

The character of the Skånians contrasts singularly with that of their northern neighbors of the provinces of Blekinge, Småland, Halland, and Bohuslän; they are quiet, phlegmatic, peaceable, and good-natured. Their farmers live well; in summer, in the height of the harvesting season, they take a meal composed of milk and soft, dark, sour rye bread and butter immediately after rising; at six or half-past six comes what they call breakfast, of about the same food, with or without coffee; at half-past ten or eleven, if they have not taken food with them, they either come home or something is sent. Dinner is at noon, when they eat either salt pork, fish, or sausages,

AN OLD HOUSE IN SKÅNE, 1558.

corned beef, or soup (according to the days), potatoes, and sour milk. At five o'clock they take another meal, consisting of cheese, butter, and bread, with a portion of *dricka*, a light small-beer; at eight o'clock is supper, consisting invariably of gröt, with either sweet or sour milk. The cows and sheep are kept on the farms all the year round.

In the southern and in some other parts of Sweden many of the names of the women are peculiar, and some of them very pretty. Among them are Signild, Hildigunda, Elna, Bengta, Ebba, Ingrid, Karna, Yra, Selma, Erika, Wendela, Thekla, Ulla, Pernilla, Gerda, Blända, Gunilla, Helfrida, Bothild, Signe, Gundela, Hildegard, Hedvig, Valborg, Disa, Thyra, Ingegerd, Gothild, Astrid, Valfrida, Yrsa, Helga, Hillevid, Illiana, Magna, Estrid, Elvira, Vendela, Hildur, Engela, Alfhild, Hertha, Freja : Syster (sister) is often used as a surname.

Among the men are the following names : Axel, Pontus, Klas, Fabian, Thure, Sixten, Malte, Hjalmar, Henning, Didrik, Sigge (very old, Odin being called Sigge Fridolfson), Fridolf, Sven, Sigurd, Sten, Ivar, Thiodolph, Gunnar, Jesper, Thorgny, Ragnvald, Alf, Göthe, Valfrid, Helge, Folke, Frithiof, Gude, Hildmar, Erland, Arvid, Elof, Bengt, Tryggve, Egil, Svante, Elof, Ulf, Björn, Styrbjörn : Bror (brother) is also used as a surname.

At a short distance from Valsjö is the small river Sissebäck, which there forms the boundary between Blekinge and Scania, which last includes the läns of Christianstad and Malmöhus.

About nine miles from Sölvesborg, and midway between it and the seaport of Åhus, is Trolle Ljungby, the largest estate in Scania, comprising over 40,000 acres; it is entailed in the family of Count Trolle Wachtmeister. The chateau is of brick, surrounded by a moat, and in the midst of a very unpicturesque, flat country. The oldest part of the present structure was built in 1633, and a later addition in 1787. The mansion has nothing remarkable in its architecture.

Among its old family portraits is one of Count Wachtmeister, who was Minister to England in the time of Cromwell. The collection includes those of several kings of Sweden, presented by themselves. There are charming paintings, the work of the present countess, and one of the count, hanging upon the walls; the old clocks and spoils of the Thirty Years' War are full of interest.

Crossing the moat, one comes to the church, where, as usual, the males and females sit apart; the pew of the countess was on one side, and that of her husband on the other; but in no way different from those occupied by the people of the place. As in most of the old churches, this contained portraits of former pastors and their families, as a sort of memorial.   In the crypt below were coffins containing the remains of members of the family who died long ago.   Two of these coffins were made of brass or copper, and among the dates I saw that of 1679.   In a wooden casket I could see the shrivelled form of a woman; a few remnants of lace around the head and some dried flowers were all that remained to mark one of the wealthy and accomplished countesses of Wachtmeister.

In many of the old chateaux of Sweden are found curious articles which, in centuries past, when superstition was rife, were held as talismans.   The destruction of so many beautiful buildings by fire has taken place where these have been removed, that the people, without being actually credulous, keep them for good-luck.   Among the objects of curiosity shown me at Trolle Ljungby was a drinking-horn and a whistle, which had the following curious history attached to them: On the road to Christianstad not far from the chateau stands a boulder thirty feet long, twenty-four feet wide, and twenty feet in height, called Maglestone.   Tradition says that at the introduction of Christianity two giants resided here.   A church was built in Åhus,* and the giants living in the parish of Jemshög becoming exceedingly angry at this innovation, threw at it two huge stones, called Maglestone and Tippelstone, intending to destroy it; but they failed to hit the mark.   It was believed in olden times that the Trolls (witches) dwelt under this stone, and at Christmas-time raised it and supported it by pillars of gold, while they danced and feasted beneath its shadow, the peasants not daring to approach.

In the year 1490 Ljungby was in the possession of Lady Sidsela Ulfstand, who, hearing that the Trolls would hold their Christmas revel under Maglestone, asked her servants if any one was willing to try to find out what they did there,

---

* Åhus is situated on the coast a few miles from Ljungby.

promising to give as a reward her best horse and a suit of clothes. A stableman said he would try. Saddling a horse, he rode to Maglestone, and as he approached it he saw it was raised and supported by pillars of gold, resplendent with lights, and the Trolls, among whom was a Christian maid who had been made a prisoner by them, were merry. When he was discovered, two men came towards him, one with a horn the other with a whistle, and asked him to drink to the health of the mountain king, and to blow at each end of the whistle. The Christian maid whispered to him: "Don't drink, but ride back home full speed." So he threw the contents behind him, spilling a few drops on the hip of the horse, burning the animal, and with horn and whistle galloped back to Ljungby, pursued by the Trolls; but Lady Sidsela ordered the draw-bridge to be raised, for Trolls cannot cross the water or run over ruts and ploughed ground. The next day a deputation of the Trolls came to the castle and asked for the return of the horn and whistle, promising in exchange to make the family the richest in the land; but their entreaties were in vain, and they retired, leaving a curse, saying that her family should become extinct, and that every time the horn was removed Ljungby would be destroyed by fire. The stableman, who had escaped, died; three times the horn has been removed, and three times the place has been destroyed by fire; great misfortune has attended the descendants of Lady Sidsela Ulfstand, and none of them are left. So the prophecy of the Trolls has been fulfilled.

The drive from Sölvesborg to Ljungby gives to the stranger a poor idea of the fertility of the province of Skåne; the soil is in many places light and sandy, with large boulders near the sea; fields and patches of tobacco are numerous in this section. Tobacco is planted extensively in many parts of Sweden, especially in the southern provinces, and is seen even around Stockholm. That raised around Åhus, and near Christianstad, is highly prized by the Swedes, its good quality being attributed to the manuring of the land with sea-weed; and this cultivation has given a high value to that otherwise poor soil.

A few miles north of Trolle Ljungby is Lake Ifö, on the

eastern side of which is the farm of Hofgården ; the house is built over the crypt in which the Bishop of Lund, Andreas Suneson, lived while afflicted with leprosy, and is now used as a cellar.   Over the entrance is cut in the stone the year 1222.

On the shore are several chateaux, among them the castle of Beckaskog, a crown residence on the narrow tract of land which divides this lake from the Opmanna. This was a favorite summer residence of the late king, Charles XV. It was in former times a monastery for the Bernardine monks. Of the former monastery buildings the old church with a tower remains. The castle has a tower five stories high. The house is of brick, forming one side of a long square, flanked by low buildings, roofed with tiles, and used as barns and stables. Through the yard a little stream of clear water runs on its way to Lake Ifö. Beckaskog, by right the residence of the colonel of the regiment of Dragoons of Skåne, comprises about 1300 acres of land. The father of King Carl leased it from the colonel, and the lease continued under him. The apartments in the mansion had a cosy look, and were notable for taste and simplicity. In this quiet retreat King Carl passed a few weeks in the summer, and often received the farmers, talking and drinking beer with them. Among the horses I saw two superb Arab stallions. There are three national stud-farms in Sweden —at Strömsholm, near Westerås ; at Ottenby, in Öland ; and at Flyinge, in Skåne, whence the stallions are sent in summer to different parts of the country for the use of farmers who are desirous to improve their breed of horses. I was surprised to find clouds of mosquitoes, the first I had met in such numbers in the South.

From the park I could see Karsholm, a castle finely situated on the opposite shore of Lake Opmanna. This property belonged to a Danish gentleman, who had made a fortune in Norway, where he also owned quite a beautiful place on the Christiania fjord.

From Ljungby the highway continues along the coast, and at almost all times views or glimpses of the sea are obtained ; following that route, one passes numerous country-seats, often hidden from view, and comes now and then to a sea-town.

Åhus was formerly an important trading-place, and is mentioned in old writings as early as 1149.

For a long distance the spire of the church of Christianstad is seen, as the city lies in the midst of a flat and rich marshy country, on the shores of the Helge. This place has a population of 9000, and was founded by the Danish king, Christian IV., when Skåne was under Denmark, and was made a fortified town ; the fortifications have now been partly pulled down

ÅHUS CHURCH.

and replaced by pleasure-grounds. It is the residence of the governor of the province, and the seat of the Superior Court for the provinces of Skåne and Blekinge. A regiment of cavalry is always stationed here, and, as in many small garrison towns, the feeling of the civilians against the military is intense: such was the case when I visited the place. Duelling in the army is unknown in Sweden and Norway; public opinion regards this custom as a relic of a barbarous age. The church is a fine type of Renaissance architecture. The letter C and arms of King Christian are found in many places on the walls. The town is on the bank of the Helge Lake, and at its upper outlet. The lake is shallow, and extensive engineering works are now employed to drain it and turn it into fruitful land. The river has been deepened, and connects the city with the thriving port of Åhus.

Many fine estates are also found around Christianstad. About three miles from the city is Råbelöf, which covers an area of about 17,000 acres of land. Iron figures on one of the outside walls of the house show the time of its construction (1637), and the letters H. W. and F. M. W. give the initials of its former owners. In ancient times it had two towers, since destroyed by fire; almost everywhere these old country-seats have been partly burned at one time or another. Four avenues lined with trees lead from the house in different directions.

The host received me with great kindness. He was of Scotch descent, and spoke English remarkably well, also German and French. He had travelled all over Europe, and in Persia, Egypt, and Algeria. The baroness spoke French admirably.* I was surprised to see on the table of the parlor a number of *Harper's Magazine*. When I expressed my astonishment, my host took occasion to bestow great praise on that publication, which he said had maintained for years the same high standard of popular and interesting matter. I was glad to hear the encomiums awarded to my friends, and to see their periodical so well appreciated in this distant region.

The mansion was simply furnished; no old portraits or paintings adorned its walls, but everywhere was an air of comfort. The front of the house overlooked a large garden protected by a hedge, and redolent with flowers, a kitchen-garden, a small pond, numerous fruit-trees, a pavilion, while trees and shrubbery were abundant. On one side the carriage-way was an open gravelled space, near the ridge of which stood a large chestnut-tree with a seat. Through the trees we had a view of the lake; behind a little lawn there was a thick grove hiding a large barn, while other spacious buildings were close at hand. Several huge bee-hive-like piles of fire-wood, chiefly birch, cut or sawed, were drying; for wood is generally used

---

* In Sweden a titled woman marrying an untitled gentleman keeps her title added to the name of her husband.

in well-regulated houses only when it has been cut two or three years, as it burns better and makes a warmer fire. The windows of my room overlooked the garden, and at night I heard at times the horn of the watchman, whose duty it was to walk around the farm to guard it against fire. This custom is prevalent on all large estates in Sweden. The watchman is required to be on duty until 4 A.M., and then he sleeps until 1 P.M., and works afterwards. But even before the specified hour, at that time of the year, as the twilight fell, a boy appeared in the garden, making a loud noise with a wooden rattle, and this was followed now and then by the firing of guns. This is done to frighten the birds, which were exceedingly numerous. The bullfinch, thrush, sparrow, oriole, several varieties of warblers, and many other birds peopled the wood outside of the garden, and made sad havoc with the cherries. The cooing of the wild-pigeon was also heard.

This estate is charged with the support of 28 soldiers, each of whom has a cottage with four acres, which must be ploughed by the owner of the estate. Certain farms are rented upon the agreement by the tenant that he will work for a given number of days during each year on the property. Peat is supplied to all the laborers, this fuel being extensively used, for forests are scarce in the South. There are about 150 people employed by the year; during the busy season 400 or 500 extra hands are hired. The farm hands have a right to about half a gallon of sweet milk daily, together with an annual portion of thirty-two bushels of rye and barley, divided into equal parts; five more of potatoes; an allowance of ten kronor for meat and fish, and a certain amount of tobacco; besides, three measures of flax-seed, and land enough to plant it, so that each man can produce the material for his own linen. In summer each hand has beer, and the supply of fuel is sufficient for his use the whole year. The men are lodged free, and the unmarried man can save 100 kronor a year out of the 150 he receives. Besides the great number of servants employed (and every farm or estate seems to have a greater number than is required), the children of the farm hands, and the sick and the poor, are under careful supervision.

The laws concerning masters and servants are strict in Sweden. After engaging a servant, the employer gives a small amount of money—generally about three kronor—to seal the bargain; when this sum has been accepted, it cannot be returned, the contract thereby becoming irrevocable on either side. After engaging a servant, the employer cannot send him or her away until the time of the contract expires; if not satisfied, the master must endure, unless he can prove before a court of justice that the man he has engaged refuses to work. If sent away before the stipulated time, the servant can recover the full amount agreed upon, together with the equivalent of his board and lodging. In the same manner, should the servant run away, he is liable to a very heavy fine, and is compelled to return. This precision has a happy effect in securing good service for the employer, and kind treatment towards the employed.

The home life of the owners on many of these large estates is still primitive, in many respects resembling the mode of living in mediæval times. The stranger is impressed by the air of comfort perceptible among them. The landholders make at home almost everything they require. Industrious habits characterize every one, from the master and mistress of the house to the humblest servant. The larger the farm or estate, the more the mistress has to superintend in the household and its economy, and these duties are never regarded as a derogation from her dignity.

Near the mansion of Råbelöf is the Economy House (name given to a building where home industries are carried on), a granite structure, in one of the rooms of which there are three looms. An experienced weaver, a woman, is engaged by the year to superintend the work. As I entered she was occupied in weaving a beautiful large linen table-cloth, while one of her assistants was making a linen cover for a carpet, and a third was busy on coarse sheeting for the beds of the working hands. The flax and hemp were raised on the farm. There were also people employed in spinning wool, and weaving cloth and carpets—all the wool used in these fabrics being the product of the farm. The head woman-servant was paid 200 kronor a year; the other females receiving from 50 to 60 kronor each. There is also a brewery, where a woman made the beer, and, when not so engaged, employed herself in weaving. The hops were grown on the estate. A bakery also was supplied with home-made flour. The amount of winter provision necessary for the household had to be carefully attended to, in order not to run short; but the proceeds from the sale of the produce of the kitchen-garden and orchards were large, and furnished the pin-money for the wife, as is the case on many of the estates.

A short distance north-west from Christianstad is situated the estate of Araslöf, belonging to Count Hamilton. It is one of the largest in Skåne, and is divided into a great number of fertile and well-cultivated farms. About fourteen miles farther north is the estate of Wanås, with a fine old chateau dating from the year 1566. It is surrounded by gardens and woods. Among the remarkable paintings which it contains is *Ecce Homo*, by Guido Reni.

The sandy and monotonous region which surrounds Åhus gives place a few miles south to a landscape which in many respects can well compare with the most favored parts of Skåne. Maltesholm is one of the finest estates entailed in the De la Gardie family, whose armorial shields are seen in many churches and chateaux belonging to that name before the "reduction." The chateau dates only from about 1700. It is approached across a valley by a road 4650 feet long, often 24 above the ground, and in some places 35 feet wide. Farther south and near the sea is the estate and chateau of Widtsköfle, with its several towers—a fine old structure, surrounded by a moat, dating from 1533. Above the gate-way is a representation of the Trinity; it is surrounded by grounds, parks, and gardens, said to be among the finest in Skåne. South-west of Widtsköfle lies the princely castle of Kristinehof, entailed in the family of Count Piper.

Journeying down the coast, one comes to the port of Cimbrishamn, with a population of about 1800 inhabitants. At a short distance is the fishing-village of Kivik, where is seen the graves of the bronze age which I have described in Vol. I.

Near it is the parish of Jerrestad, one of the few places of
Skåne where the ancient costume is still in use among the

COSTUME OF JERRESTAD.

peasants. The men wear light yellow leather breeches, and
the women woollen outside garments of variegated colors, with
white skirts over the petticoats.

A few miles south-west, near the high-road, is the estate of
Glimminge, with a castle, one of the two left in Sweden in its
original state, showing the mode of building fortified houses
during mediæval times, and therefore one of the most remarkable, perhaps, in the country. It was built during the fourteenth century.

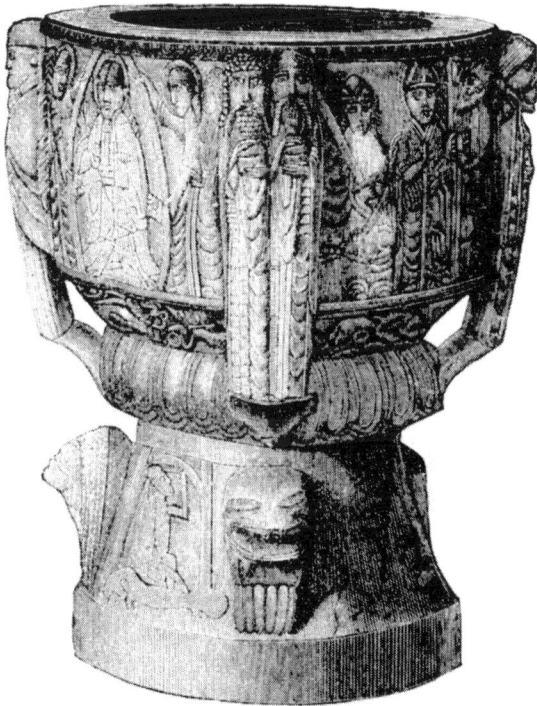

BAPTISMAL FONT OF STONE IN TRYDE CHURCH, SKÅNE.

Thirty miles south-west of Cimbrishamn is the town of
Ystad (lat. 55° 25'), with a population of nearly 7000. It has a
commodious harbor, and exports much grain, especially to England. There is a charming walk along the beach, a public garden, and a fine cemetery; there are two churches, one dating
from about 1200. The chalk cliffs of Denmark (isle of Möen)
are seen, looking very white in the dazzling sun. From Ystad
we have now entered Malmö län, the most thickly settled and

fertile part of Skåne, containing a population of 181 to the square mile. On its seaboard are several thriving corn-exporting towns.

Tosterup is eight miles from Ystad, with a castle and towers, from which a magnificent view is had over the surrounding plain and the Baltic. Among the chateaux in the neighborhood are Charlottenlund, with pleasure-park and gardens, from which there is an extensive view of the sea; Marvinsholm, built in 1644–48, with a moat spanned by a stone bridge; and Krageholm, the property of Count Piper, with its trees clipped to form rooms and passages. A few miles farther north another branch of the same family own the estates of Snogeholm and Söfdeborg, the latter with a chateau of the seventeenth century, decorated and furnished in the Netherland style of the sixteenth century: here are fine historical portraits, among them those of the Königsmark family, including that of the fair Aurora; the knight's hall was once of great magnificence, ornamented with copper sheets, which, when the wind struck them, made an æolian music. Farther north is Öfvedskloster, with a very fine chateau and a grand forest, in which roam a peculiar breed of milk-white deer, of which there are only two or three herds in Sweden. In a more westerly direction from Ystad is Svaneholm, on an island in the beautiful Svanesjö, besides a number of other estates.

From the roads, winding their tortuous ways along the shores of southern and western Scania, the eye, wandering across the water, sees the coast of Denmark, a kingdom inhabited by a race worthy of their ancestors of old. Looking at that land, the memory of the daring and mighty deeds of their forefathers came back vividly to my mind; the brilliant record of their great past, with the grand results which followed the outgrowth of their tremendous energy, as seen in the great empires which have risen and inherited their blood, appeared in a panorama of majestic outlines. History unfolded itself. Uncovering my head reverently, I exclaimed, Land of the Danes! Scandinavian country! ancient home of Vikings! I salute thee! and equally with thy twin sisters, Sweden and Norway, I wish thee happiness and prosperity!

CHAPTER XL.

A flat, low Coast.—Skanör and Falsterbo.—Their Antiquity.—Malmö.—City Hall of Malmö.—Guilds in Northern Europe.—Malmö Castle.—Landskrona.—The Island of Hven.—Birthplace of Tycho Brahe.—Helsingborg.—A Beautiful Neighborhood.—Castles, Chateaux.—The Coal-mines of Höganäs.—The University Town of Lund.—Cathedral of St. Lars.—Estates around Lund.—Örtofta.—Skarhult.—Löberöd.—Trollenäs.—Trollcholm.—The Promontory of Kullen.—A Fine View.—Leaving Scandinavia.—Farewell.

FROM the dangerous Sandhammar reef, some seventeen miles east of Ystad, the low coast of Skåne runs east and west for about seventy miles. At the fishing-village of Smygge (lat. 55° 20′), the most southerly point of Sweden is reached. Here the sun rises on June 23d at 3.18 A.M., and sets at 8.46 P.M.; on September 23d it rises at 5.49 A.M., and sets at 5.55 P.M.; while on the shortest day, December 23d, it rises at 8.31 A.M., and sets at 3.27 P.M. What a contrast between this southern shore of the peninsula and the northern! Here fruitful fields, orchards, and hamlets embosomed in trees; there a stern, dark, rocky coast, terminating in the weird North Cape. Trelleborg (lat. 55° 22′) is the most southerly town of Sweden, with a population of 2100. In the midst of two clumps of trees are seen two spires: these belong to the churches of the old towns of Skanör and Falsterbo, once rich and powerful, but now insignificant villages; the first having a population of 750, and the second, of 300. They have a common cemetery, burgomaster, and poor-house. There is neither druggist nor doctor, and sometimes a year or two passes without a death. For more than a generation not a person has been imprisoned even for the most trivial offence. The people are temperate; they do not allow a liquor-shop in their midst. A more primitive community can hardly be found; but, like the rest of their countrymen, they indulge in innocent recreations on Sunday afternoons. Both places flourished in the beginning of the Christian era, and their fairs once were among the most popular in Scandinavia. Hollanders and merchants of the Hanseatic League owned large establishments. The herring-fisheries were very extensive, the shoals said to be often so thick that the boats could hardly row among them; but the fish have disappeared. Their ports were deep and safe; Falsterbo, especially, had a magnificent harbor, but in 1631 a furious tempest swept the sand from the downs and shores, and filled it, covering, besides, the fertile lands around: dangerous reefs now line the coast.

CHURCH OF SKANÖR.

Most of the male population is a seafaring one; their sailors are considered among the best in Skåne, and many men have their homes here. The church of Skanör is an interesting old edifice, possessing among its relics an ancient stone font, with the effigies of a number of kings, among them St. Olaf. From Falsterbo the coast trends north, and forms with the Danish shores the Öresund Sound, where, for a distance of about seventy miles, a charming panorama greets the eye.

Some fifteen miles from Skanör, nearly opposite Copenhagen, is the city of Malmö, in lat. 55° 36', with a population
of 36,000. It is one of the most flourishing towns of Scandinavia, exporting annually great quantities of grain and spirits.

INTERIOR OF SKANÖR CHURCH.

It is the largest city in Southern Sweden, and is rising in importance yearly by the extension of its commerce and man-

ufactures. It contains a cotton-mill, a machine shop, a glove factory, and other industrial establishments. It was known in 1259 under the name of Malmenhauge; its fortifications were finished in 1434. The Church of St. Peter, founded in 1319, and rebuilt in 1847–53, is worth a visit, its transepts being extremely beautiful and light in form. It is in pure pointed-arch style, and was founded in 1319: in this church the Lutheran confession was first promulgated. The Rådhus (City Hall) was built in 1546, and renovated in 1867–69, in Renaissance style. It is remarkable not only for its handsome exterior but for its magnificent festival hall, the so-called Knutshall (Canute's Hall), in which formerly the St. Knut Guild held its meetings: this is 100 feet long, 19 wide, and 12 high. The St. Knut Guild was a powerful society, every member of which was equal to six witnesses before a court of justice. These guilds were exceedingly popular in Northern Europe, and were numerous. Wisby, as has already been said, possessed many of them, each under a patron saint; but religion comprised a very small part of the system under which they were established, conviviality being apparently the chief object of their members. The beautiful drinking-cups of the order, preserved in Malmö, furnish evidence on this point. The ancient guild of St. Knut was founded in 1100, and the branch in Malmö dates from about 1360. The regulations of the brotherhood bound its members to help one another. When a brother was to appear before the king, a court of justice, or a bishop, twelve of his fellows accompanied him, armed to the teeth, and did not leave him until he was safe. If one of their number killed a man, all were bound to aid him in his flight, providing him with a horse or other means of escape; for in those days the taking of human life for revenge was not considered disgraceful, and in nothing, perhaps, has greater progress been made than in the protection of life. Kings, princes, and princesses who loved the pleasure of the table and convivial life joined these fraternities.

Malmö Castle, dating from 1537, serves at present as barracks for the garrison of the town, and as a prison. In the castle Count Bothwell, the third husband of Mary Stuart, was kept a prisoner. Towards the end of the sixteenth century the herring-fishery, once a source of great profit, fell off. After the terrible plague which swept over the country Malmö rapidly dwindled. At the end of the seventeenth century the town numbered only 2000 inhabitants, but it is again rising fast into prosperity.

The surroundings of Malmö are flat and bare of trees, but, like the greater part of Southern Skåne, very fertile. There are no large estates in its immediate neighborhood, and the farms, as a general rule, are small. But a few miles south-east are a number of estates, among them Torup, a chateau surrounded by a moat, with its pinnacled gables, and solid round and octagonal watch-towers, which have stood the blasts of over three centuries; it lies in a meadow encompassed by beech woods. Börringekloster, Skabersjö, and many others are found in that vicinity.

North of Malmö is the town of Landskrona, founded in 1413 by King Erik XIII., with a population of nearly 9000 inhabitants. The harbor is good; the manufacture of beet-sugar is carried on here. The fort, built in 1543, surrounded by a moat, still remains, and is now used as a prison for criminals under long sentence. These are constantly employed, and a careful register of their conduct is kept. A few miles north of the city, in the sound, is the island of Hven, where the renowned astronomer Tycho Brahe lived; but few traces remain of his princely castle, Uranienborg, and observatory of Stelleborg. About fourteen miles north-east of Landskrona lies the estate of Knutstorp, remarkable as the birthplace of Tycho Brahe.

Continuing the sail, one comes to Helsingborg, with a population of 9000, in the narrowest part of the Öresund, which here has a width of about three miles. The harbor is fine, and the town flourishing. In olden times, like other cities of the southern peninsula, it was an important trading mart, but has gradually deteriorated. The old town was situated where the tower of Kärnan still stands; but, after a great fire in 1425, it was rebuilt on the present site. Three miles south-east of Helsingborg, in an exceedingly pretty neighborhood, is the mineral spring of Ramlösa. The spring issues from a sandstone rock about eighteen feet high, and is efficacious in the cure of many diseases. The place has a beautiful park, and offers from several points very fine views.

About four miles from the city is the new palace of Sofiero, the summer residence of the present queen. The view over the sound is magnificent. About two miles beyond one comes to the fine estate of Kulla-Gunnarstorp, belonging to Baron Platen, with an old castle erected in 1562, and a new one which is one of the most valuable and beautiful of Sweden. Farther on is the estate of Wrams Gunnarstorp, with considerable forest, and surrounded by a beautiful country. Following the coast northward, about fifteen miles from Helsingborg are the coal-mines of Höganäs, which were worked as early as 1650, and which now have a depth of 320 feet. The coal in quality is inferior to the English. The mine also yields fire-clays, from which bricks and stoneware are manufactured: the works form quite a little town. Here one sees the same thoughtful care, met everywhere in Sweden, of the employers towards their workingmen. Everything is done to elevate them; their houses are clean and healthy; a public garden has been made for their benefit, and the miners and their families are contented and happy; schools for them are not forgotten, and there is also a church.

Ten miles north-east of Malmö, on the line of railway to Stockholm, is the city of Lund, formerly called Lunden, "the grove," and Londinum Gothorum — the only inland city of Skåne except Christianstad: this place is said to have had 200,000 inhabitants. There is an old saying that when Christ was born Skanör and Lund were already in harvest, meaning that they were already prosperous. About the year 900 it is mentioned as rich and fortified. It is situated in a fertile plain, on the little river Höjeå, which formerly was navigable for large vessels; during Viking times their fleets sailed up to the town. In 1048 it received its first bishop, Henrik, under whom the cathedral was commenced; in 1107 it became the seat of the first archbishop, Asker, who was primate of the North. Lund was then called *Metropolis Daniæ*, and was the place of residence and coronation of many kings. After the mediæval age it began to decline rapidly, so that when acquired by the Swedes, in 1652, it was little more than a village. It soon after began to rise again; in 1668 a university was inaugurated there, and at present the city is constantly advancing. Here are the principal hospitals of Skåne, the numerous university buildings, many lower schools, and an institute for the deaf and dumb. This old university town has now a population of nearly 12,000. The chief building of interest is the Cathedral of St. Lars, 271 feet long and 72 high, in the shape of a cross, of pure round-arched style, with two towers formerly surmounted by high spires; it was inaugurated in 1145. The inner perspective of the church is very fine, which is probably caused by its being wider at the west end than at the east; besides which, the floor imperceptibly rises from the sides towards the middle about a foot and a half. The chancel is the most beautiful and majestic part of the church, with its open rows of pillars and its pinnacles symbolizing the thorn-crown of Christ. The inner vault of the structure rests on 18 pillars, in two rows. The pulpit and altar ornaments are of the mediæval age, and are quite valuable. Perhaps more remarkable than the church itself is the crypt, extending under the entire chancel, with a length of 126 feet, 36 in width and 14 in height. It is lighted by 10 windows, and is supported by 24 pillars; it is one of the largest crypts in the world. The university has a fine library, and an historical museum of Northern antiquities.

The country around Lund is rich in fine estates with old chateaux. On the line of the railroad, about six miles distant, is the castle of Örtofta, on the bank of the Brå River. It was built at the beginning of the sixteenth century, and in public documents the estate is mentioned as early as 1381. Many historical memories are connected with it. Örtofta was the only property in Skåne whose owner had birkerätt, *i. e.*, full jurisdiction over his dependents and subordinates, and the right to all fines; he was free from taxes, but instead had to maintain a court-house and a place of execution: this right was in force as late as the seventeenth century. The estate belongs

to Count Dücker. Around Örtofta are found several grave-
mounds, and near it is the estate of Hviderup, with a castle
built in the sixteenth century: this has for nearly 250 years
belonged to the baronial family of Ramel. South-east of Lund,
between Lund and Ystad, is Dalby Church, formerly a monastery; under the tower is a crypt like that of Lund; in the
church lies buried the Danish king, Harold Heine, who died
in 1080.

ÖRTOFTA.

Skarhult is a good specimen of the architecture of the fourteenth century, with lofty towers, pitched roofs, and peculiar
chimneys; above the archway of the main court, and between
two sculptured coats of arms, is the date (1562) when it was
completed. Not far from Skarhult is the large estate of Löberöd, with a castle, from which in clear weather one can see
across the Skåne plain and the Sound to Copenhagen. The
estate is entailed in the De la Gardie family, which is of

French extraction, and whose history is full of romance. Few places in the country contain more objects of historical interest than Löberöd; they are chiefly trophies of the Thirty Years' War, including cabinets filled with treasure, old furniture, and paintings of the Dutch and Flemish schools.

Trollenäs, with a large mansion erected in 1559 by Tage Tott, was formerly called Näs, and has always belonged to the families of Tott and Trolle, in which latter it is now entailed. It has very fine parks and gardens, and traces of the former fortifications are still seen. Charles XI. had his headquarters here in April, 1677. Trolleholm, about twenty miles north of Lund, is a large estate, comprising nearly 22,000 acres. The castle has four towers, and is surrounded by a moat with two stone bridges; the garden is large and fine.

Near and on the shores of the pretty Ringsjö are situated many fine estates with old chateaux: among these are Bosjökloster, Fulltofta, and Ousbyholm. The first is very old, and formerly was a nunnery: on this estate is found one of the largest trees in Sweden, an oak measuring forty feet in circumference near the root.

One of the most picturesque places in Skåne is the promontory of Kullen, extending into the Öresund, and the most north-western point of the province. Its extremity was formerly an island, separated from the main-land by a creek. The promontory is composed of several steep granite hills, rising like an amphitheatre, the highest being more than 600 feet above the sea: on this point is a light-house. At the base of the mountains on the north side near the sea is the Trollhålet (the witch-hole), a grotto about 100 feet deep. To one who has been wandering through level and monotonous plains, and along the flat shores of Skåne, great, indeed, is the change to this promontory. From the highest point of Kullen the scenery is charming and the view extensive, including the shores of Skeldervik, with its fishing hamlets and farms, green hills clad with beech and oak, and fertile meadows— the Cattegat, and beyond the Öresund, whose shores are lost in the distance—the coast of Jutland, with Kroneborg and Helsingör. Among the castles in its neighborhood are Krapperup, with its towers and ramparts, park and garden; Vege-holm, built in 1530 on the island of that name, whose fortifications have disappeared.

As I stood upon the heights of Kullen, how beautiful was the scene! Not a ripple disturbed the sea; the sun, gorgeously red, was sinking slowly below the horizon. How calm was that summer evening on the Cattegat, where in olden times the Viking fleets sailed on their voyages for conquest and plunder! As night advanced, the outlines of the coast became dimmer, and at last were lost in darkness, but with here and there a bright light to guide the mariner.

Though I have left much unsaid, I must close these volumes. Farewell, Scandinavia—Land of the Midnight Sun! I have wandered over thy country from north to south; I have seen thy gay cities and quiet villages, thy fruitful farms, thy humble cottages; I have sailed upon thy fjords and lakes; I have wended my way in the midst of thy beautiful valleys and dales; I have clambered over thy majestic mountains; I have gazed with awe and wonder upon thy noble glaciers; I have stood upon thy grand and rugged coasts and watched the storm-tossed sea as it dashed with fury upon thy shores.

Never shall I forget the kindness and hospitality of thy people. The lofty and the lowly—king and peasant—have united to welcome the stranger who landed among them. The many happy days spent among thy good and noble people will never be forgotten. The memory of the dear friends who have been so kind to me will always be cherished.

INDEX.

THE END.

LONDON: PRINTED BY WILLIAM CLOWES AND SONS, LIMITED, STAMFORD STREET
AND CHARING CROSS.

50, ALBEMARLE STREET, LONDON.
October, 1881.

MR. MURRAY'S

GENERAL LIST OF WORKS.

ALBERT MEMORIAL. A Descriptive and Illustrated Account of the National Monument erected to the PRINCE CONSORT at Kensington. Illustrated by Engravings of its Architecture, Decorations, Sculptured Groups, Statues, Mosaics, Metalwork &c. With Descriptive Text. By DOYNE C. BELL. With 24 Plates. Folio. 12*l*. 12*s*.

——— HANDBOOK TO. Post 8vo. 1*s*.; or Illustrated Edition, 2*s*. 6*d*.

——— ——— (PRINCE) SPEECHES AND ADDRESSES. Fcap. 8vo. 1*s*.

ABBOTT (REV. J.). Memoirs of a Church of England Missionary in the North American Colonies. Post 8vo. 2*s*.

ABERCROMBIE (JOHN). Enquiries concerning the Intellectual Powers and the Investigation of Truth. Fcap. 8vo. 3*s*. 6*d*.

ACLAND (REV. CHARLES). Popular Account of the Manners and Customs of India. Post 8vo. 2*s*.

ÆSOP'S FABLES. A New Version. By Rev. THOMAS JAMES. With 100 Woodcuts, by TENNIEL and WOLF. Post 8vo. 2*s*. 6*d*.

AGRICULTURAL (ROYAL) JOURNAL. *(Published half-yearly.)*

AMBER-WITCH (THE). A most interesting Trial for Witchcraft. Translated by LADY DUFF GORDON. Post 8vo. 2*s*.

APOCRYPHA: With a Commentary Explanatory and Critical, by various Writers. Edited by REV. HENRY WACE. 2 Vols. Medium 8vo.   [*In the Press.*

ARISTOTLE. [See GROTE, HATCH.]

ARMY LIST (THE). *Published Monthly by Authority.*

——— ——— (THE NEW OFFICIAL). *Published Quarterly.* Royal 8vo. 15*s*.

ARTHUR'S (LITTLE) History of England. By LADY CALLCOTT. *New Edition, continued to* 1872. With 36 Woodcuts. Fcap. 8vo. 1*s*. 6*d*.

ATKINSON (DR. R.) Vie de Seint Auban. A Poem in Norman-French. Ascribed to MATTHEW PARIS. With Concordance, Glossary and Notes. Small 4to. 10*s*. 6*d*.

AUSTIN (JOHN). LECTURES ON GENERAL JURISPRUDENCE; or, the Philosophy of Positive Law. Edited by ROBERT CAMPBELL. 2 Vols. 8vo. 32*s*.

——— STUDENT'S EDITION, compiled from the above work, by ROBERT CAMPBELL. Post 8vo. 12*s*.

——— Analysis of. By GORDON CAMPBELL. Post 8vo. 6*s*.

B

ADMIRALTY PUBLICATIONS; Issued by direction of the Lords
  Commissioners of the Admiralty:—
  CHALLENGER EXPEDITION, 1873—1876 : Report of the Scientific
    Results of. Zoology. Vol. I. 37s. 6d. Vol. II. 50s.
  A MANUAL OF SCIENTIFIC ENQUIRY, for the Use of Travellers.
    Fourth Edition. Edited by ROBERT MAIN, M.A. Woodcuts. Post
    8vo. 3s. 6d.
  GREENWICH ASTRONOMICAL OBSERVATIONS, 1841 to 1847,
    and 1847 to 1877. Royal 4to. 20s. each.
  GREENWICH ASTRONOMICAL RESULTS, 1847 to 1877. 4to. 3s.
    each.
  MAGNETICAL AND METEOROLOGICAL OBSERVATIONS, 1844
    to 1877. Royal 4to. 20s. each.
  MAGNETICAL AND METEOROLOGICAL RESULTS, 1848 to 1877.
    4to. 3s. each.
  APPENDICES TO OBSERVATIONS.
    1837. Logarithms of Sines and Cosines in Time. 3s.
    1842. Catalogue of 1439 Stars, from Observations made in 1836.
        1841. 4s.
    1845. Longitude of Valentia (Chronometrical). 3s.
    1847. Description of Altazimuth. 3s.
        Description of Photographic Apparatus. 2s.
    1851. Maskelyne's Ledger of Stars. 3s.
    1852. I. Description of the Transit Circle. 3s.
    1853. Bessel's Refraction Tables. 3s.
    1854. I. Description of the Reflex Zenith Tube. 3s.
        II. Six Years' Catalogue of Stars, from Observations. 1848
        to 1853. 4s.
    1860. Reduction of Deep Thermometer Observations. 2s.
    1862. II. Plan of Ground and Buildings of Royal Observatory,
        Greenwich. 3s.
        III. Longitude of Valentia (Galvanic). 2s.
    1864. I. Moon's Semi-diameter, from Occultations. 2s.
        II. Reductions of Planetary Observations. 1831 to 1835. 2s.
    1868. I. Corrections of Elements of Jupiter and Saturn. 2s.
        II. Second Seven Years' Catalogue of 2760 Stars. 1861-7. 4s.
        III. Description of the Great Equatorial. 3s.
    1871. Water Telescope. 3s.
    1873. Regulations of the Royal Observatory. 2s.
    1876. II. Nine Years' Catalogue of 2263 Stars. (1861-67.) 4s.
    Cape of Good Hope Observations (Star Ledgers) : 1856 to 1863. 2s.
    ———— —   —— 1856. 5s.
    ———————— Astronomical Results. 1857 to 1858. 5s.
    Cape Catalogue of 1159 Stars, reduced to the Epoch 1860. 3s.
    Cape of Good Hope Astronomical Results. 1859 to 1860. 5s.
    ——————————————————— 1871 to 1873. 5s.
    ——————   1874 to 1876. 5s. each.
    Report on Teneriffe Astronomical Experiment. 1856. 5s.
    Paramatta Catalogue of 7385 Stars. 1822 to 1826. 4s.
  REDUCTION OF THE OBSERVATIONS OF PLANETS. 1750 to
    1830. Royal 4to. 20s. each.
    ——————————————— LUNAR OBSERVATIONS. 1750
    to 1830. 2 Vols. Royal 4to. 20s. each.
    ——————————— 1831 to 1851. 4to. 10s. each.
    —————— GREENWICH METEOROLOGICAL OBSERVA-
    TIONS. Chiefly 1847 to 1873. 5s.
  ARCTIC PAPERS. 13s. 6d.
  BERNOULLI'S SEXCENTENARY TABLE. 1779. 4to. 5s.
  BESSEL'S AUXILIARY TABLES FOR HIS METHOD OF CLEAR-
    ING LUNAR DISTANCES. 8vo. 2s.
  ENCKE'S BERLINER JAHRBUCH, for 1830. *Berlin*, 1828. 8vo. 9s.
  HANNYNGTON'S HAVERSINES.
  HANSEN'S TABLES DE LA LUNE. 4to. 20s.
  LAX'S TABLES FOR FINDING THE LATITUDE AND LONGI-
    TUDE. 1821. 8vo. 10s.

ADMIRALTY PUBLICATIONS—*continued.*

LUNAR OBSERVATIONS at GREENWICH. 1783 to 1819. Compared with the Tables, 1821. 4to. 7s. 6d.

MACLEAR ON LACAILLE'S ARC OF MERIDIAN. 2 Vols. 20s. each.

MAYER'S DISTANCES of the MOON'S CENTRE from the PLANETS. 1822, 3s.; 1823, 4s. 6d. 1824 to 1835. 8vo. 4s. each.

MAYER'S TABULÆ MOTUUM SOLIS ET LUNÆ. 1770. 5s.

———— ASTRONOMICAL OBSERVATIONS MADE AT GÖTTINGEN, from 1756 to 1761. 1826. Folio. 7s. 6d.

NAUTICAL ALMANACS, from 1767 to 1884. 2s. 6d. each.

———————————— SELECTIONS FROM, up to 1812. 8vo. 5s. 1834-54. 5s.

———————————— SUPPLEMENTS, 1828 to 1833, 1837 and 1838. 2s. each.

———————————— TABLE requisite to be used with the N.A. 1781. 8vo. 5s.

SABINE'S PENDULUM EXPERIMENTS to DETERMINE THE FIGURE OF THE EARTH. 1825. 4to. 40s.

SHEPHERD'S TABLES for CORRECTING LUNAR DISTANCES. 1772. Royal 4to. 21s.

———————————— TABLES, GENERAL, of the MOON'S DISTANCE from the SUN, and 10 STARS. 1787. Folio. 5s. 6d.

TAYLOR'S SEXAGESIMAL TABLE. 1780. 4to. 15s.

———————————— TABLES OF LOGARITHMS. 4to. 60s.

TIARK'S ASTRONOMICAL OBSERVATIONS tor the LONGITUDE of MADEIRA. 1822. 4to. 5s.

———————————— CHRONOMETRICAL OBSERVATIONS for DIFFERENCES of LONGITUDE between DOVER, PORTSMOUTH, and FALMOUTH. 1823. 4to. 5s.

VENUS and JUPITER: OBSERVATIONS of, compared with the TABLES. London, 1822. 4to. 2s.

WALES AND BAYLY'S ASTRONOMICAL OBSERVATIONS. 1777. 4to. 21s.

———————————— REDUCTION OF ASTRONOMICAL OBSERVATIONS MADE IN THE SOUTHERN HEMISPHERE. 1764—1771. 1788. 4to. 10s. 6d.

BARBAULD (MRS.). Hymns in Prose for Children. With 100 Illustrations. 16mo. 3s. 6d.

BARCLAY (BISHOP). Selected Extracts from the Talmud, illustrating the Teaching of the Bible. With an Introduction. 8vo. 14s.

BARKLEY (H. C.). Five Years among the Bulgarians and Turks between the Danube and the Black Sea. Post 8vo. 10s. 6d.

— ———   —   Bulgaria Before the War ; during a Seven Years' Experience of European Turkey and its Inhabitants. Post 8vo. 10s. 6d.

———————————— My Boyhood : a True Story. Illustrations. Post 8vo. 6s.

BARROW (JOHN). Life, Exploits, and Voyages of Sir Francis Drake. Post 8vo. 2s.

BARRY (CANON). The Manifold Witness for Christ. An Attempt to Exhibit the Combined Force of various Evidences, Direct and Indirect, of Christianity. 8vo. 12s.

———————————— (EDW.), R.A. Lectures on Architecture, delivered before the Royal Academy. With Memoir and Illustrations. 8vo.

BATES (H. W.). Records of a Naturalist on the Amazons during Eleven Years' Adventure and Travel. Illustrations. Post 8vo. 7s. 6d.

BAX (CAPT.). Russian Tartary, Eastern Siberia, China, Japan, &c. Illustrations. Cr. 8vo. 12s.

BELCHER (LADY). Account of the Mutineers of the 'Bounty,' and their Descendants; with their Settlements in Pitcairn and Norfolk Islands. Illustrations. Post 8vo. 12s.

BELL (Sir Chas.). Familiar Letters. Portrait. Post 8vo. 12s.

———— (Doyne C.). Notices of the Historic Persons buried in the Chapel of St. Peter ad Vincula, in the Tower of London, with an account of the discovery of the supposed remains of Queen Anne Boleyn. With Illustrations. Crown 8vo. 14s.

BERTRAM (Jas. G.). Harvest of the Sea: an Account of British Food Fishes, including Fisheries and Fisher Folk. Illustrations. Post 8vo. 9s.

BIBLE COMMENTARY. The Old Testament. Explanatory and Critical. With a Revision of the Translation. By BISHOPS and CLERGY of the ANGLICAN CHURCH. Edited by F. C. Cook, M.A., Canon of Exeter. 6 Vols. Medium 8vo. 6l. 15s.

Vol. I. 30s.	Genesis. Exodus. Leviticus. Numbers. Deuteronomy.	Vol. IV. 24s.	Job. Psalms. Proverbs. Ecclesiastes. Song of Solomon.
Vols. II. and III. 36s.	Joshua, Judges, Ruth, Samuel, Kings, Chronicles, Ezra, Nehemiah, Esther.	Vol. V. 20s.	Isaiah. Jeremiah.
		Vol. VI. 25s.	Ezekiel. Daniel. Minor Prophets.

BIBLE COMMENTARY. The New Testament. 4 Vols. Medium 8vo.

| Vol. I. 18s. | Introduction. St. Matthew. St. Mark. St. Luke. | Vol. III. | Romans, Corinthians, Galatians, Philippians, Ephesians, Colossians, Thessalonians, Pastoral Epistles, Philemon. |
| Vol. II. 20s. | St. John. Acts. | Vol. IV. | Hebrews, St. James, St. Peter, St. John, St. Jude, Revelation. |

———— The Student's Edition. Abridged and Edited by John M. Fuller, M.A., Vicar of Bexley. (To be completed in 6 Volumes.) Vols. I. to IV. Crown 8vo. 7s. 6d. each.

BIGG-WITHER (T. P.). Pioneering in South Brazil; Three Years of Forest and Prairie Life in the Province of Parana. Map and Illustrations. 2 vols. Crown 8vo. 24s.

BIRD (Isabella). Hawaiian Archipelago; or Six Months among the Palm Groves, Coral Reefs, and Volcanoes of the Sandwich Islands. Illustrations. Crown 8vo. 7s. 6d.

———— Unbeaten Tracks in Japan: Travels of a Lady in the interior, including Visits to the Aborigines of Yezo and the Shrines of Nikko and Ise. Illustrations. 2 Vols. Crown 8vo. 24s.

———— A Lady's Life in the Rocky Mountains. Illustrations. Post 8vo.

BISSET (Sir John). Sport and War in South Africa from 1834 to 1867, with a Narrative of the Duke of Edinburgh's Visit. Illustrations. Crown 8vo. 14s.

BLUNT (Lady Anne). The Bedouins of the Euphrates Valley. With some account of the Arabs and their Horses. Illustrations. 2 Vols. Crown 8vo. 24s.

———— A Pilgrimage to Nejd, the Cradle of the Arab Race, and a Visit to the Court of the Arab Emir. Illustrations. 2 Vols. Post 8vo. 24s

BLUNT (Rev. J. J.). Undesigned Coincidences in the Writings of the Old and New Testaments, an Argument of their Veracity. Post 8vo. 6s.

———— History of the Christian Church in the First Three Centuries. Post 8vo. 6s.

———— Parish Priest; His Duties, Acquirements, and Obligations. Post 8vo. 6s.

———— University Sermons. Post 8vo. 6s.

BOOK OF COMMON PRAYER. Illustrated with Coloured Borders, Initial Letters, and Woodcuts. 8vo. 18s.

BORROW (George). Bible in Spain; or the Journeys, Adventures, and Imprisonments of an Englishman in an Attempt to circulate the Scriptures in the Peninsula. Post 8vo. 5s.

———— Gypsies of Spain : their Manners, Customs, Religion, and Language. With Portrait. Post 8vo. 5s.

———— Lavengro ; The Scholar—The Gypsy—and the Priest. Post 8vo. 5s.

———— Romany Rye—a Sequel to "Lavengro." Post 8vo. 5s.

———— Wild Wales : its People, Language, and Scenery. Post 8vo. 5s.

———— Romano Lavo-Lil ; Word-Book of the Romany, or English Gypsy Language; with Specimens of their Poetry, and an account of certain Gypsyries. Post 8vo. 10s. 6d.

BOSWELL'S Life of Samuel Johnson, LL.D. Including the Tour to the Hebrides. Edited by Mr. Croker. *Seventh Edition.* Portraits. 1 vol. Medium 8vo. 12s.

BRACE (C. L.). Manual of Ethnology; or the Races of the Old World. Post 8vo. 6s.

BREWER (Rev. J. S.). English Studies, or Essays on English History and Literature. 8vo. 14s Contents : –

New Sources of English History.	The Stuarts.
Green's Short History of the English People.	Shakspeare.
Royal Supremacy.	Study of History and English History.
Hatfield House.	Ancient London.

BRITISH ASSOCIATION REPORTS. 8vo.

York and Oxford, 1831-32, 13s. 6d.	Dublin, 1857, 15s.
Cambridge, 1833, 12s.	Leeds, 1858. 20s.
Edinburgh, 1834, 15s.	Aberdeen, 1859, 15s.
Dublin, 1835, 13s. 6d.	Oxford, 1860, 25s.
Bristol, 1836, 12s.	Manchester, 1861, 15s.
Liverpool, 1837, 16s. 6d.	Cambridge, 1862, 20s.
Newcastle, 1838, 15s.	Newcastle, 1863, 25s.
Birmingham, 1839, 13s. 6d.	Bath, 1864, 18s.
Glasgow, 1840, 15s.	Birmingham, 1865. 25s.
Plymouth, 1841, 13s. 6d.	Nottingham. 1866, 24s.
Manchester, 1842, 10s. 6d.	Dundee, 1867, 26s.
Cork, 1843, 12s.	Norwich, 1868, 25s.
York, 1844, 20s.	Exeter, 1869, 22s.
Cambridge, 1845, 12s.	Liverpool, 1870, 18s.
Southampton, 1846, 15s.	Edinburgh, 1871, 16s.
Oxford, 1847, 18s.	Brighton, 1872. 24s.
Swansea, 1848, 9s.	Bradford, 1873, 25s.
Birmingham, 1849, 10s.	Belfast, 1874, 25s.
Edinburgh, 1850, 15s.	Bristol, 1875, 25s.
Ipswich, 1851, 16s. 6d.	Glasgow. 1876, 25s.
Belfast, 1852, 15s.	Plymouth, 1877. 24s.
Hull, 1853, 10s. 6d.	Dublin, 1878, 24s.
Liverpool, 1854, 18s.	Sheffield, 1879, 24s.
Glasgow, 1855. 15s.	Swansea, 1880, 24s.
Cheltenham, 1856, 18s.	

BRUGSCH (Professor). A History of Egypt, under the Pharaohs. Derived entirely from Monuments, with a Memoir on the Exodus of the Israelites. Translated by Philip Smith, B.A. 2nd Edition. Maps. 2 vols. 8vo. 32s.

BUNBURY (E. H.). A History of Ancient Geography, among the Greeks and Romans, from the Earliest Ages till the Fall of the Roman Empire. With Index and 20 Maps. 2 Vols. 8vo. 42s.

BURBIDGE (F. W.). The Gardens of the Sun: or A Naturalist's Journal on the Mountains and in the Forests and Swamps of Borneo and the Sulu Archipelago. With Illustrations. Crown 8vo. 14s.

BURCKHARDT'S Cicerone; or Art Guide to Painting in Italy. Translated from the German by Mrs. A. Clough. New Edition, revised by J. A. Crowe. Post 8vo. 6s.

BURN (Col.). Dictionary of Naval and Military Technical Terms, English and French—French and English. Crown 8vo. 15s.

BUTTMANN'S Lexilogus; a Critical Examination of the Meaning of numerous Greek Words, chiefly in Homer and Hesiod. By Rev. J. R. Fishlake. 8vo. 12s.

BUXTON (Charles). Memoirs of Sir Thomas Fowell Buxton, Bart. Portrait. 8vo. 16s. *Popular Edition.* Fcap. 8vo. 5s.

———— (Sydney C.). A Handbook to the Political Questions of the Day; with the Arguments on Either Side. 8vo. 5s.

BYLES (Sir John). Foundations of Religion in the Mind and Heart of Man. Post 8vo. 6s.

BYRON'S (Lord) LIFE AND WORKS :—

LIFE, LETTERS, AND JOURNALS. By Thomas Moore. *Cabinet Edition.* Plates. 6 Vols. Fcap. 8vo. 18s.; or One Volume, Portraits. Royal 8vo., 7s. 6d.

LIFE AND POETICAL WORKS. *Popular Edition.* Portraits. 2 vols. Royal 8vo. 15s.

POETICAL WORKS. *Library Edition.* Portrait. 6 Vols. 8vo. 45s.

POETICAL WORKS. *Cabinet Edition.* Plates. 10 Vols. 12mo. 30s.

POETICAL WORKS. *Pocket Ed.* 8 Vols. 16mo. In a case. 21s.

POETICAL WORKS. *Popular Edition.* Plates. Royal 8vo. 7s. 6d.

POETICAL WORKS. *Pearl Edition.* Crown 8vo. 2s. 6d.

CHILDE HAROLD. With 80 Engravings. Crown 8vo. 12s.

CHILDE HAROLD. 16mo. 2s. 6d.

CHILDE HAROLD. Vignettes. 16mo. 1s.

CHILDE HAROLD. Portrait. 16mo. 6d.

TALES AND POEMS. 16mo. 2s. 6d.

MISCELLANEOUS. 2 Vols. 16mo. 5s.

DRAMAS AND PLAYS. 2 Vols. 16mo. 5s.

DON JUAN AND BEPPO. 2 Vols. 16mo. 5s.

BEAUTIES. Poetry and Prose. Portrait. Fcap. 8vo. 3s. 6d.

CAMPBELL (Lord). Life : Based on his Autobiography, with selections from Journals, and Correspondence. Edited by Mrs. Hardcastle. Portrait. 2 Vols. 8vo. 30s.

———— Lord Chancellors and Keepers of the Great Seal of England. From the Earliest Times to the Death of Lord Eldon in 1838. 10 Vols. Crown 8vo. 6s. each.

— ———— Chief Justices of England. From the Norman Conquest to the Death of Lord Tenterden. 4 Vols. Crown 8vo. 6s. each.

———— (Thos.) Essay on English Poetry. With Short Lives of the British Poets. Post 8vo. 3s. 6d.

CARNARVON (LORD). Portugal, Gallicia, and the Basque Provinces. Post 8vo. 3s. 6d.

———————The Agamemnon : Translated from Æschylus. 8m. 8vo. 6s.

CARNOTA (CONDE DA). Memoirs of the Life and Eventful Career of F.M. the Duke of Saldanha ; Soldier and Statesman. With Selections from his Correspondence. 2 Vols. 8vo. 32s.

CARTWRIGHT (W. C.). The Jesuits : their Constitution and Teaching. An Historical Sketch. 8vo. 9s.

CAVALCASELLE'S WORKS. [See CROWE.]

CESNOLA (GEN.). Cyprus ; its Ancient Cities, Tombs, and Temples. Researches and Excavations during Ten Years' Residence in that Island. With 400 Illustrations. Medium 8vo. 50s.

CHILD (CHAPLIN). Benedicite ; or, Song of the Three Children ; being Illustrations of the Power, Beneficence, and Design manifested by the Creator in his Works. Post 8vo. 6s.

CHISHOLM (Mrs.). Perils of the Polar Seas ; True Stories of Arctic Discovery and Adventure. Illustrations. Post 8vo. 6s.

CHURTON (ARCHDEACON). Poetical Remains, Translations and Imitations. Portrait. Post 8vo. 7s. 6d.

CLASSIC PREACHERS OF THE ENGLISH CHURCH. Being Lectures delivered at St. James', Westminster, in 1877-8. By Eminent Divines. With Introduction by J. E. Kempe. 2 Vols. Post 8vo. 7s. 6d. each.

CLIVE'S (LORD) Life. By REV. G. R. GLEIG. Post 8vo. 3s. 6d.

CLODE (C. M.). Military Forces of the Crown ; their Administration and Government. 2 Vols. 8vo. 21s. each.

——— Administration of Justice under Military and Martial Law, as applicable to the Army, Navy, Marine, and Auxiliary Forces. 8vo. 12s.

COLERIDGE'S (SAMUEL TAYLOR) Table-Talk. Portrait. 12mo. 3s. 6d.

COLONIAL LIBRARY. [See Home and Colonial Library.]

COMPANIONS FOR THE DEVOUT LIFE. Lectures on well-known Devotional Works. By Eminent Divines. With Preface by J. E. Kempe, M.A. Crown 8vo. 6s.

DE IMITATIONE CHRISTI.	THEOLOGIA GERMANICA.
PENSÉES OF BLAISE PASCAL.	FÉNÉLON'S ŒUVRES SPIRITUELLES.
S. FRANÇOIS DE SALES.	ANDREWES' DEVOTIONS.
BAXTER'S SAINTS' REST.	CHRISTIAN YEAR.
S. AUGUSTINE'S CONFESSIONS.	PARADISE LOST.
JEREMY TAYLOR'S HOLY LIVING AND	PILGRIM'S PROGRESS.
DYING.	PRAYER BOOK.

CONVOCATION PRAYER-BOOK. (See Prayer-Book.)

COOKE (E. W.). Leaves from my Sketch-Book. Being a Selection from Sketches made during many Tours. With Descriptive Text. 50 Plates. 2 Vols. Small folio. 31s. 6d. each.

COOKERY (MODERN DOMESTIC). Founded on Principles of Economy and Practical Knowledge. By a Lady. Woodcuts. Fcap. 8vo. 5s.

CRABBE (REV. GEORGE). Life & Poetical Works. Illustrations. Royal 8vo. 7s.

CRIPPS (WILFRED). Old English Plate : Ecclesiastical, Decorative, and Domestic, its Makers and Marks. With a Complete Table of Date Letters, &c. New Edition. With 70 Illustrations. Medium 8vo. 16s.

——— Old French Plate ; Furnishing Tables of the Paris Date Letters, and Facsimiles of Other Marks. With Illustrations. 8vo. 8s. 6d.

CROKER (J. W.). Progressive Geography for Children. 18mo. 1s. 6d.

———— Boswell's Life of Johnson. Including the Tour to the Hebrides. *Seventh Edition.* Portraits. 8vo. 12s.

———— Historical Essay on the Guillotine. Fcap. 8vo. 1s.

CROWE AND CAVALCASELLE. Lives of the Early Flemish Painters. Woodcuts. Post 8vo, 7s. 6d.; or Large Paper, 8vo, 15s.

———— History of Painting in North Italy, from 14th to 16th Century. With Illustrations. 2 Vols. 8vo. 42s.

———— Life and Times of Titian, with some Account of his Family, chiefly from new and unpublished records. With Portrait and Illustrations. 2 vols. 8vo.

CUMMING (R. GORDON). Five Years of a Hunter's Life in the Far Interior of South Africa. Woodcuts. Post 8vo. 6s.

CUNYNGHAME (SIR ARTHUR). Travels in the Eastern Caucasus, on the Caspian and Black Seas, in Daghestan and the Frontiers of Persia and Turkey. Illustrations. 8vo. 18s.

CURTIUS' (PROFESSOR) Student's Greek Grammar, for the Upper Forms. Edited by DR. WM. SMITH. Post 8vo. 6s.

———— Elucidations of the above Grammar. Translated by EVELYN ABBOT. Post 8vo. 7s. 6d.

———— Smaller Greek Grammar for the Middle and Lower Forms. Abridged from the larger work. 12mo. 3s. 6d.

———— Accidence of the Greek Language. Extracted from the above work. 12mo. 2s. 6d.

———— Principles of Greek Etymology. Translated by A. S. WILKINS, M.A., and E. B. ENGLAND, M.A. 2 vols. 8vo. 15s. each.

———— The Greek Verb, its Structure and Development. Translated by A. S. WILKINS, M.A., and E. B. ENGLAND, M.A. 8vo. 18s.

CURZON (HON. ROBERT). Visits to the Monasteries of the Levant. Illustrations. Post 8vo. 7s. 6d.

CUST (GENERAL). Warriors of the 17th Century—The Thirty Years' War. 2 Vols. 16s. Civil Wars of France and England. 2 Vols. 16s. Commanders of Fleets and Armies. 2 Vols. 18s.

———— Annals of the Wars—18th & 19th Century. With Maps. 9 Vols. Post 8vo. 5s. each.

DAVY (SIR HUMPHRY). Consolations in Travel; or, Last Days of a Philosopher. Woodcuts. Fcap. 8vo. 3s. 6d.

———— Salmonia; or, Days of Fly Fishing. Woodcuts. Fcap. 8vo. 3s. 6d.

DE COSSON (E. A.). The Cradle of the Blue Nile; a Journey through Abyssinia and Soudan, and a Residence at the Court of King John of Ethiopia. Map and Illustrations. 2 vols. Post 8vo. 21s.

DENNIS (GEORGE). The Cities and Cemeteries of Etruria. A new Edition, revised, recording all the latest Discoveries. With 20 Plans and 200 Illustrations. 2 vols. Medium 8vo. 42s.

DENT (EMMA). Annals of Winchcombe and Sudeley. With 120 Portraits, Plates and Woodcuts. 4to. 42s.

DERBY (EARL OF). Iliad of Homer rendered into English Blank Verse. With Portrait. 2 Vols. Post 8vo. 10s.

DARWIN'S (CHARLES) WORKS:—

JOURNAL OF A NATURALIST DURING A VOYAGE ROUND THE
WORLD. Crown 8vo. 9s.

ORIGIN OF SPECIES BY MEANS OF NATURAL SELECTION; or, the
Preservation of Favoured Races in the Struggle for Life. Woodcuts.
Crown 8vo. 7s. 6d.

VARIATION OF ANIMALS AND PLANTS UNDER DOMESTICATION.
Woodcuts. 2 Vols. Crown 8vo. 18s.

DESCENT OF MAN, AND SELECTION IN RELATION TO SEX.
Woodcuts. Crown 8vo. 9s.

EXPRESSIONS OF THE EMOTIONS IN MAN AND ANIMALS. With
Illustrations. Crown 8vo. 12s.

VARIOUS CONTRIVANCES BY WHICH ORCHIDS ARE FERTILIZED
BY INSECTS. Woodcuts. Crown 8vo. 9s.

MOVEMENTS AND HABITS OF CLIMBING PLANTS. Woodcuts,
Crown 8vo. 6s.

INSECTIVOROUS PLANTS. Woodcuts. Crown 8vo. 14s.

EFFECTS OF CROSS AND SELF-FERTILIZATION IN THE VEGETABLE
KINGDOM. Crown 8vo. 12s.

DIFFERENT FORMS OF FLOWERS ON PLANTS OF THE SAME
SPECIES. Crown 8vo. 10s. 6d.

POWER OF MOVEMENT IN PLANTS. Woodcuts. Cr. 8vo. 15s.

THE FORMATION OF VEGETABLE MOULD THROUGH THE ACTION OF
WORMS; with Observations on their Habits. Post 8vo.

LIFE OF ERASMUS DARWIN. With a Study of his Works by
ERNEST KRAUSE. Portrait. Crown 8vo. 7s. 6d.

FACTS AND ARGUMENTS FOR DARWIN. By FRITZ MULLER.
Translated by W. S. DALLAS. Woodcuts. Post 8vo. 6s.

DERRY (BISHOP OF). Witness of the Psalms to Christ and Christianity. The Bampton Lectures for 1876. 8vo. 14s.

DEUTSCH (EMANUEL). Talmud, Islam, The Targums and other
Literary Remains. With a brief Memoir. 8vo. 12s.

DILKE (SIR C. W.). Papers of a Critic. Selected from the
Writings of the late CHAS. WENTWORTH DILKE. With a Biographi-
cal Sketch. 2 Vols. 8vo. 24s.

DOG-BREAKING. [See HUTCHINSON.]

DOMESTIC MODERN COOKERY. Founded on Principles of
Economy and Practical Knowledge, and adapted for Private Families.
Woodcuts. Fcap. 8vo. 5s.

DOUGLAS'S (SIR HOWARD) Theory and Practice of Gunnery.
Plates. 8vo. 21s.

———————— (WM.) Horse-Shoeing; As it Is, and As it Should be.
Illustrations. Post 8vo. 7s. 6d.

DRAKE'S (SIR FRANCIS) Life, Voyages, and Exploits, by Sea and
Land. By JOHN BARROW. Post 8vo. 2s.

DRINKWATER (JOHN). History of the Siege of Gibraltar,
1779-1783. With a Description and Account of that Garrison from the
Earliest Periods. Post 8vo. 2s.

DUCANGE'S MEDIÆVAL LATIN-ENGLISH DICTIONARY. Re-arranged
  and Edited, in accordance with the modern Science of Philology, by Rev.
  E. A. DAYMAN and J. H. HESSELS. Small 4to.   [*In Preparation*.

DU CHAILLU (PAUL B.). The Land of the Midnight Sun; Summer
  and Winter Journeys through Sweden, Norway, Lapland, and Northern
  Finland, with Descriptions of the Inner Life of the People, their
  Manners and Customs, the Primitive Antiquities, &c., &c. With Map
  and 235 Illustrations. 2 Vols. 8vo.

———————— EQUATORIAL AFRICA, with Accounts of the
  Gorilla, the Nest-building Ape, Chimpanzee, Crocodile, &c. Illustrations. 8vo. 21s.

———————— Journey to Ashango Land; and Further Pene-
  tration into Equatorial Africa. Illustrations. 8vo. 21s.

DUFFERIN (LORD). Letters from High Latitudes; a Yacht
  Voyage to Iceland, Jan Mayen, and Spitzbergen. Woodcuts. Post
  8vo. 7s. 6d.

———————— Speeches and Addresses, Political and Literary,
  delivered in the House of Lords, in Canada, and elsewhere. 8vo.
                                                       [*In the Press*.

DUNCAN (MAJOR). History of the Royal Artillery. Compiled from the Original Records. Portraits. 2 Vols. 8vo. 18s.

———————— English in Spain; or, The Story of the War of Succession, 1834-1840. Compiled from the Reports of the British Commissioners. With Illustrations. 8vo. 10s.

DÜRER (ALBERT); his Life, with a History of his Art. By DR.
  THAUSING, Keeper of Archduke Albert's Art Collection at Vienna.
  Translated from the German. With Portrait and Illustrations. 2 vols.
  Medium 8vo.

EASTLAKE (SIR CHARLES). Contributions to the Literature of
  the Fine Arts. With Memoir of the Author, and Selections from his
  Correspondence. By LADY EASTLAKE. 2 Vols. 8vo. 24s.

EDWARDS (W. H.). Voyage up the River Amazon, including a
  Visit to Para. Post 8vo. 2s.

ELDON'S (LORD) Public and Private Life, with Selections from
  his Diaries, &c. By HORACE TWISS. Portrait. 2 Vols. Post 8vo. 21s.

ELGIN (LORD). Letters and Journals. Edited by THEODORE
  WALROND. With Preface by Dean Stanley. 8vo. 14s.

ELLESMERE (LORD). Two Sieges of Vienna by the Turks.
  Translated from the German. Post 8vo. 2s

ELLIS (W.). Madagascar Revisited. The Persecutions and
  Heroic Sufferings of the Native Christians. Illustrations. 8vo. 16s.

———— Memoir. By HIS SON. With his Character and
  Work. By REV. HENRY ALLON, D.D. Portrait. 8vo. 10s. 6d.

———————— (ROBINSON) Poems and Fragments of Catullus. 16mo. 5s.

ELPHINSTONE (HON. MOUNTSTUART). History of India—the
  Hindoo and Mahomedan Periods. Edited by PROFESSOR COWELL.
  Map. 8vo. 18s.

————   — (H. W.). Patterns for Turning; Comprising
  Elliptical and other Figures cut on the Lathe without the use of any
  Ornamental Chuck. With 70 Illustrations. Small 4to. 15s.

ELTON (CAPT.) and H. B. COTTERILL. Adventures and
  Discoveries Among the Lakes and Mountains of Eastern and Central
  Africa. With Map and Illustrations. 8vo. 21s.

ENGLAND. [See ARTHUR, CROKER, HUME, MARKHAM, SMITH,
  and STANHOPE.]

ESSAYS ON CATHEDRALS. Edited, with an Introduction.
  By DEAN HOWSON. 8vo. 12s.

FERGUSSON (James). History of Architecture in all Countries from the Earliest Times. With 1,600 Illustrations. 4 Vols. Medium 8vo.
I. & II. Ancient and Mediæval. 63s.
III. Indian & Eastern. 42s.   IV. Modern. 31s. 6d.

———————— Rude Stone Monuments in all Countries; their Age and Uses. With 230 Illustrations. Medium 8vo. 24s.

———————— Holy Sepulchre and the Temple at Jerusalem. Woodcuts. 8vo. 7s. 6d.

———————— Temples of the Jews and other buildings in the Haram Area at Jerusalem. With Illustrations. 4to. 42s.

FLEMING (Professor). Student's Manual of Moral Philosophy. With Quotations and References. Post 8vo. 7s. 6d.

FLOWER GARDEN. By Rev. Thos. James. Fcap. 8vo. 1s.

FORBES (Capt.) British Burma and its People; Native Manners, Customs, and Religion. Cr. 8vo. 10s. 6d.

FORD (Richard). Gatherings from Spain. Post 8vo. 3s. 6d.

FORSTER (John). The Early Life of Jonathan Swift. 1667-1711. With Portrait. 8vo. 15s.

FORSYTH (William). Hortensius; an Historical Essay on the Office and Duties of an Advocate. Illustrations. 8vo. 7s. 6d.

———————— Novels and Novelists of the 18th Century, in Illustration of the Manners and Morals of the Age. Post 8vo. 10s. 6d.

FRANCE (History of). [See Jervis— Markham— Smith— Students'—Tocqueville.]

FRENCH IN ALGIERS; The Soldier of the Foreign Legion— and the Prisoners of Abd-el-Kadir. Translated by Lady Duff Gordon. Post 8vo. 2s.

FRERE (Sir Bartle). Indian Missions. Small 8vo. 2s. 6d.

— ———— Eastern Africa as a Field for Missionary Labour. With Map. Crown 8vo. 5s.

———————— Bengal Famine. How it will be Met and How to Prevent Future Famines in India. With Maps. Crown 8vo. 5s.

———— (M.). Old Deccan Days, or Hindoo Fairy Legends current in Southern India, with Introduction by Sir Bartle Frere. With 50 Illustrations. Post 8vo. 7s. 6d.

GALTON (F.). Art of Travel; or, Hints on the Shifts and Contrivances available in Wild Countries. Woodcuts. Post 8vo. 7s. 6d.

GEOGRAPHY. [See Bunbury— Croker— Richardson — Smith —Students'.]

GEOGRAPHICAL SOCIETY'S JOURNAL. (*Published Yearly.*)

GEORGE (Ernest). The Mosel; a Series of Twenty Etchings, with Descriptive Letterpress. Imperial 4to. 42s.

———————— Loire and South of France; a Series of Twenty Etchings, with Descriptive Text. Folio. 42s.

GERMANY (History of). [See Markham.]

GIBBON (Edward). History of the Decline and Fall of the Roman Empire. Edited by Milman, Guizot, and Dr. Wm. Smith. Maps. 8 Vols. 8vo. 60s.

———————— The Student's Edition; an Epitome of the above work, incorporating the Researches of Recent Commentators. By Dr. Wm. Smith. Woodcuts. Post 8vo. 7s. 6d.

GIFFARD (Edward). Deeds of Naval Daring; or, Anecdotes of the British Navy. Fcap. 8vo. 3s. 6d.

GILL (CAPT. WM). The River of Golden Sand. Narrative
of a Journey through China to Burmah. With a Preface by Col. H.
Yule, C.B. Maps and Illustrations. 2 Vols. 8vo. 30s.

———— (MRS.). Six Months in Ascension. An Unscientific Account of a Scientific Expedition. Map. Crown 8vo. 9s.

GLADSTONE (W. E.). Rome and the Newest Fashions in
Religion. Three Tracts. 8vo. 7s. 6d.

———————— Gleanings of Past Years, 1843-78. 7 vols. Small
8vo. 2s. 6d. each. I. The Throne, the Prince Consort, the Cabinet and
Constitution. II. Personal and Literary. III. Historical and Specu-
lative. IV. Foreign. V. and VI. Ecclesiastical. VII. Miscellaneous.

GLEIG (G. R.). Campaigns of the British Army at Washington
and New Orleans. Post 8vo. 2s.

———— Story of the Battle of Waterloo. Post 8vo. 3s. 6d.

———— Narrative of Sale's Brigade in Affghanistan. Post 8vo. 2s.

———— Life of Lord Clive. Post 8vo. 3s. 6d.

———— Sir Thomas Munro. Post 8vo. 3s. 6d.

GLYNNE (SIR STEPHEN R.). Notes on the Churches of Kent.
With Preface by W. H. Gladstone, M.P. Illustrations. 8vo. 12s.

GOLDSMITH'S (OLIVER) Works. Edited with Notes by PETER
CUNNINGHAM. Vignettes. 4 Vols. 8vo. 30s.

GOMM (FIELD-MARSHAL SIR WM. M.), Commander-in-Chief in
India, Constable of the Tower, and Colonel of the Coldstream Guards.
His Letters and Journals. 1799 to 1815. Edited by F.C. Carr Gomm.
With Portrait. 8vo.

GORDON (SIR ALEX.). Sketches of German Life, and Scenes
from the War of Liberation. Post 8vo. 3s. 6d.

———— (LADY DUFF) Amber-Witch: A Trial for Witchcraft. Post 8vo. 2s.

———— French in Algiers. 1. The Soldier of the Foreign
Legion. 2. The Prisoners of Abd-el-Kadir. Post 8vo. 2s.

GRAMMARS. [See CURTIUS; HALL; HUTTON; KING EDWARD;
LEATHES; MAETZNER; MATTHIÆ; SMITH.]

GREECE (HISTORY OF). [See GROTE—SMITH—STUDENTS'.]

GROTE'S (GEORGE) WORKS :—

HISTORY OF GREECE. From the Earliest Times to the close
of the generation contemporary with the Death of Alexander the Great.
Library Edition. Portrait, Maps, and Plans. 10 Vols. 8vo. 120s.
Cabinet Edition. Portrait and Plans. 12 Vols. Post 8vo. 6s. each.

PLATO, and other Companions of Socrates. 3 Vols. 8vo. 45s.

ARISTOTLE. With additional Essays. 8vo. 18s.

MINOR WORKS. Portrait. 8vo. 14s.

LETTERS ON SWITZERLAND IN 1847. 6s.

PERSONAL LIFE. Portrait. 8vo. 12s.

GROTE (MRS.). A Sketch. By LADY EASTLAKE. Crown 8vo. 6s.

HALL'S (T. D.) School Manual of English Grammar. With
Copious Exercises. 12mo. 3s. 6d.

———— Manual of English Composition. With Copious Illustrations and Practical Exercises. 12mo. 3s. 6d.

———— Primary English Grammar for Elementary Schools.
Based on the larger work. 16mo. 1s.

———— Child's First Latin Book, comprising a full Practice of
Nouns, Pronouns, and Adjectives, with the Active Verbs. 16mo. 2s.

HALLAM'S (Henry) WORKS :—

The Constitutional History of England, from the Accession of Henry the Seventh to the Death of George the Second. *Library Edition*. 3 Vols. 8vo. 3 ls. *Cabinet Edition*, 3 Vols. Post 8vo. 12s. *Student's Edition*, Post 8vo. 7s. 6d.

History of Europe during the Middle Ages. *Library Edition*, 3 Vols. 8vo. 30s. *Cabinet Edition*, 3 Vols. Post 8vo. 12s. *Student's Edition*, Post 8vo. 7s. 6l.

Literary History of Europe during the 15th, 16th, and 17th Centuries. *Library Edition*, 3 Vols. 8vo. 36s. *Cabinet Edition*, 4 Vols. Post 8vo. 16s.

HALLAM'S (Arthur) Literary Remains; in Verse and Prose. Portrait. Fcap. 8vo. 3s. 6d.

HAMILTON (Gen. Sir F. W.). History of the Grenadier Guards. From Original Documents, &c. With Illustrations. 3 Vols. 8vo. 63s.

—————— (Andrew). Rheinsberg: Memorials of Frederick the Great and Prince Henry of Prussia. 2 Vols. Crown 8vo. 21s.

HART'S ARMY LIST. (*Published Quarterly and Annually*.)

HATCH (W. M.). The Moral Philosophy of Aristotle, consisting of a translation of the Nichomachean Ethics, and of the Paraphrase attributed to Andronicus, with an Introductory Analysis of each book. 8vo. 18s.

HATHERLEY (Lord). The Continuity of Scripture, as Declared by the Testimony of our Lord and of the Evangelists and Apostles. 8vo. 6s. *Popular Edition*. Post 8vo. 2s. 6d.

HAY (Sir J. H. Drummond). Western Barbary, its Wild Tribes and Savage Animals. Post 8vo. 2s.

HAYWARD (A.). Sketches of Eminent Statesmen and Writers, with other Essays. Reprinted from the "Quarterly Review." Contents: Thiers, Bismarck, Cavour, Metternich, Montalembert, Melbourne, Wellesley, Byron and Tennyson, Venice, St. Simon, Sevigné, Du Deffand, Holland House, Strawberry Hill. 2 Vols. 8vo. 28s.

HEAD'S (Sir Francis) WORKS :—

The Royal Engineer. Illustrations. 8vo. 12s.

Life of Sir John Burgoyne. Post 8vo. 1s.

Rapid Journeys across the Pampas. Post 8vo. 2s.

Bubbles from the Brunnen of Nassau. Illustrations. Post 8vo. 7s. 6d.

Stokers and Pokers; or, the London and North Western Railway. Post 8vo. 2s.

HEBER'S (Bishop) Journals in India. 2 Vols. Post 8vo. 7s.

—————— Poetical Works. Portrait. Fcap. 8vo. 3s. 6d.

—————— Hymns adapted to the Church Service. 16mo. 1s. 6d.

HERODOTUS. A New English Version. Edited, with Notes and Essays, Historical, Ethnographical, and Geographical, by Canon Rawlinson, Sir H. Rawlinson and Sir J. G. Wilkinson. Maps and Woodcuts. 4 Vols. 8vo. 48s.

HERRIES (Rt. Hon. John). Memoir of his Public Life during the Reigns of George III. and IV., William IV., and Queen Victoria. Founded on his Letters and other Unpublished Documents. By his son, Edward Herries, C.B. 2 vols. 8vo. 24s.

HERSCHEL'S (Caroline) Memoir and Correspondence. By Mrs. John Herschel. With Portraits. Crown 8vo. 7s. 6d.

FOREIGN HANDBOOKS.

HAND-BOOK—TRAVEL-TALK. English, French, German, and Italian. 18mo. 3s. 6d.

——————— HOLLAND AND BELGIUM. Map and Plans. Post 8vo. 6s.

——————— NORTH GERMANY and THE RHINE,— The Black Forest, the Hartz, Thüringerwald, Saxon Switzerland, Rügen, the Giant Mountains, Taunus, Odenwald, Elass, and Lothringen. Map and Plans. Post 8vo. 10s.

——————— SOUTH GERMANY,—Wurtemburg, Bavaria, Austria, Styria, Salzburg, the Alps, Tyrol, Hungary, and the Danube, from Ulm to the Black Sea. Maps and Plans. Post 8vo. 10s.

——————— PAINTING. German, Flemish, and Dutch Schools. Illustrations. 2 Vols. Post 8vo. 24s.

——————— LIVES AND WORKS OF EARLY FLEMISH Painters. Illustrations. Post 8vo. 7s. 6d.

——————— SWITZERLAND, Alps of Savoy, and Piedmont. In Two Parts. Maps and Plans. Post 8vo. 10s.

——————— FRANCE, Part I. Normandy, Brittany, the French Alps, the Loire, Seine, Garonne, and Pyrenees. Maps and Plans. Post 8vo. 7s. 6d.

——————————————— Part II. Central France, Auvergne, the Cevennes, Burgundy, the Rhone and Saone, Provence, Nimes, Arles, Marseilles, the French Alps, Alsace, Lorraine, Champagne, &c. Maps and Plans. Post 8vo. 7s. 6d.

——————— MEDITERRANEAN—its Principal Islands, Cities, Seaports, Harbours, and Border Lands. For travellers and yachtsmen, with nearly 50 Maps and Plans. Post 8vo. 20s.

——————— ALGERIA AND TUNIS. Algiers, Constantine, Oran, the Atlas Range. Maps and Plans. Post 8vo. 10s.

——————— PARIS, and its Environs. Maps and Plans. 16mo. 3s. 6d.

——————— SPAIN, Madrid, The Castiles, The Basque Provinces, Leon, The Asturias, Galicia, Estremadura, Andalusia, Ronda, Granada, Murcia, Valencia, Catalonia, Aragon, Navarre, The Balearic Islands, &c. &c. Maps and Plans. Post 8vo. 20s.

——————— PORTUGAL, Lisbon, Porto, Cintra, Mafra, &c. Map and Plan. Post 8vo. 12s.

——————— NORTH ITALY, Turin, Milan, Cremona, the Italian Lakes, Bergamo, Brescia, Verona, Mantua, Vicenza, Padua, Ferrara, Bologna, Ravenna, Rimini, Piacenza, Genoa, the Riviera, Venice, Parma, Modena, and Romagna. Maps and Plans. Post 8vo. 10s.

——————— CENTRAL ITALY, Florence, Lucca, Tuscany, The Marches, Umbria, &c. Maps and Plans. Post 8vo. 10s.

——————— ROME AND ITS ENVIRONS. With 50 Maps and Plans. Post 8vo. 10s.

——————— SOUTH ITALY, Naples, Pompeii, Herculaneum, and Vesuvius. Maps and Plans. Post 8vo. 10s.

——————— PAINTING. The Italian Schools. Illustrations. 2 Vols. Post 8vo. 30s.

——————— LIVES OF ITALIAN PAINTERS, from Cimabue to Bassano. By Mrs. Jameson. Portraits. Post 8vo. 12s.

——————— NORWAY, Christiania, Bergen, Trondhjem. The Fjelds and Fjords. Maps and Plans. Post 8vo. 9s.

——————— SWEDEN, Stockholm, Upsala, Gothenburg, the Shores of the Baltic, &c. Maps and Plan. Post 8vo. 6s.

HAND-BOOK—DENMARK, Sleswig, Holstein, Copenhagen, Jutland, Iceland. Maps and Plans. Post 8vo. 6s.

———— RUSSIA, St. Petersburg, Moscow, Poland, and Finland. Maps and Plans. Post 8vo. 18s.

———— GREECE, the Ionian Islands, Continental Greece, Athens, the Peloponnesus, the Islands of the Ægean Sea. Albania, Thessaly, and Macedonia. Maps, Plans, and Views. Post 8vo.

———— TURKEY IN ASIA—Constantinople, the Bosphorus, Dardanelles, Brousa, Plain of Troy, Crete, Cyprus, Smyrna, Ephesus, the Seven Churches, Coasts of the Black Sea, Armenia, Euphrates Valley. Route to India, &c. Maps and Plans. Post 8vo. 15s.

———— EGYPT, including Descriptions of the Course of the Nile through Egypt and Nubia, Alexandria, Cairo, and Thebes, the Suez Canal, the Pyramids, the Peninsula of Sinai, the Oases, the Fyoom, &c. In Two Parts. Maps and Plans. Post 8vo. 15s.

———— HOLY LAND—Syria, Palestine, Peninsula of Sinai. Edom, Syrian Deserts, Petra, Damascus; and Palmyra. Maps and Plans. Post 8vo. 20s. *.* Travelling Map of Palestine. In a case. 12s.

———— INDIA. Maps and Plans. Post 8vo. Part I. Bombay, 15s. Part II. Madras, 15s. Part III. Bengal.

ENGLISH HAND-BOOKS.

HAND-BOOK—ENGLAND AND WALES. An Alphabetical Hand-Book. Condensed into One Volume for the Use of Travellers. With a Map. Post 8vo. 10s.

———— MODERN LONDON. Maps and Plans. 16mo. 3s. 6d.

———— ENVIRONS OF LONDON within a circuit of 20 miles. 2 Vols. Crown 8vo. 21s.

———— ST. PAUL'S CATHEDRAL. 20 Illustrations. Crown 8vo. 10s. 6d.

———— EASTERN COUNTIES, Chelmsford, Harwich, Colchester, Maldon, Cambridge, Ely, Newmarket, Bury St. Edmunds, Ipswich, Woodbridge, Felixstowe, Lowestoft, Norwich, Yarmouth, Cromer, &c. Map and Plans. Post 8vo. 12s

———— CATHEDRALS of Oxford, Peterborough, Norwich, Ely, and Lincoln. With 90 Illustrations. Crown 8vo. 21s.

———— KENT, Canterbury, Dover, Ramsgate, Sheerness, Rochester, Chatham, Woolwich. Maps and Plans. Post 8vo. 7s. 6d.

———— SUSSEX, Brighton, Chichester, Worthing, Hastings, Lewes, Arundel, &c. Maps and Plans. Post 8vo. 6s.

———— SURREY AND HANTS, Kingston, Croydon, Reigate, Guildford, Dorking, Boxhill, Winchester, Southampton, New Forest, Portsmouth, Isle of Wight, &c. Maps and Plans. Post 8vo. 10s.

———— BERKS, BUCKS, AND OXON, Windsor, Eton, Reading, Aylesbury, Uxbridge, Wycombe, Henley, the City and University of Oxford, Blenheim, and the Descent of the Thames. Maps and Plans. Post 8vo.

———— WILTS, DORSET, AND SOMERSET, Salisbury, Chippenham, Weymouth, Sherborne, Wells, Bath, Bristol, Taunton, &c. Map. Post 8vo. 10s.

———— DEVON, Exeter, Ilfracombe, Linton, Sidmouth, Dawlish, Teignmouth, Plymouth, Devonport, Torquay. Maps and Plans. Post 8vo. 7s. 6d.

HAND-BOOK—CORNWALL, Launceston, Penzance, Falmouth, the Lizard, Land's End, &c. Maps. Post 8vo. 6s.

——————CATHEDRALS of Winchester, Salisbury, Exeter, Wells, Chichester, Rochester. Canterbury, and St. Albans. With 130 Illustrations. 2 Vols. Cr. 8vo. 36s. St. Albans separately, cr. 8vo. 6s.

——————GLOUCESTER, HEREFORD, AND WORCESTER, Cirencester, Cheltenham. Stroud, Tewkesbury, Leominster, Ross, Malvern, Kidderminster, Dudley, Bromsgrove, Evesham. Map. Post 8vo.

——————CATHEDRALS of Bristol, Gloucester, Hereford, Worcester, and Lichfield. With 50 Illustrations. Crown 8vo. 16s.

——————NORTH WALES, Bangor, Carnarvon, Beaumaris, Snowdon, Llanberis. Dolgelly, Cader Idris, Conway, &c. Map. Post 8vo. 7s.

——————SOUTH WALES, Monmouth, Llandaff, Merthyr, Vale of Neath, Pembroke, Carmarthen, Tenby, Swansea, The Wye, &c. Map. Post 8vo. 7s.

——————CATHEDRALS OF BANGOR, ST. ASAPH, Llandaff, and St. David's. With Illustrations. Post 8vo. 15s.

——————NORTHAMPTONSHIRE AND RUTLAND— Northampton, Peterborough, Towcester, Daventry, Market Harborough, Kettering, Wallingborough, Thrapston, Stamford, Uppingham, Oakham. Maps. Post 8vo. 7s. 6d.

——————DERBY, NOTTS, LEICESTER, STAFFORD, Matlock, Bakewell, Chatsworth, The Peak. Buxton, Hardwick, Dove Dale, Ashborne, Southwell, Mansfield, Retford, Burton, Belvoir, Melton Mowbray, Wolverhampton, Lichfield, Walsall, Tamworth. Map. Post 8vo. 9s.

——————SHROPSHIRE AND CHESHIRE, Shrewsbury, Ludlow, Bridgnorth, Oswestry, Chester, Crewe, Alderley, Stockport, Birkenhead. Maps and Plans. Post 8vo. 6s.

——————LANCASHIRE, Warrington, Bury, Manchester, Liverpool, Burnley, Clitheroe, Bolton, Blackburn, Wigan, Preston, Rochdale, Lancaster, Southport, Blackpool, &c. Maps and Plans. Post 8vo. 7s. 6d.

——————YORKSHIRE, Doncaster, Hull, Selby, Beverley, Scarborough, Whitby, Harrogate, Ripon, Leeds, Wakefield, Bradford, Halifax, Huddersfield, Sheffield. Map and Plans. Post 8vo. 12s.

——————CATHEDRALS of York, Ripon, Durham, Carlisle, Chester, and Manchester. With 60 Illustrations. 2 Vols. Cr. 8vo. 21s.

——————DURHAM AND NORTHUMBERLAND, Newcastle, Darlington, Gateshead, Bishop Auckland, Stockton, Hartlepool, Sunderland, Shields, Berwick-on-Tweed, Morpeth, Tynemouth, Coldstream, Alnwick, &c. Map. Post 8vo. 9s.

——————WESTMORLAND AND CUMBERLAND—Lancaster, Furness Abbey, Ambleside, Kendal, Windermere, Coniston, Keswick, Grasmere, Ulswater, Carlisle, Cockermouth, Penrith, Appleby. Map. Post 8vo.

₊ MURRAY'S MAP OF THE LAKE DISTRICT, on canvas. 3s. 6d.

——————SCOTLAND, Edinburgh, Melrose, Kelso, Glasgow, Dumfries, Ayr, Stirling, Arran, The Clyde, Oban, Inverary, Loch Lomond, Loch Katrine and Trossachs, Caledonian Canal, Inverness, Perth, Dundee, Aberdeen, Braemar, Skye, Caithness, Ross, Sutherland, &c. Maps and Plans. Post 8vo. 9s.

——————IRELAND, Dublin, Belfast, the Giant's Causeway, Donegal, Galway, Wexford, Cork, Limerick. Waterford. Killarney, Bantry, Glengariff, &c. Maps and Plans. Post 8vo. 10s.

HOME AND COLONIAL LIBRARY. A Series of Works adapted for all circles and classes of Readers, having been selected for their acknowledged interest, and ability of the Authors. Post 8vo. Published at 2s. and 3s. 6d. each, and arranged under two distinctive heads as follows :—

CLASS A.

HISTORY, BIOGRAPHY, AND HISTORIC TALES.

1. SIEGE OF GIBRALTAR. By JOHN DRINKWATER. 2s.

2. THE AMBER-WITCH. By LADY DUFF GORDON. 2s.

3. CROMWELL AND BUNYAN. By ROBERT SOUTHEY. 2s.

4. LIFE OF SIR FRANCIS DRAKE. By JOHN BARROW. 2s.

5. CAMPAIGNS AT WASHINGTON. By REV. G. R. GLEIG. 2s.

6. THE FRENCH IN ALGIERS. By LADY DUFF GORDON. 2s.

7. THE FALL OF THE JESUITS. 2s.

8. LIVONIAN TALES. 2s.

9. LIFE OF CONDÉ. By LORD MAHON. 3s. 6d.

10. SALE'S BRIGADE. By REV. G. R. GLEIG. 2s.

11. THE SIEGES OF VIENNA. By LORD ELLESMERE. 2s.

12. THE WAYSIDE CROSS. By CAPT. MILMAN. 2s.

13. SKETCHES OF GERMAN LIFE. By SIR A. GORDON. 3s. 6d.

14. THE BATTLE OF WATERLOO. By REV. G. R. GLEIG. 3s. 6d.

15. AUTOBIOGRAPHY OF STEFFENS. 2s.

16. THE BRITISH POETS. By THOMAS CAMPBELL. 3s. 6d.

17. HISTORICAL ESSAYS. By LORD MAHON. 3s. 6d.

18. LIFE OF LORD CLIVE. By REV. G. R. GLEIG. 3s. 6d.

19. NORTH - WESTERN RAILWAY. By SIR F. B. HEAD. 2s.

20. LIFE OF MUNRO. By REV. G. R. GLEIG. 3s. 6d.

CLASS B.

VOYAGES, TRAVELS, AND ADVENTURES.

1. BIBLE IN SPAIN. By GEORGE BORROW. 3s. 6d.

2. GYPSIES OF SPAIN. By GEORGE BORROW. 3s. 6d.

3 & 4. JOURNALS IN INDIA. By BISHOP HEBER. 2 Vols. 7s.

5. TRAVELS IN THE HOLY LAND. By IRBY and MANGLES. 2s.

6. MOROCCO AND THE MOORS. By J. DRUMMOND HAY. 2s.

7. LETTERS FROM THE BALTIC. By a LADY.

8. NEW SOUTH WALES. By MRS. MEREDITH. 2s.

9. THE WEST INDIES. By M. G. LEWIS. 2s.

10. SKETCHES OF PERSIA. By SIR JOHN MALCOLM. 3s. 6d.

11. MEMOIRS OF FATHER RIPA. 2s.

12 & 13. TYPEE AND OMOO. By HERMANN MELVILLE. 2 Vols. 7s.

14. MISSIONARY LIFE IN CANADA. By REV. J. ABBOTT. 2s.

15. LETTERS FROM MADRAS. By a LADY. 2s.

16. HIGHLAND SPORTS. By CHARLES ST. JOHN. 3s. 6d.

17. PAMPAS JOURNEYS. By SIR F. B. HEAD. 2s.

18. GATHERINGS FROM SPAIN. By RICHARD FORD. 3s. 6d.

19. THE RIVER AMAZON. By W. H. EDWARDS. 2s.

20. MANNERS & CUSTOMS OF INDIA. By REV. C. ACLAND. 2s.

21. ADVENTURES IN MEXICO. By G. F. RUXTON. 3s. 6d.

22. PORTUGAL AND GALICIA. By LORD CARNARVON. 3s. 6d.

23. BUSH LIFE IN AUSTRALIA. By REV. H. W. HAYGARTH. 2s.

24. THE LIBYAN DESERT. By BAYLE ST. JOHN. 2s.

25. SIERRA LEONE. By A LADY. 3s. 6d.

** Each work may be had separately.

c

HOLLWAY (J. G.). A Month in Norway. Fcap. 8vo. 2s.

HONEY BEE. By Rev. Thomas James. Fcap. 8vo. 1s.

HOOK (Dean). Church Dictionary. 8vo. 16s.

—— (Theodore) Life. By J. G. Lockhart. Fcap. 8vo. 1s.

HOPE (A. J. Beresford). Worship in the Church of England. 8vo. 9s., or, *Popular Selections from.* 8vo. 2s. 6d.

HORACE; a New Edition of the Text. Edited by Dean Milman. With 100 Woodcuts. Crown 8vo. 7s. 6d.

HOUGHTON'S (Lord) Monographs, Personal and Social. With Portraits. Crown 8vo. 10s. 6d.

—————— Poetical Works. *Collected Edition.* With Portrait. 2 Vols. Fcap. 8vo. 12s.

HOUSTOUN (Mrs.). Twenty Years in the Wild West of Ireland, or Life in Connaught. Post 8vo. 9s.

HUME (The Student's). A History of England, from the Invasion of Julius Cæsar to the Revolution of 1688. New Edition, revised, corrected, and continued to the Treaty of Berlin, 1878. By J. S. Brewer, M.A. With 7 Coloured Maps & 70 Woodcuts. Post 8vo. 7s. 6d.

HUTCHINSON (Gen.). Dog Breaking, with Odds and Ends for those who love the Dog and the Gun. With 40 Illustrations. Crown 8vo. 7s. 6d.

HUTTON (H. E.). Principia Græca; an Introduction to the Study of Greek. Comprehending Grammar, Delectus, and Exercise-book, with Vocabularies. *Sixth Edition.* 12mo. 3s. 6d.

HYMNOLOGY, Dictionary of. See Julian.

INDIA. [See Elphinstone, Hand-book, Temple.]

IRBY AND MANGLES' Travels in Egypt, Nubia, Syria, and the Holy Land. Post 8vo. 2s.

JAMESON (Mrs.). Lives of the Early Italian Painters— and the Progress of Painting in Italy—Cimabue to Bassano. With 50 Portraits. Post 8vo. 12s.

JAPAN. [See Bird, Mossman, Mounsey, Reed.]

JENNINGS (Louis J.). Field Paths and Green Lanes in Surrey and Sussex. Illustrations. Post 8vo. 10s. 6d.

—————— Rambles among the Hills in the Peak of Derbyshire and on the South Downs. With sketches of people by the way. With 23 Illustrations. Post 8vo. 12s.

JERVIS (Rev. W. H.). The Gallican Church, from the Concordat of Bologna, 1516, to the Revolution. With an Introduction. Portraits. 2 Vols. 8vo. 28s.

JESSE (Edward). Gleanings in Natural History. Fcp. 8vo. 3s. 6d.

JEX-BLAKE (Rev. T. W.). Life in Faith: Sermons Preached at Cheltenham and Rugby. Fcap. 8vo. 3s. 6d.

JOHNSON'S (Dr. Samuel) Life. By James Boswell. Including the Tour to the Hebrides. Edited by Mr. Croker. 1 vol. Royal 8vo. 12s.

JULIAN (Rev. John J.). A Dictionary of Hymnology. A Companion to Existing Hymn Books. Setting forth the Origin and History of the Hymns contained in the Principal Hymnals used by the Churches of England, Scotland, and Ireland, and various Dissenting Bodies, with Notices of their Authors. Post 8vo. [*In the Press.*]

JUNIUS' Handwriting Professionally investigated. By Mr. Chabot, Expert. With Preface and Collateral Evidence, by the Hon. Edward Twisleton. With Facsimiles, Woodcuts, &c. 4to. £3 3s.

KERR (ROBERT). Small Country House. A Brief Practical Discourse on the Planning of a Residence from 2000*l.* to 5000*l.* With Supplementary Estimates to 7000*l.* Post 8vo. 3*s.*

———— (R. MALCOLM). Student's Blackstone. A Systematic Abridgment of the entire Commentaries, adapted to the present state of the law. Post 8vo. 7*s.* 6*d.*

KING EDWARD VITH's Latin Grammar. 12mo. 3*s.* 6*d.*

———— ———— First Latin Book. 12mo. 2*s.* 6*d.*

KING (R. J.). Archæology, Travel and Art; being Sketches and Studies, Historical and Descriptive. 8vo. 12*s.*

KIRK (J. FOSTER). History of Charles the Bold, Duke of Burgundy. Portrait. 3 Vols. 8vo. 45*s.*

KIRKES' Handbook of Physiology. Edited by W. MORRANT BAKER, F.R.C.S. With 400 Illustrations. Post 8vo. 14*s.*

KUGLER'S Handbook of Painting.—The Italian Schools. Revised and Remodelled from the most recent Researches. By LADY EASTLAKE. With 140 Illustrations. 2 Vols. Crown 8vo. 30*s.*

———— Handbook of Painting.—The German, Flemish, and Dutch Schools. Revised and in part re-written. By J. A. CROWE. With 60 Illustrations. 2 Vols. Crown 8vo. 24*s.*

LANE (E. W.). Account of the Manners and Customs of Modern Egyptians. With Illustrations. 2 Vols. Post 8vo. 12*s*

LAWRENCE (SIR GEO.). Reminiscences of Forty-three Years' Service in India: including Captivities in Cabul among the Affghans and among the Sikhs, and a Narrative of the Mutiny in Rajputana. Crown 8vo. 10*s.* 6*d.*

LAYARD (A. H.). Nineveh and its Remains; a Popular Account of Researches and Discoveries amidst the Ruins of Assyria. With Illustrations. Post 8vo. 7*s* 6*d.*

———— Nineveh and Babylon; A Popular Account of Discoveries in the Ruins, with Travels in Armenia, Kurdistan and the Desert, during a Second Expedition to Assyria. With Illustrations. Post 8vo. 7*s.* 6*d.*

LEATHES' (STANLEY). Practical Hebrew Grammar. With the Hebrew Text of Genesis i.—vi., and Psalms i.—vi. Grammatical Analysis and Vocabulary. Post 8vo. 7*s.* 6*d.*

LENNEP (REV. H. J. VAN). Missionary Travels in Asia Minor. With Illustrations of Biblical History and Archæology. With Map and Woodcuts. 2 Vols. Post 8vo. 24*s.*

———— Modern Customs and Manners of Bible Lands in Illustration of Scripture. With Coloured Maps and 300 Illustrations. 2 Vols. 8vo. 21*s.*

LESLIE (C. R.). Handbook for Young Painters. Illustrations. Post 8vo. 7*s.* 6*d.*

———— Life and Works of Sir Joshua Reynolds. Portraits. 2 Vols. 8vo. 42*s.*

LETO (POMPONIO). Eight Months at Rome during the Vatican Council. 8vo. 12*s.*

LETTERS FROM THE BALTIC. By a LADY. Post 8vo. 2*s.*

———— MADRAS. By a LADY. Post 8vo. 2*s.*

———— SIERRA LEONE. By a LADY. Post 8vo. 3*s.* 6*d.*

LEVI (LEONE). History of British Commerce: and Economic Progress of the Nation, from 1763 to 1878. 8vo. 18*s.*

LEX SALICA; the Ten Texts with the Glosses and the Lex Emendata. Synoptically edited by J. H. HESSELS. With Notes on the Frankish Words in the Lex Salica by H. KERN, of Leyden. 4to. 42*s.*

LIDDELL (DEAN). Student's History of Rome, from the earliest
Times to the establishment of the Empire. Woodcuts. Post 8vo. 7s. 6d.

LISPINGS from LOW LATITUDES; or, the Journal of the Hon.
Impulsia Gushington. Edited by LORD DUFFERIN. With 24 Plates. 4to. 21s.

LIVINGSTONE (DR). First Expedition to Africa, 1840–56.
Illustrations. Post 8vo. 7s. 6d.

———————— Second Expedition to Africa, 1858–64. Illustrations. Post 8vo. 7s. 6d.

———— Last Journals in Central Africa, from 1865 to
his Death. Continued by a Narrative of his last moments and sufferings.
By Rev. HORACE WALLER. Maps and Illustrations. 2 Vols. 8vo. 15s.

———————— Personal Life. From his unpublished Journals
and Correspondence. By Wm. G. Blaikie, D D. With Map and
Portrait. 8vo. 15s.

LIVINGSTONIA. Journal of Adventures in Exploring Lake
Nyassa, and Establishing a Missionary Settlement there. By E. D.
YOUNG, R.N. Maps. Post 8vo. 7s. 6d.

LIVONIAN TALES. By the Author of "Letters from the
Baltic." Post 8vo. 2s.

LOCKHART (J. G.). Ancient Spanish Ballads. Historical and
Romantic. Translated, with Notes. Illustrations. Crown 8vo. 5s.

———————— Life of Theodore Hook. Fcap. 8vo. 1s.

LOUDON (MRS.). Gardening for Ladies. With Directions and
Calendar of Operations for Every Month Woodcuts. Fcap. 8vo. 3s. 6d.

LYELL (SIR CHARLES). Principles of Geology; or, the Modern
Changes of the Earth and its Inhabitants considered as illustrative of
Geology. With Illustrations. 2 Vols. 8vo. 32s.

———————— Student's Elements of Geology. With Table of British
Fossils and 600 Illustrations. Third Edition. Revised. Post 8vo. 9s.

———————— Life and Letters. Edited by his sister-in-law, MRS.
LYELL. With Portrait. 2 Vols. 8vo.

———— (K. M.). Geographical Handbook of Ferns. With Tables
to show their Distribution. Post 8vo. 7s. 6d.

LYTTON (LORD). A Memoir of Julian Fane. With Portrait. Post
8vo. 5s.

McCLINTOCK (SIR L.). Narrative of the Discovery of the
Fate of Sir John Franklin and his Companions in the Arctic Seas.
With Illustrations. Post 8vo. 7s. 6d.

MACDOUGALL (COL.). Modern Warfare as Influenced by Modern
Artillery. With Plans. Post 8vo. 12s.

MACGREGOR (J.). Rob Roy on the Jordan, Nile, Red Sea, Gen-
nesareth, &c. A Canoe Cruise in Palestine and Egypt and the Waters
of Damascus. With 70 Illustrations. Crown 8vo. 7s. 6d.

MAETZNER'S ENGLISH GRAMMAR. A Methodical, Analytical,
and Historical Treatise on the Orthography, Prosody, Inflections, and
Syntax. By CLAIR J. GRECE, LL.D. 3 Vols. 8vo. 36s.

MAHON (LORD), see STANHOPE.

MAINE (SIR H. SUMNER). Ancient Law: its Connection with the
Early History of Society, and its Relation to Modern Ideas. 8vo. 12s.

———————— Village Communities in the East and West. 8vo. 12s.

———————— Early History of Institutions. 8vo. 12s.

MALCOLM (SIR JOHN). Sketches of Persia. Post 8vo. 3s. 6d.

MANSEL (DEAN). Limits of Religious Thought Examined.
Post 8vo. 8s. 6d.

———————— Letters, Lectures, and Reviews. 8vo. 12s.

MANUAL OF SCIENTIFIC ENQUIRY. For the Use of Travellers. Edited by Rev. R. Main. Post 8vo. 3s. 6d. (*Published by order of the Lords of the Admiralty.*)

MARCO POLO. The Book of Ser Marco Polo, the Venetian. Concerning the Kingdoms and Marvels of the East. A new English Version. Illustrated by the light of Oriental Writers and Modern Travels. By Col. Henry Yule. Maps and Illustrations. 2 Vols. Medium 8vo. 63s.

MARKHAM (Mrs.). History of England. From the First Invasion by the Romans. Woodcuts. 12mo. 3s. 6d.

———— History of France. From the Conquest by the Gauls. Woodcuts. 12mo. 3s. 6d.

———— History of Germany. From the Invasion by Marius. Woodcuts. 12mo. 3s. 6d.

———— (Clements R.). A Popular Account of Peruvian Bark and its introduction into British India. With Maps. Post 8vo. 14s.

MARRYAT (Joseph). History of Modern and Mediæval Pottery and Porcelain. With a Description of the Manufacture. Plates and Woodcuts. 8vo. 42s.

MARSH (G. P.). Student's Manual of the English Language. Edited with Additions. By Dr. Wm. Smith. Post 8vo. 7s. 6d.

MASTERS in English Theology. 'Lectures delivered at King's College, London, in 1877, by Eminent Divines. With Introduction by Canon Barry. Post 8vo. 7s. 6d.

MATTHIÆ'S Greek Grammar. Abridged by Blomfield. Revised by E. S. Crooke. 12mo. 4s.

MAUREL'S Character, Actions, and Writings of Wellington. Fcap. 8vo. 1s. 6d.

MAYO (Lord). Sport in Abyssinia; or, the Mareb and Tackazzee. With Illustrations. Crown 8vo. 12s.

MEADE (Hon. Herbert). Ride through the Disturbed Districts of New Zealand, with a Cruise among the South Sea Islands. With Illustrations. Medium 8vo. 12s.

MELVILLE (Hermann). Marquesas and South Sea Islands. 2 Vols. Post 8vo. 7s.

MEREDITH (Mrs. Charles). Notes and Sketches of New South Wales. Post 8vo. 2s.

MICHAEL ANGELO, Sculptor, Painter, and Architect. His Life and Works. By C. Heath Wilson. Illustrations. Royal 8vo.

MIDDLETON (Chas. H.) A Descriptive Catalogue of the Etched Work of Rembrandt, with Life and Introductions. With Explanatory Cuts. Medium 8vo. 31s. 6d.

MILLINGTON (Rev. T. S.). Signs and Wonders in the Land of Ham, or the Ten Plagues of Egypt, with Ancient and Modern Illustrations. Woodcuts. Post 8vo. 7s. 6d.

MIVART (St. George). Lessons from Nature; as manifested in Mind and Matter. 8vo. 15s.

———— The Cat. An Introduction to the Study of Backboned Animals, especially Mammals. With 200 Illustrations. Medium 8vo. 30s.

MOORE (Thomas). Life and Letters of Lord Byron. *Cabinet Edition.* With Plates. 6 Vols. Fcap. 8vo. 18s.; *Popular Edition,* with Portraits. Royal 8vo. 7s. 6d.

MORESBY (Capt.), R.N. Discoveries in New Guinea, Polynesia, Torres Straits, &c., during the cruise of H.M.S. Basilisk. Map and Illustrations. 8vo. 15s.

MILMAN'S (Dean) WORKS :—

> History of the Jews, from the earliest Period down to Modern Times. 3 Vols. Post 8vo. 18s.

> Early Christianity, from the Birth of Christ to the Abolition of Paganism in the Roman Empire. 3 Vols. Post 8vo. 18s.

> Latin Christianity, including that of the Popes to the Pontificate of Nicholas V. 9 Vols. Post 8vo. 54s.

> Handbook to St. Paul's Cathedral. Woodcuts. Crown 8vo. 10s. 6d.

> Quinti Horatii Flacci Opera. Woodcuts. Sm. 8vo. 7s. 6d.

> Fall of Jerusalem. Fcap. 8vo. 1s.

> ———— (Capt. E. A.) Wayside Cross. Post 8vo. 2s.

> ———— (Bishop, D.D.,) Life. With a Selection from his Correspondence and Journals. By his Sister. Map. 8vo. 12s.

MOSSMAN (Samuel). New Japan; the Land of the Rising Sun; its Annals during the past Twenty Years, recording the remarkable Progress of the Japanese in Western Civilisation. With Map. 8vo. 15s.

MOTLEY (J. L.). History of the United Netherlands: from the Death of William the Silent to the Twelve Years' Truce, 1609. Portraits. 4 Vols. Post 8vo. 6s. each.

> ———— Life and Death of John of Barneveld, Advocate of Holland. With a View of the Primary Causes and Movements of the Thirty Years' War. Illustrations. 2 Vols. Post 8vo. 12s.

MOZLEY (Canon). Treatise on the Augustinian doctrine of Predestination. Crown 8vo. 9s.

MUIRHEAD (Jas.). The Vaux-de-Vire of Maistre Jean Le Houx, Advocate of Vire. Translated and Edited. With Portrait and Illustrations. 8vo. 21s.

MUNRO'S (General) Life and Letters. By Rev. G. R. Gleig. Post 8vo. 3s. 6d.

MURCHISON (Sir Roderick). Siluria; or, a History of the Oldest rocks containing Organic Remains. Map and Plates. 8vo. 18s.

> ———— Memoirs. With Notices of his Contemporaries, and Rise and Progress of Palæozoic Geology. By Archibald Geikie. Portraits. 2 Vols. 8vo. 30s.

MURRAY (A. S.). A History of Greek Sculpture, from the Earliest Times down to the Age of Pheidias. With Illustrations. Roy. 8vo. 21s.

MUSTERS' (Capt.) Patagonians; a Year's Wanderings over Untrodden Ground from the Straits of Magellan to the Rio Negro. Illustrations. Post 8vo. 7s. 6d.

NAPIER (Sir Wm.). English Battles and Sieges of the Peninsular War. Portrait. Post 8vo. 9s.

NAPOLEON at Fontainebleau and Elba. Journal of Occurrences and Notes of Conversations. By Sir Neil Campbell. Portrait. 8vo. 15s.

NARES (Sir George), R.N. Official Report to the Admiralty of the recent Arctic Expedition. Map. 8vo. 2s. 6d.

NAUTICAL ALMANAC (The). (By Authority.) 2s. 6d.

NAVY LIST. (Monthly and Quarterly.) Post 8vo.

NEW TESTAMENT. With Short Explanatory Commentary. By ARCHDEACON CHURTON, M.A., and the BISHOP OF ST. DAVID'S. With 110 authentic Views, &c. 2 Vols. Crown 8vo. 21s. bound.

NEWTH (SAMUEL). First Book of Natural Philosophy ; an Introduction to the Study of Statics, Dynamics, Hydrostatics, Light, Heat, and Sound, with numerous Examples. Small 8vo. 3s. 6d.

———————— Elements of Mechanics, including Hydrostatics, with numerous Examples. Small 8vo. 8s. 6d.

———————— Mathematical Examples. A Graduated Series of Elementary Examples in Arithmetic, Algebra, Logarithms, Trigonometry, and Mechanics. Small 8vo. 8s. 6d.

NICOLAS (SIR HARRIS). Historic Peerage of England. Exhibiting the Origin, Descent, and Present State of every Title of Peerage which has existed in this Country since the Conquest. By WILLIAM COURTHOPE. 8vo. 30s.

NILE GLEANINGS. [See STUART.]

NIMROD, On the Chace—Turf—and Road. With Portrait and Plates. Crown 8vo. 5s. Or with Coloured Plates, 7s. 6d.

NORDHOFF (CHAS.). Communistic Societies of the United States; including Detailed Accounts of the Shakers, The Amana, Oneida, Bethell, Aurora, Icarian and other existing Societies. With 40 Illustrations. 8vo. 15s.

NORTHCOTE'S (SIR JOHN) Notebook in the Long Parliament. Containing Proceedings during its First Session, 1640. Edited, with a Memoir, by A. H. A. Hamilton. Crown 8vo. 9s.

OWEN (LIEUT.-COL.). Principles and Practice of Modern Artillery, including Artillery Material, Gunnery, and Organisation and Use of Artillery in Warfare. With Illustrations. 8vo. 15s.

OXENHAM (REV. W.). English Notes for Latin Elegiacs ; designed for early Proficients in the Art of Latin Versification, with Prefatory Rules of Composition in Elegiac Metre. 12mo. 3s. 6d.

PAGET (LORD GEORGE). The Light Cavalry Brigade in the Crimea. Containing Extracts from Journal and Correspondence. Map. Crown 8vo. 10s. 6d.

PALGRAVE (R. H. I.). Local Taxation of Great Britain and Ireland. 8vo. 5s.

PALLISER (MRS.). Mottoes for Monuments, or Epitaphs selected General Use and Study. With Illustrations. Crown 8vo. 7s. 6d.

PARIS (DR.) Philosophy in Sport made Science in Earnest ; or, the First Principles of Natural Philosophy inculcated by aid of the Toys and Sports of Youth. Woodcuts. Post 8vo. 7s. 6d.

PARKYNS' (MANSFIELD) Three Years' Residence in Abyssinia : with Travels in that Country. With Illustrations. Post 8vo. 7s. 6d.

PEEL'S (SIR ROBERT) Memoirs. 2 Vols. Post 8vo. 15s.

PENN (RICHARD). Maxims and Hints for an Angler and Chessplayer. Woodcuts. Fcap. 8vo. 1s.

PERCY (JOHN, M.D.). METALLURGY. Fuel, Wood, Peat, Coal, Charcoal, Coke. Fire-Clays. Illustrations. 8vo. 30s.

———————— Lead, including part of Silver. Illustrations. 8vo. 30s.

———————— Silver and Gold. Part I. Illustrations. 8vo. 30s.

PERRY (REV. CANON). Life of St. Hugh of Avalon, Bishop of Lincoln. Post 8vo. 10s. 6d.

———————— History of the English Church. See STUDENTS' Manuals.

PHILLIPS (SAMUEL). Literary Essays from " The Times." With Portrait. 2 Vols. Fcap. 8vo. 7s.

PIGAFETTA (Filippo). The Kingdom of Congo, and of the Surrounding Countries. Translated and edited by Margarite Hutchinson. With Preface by Sir T. Fowell Buxton. Maps. 8vo. 10s. 6d.

POPE'S (Alexander) Works. With Introductions and Notes, by Rev. Whitwell Elwin. Vols. I., II., VI., VII., VIII. With Portraits. 8vo. 10s. 6d. each.

PORTER (Rev. J. L.). Damascus, Palmyra, and Lebanon. With Travels among the Giant Cities of Bashan and the 'Hauran. Map and Woodcuts. Post 8vo. 7s. 6d.

PRAYER-BOOK (Illustrated), with Borders, Initials, Vignettes, &c. Edited, with Notes, by Rev. Thos. James. Medium 8vo. 18s. cloth ; 31s. 6d. calf ; 36s. morocco.

————— (The Convocation), with altered rubrics, showing the book if amended in conformity with the recommendations of the Convocations of Canterbury and York in 1879. Post 8vo. 5s.

PRINCESS CHARLOTTE OF WALES. A Brief Memoir. With Selections from her Correspondence and other unpublished Papers. By Lady Rose Weigall. With Portrait. 8vo. 8s. 6d.

PRIVY COUNCIL JUDGMENTS in Ecclesiastical Cases relating to Doctrine and Discipline. With Historical Introduction, by G. C. Brodrick and W. H. Fremantle. 8vo. 10s. 6d.

PSALMS OF DAVID. With Notes Explanatory and Critical by the Dean of Wells, Canon Elliott, and Canon Cook. Medium 8vo. 10s. 6d.

PUSS IN BOOTS. With 12 Illustrations. By Otto Speckter. 16mo. 1s. 6d. Or coloured, 2s. 6d.

QUARTERLY REVIEW (The). 8vo. 6s.

RAE (Edward). Country of the Moors. A Journey from Tripoli in Barbary to the Holy City of Kairwan. Map and Etchings. Crown 8vo. 12s.

————— The White Sea Peninsula. Journey to the White Sea, and the Kola Peninsula. With Illustrations. Crown 8vo. [In the Press.

RAMBLES in the Syrian Deserts. Post 8vo. 10s. 6d.

RASSAM (Hormuzd). British Mission to Abyssinia. With Notices of the Countries from Massowah to Magdala. Illustrations. 2 Vols. 8vo. 28s.

RAWLINSON'S (Canon) Herodotus. A New English Version. Edited with Notes and Essays. Maps and Woodcut. 4 Vols. 8vo. 48s.

————— Five Great Monarchies of Chaldæa, Assyria, Media, Babylonia, and Persia. With Maps and Illustrations. 3 Vols. 8vo. 42s.

————— (Sir Henry) England and Russia in the East ; a Series of Papers on the Political and Geographical Condition of Central Asia. Map. 8vo. 12s.

REED (Sir E. J.) Iron-Clad Ships ; their Qualities, Performances, and Cost. With Chapters on Turret Ships, Iron-Clad Rams, &c. With Illustrations. 8vo. 12s.

————— Letters from Russia in 1875. 8vo. 5s.

————— Japan : Its History, Traditions, and Religions. With Narrative of a Visit in 1879. Illustrations. 2 Vols. 8vo. 28s.

REJECTED ADDRESSES (The). By James and Horace Smith. Woodcuts. Post 8vo. 3s. 6d. ; or Popular Edition, Fcap. 8vo. 1s.

REMBRANDT. See Middleton.

REYNOLDS' (Sir Joshua) Life and Times. By C. R. Leslie, R.A. and Tom Taylor. Portraits. 2 Vols. 8vo. 42s.

RICARDO'S (David) Political Works. With a Notice of his Life and Writings. By J. R. M'Culloch. 8vo. 16s.

RIPA (Father). Thirteen Years at the Court of Peking. Post
8vo. 2s.

ROBERTSON (Canon). History of the Christian Church, from the
Apostolic Age to the Reformation, 1517. 8 Vols. Post 8vo. 6s. each.

ROBINSON (Rev. Dr.). Biblical Researches in Palestine and the
Adjacent Regions, 1838—52. Maps. 3 Vols. 8vo. 42s.

—— (Wm.) Alpine Flowers for English Gardens. With
70 Illustrations. Crown 8vo. 7s. 6d.

———————— Sub-Tropical Garden. Illustrations. Small 8vo. 5s.

ROBSON (E. R.). School Architecture. Remarks on the
Planning, Designing, Building, and Furnishing of School-houses.
Illustrations. Medium 8vo. 18s.

ROME (History of). See Gibbon—Liddell—Smith—Students'.

ROYAL SOCIETY CATALOGUE OF SCIENTIFIC PAPERS.
8 vols. 8vo. 20s. each. Half morocco, 28s. each.

RUXTON (Geo. F.). Travels in Mexico; with Adventures among Wild
Tribes and Animals of the Prairies and Rocky Mountains. Post 8vo. 3s. 6d.

ST. HUGH OF AVALON, Bishop of Lincoln; his Life by G. G.
Perry, Canon of Lincoln. Post 8vo. 10s. 6d.

ST. JOHN (Charles). Wild Sports and Natural History of the
Highlands of Scotland. Illustrated Edition. Crown 8vo. 15s. *Cheap
Edition*, Post 8vo. 3s. 6d.

———————— (Bayle) Adventures in the Libyan Desert. Post 8vo. 2s.

SALDANHA (Duke of). See Carnota.

SALE'S (Sir Robert) Brigade in Affghanistan. With an Account of
the Defence of Jellalabad. By Rev. G. R. Gleig. Post 8vo. 2s.

SCEPTICISM IN GEOLOGY; and the Reasons for It. An
assemblage of facts from Nature combining to refute the theory of
"Causes now in Action." By Verifier. Woodcuts. Crown 8vo. 6s.

SCOTT (Sir Gilbert). Lectures on the Rise and Development
of Mediæval Architecture. Delivered at the Royal Academy. With
400 Illustrations. 2 Vols. Medium 8vo. 42s.

SCHLIEMANN (Dr. Henry). Troy and Its Remains. A Narra-
tive of Researches and Discoveries made on the Site of Ilium, and in the
Trojan Plain. With 500 Illustrations. Medium 8vo. 42s.

———————— Ancient Mycenæ and Tiryns. With 500 Illustrations. Medium 8vo. 50s.

Ilios; the City and Country of the Trojans,
including all Recent Discoveries and Researches made on the Site
of Troy and the Troad. With an Autobiography. With 2000 Illustrations. Imperial 8vo. 50s.

SCHOMBERG (General). The Odyssey of Homer, rendered
into English blank verse. Books I—XII. 8vo. 12s.

SEEBOHM (Henry). Siberia in Europe; a Naturalist's Visit to
the Valley of the Petchora in N.E. Russia. With notices of Birds and
their migrations. With Map and Illustrations. Crown 8vo. 11s.

SELBORNE (Lord). Notes on some Passages in the Liturgical
History of the Reformed English Church. 8vo. 6s.

SHADOWS OF A SICK ROOM. Preface by Canon Liddon.
16mo. 2s. 6d.

SHAH OF PERSIA'S Diary during his Tour through Europe in
1873. Translated from the Original. By J. W. Redhouse. With
Portrait and Coloured Title. Crown 8vo. 12s.

SHAW (T. B.). Manual of English Literature. Post 8vo. 7s. 6d.

———————— Specimens of English Literature. Selected from the
Chief Writers. Post 8vo. 7s. 6d.

SHAW (ROBERT). Visit to High Tartary, Yarkand, and Kashgar (formerly Chinese Tartary), and Return Journey over the Karakorum Pass. With Map and Illustrations. 8vo. 16s.

SIERRA LEONE; Described in Letters to Friends at Home. By A LADY. Post 8vo. 3s. 6d.

SIMMONS (CAPT.). Constitution and Practice of Courts-Martial. 8vo. 15s.

SMILES' (SAMUEL, LL.D.) WORKS :—

    BRITISH ENGINEERS; from the Earliest Period to the death of the Stephensons. With Illustrations. 5 Vols. Crown 8vo. 7s. 6d. each.

    LIFE OF GEORGE STEPHENSON. Post 8vo. 3s. 6d.

    LIFE OF A SCOTCH NATURALIST (THOS. EDWARD). Illustrations. Crown 8vo. 10s. 6d.

    LIFE OF A SCOTCH GEOLOGIST AND BOTANIST (ROBERT DICK). Illustrations. Crown 8vo. 12s.

    HUGUENOTS IN ENGLAND AND IRELAND. Crown 8vo. 7s. 6d.

    SELF-HELP. With Illustrations of Conduct and Perseverance. Post 8vo. 6s. Or in French, 5s.

    CHARACTER. A Sequel to "SELF-HELP." Post 8vo. 6s.

    THRIFT. A Book of Domestic Counsel. Post 8vo. 6s.

    DUTY. With Illustrations of Courage, Patience, and Endurance. Post 8vo. 6s.

    INDUSTRIAL BIOGRAPHY; or, Iron Workers and Tool Makers. Post 8vo. 6s.

    BOY'S VOYAGE ROUND THE WORLD. Illustrations. Post 8vo. 6s.

SMITH (DR. GEORGE) Student's Manual of the Geography of India. Post 8vo.

———— Life of John Wilson, D.D. (Bombay), Missionary and Philanthropist. Portrait. Post 8vo. 9s.

———— (PHILIP). History of the Ancient World, from the Creation to the Fall of the Roman Empire, A.D. 476. 3 Vols. 8vo. 31s. 6d.

SMITH'S (DR. WM.) DICTIONARIES :—

    DICTIONARY OF THE BIBLE; its Antiquities, Biography, Geography, and Natural History. Illustrations. 3 Vols. 8vo. 105s.

    CONCISE BIBLE DICTIONARY. With 300 Illustrations. Medium 8vo. 21s.

    SMALLER BIBLE DICTIONARY. With Illustrations. Post 8vo. 7s. 6d.

    CHRISTIAN ANTIQUITIES. Comprising the History, Institutions, and Antiquities of the Christian Church. With Illustrations. 2 Vols. Medium 8vo. 3l. 13s. 6d.

    CHRISTIAN BIOGRAPHY, LITERATURE, SECTS, AND DOCTRINES; from the Times of the Apostles to the Age of Charlemagne. Medium 8vo. Vols. I. & II. 31s. 6d. each. (To be completed in 4 Vols.)

    GREEK AND ROMAN ANTIQUITIES. With 500 Illustrations. Medium 8vo. 28s.

    GREEK AND ROMAN BIOGRAPHY AND MYTHOLOGY. With 600 Illustrations. 3 Vols. Medium 8vo. 4l. 4s.

    GREEK AND ROMAN GEOGRAPHY. 2 Vols. With 500 Illustrations. Medium 8vo. 56s.

    ATLAS OF ANCIENT GEOGRAPHY—BIBLICAL AND CLASSICAL. Folio. 6l. 6s.

    CLASSICAL DICTIONARY OF MYTHOLOGY, BIOGRAPHY, AND GEOGRAPHY. 1 Vol. With 750 Woodcuts. 8vo. 18s.

SMITH'S (DR. WM.) DICTIONARIES— *continued.*

SMALLER CLASSICAL DICTIONARY. With 200 Woodcuts. Crown 8vo. 7s. 6d.

SMALLER GREEK AND ROMAN ANTIQUITIES. With 200 Woodcuts. Crown 8vo. 7s. 6d.

COMPLETE LATIN-ENGLISH DICTIONARY. With Tables of the Roman Calendar, Measures, Weights, and Money. 8vo. 21s.

SMALLER LATIN-ENGLISH DICTIONARY. 12mo. 7s. 6d.

COPIOUS AND CRITICAL ENGLISH-LATIN DICTIONARY. 8vo. 21s.

SMALLER ENGLISH-LATIN DICTIONARY. 12mo. 7s. 6d.

SMITH'S (DR. WM.) ENGLISH COURSE:—

SCHOOL MANUAL OF ENGLISH GRAMMAR, WITH COPIOUS EXERCISES. Post 8vo. 3s. 6d.

PRIMARY ENGLISH GRAMMAR. 16mo. 1s.

MANUAL OF ENGLISH COMPOSITION. With Copious Illustrations and Practical Exercises. 12mo. 3s. 6d.

PRIMARY HISTORY OF BRITAIN. 12mo. 2s. 6d.

SCHOOL MANUAL OF MODERN GEOGRAPHY, PHYSICAL AND Political. Post 8vo. 5s.

A SMALLER MANUAL OF MODERN GEOGRAPHY. 16mo. 2s. 6d.

SMITH'S (DR. WM.) FRENCH COURSE:—

FRENCH PRINCIPIA. Part I. A First Course, containing a Grammar, Delectus, Exercises, and Vocabularies. 12mo. 3s. 6d.

APPENDIX TO FRENCH PRINCIPIA. Part I. Containing additional Exercises, with Examination Papers. 12mo. 2s. 6d.

FRENCH PRINCIPIA. Part II. A Reading Book, containing Fables, Stories, and Anecdotes, Natural History, and Scenes from the History of France. With Grammatical Questions, Notes and copious Etymological Dictionary. 12mo. 4s. 6d.

FRENCH PRINCIPIA. Part III. Prose Composition, containing a Systematic Course of Exercises on the Syntax, with the Principal Rules of Syntax. 12mo. [*In the Press.*]

STUDENT'S FRENCH GRAMMAR. By C. HERON-WALL. With Introduction by M. Littré. Post 8vo. 7s. 6d.

SMALLER GRAMMAR OF THE FRENCH LANGUAGE. Abridged from the above. 12mo. 3s. 6d.

SMITH'S (DR. WM.) GERMAN COURSE:—

GERMAN PRINCIPIA. Part I. A First German Course, containing a Grammar. Delectus, Exercise Book, and Vocabularies. 12mo. 3s. 6d.

GERMAN PRINCIPIA. Part II. A Reading Book; containing Fables, Stories, and Anecdotes, Natural History, and Scenes from the History of Germany. With Grammatical Questions, Notes, and Dictionary. 12mo. 3s. 6d.

PRACTICAL GERMAN GRAMMAR. Post 8vo. 3s. 6d.

SMITH'S (DR. WM.) ITALIAN COURSE:—

ITALIAN PRINCIPIA. An Italian Course, containing a Grammar, Delectus, Exercise Book, with Vocabularies, and Materials for Italian Conversation. By Signor RICCI, Professor of Italian at the City of London College. 12mo. 3s. 6d.

ITALIAN PRINCIPIA. Part II. A First Italian Reading Book, containing Fables, Anecdotes, History, and Passages from the best Italian Authors, with Grammatical Questions, Notes, and a Copious Etymological Dictionary. By SIGNOR RICCI. 12mo. 3s. 6d.

SMITH'S (DR. WM.) LATIN COURSE:—

THE YOUNG BEGINNER'S FIRST LATIN BOOK : Containing the Rudiments of Grammar, Easy Grammatical Questions and Exercises, with Vocabularies. Being a Stepping stone to Principia Latina, Part 1, for Young Children. 12mo. 2s.

THE YOUNG BEGINNER'S SECOND LATIN BOOK : Containing an easy Latin Reading Book, with an Analysis of the Sentences, Notes, and a Dictionary. Being a Stepping stone to Principia Latina, Part II., for Young Children. 12mo. 2s.

PRINCIPIA LATINA. Part I. First Latin Course, containing a Grammar, Delectus, and Exercise Book. with Vocabularies. 12mo. 3s. 6d.
. In this Edition the Cases of the Nouns, Adjectives, and Pronouns are arranged both as in the ORDINARY GRAMMARS and as in the PUBLIC SCHOOL PRIMER, together with the corresponding Exercises

APPENDIX TO PRINCIPIA LATINA. Part I.; being Additional Exercises, with Examination Papers. 12mo. 2s 6d.

PRINCIPIA LATINA. Part II. A Reading-book of Mythology, Geography, Roman Antiquities, and History. With Notes and Dictionary. 12mo. 3s. 6d.

PRINCIPIA LATINA. Part III. A Poetry Book. Hexameters and Pentameters; Eclog. Ovidianæ: Latin Prosody. 12mo. 3s. 6d.

PRINCIPIA LATINA. Part IV. Prose Composition. Rules of Syntax with Examples, Explanations of Synonyms, and Exercises on the Syntax. 12mo. 3s. 6d.

PRINCIPIA LATINA. Part V. Short Tales and Anecdotes for Translation into Latin. 12mo. 3s.

LATIN-ENGLISH VOCABULARY AND FIRST LATIN-ENGLISH DICTIONARY FOR PHÆDRUS, CORNELIUS NEPOS, AND CÆSAR. 12mo. 3s. 6d.

STUDENT'S LATIN GRAMMAR. For the Higher Forms. Post 8vo. 6s.

SMALLER LATIN GRAMMAR. For the Middle and Lower Forms. 12mo. 3s. 6d.

TACITUS, Germania, Agricola, &c. With English Notes. 12mo. 3s. 6d.

SMITH'S (DR. WM.) GREEK COURSE:—

INITIA GRÆCA. Part I. A First Greek Course, containing a Grammar, Delectus, and Exercise-book. With Vocabularies. 12mo. 3s. 6d.

APPENDIX TO INITIA GRÆCA. Part I. Containing additional Exercises. With Examination Papers. Post 8vo. 2s. 6d.

INITIA GRÆCA. Part II. A Reading Book. Containing Short Tales, Anecdotes, Fables, Mythology, and Grecian History. 12mo. 3s. 6d.

INITIA GRÆCA. Part III. Prose Composition. Containing the Rules of Syntax, with copious Examples and Exercises. 12mo. 3s. 6d.

STUDENT'S GREEK GRAMMAR. For the Higher Forms. By CURTIUS. Post 8vo. 6s.

SMALLER GREEK GRAMMAR. For the Middle and Lower Forms. 12mo. 3s. 6d.

GREEK ACCIDENCE. 12mo. 2s. 6d.

PLATO, Apology of Socrates, &c. With Notes. 12mo. 3s. 6d.

SMITH'S (DR. WM.) SMALLER HISTORIES:—

SCRIPTURE HISTORY. Woodcuts. 16mo. 3s. 6d.

ANCIENT HISTORY. Woodcuts. 16mo. 3s. 6d.

ANCIENT GEOGRAPHY. Woodcuts. 16mo. 3s. 6d.

MODERN GEOGRAPHY. 16mo. 2s. 6d.

GREECE. Maps and Woodcuts. 16mo. 3s. 6d.

ROME. Maps and Woodcuts. 16mo. 3s. 6d.

SMITH'S (Dr. Wm.) Smaller Histories—*continued.*
    Classical Mythology. Woodcuts. 16mo. 3s. 6d.
    England. Maps and Woodcuts. 16mo. 3s. 6d.
    English Literature. 16mo. 3s. 6d.
    Specimens of English Literature. 16mo. 3s. 6d.

SOMERVILLE (Mary). Personal Recollections from Early Life to Old Age. Portrait. Crown 8vo. 12s.
———————— Physical Geography. Portrait. Post 8vo. 9s.
———————— Connexion of the Physical Sciences. Post 8vo. 9s.
———————— Molecular & Microscopic Science. Illustrations. 2 Vols. Post 8vo. 21s.

SOUTH (John F.). Household Surgery; or, Hints for Emergencies. With Woodcuts. Fcap. 8vo. 3s. 6d.

SOUTHEY (Robt). Lives of Bunyan and Cromwell. Post 8vo. 2s.

STAEL (Madame de). *See* Stevens.

STANHOPE'S (Earl) WORKS:—
    History of England from the Reign of Queen Anne to the Peace of Versailles, 1701-83. 9 vols. Post 8vo. 5s. each.
    Life of William Pitt. Portraits. 3 Vols. 8vo. 36s.
    Miscellanies. 2 Vols. Post 8vo. 13s.
    British India, from its Origin to 1783. Post 8vo. 3s. 6d.
    History of "Forty-Five." Post 8vo. 3s.
    Historical and Critical Essays. Post 8vo. 3s. 6d.
    French Retreat from Moscow, and other Essays. Post 8vo. 7s. 6d.
    Life of Belisarius. Post 8vo. 10s. 6d.
    Life of Condé. Post 8vo. 3s. 6d.
    Story of Joan of Arc. Fcap. 8vo. 1s.
    Addresses on Various Occasions. 16mo. 1s.

STANLEY'S (Dean) WORKS:—
    Sinai and Palestine. Maps. 8vo. 14s.
    Bible in the Holy Land; Extracted from the above Work. Woodcuts. Fcap. 8vo. 2s. 6d.
    Eastern Church. 8vo. 12s.
    Jewish Church. From the Earliest Times to the Christian Era. 3 Vols. 8vo. 38s.
    Church of Scotland. 8vo. 7s. 6d.
    Epistles of St. Paul to the Corinthians. 8vo. 18s.
    Life of Dr. Arnold. Portrait. 2 vols. Cr. 8vo. 12s.
    Canterbury Cathedral. Illustrations. Post 8vo. 7s. 6d.
    Westminster Abbey. Illustrations. 8vo. 15s.
    Sermons during a Tour in the East. 8vo. 9s.
    Memoir of Edward, Catherine, and Mary Stanley. Cr. 8vo. 9s.
    Christian Institutions. Essays on Ecclesiastical Subjects. 8vo. 12s.

STEPHENS (Rev. W. R. W.). Life and Times of St. John Chrysostom. A Sketch of the Church and the Empire in the Fourth Century. Portrait. 8vo. 12s.

STEVENS (Dr. A.). Madame de Staël; a Study of her Life and Times. The First Revolution and the First Empire. Portraits. 2 Vols. Crown 8vo. 24s.

STRATFORD de REDCLIFFE (Lord). The Eastern Question.
 Being a Selection from his Writings during the last Five Years of his
 Life. With a Preface by Dean Stanley. With Map, 8vo. 9s.

STREET (G. E.). Gothic Architecture in Spain. Illustrations.
 Royal 8vo. 30s.

——————— —— —— —— Italy, chiefly in Brick and
 Marble. With Notes on North of Italy. Illustrations. Royal 8vo. 26s.

——————— Rise of Styles in Architecture. With Illustrations. 8vo.

STUART (Villiers). Nile Gleanings: The Ethnology, History,
 and Art of Ancient Egypt, as Revealed by Paintings and Bas-
 Reliefs. With Descriptions of Nubia and its Great Rock Temples,
 59 Coloured Illustrations, &c. Medium 8vo. 31s. 6d.

STUDENTS' MANUALS :—

 Old Testament History; from the Creation to the Return of
  the Jews from Captivity. Maps and Woodcuts. Post 8vo. 7s. 6d.

 New Testament History. With an Introduction connecting
  the History of the Old and New Testaments. Maps and Woodcuts.
  Post 8vo. 7s. 6d.

 Evidences of Christianity. By Rev. H. Wace. Post 8vo.

 Ecclesiastical History. The Christian Church during the
  First Ten Centuries; From its Foundation to the full establishment
  of the Holy Roman Empire and the Papal Power. Post 8vo. 7s. 6d.

 History of the Early English Church, First Period, from
  the planting of the Church in Britain to the Accession of Henry VIII.
  By Canon Perry. Post 8vo. 7s. 6d.

 English Church History, Second Period, from the accession
  of Henry VIII. to the silencing of Convocation in the 18th Century. By
  Canon Perry. Post 8vo. 7s. 6d.

 Ancient History of the East; Egypt, Assyria, Babylonia,
  Media, Persia, Asia Minor. and Phœnicia. Woodcuts. Post 8vo. 7s. 6d.

 Ancient Geography. By Canon Bevan. Woodcuts. Post
  8vo. 7s. 6d.

 History of Greece; from the Earliest Times to the Roman
  Conquest. By Wm. Smith, D.C.L. Woodcuts. Crown 8vo. 7s. 6d.
   „ Questions on the above Work, 12mo. 2s.

 History of Rome; from the Earliest Times to the Establishment of the Empire. By Dean Liddell. Woodcuts. Crown 8vo. 7s. 6d.

 Gibbon's Decline and Fall of the Roman Empire. Woodcuts.
  Post 8vo. 7s. 6d.

 Hallam's History of Europe during the Middle Ages.
  Post 8vo. 7s. 6d.

 History of Modern Europe, from the end of the Middle
  Ages to the Treaty of Berlin, 1878. Post 8vo.   [In the Press.

 Hallam's History of England; from the Accession of
  Henry VII. to the Death of George II. Post 8vo. 7s. 6d.

 Hume's History of England from the Invasion of Julius
  Cæsar to the Revolution in 1688. Revised, corrected, and continued
  down to the Treaty of Berlin, 1878. By J. S. Brewer, M.A. With
  7 Coloured Maps & 70 Woodcuts. Post 8vo. 7s. 6d.
   „ Questions on the above Work, 12mo. 2s.

 History of France; from the Earliest Times to the Establishment of the Second Empire, 1852. By H. W. Jervis. Woodcuts.
  Post 8vo. 7s. 6d.

 English Language. By Geo. P. Marsh. Post 8vo. 7s. 6d.

 English Literature. By T. B. Shaw, M.A. Post 8vo. 7s. 6d.

 Specimens of English Literature. By T. B. Shaw. Post 8vo.
  7s. 6d.

STUDENTS' MANUALS—*continued.*

    MODERN GEOGRAPHY ; Mathematical, Physical and Descriptive.
        By CANON BEVAN. Woodcuts. Post 8vo. 7s. 6d.

    GEOGRAPHY OF INDIA. By Dr. GEORGE SMITH, LL.D. P. st. 8vo.
        7s. 6d.   [*In the Press.*

    MORAL PHILOSOPHY. By WM. FLEMING. Post 8vo. 7s. 6d.

    BLACKSTONE'S COMMENTARIES. By MALCOLM KERR. Post 8vo.
        7s. 6d.

SUMNER'S (BISHOP) Life and Episcopate during 40 Years. By
    Rev. G. H. SUMNER. Portrait. 8vo. 14s.

SWAINSON (CANON). Nicene and Apostles' Creeds; Their
    Literary History : together with some Account of "The Creed of St.
    Athanasius." 8vo. 16s.

SWIFT (JONATHAN). Life of. By HENRY CRAIK, B.A.

SYBEL (VON) History of Europe during the French Revolution,
    1789—1795. 4 Vols. 8vo. 48s.

SYMONDS' (REV. W.) Records of the Rocks; or Notes on the
    Geology, Natural History, and Antiquities of North and South Wales,
    Siluria, Devon, and Cornwall. With Illustrations. Crown 8vo. 12s.

TALMUD. See BARCLAY ; DEUTSCH.

TEMPLE (SIR RICHARD). India in 1880. With Maps. 8vo. 16s.

———— Men and Events of My Time in India. 8vo.

THIBAUT'S (ANTOINE) Purity in Musical Art. Translated from
    the German. With a prefatory Memoir by W. H. Gladstone, M.P.
    Post 8vo. 7s. 6d.

THIELMANN (BARON). Journey through the Caucasus to
    Tabreez, Kurdistan, down the Tigris and Euphrates to Nineveh and
    Babylon, and across the Desert to Palmyra. Translated by CHAS.
    HENEAGE. Illustrations. 2 Vols. Post 8vo. 18s.

THOMSON (ARCHBISHOP). Lincoln's Inn Sermons. 8vo. 10s. 6d.

————————— Life in the Light of God's Word. Post 8vo. 5s.

—————————— Word, Work, & Will : Collected Essays. Crown 8vo. 9s.

TITIAN'S LIFE AND TIMES. With some account of his
    Family, chiefly from new and unpublished Records. By CROWE and
    CAVALCASELLE. With Portrait and Illustrations. 2 Vols. 8vo.

TOCQUEVILLE'S State of Society in France before the Revolution,
    1789, and on the Causes which led to that Event. Translated by HENRY
    REEVE. 8vo. 14s.

TOMLINSON (CHAS.); The Sonnet; Its Origin, Structure, and Place
    in Poetry. With translations from Dante, Petrarch, &c. Post 8vo. 9s.

TOZER (REV. H. F.) Highlands of Turkey, with Visits to Mounts
    Ida, Athos, Olympus, and Pelion. 2 Vols. Crown 8vo. 24s.

———— Lectures on the Geography of Greece. Map. Post
    8vo. 9s.

TRISTRAM (CANON). Great Sahara. Illustrations. Crown 8vo. 15s.

———————— Land of Moab ; Travels and Discoveries on the East
    Side of the Dead Sea and the Jordan. Illustrations. Crown 8vo. 15s.

TRURO (BISHOP OF). The Cathedral: its Necessary Place in
    the Life and Work of the Church. Crown 8vo. 6s.

TWENTY YEARS' RESIDENCE among the Greeks, Albanians,
    Turks, Armenians, and Bulgarians. By an ENGLISH LADY. 2 Vols.
    Crown 8vo. 21s.

TWINING (REV. THOS.) Selections from His Correspondence. 8vo.

TWISS' (HORACE) Life of Lord Eldon. 2 Vols. Post 8vo. 21s.

TYLOR (E. B.) Researches into the Early History of Mankind, and Development of Civilization. 3rd Edition Revised. 8vo. 12s.

———————— Primitive Culture; the Development of Mythology, Philosophy, Religion, Art, and Custom. 2 Vols. 8vo. 24s.

VATICAN COUNCIL. *See* LETO.

VIRCHOW (PROFESSOR). The Freedom of Science in the Modern State. Fcap. 8vo. 2s.

WACE (REV. HENRY). The Gospel and its Witnesses: the Principal Facts in the Life of our Lord, and the Authority of the Evangelical Narratives. 8vo.

WELLINGTON'S Despatches during his Campaigns in India, Denmark, Portugal, Spain, the Low Countries, and France. 8 Vols. 8vo. 20s. each.

———————— Supplementary Despatches, relating to India, Ireland, Denmark, Spanish America, Spain, Portugal, France, Congress of Vienna, Waterloo and Paris. 14 Vols. 8vo. 20s. each. *⁎* An Index. 8vo. 20s.

———————— Civil and Political Correspondence. Vols. I. to VIII. 8vo. 20s. each.

———————— Speeches in Parliament. 2 Vols. 8vo. 42s.

WHEELER (G.). Choice of a Dwelling. Post 8vo. 7s. 6d.

WHITE (W. H.). Manual of Naval Architecture, for the use of Naval Officers, Shipowners, Shipbuilders, and Yachtsmen. Illustrations. 8vo. 24s.

WHYMPER (EDWARD). The Ascent of the Matterhorn. With 100 Illustrations. Medium 8vo. 10s. 6d.

WILBERFORCE'S (BISHOP) Life of William Wilberforce. Portrait. Crown 8vo. 6s.

———————— (SAMUEL, LL.D.), Lord Bishop of Oxford and Winchester; his Life. By Canon ASHWELL, D.D., and R. G. WILBERFORCE. With Portraits and Woodcuts. Vols. I. and II. 8vo. 15s. each.

WILKINSON (SIR J. G.). Manners and Customs of the Ancient Egyptians, their Private Life, Laws, Arts, Religion, &c. A new edition. Edited by SAMUEL BIRCH, LL.D. Illustrations. 3 Vols. 8vo. 84s.

———————— Popular Account of the Ancient Egyptians. With 500 Woodcuts. 2 Vols. Post 8vo. 12s.

WILSON (JOHN, D.D.). *See* SMITH (GEO.).

WOOD'S (CAPTAIN) Source of the Oxus. With the Geography of the Valley of the Oxus. By COL. YULE. Map. 8vo. 12s.

WORDS OF HUMAN WISDOM. Collected and Arranged by E. S. With a Preface by CANON LIDDON. Fcap. 8vo. 3s. 6d

YORK (ARCHBISHOP OF). Collected Essays. Contents.—Synoptic Gospels. Death of Christ. God Exists. Worth of Life. Design in Nature. Sports and Pastimes. Emotions in Preaching. Defects in Missionary Work. Limits of Philosophical Enquiry. Crown 8vo. 9s.

YULE (COLONEL). Book of Marco Polo. Illustrated by the Light of Oriental Writers and Modern Travels. With Maps and 80 Plates. 2 Vols. Medium 8vo. 63s.

———————— A. F. A Little Light on Cretan Insurrection. Post 8vo. 2s. 6d.

BRADBURY, AGNEW, & CO., PRINTERS, WHITEFRIARS.

5720086R00311

Printed in Great Britain
by Amazon.co.uk, Ltd.,
Marston Gate.